# U.S. Ratification of the International Covenants on Human Rights

The American Society of International Law

# U.S. Ratification of the International Covenants on Human Rights

Edited by
Hurst Hannum
and
Dana D. Fischer



Transnational Publishers, Inc.
Irvington-on-Hudson, New York

**Library of Congress Cataloging-in-Publication Data**

U.S. ratification of the human rights covenants / edited by
Hurst Hannum
p. cm.
ISBN 0-941320-79-0
1. Human rights. 2. Human rights--United States.
3. International and municipal law--United States. I. Hannum,
Hurst. II. Fisher, Dana D. III. Title: United States ratifications
of the human rights covenants.
K3240.6.U18 1993
341.4'81--dc20 92-33196
CIP



Manufactured in the United States of America

# CONTENTS

# ACKNOWLEDGMENTS

While in appearance a jointly edited project, this book in fact results from two quite distinct efforts. The first, under the editorship of Dana D. Fischer, resulted in production of a substantial and nearly final manuscript in 1983. The effort to bring that manuscript promptly to publication was frustrated, however, for various unavoidable reasons. Principal among these were the substantial changes in United States law, policy and practice in certain areas dealt with in this book that took place in the early years of the Reagan Administration. These required a further round of sometimes extensive rewriting by some authors. At the same time, the prospects of a significant investment of effort by either the Executive Branch or the Congress to obtain ratification of the Covenants had reached a low ebb. This raised questions about the desirability of producing a book that might again become obsolete in important respects before the time of its potential maximum impact had arrived.

In 1989 I assumed direction of the then necessary process of revision. The bulk of the work, however, resulted from the efforts of Dana Fischer and the original contributors over a decade ago, and the present version would not have been possible without their enthusiasm and dedication.

A great debt of gratitude obviously is owed to the initial contributors, particularly to those who were willing and able to revise their sections for the edition reincarnated in 1989-91. A similar debt is owed to those new contributors who were willing to offer their talents in revising or rewriting material which the original author was unable to complete. Each section or chapter is very much the work of the author(s) noted, and, while there is likely to be general agreement among the authors with the analyses adopted by their colleagues, no corporate responsibility for the substance of the text should be implied.

The one constant throughout this process has been the American Society of International Law and its Executive Director, John Lawrence Hargrove. It has been through Larry's persistence and tenacity that the present work has been made possible. Special thanks also are due to Sandra Liebel, who expertly turned an unwieldy, much-edited, and pre-computerized collection of several hundred pages into a real manuscript.

Finally, the Society and all concerned with this book are grateful to the Ford Foundation, for the initial, major grant in the Advancement of Human Rights for the grant which made possible its completion.

Hurst Hannum
*The Fletcher School of Law and Diplomacy*
November, 1992

# PART I
# THE POLITICAL FRAMEWORK

# I
# THE POLITICAL FRAMEWORK

*Hurst Hannum and Dana D. Fischer*

From the assertion in the Declaration of Independence of the rights to life, liberty, and the pursuit of happiness to twentieth century concerns with democracy around the world, the concept of human rights has been a central component of the government of the United States. As noted below, the United States has not hesitated to raise human rights issues internationally, and we were among those who insisted that a place be found for human rights in the United Nations Charter.

However, despite U.S. participation in such international organizations as the United Nations and the ongoing Conference on Security and Cooperation in Europe, most U.S. activity in the human rights area is unilateral or bilateral. There has been no sustained commitment to shape according to our own values those international institutions which oversee or interpret human rights norms.

The opportunity to participate fully in the implementation of international human rights norms has been present at least since the mid-1960s, when the two fundamental international human rights treaties were adopted by the U.N. General Assembly: the International Covenant on Civil and Political Rights[1] ("CPR Covenant") and its

[1] International Covenant on Civil and Political Rights, *adopted* 16 Dec. 1966, *entered into force* 23 Mar. 1976, *entered into force for the U.S.* 8 June 1992, 999 U.N.T.S. 171 (1966).

Optional Protocol and the International Covenant on Economic, Social and Cultural Rights ("ESC Covenant").[2] While several other international treaties dealing with more specific aspects of human rights have been adopted since the mid-1960s,[3] the United States has become a party to only five human rights treaties in the past two decades.[4] It ratified the CPR Covenant only in 1992, although the Covenant had been submitted to the Senate for advice and consent in 1979.

The CPR Covenant and ESC Covenant translate political pronouncements and aspirations into binding treaty language. They also create or designate institutions to oversee their implementation, participation in which is limited to States Parties to the treaties. Non-ratification by the United States has meant continued exclusion from these oversight bodies and the limitation of American influence to political arenas in which semantic shadow-boxing or generalities may consume much energy but yield little real result.

The Covenants are the product of generations of evolving law and three decades of negotiations in which the United States figured prominently. The history which follows offers a legal and political perspective on the issue of U.S. ratification.

[2] International Covenant on Economic, Social and Cultural Rights, *adopted* 16 Dec. 1966, *entered into force* 3 Jan. 1976, 999 U.N.T.S. 3 (1966).

[3] Several of these treaties have been signed by the President and submitted to the Senate for its advice and consent: International Convention on the Elimination of All Forms of Racial Discrimination, *adopted* 21 Dec. 1965, *entered into force* 4 Jan. 1969, 660 U.N.T.S. 195; Convention on the Elimination of All Forms of Discrimination Against Women, *adopted* 18 Dec. 1979, *entered into force* 3 Sept. 1981, G.A. Res. 34/180, 34 U.N. GAOR, Supp. (No. 46) 193 (1979); American Convention on Human Rights, *signed* 22 Nov. 1969, *entered into force* 18 July 1978, O.A.S.T.S. No. 36, p.1, O.A.S. Off. Rec. OEA/Ser. L/V/II.23, doc. 21, rev. 6.

[4] Protocol Relating to the Status of Refugees, *opened for signature* 31 Jan. 1967, *entered into force for the U.S.* 1 Nov. 1968, 19 U.S.T. 6223, T.I.A.S. No. 6577; Convention on the Political Rights of Women, *opened for signature* 31 Mar. 1953, *entered into force for the U.S.* 7 July 1976, 27 U.S.T. 8289, T.I.A.S. No. 8289, 193 U.N.T.S. 135; Convention on the Prevention and Punishment of the Crime of Genocide, *opened for signature* 9 Dec. 1948, *entered into force for the U.S.* 23 Feb. 1989, 78 U.N.T.S. 277; Convention against Torture and Other Cruel, Inhuman or Degrading Treatment or Punishment, *adopted* 10 Dec. 1984, *entered into force* 28 June 1987, G.A. Res. 39/46, 39 U.N. GAOR, Supp. (No. 51) at 197 (1984), Senate consent to ratification given Nov. 1990; CPR Covenant, *supra* note 1.

## 1.1 ORIGIN AND DEVELOPMENT OF THE INTERNATIONAL PROTECTION OF HUMAN RIGHTS

Expressions of the concept of human rights or closely related ideas can be found throughout history.[5] Earlier formulations have their roots in the Stoic concept of universal justice and in medieval notions of natural law, and assert that universal standards are applicable to all human societies. The seventeenth century brought a shift of emphasis away from natural law and toward a theory of natural rights. In the effort to counter claims of divine right, the idea was developed in Europe that every human being has rights that are to be recognized—not conferred—by the State. The idea of "inalienable" human rights was a moving force in the English civil war as well as the American and French revolutions.

The shift from the term natural law to that of natural rights marks a change in political and social values, the future importance of which was not confined to the West. Natural rights was one of the handful of doctrines that served to moderate the practice of colonial governments in Africa and Asia and was often adopted by the native leadership of colonial countries in their struggle for independence.

The doctrine of natural rights affected the development of customary law pertaining to the protection of aliens. International legal publicists asserted that all persons, both nationals of a State and aliens, were entitled to certain natural rights. It followed that whoever ill-treats a citizen indirectly injures the State of his nationality and that the State concerned has a right to protect its citizen. Long before international law sought to secure fundamental rights of the individual against his own State, this provided a degree of protection for the individual in his capacity as an alien. The paradoxical result was that "[t]he individual in his capacity as an alien enjoy[ed] a larger measure of protection by international law than in his character as a citizen of his own State."[6]

The principal goal of the contemporary international human rights movement is "to accord nationals the same protection formerly only accorded to aliens, while at the same time raising the standard of

[5] *See generally,* e.g., L. HENKIN, THE RIGHTS OF MAN TODAY (1978); L. SOHN AND T. BUERGENTHAL, INTERNATIONAL PROTECTION OF HUMAN RIGHTS 1-21 (1973); P. SIEGHART, THE INTERNATIONAL LAW OF HUMAN RIGHTS 3-23; Shestack, *The Jurisprudence of Human Rights,*in 1 HUMAN RIGHTS IN INTERNATIONAL LAW, LEGAL AND POLICY ISSUES 69-113 (T. Meron ed. 1984).

[6] H. LAUTERPACHT, INTERNATIONAL LAW AND HUMAN RIGHTS 121 (1950, 1968).

protection for all humans beings, nationals as well as aliens, far beyond the minimum international standard developed under earlier customary law."[7] In short, it seeks to dispense with nationality as the condition of protection.

The rudiments of international concern for individual human rights can be traced back as far as the middle of the seventeenth century to the end of the religious wars in Europe. The Treaty of Westphalia in 1648 established the principle of equality of rights for those of the Catholic and Protestant faiths. Both the Congress of Vienna in 1815 and the Congress of Berlin in 1878 provided for the individual's rights to exercise his religion freely.

Slavery was another object of international concern. Around the turn of the nineteenth century, Quaker movements advocated its abolition. Later, in the 1890 Brussels Agreement, sixteen countries agreed to cease slave trading and submit to a degree of international supervision. The various anti-slavery movements culminated in a League of Nations Anti-Slavery Convention in 1926. During the nineteenth century, some concern also developed for individual rights with respect to navigating Europe's rivers. The Final Act of the Congress of Vienna and the 1856 Treaty of Paris established commissions to enforce these rights. The 1856 Declaration of Paris, the 1864 Convention, and the 1868 Declaration of St. Petersburg led to the adoption of detailed rules of war, many of which concerned the treatment of individuals, by the Hague Conferences of 1899 and 1907. Reaction to Turkish atrocities in Armenia in 1864 and in Bulgaria in 1876 resulted in the establishment of international commissions of inquiry. Before World War I, a similar European commission investigated Russian massacres of Armenians in Russia.

The Treaty of Versailles and the "minorities treaties" adopted subsequently obliged some States to respect the rights of members of minorities living within their boundaries. The post-World War I territorial settlements also afforded some recognition to the principle of self-determination. While the League of Nations Covenant did not mention human rights, its mandate system did stipulate the right to "just" treatment for individuals in territories under mandate. The International Labour Organisation, created in 1919, developed standards for humane labor conditions and measures to effect that goal. At

[7] McDougal, Lasswell and Chen, *The Protection of Aliens from Discrimination and World Public Order: Responsibility of States Conjoined with Human Rights,* 70 AJIL 464 (1976).

best, however, these were intermittent, if salutory, developments. It was not until the founding of the United Nations that the rights of the individual became a primary concern of international law.

## 1.2 ORIGIN AND DEVELOPMENT OF THE HUMAN RIGHTS COVENANTS

Interest in securing human rights on a global level is essentially an extension of the 300-year domestic effort to promote and expand such rights. Events during World War II, which caused the peoples of the world and their leaders to recoil in horror, hastened this development. It is no accident that a significant mission of the United Nations, as conceived in San Francisco, was the promotion and protection of human rights. The Preamble and Articles 55 and 56 of the U.N. Charter make clear that international protection of human rights is one of the organization's highest priorities.

In San Francisco, the United States and several other countries proposed that a Bill of Human Rights be included in the Charter or be annexed to it. While this proposal was unsuccessful, Article 68 of the Charter did require establishment of a commission on human rights.[8] In 1947, the newly established commission decided that an "International Bill of Rights," consisting of a declaration and subsequent convention, should be adopted. The first phase was completed when, on December 10, 1948, the General Assembly adopted without a dissenting vote the Universal Declaration of Human Rights, which includes civil, political, economic, social and cultural rights.[9]

It was always intended that a treaty should be drafted to make enforceable those rights laid down in the Declaration. The Covenants on Civil and Political Rights and on Economic, Social, and Cultural Rights, respectively, are the fulfillment of that intent. The main issues confronted in the drafting process demonstrate that the two treaties reflect American interests and embody more American values than the United States could ever expect to renegotiate today.

Originally, there was to have been only one treaty. Drafting began immediately after the Declaration was completed and lasted until the

[8] For a more detailed exposition of the commission's early history, *see* H. TOLLEY, JR., THE U.N. COMMISSION ON HUMAN RIGHTS 1-13 (1987).

[9] Universal Declaration of Human Rights, *adopted* 10 Dec. 1948, G.A. Res. 217A (III), at 71, U.N. Doc. A/810 (1948).

end of 1966. During this period, U.N. membership more than doubled and the Cold War intensified. These and other developments confounded what, under the best of circumstances, would have been a complex set of multilateral negotiations. The difficulties of reaching a consensus at any level were immense. Some States insisted that implementation machinery was essential; others vehemently opposed provision for such machinery. Some States were unwilling to commit themselves to legally binding clauses concerning economic, social, and cultural rights; other States insisted that such clauses must be included. In 1951, after 73 articles had been drafted, the U.N. General Assembly voted to ask the Commission to draft two treaties, one on civil and political rights and the other on economic, social, and cultural rights.

The Commission on Human Rights completed the drafting of the two treaties in 1954. The following year the Third Committee of the General Assembly began what would be a 12-year debate. At its 1963 session, it completed consideration of the substantive provisions of both Covenants. Preceding adoption of the Covenants by the General Assembly in 1966, there already were expressions of dissatisfaction that the texts were inadequate and out-of-date. Nevertheless, the consensus held, and both Covenants were adopted and opened for signature. Ten years later, both entered into force.

## 1.3 COMPLIANCE MECHANISMS

While the drafting committee of the Human Rights Commission agreed that observance of the rights to be incorporated in the proposed international bill of human rights must be assured, it could not agree on the method of doing it.[10] The problem was balancing the requirement of an effective implementation procedure with the need for securing the widest possible acceptance of the treaties. The United States was among those States urging that implementation procedures should develop gradually in the light of experience.

[10] *See* L. Sohn, *A Short History of United Nations Documents on Human Rights,* THE UNITED NATIONS AND HUMAN RIGHTS 39 (Eighteenth Report of the Commission to Study the Organization of Peace, 1968); Schwelb, *The International Measures of Implementation of the International Covenant on Civil and Political Rights and of the Optional Protocol, 12* TEX. INT'L J. *141 (1977);* Robertson, *The Implementation System: International Measures,* in THE INTERNATIONAL BILL OF RIGHTS: THE COVENANT ON CIVIL AND POLITICAL RIGHTS, 332 (L. Henkin ed. 1981).

The Third Committee of the General Assembly substantially amended the implementation provisions contained in the draft CPR Covenant proposed by the Commission on Human Rights.[11] There was considerable sympathy on the part of newly independent members of the Commission for a system of implementation consisting of a compulsory reporting procedure with an optional fact-finding and conciliation procedure to be set in motion solely by those States Parties willing to accept such supplementary obligations. Some States also favored the inclusion in the proposed system of an optional clause concerning individual petitions.

The Third Committee decided that the proposed Human Rights Committee would be composed of eighteen nationals of the States Parties, who would be elected by secret ballot from a list of persons nominated by the States Parties. The members of the Human Rights Committee would serve in their personal capacities. The Committee's function with regard to the reporting procedure would be to "study" the reports submitted by the Parties and make "general comments" to the States regarding the reports.

A French proposal for a mandatory system of fact-finding and conciliation was rejected in favor of an Afro-Asian proposal for an optional system. Under Article 41 of the CPR Covenant, a State may declare that it recognizes the competence of the Human Rights Committee to receive and consider communications which allege that another State is not fulfilling its obligations under the Covenant. The Committee will accept a communication only from a State Party which has made a declaration recognizing the competence of the Committee in regard to itself, and the Covenant may make its good offices available to the States Parties concerned. After rejecting a Chilean proposal for compulsory conciliation, the Third Committee approved another Afro-Asian proposal, with several important amendments by the United States, for an *ad hoc* Conciliation Commission.[12] Neither the interstate communication procedure nor the provisions for a Conciliation Commission has yet been invoked. The provision for vesting in the individual the right of direct recourse to the Human Rights Committee was considered too radical for inclusion within the

[11] Early U.N. debates on the CPR Covenant's implementation procedures are collected and excerpted in M. BOSSUYT, GUIDE TO THE "*TRAVAUX PRÉPARATOIRES*" OF THE INTERNATIONAL COVENANT ON CIVIL AND POLITICAL RIGHTS 615-33 (art. 40), 635-91 (art. 41), 793-818 (Optional Protocol) (1987).

[12] *See* CPR Covenant, art. 42; BOSSUYT, *supra* note 11, at 689-716.

Covenant, even as another optional clause. Fearing that a petition clause might so limit ratifications as to jeopardize the Covenant's entry into force, a Lebanese proposal was accepted which embodied the right of individual petition in a separate protocol to be annexed to the Covenant.[13] The Optional Protocol recognizes the competence of the Human Rights Committee to consider communications from individuals subject to the jurisdiction of an adhering State Party who claim to be victims of a violation by that State Party of the rights set forth in the Covenant. The Committee considers individual communications in closed meetings after which it forwards its views to the State concerned and the complainant.[14]

As a restraint on the conduct of States, a reporting requirement is the weakest of the range of implementation techniques. However, because of the optional character of both interstate complaints and individual petitions as implementation techniques, the examination of reports by the State Parties under Article 40 of the CPR Covenant has become the major component of the work of the Human Rights Committee.[15] Following an initial report, which is to be submitted within one year of the Covenant's entry into force for the State concerned, periodic reports are to be submitted to and reviewed by the Committee every five years.

Unlike the CPR Covenant, the ESC Covenant does not specifically create a new institution to oversee its implementation. Instead, it provides merely that States Parties are to submit reports for consideration by the U.N. Economic and Social Council (ECOSOC). There is no provision for individual or interstate communications alleging non-compliance with the ESC Covenant, although provision is made for participation in the review process by appropriate U.N. specialized agencies.

Following highly unsatisfactory attempts from 1979 to 1986 by an ECOSOC working group (composed initially of government representatives and later by independent experts) to consider State reports,

[13] *See* Bossuyt, *supra* note 11, at 793-818.

[14] The Committee's rules of procedure and activities under the Optional Protocol are summarized in Human Rights Committee, Selected Decisions Under the Optional Protocol (Vol. 1: U.N. Sales No. E.84.XIV.2, 1985; Vol. 2: U.N. Sales No. E.89-XIV.1, 1990).

[15] *See infra*, sec. 3.5.; Fischer, *Reporting Under the Covenant on Civil and Political Rights: The First Five Years of the Human Rights Committee,* 76 AJIL 141 (1982); Gomez del Prado, *United Nations Conventions on Human Rights: The Practice of the Human Rights Committee and the Committee on the Elimination of Racial Discrimination in Dealing with Reporting Obligations of States Parties,* 7 Hum. Rts. Q. 492 (1985).

ECOSOC created a new expert Committee on Economic, Social and Cultural Rights in May 1986.[16] The new committee has adopted a five-year cycle of periodic reports similar to that of the Human Rights Committee, although it faces a mounting backlog of reports to consider and currently meets for only three weeks each year.[17]

## 1.4 THE PRESENT STATUS OF THE COVENANTS

In December 1966, the General Assembly adopted the two Human Rights Covenants and the Optional Protocol. Where the Universal Declaration of Human Rights was approved by less than fifty votes, with eight significant abstentions, 105 States voted for the Covenants, with only a few States (e.g., Portugal and South Africa) daring to be absent.

As of June, 1992, there were 111 States Parties to the CPR Covenant and 113 States Parties to the ESC Covenant. The Optional Protocol to the CPR Covenant has been accepted by 59 States, and 33 States have made the declaration accepting the possibility of interstate complaints under Article 41 of the CPR Covenant. A second Optional Protocol abolishing capitol punishment entered into force in 1991 and has been ratified by 12 states.

A broad cross-section of States has ratified both Covenants, underscoring their global acceptance. Virtually all of the Western countries are parties, with the notable exception of the United States until 1992; the Russian Federation and all of the Eastern European countries also are parties. A majority of the States Parties to the two Covenants are from developing countries in Africa, Asia, and Latin America.

As discussed below in chapter 5, Presidents Carter and Bush suggested a series of reservations, declarations, and understandings to the Covenants when they were submitted to the Senate for advice and consent.[18] As of September 1, 1987, only 18 of 90 States Parties to the

[16] *See infra,* chap. 4, sec. 4.5; Alston, *Out of the Abyss: The Challenges Confronting the New U.N. Committee on Economic, Social and Cultural Rights,* 9 HUM. RTS. Q. 332 (1987).

[17] *See, e.g.,* Committee on Economic, Social and Cultural Rights, *Report on the Second Session,* 1988 U.N. ESCOR, Supp. (No. 4) at 58-65, U.N. Doc. E/1988/14 (1988); *id., Report on the Fourth Session,* 1990 U.N. ESCOR, Supp. (No. 3) at 6-12, U.N. Doc. E/1990/23 (1990).

[18] President Carter's recommendations are found in Message of the President Transmitting Four Treaties Pertaining to Human Rights, S. EXEC. DOC. No. 95-C, D, E & F, 95th Cong. 2d Sess. (1978). The Bush Administration's generally similar recommendations are contained in International Covenant on Civil and Political Rights, S. EXEC. DOC. No. 102-23, 102d Cong. 2d Sess, 6-21 (1992).

ESC Covenant (20%) ratified with reservations; 25 of the 86 parties to the CPR Covenant (29%) filed reservations.[19]

Among the States filing reservations to the ESC Covenant, more than half (20) maintain a single substantive reservation. Nine reservations concern Article 8(1)(d), guaranteeing the right to strike. Other provisions which are the subject of more than one reservation are the rights to education (7 reservations), paid maternity leave (4), and remuneration for public holidays (3).

Over half the reservations to the CPR Covenant concern two articles, both of which establish norms of criminal procedure. More than 20 reservations have been filed with respect to the requirements of segregating convicted from accused and juvenile from adult prisoners. Even more States have declined to accept certain provisions of Article 14, most often the requirement that free legal assistance be provided to an accused.

Finally, several States which are parties to the European Convention on Human Rights have limited their acceptance of the Optional Protocol to those cases which have not been examined by "another procedure of international investigation or settlement," thus avoiding the same situation being brought before both the Human Rights Committee and the European Convention human rights machinery.

## 1.5 UNITED STATES POLICY AND HUMAN RIGHTS

### 1.5.1 American Leadership

While the Carter Administration deserves credit for revitalizing American interest in human rights, its advocacy of human rights drew upon traditional American values and represented the continuation of a long-standing, bipartisan foreign policy interest.

Virtually since its inception, the United States has been a proponent of the international protection of human rights. The United States was among the first States to promote the right of self-determination, the free exercise of religion, and the right to be free from racial discrimination. In the last century, the United States expressed

[19] UNITED NATIONS, STATUS OF INTERNATIONAL INSTRUMENTS 1-89, U.N. Sales No. E.87.XIV.2 (1987); *also see* Shelton, *State Practice on Reservations to Human Rights Treaties,* 1 CANADIAN HUM. RTS. Y.B. 205 (1983). Five States subsequently withdrew reservations they had filed to the CPR Covenant, thus reducing to 23% the number of States with reservations.

concern over the treatment of Jews in Eastern Europe and on several occasions made formal protests to the governments of Romania and Russia. The United States sought through diplomatic means to halt the Turkish massacre of some 200,000 Armenians prior to World War I.

After World War I, President Woodrow Wilson contributed to the first truly international formulation of human rights reflected in the "minorities treaties" between the Allied and Associated Powers and a number of defeated States. In 1929, the United States ratified an international convention abolishing slavery.

As World War II began, President Roosevelt gave new prominence to the role of human rights in international relations in his "Four Freedoms" message to Congress. The United States, he said, looked to a future world founded on four essential freedoms: freedom of speech and expression, freedom of worship, freedom from want, and freedom from fear. "Freedom," said Roosevelt, "means the supremacy of human rights everywhere."[20]

At the 1945 San Francisco Conference, which adopted the United Nations Charter, Secretary of State Edward R. Stettinius expressed the hope that the proposed U.N. Commission on Human Rights would "promptly undertake to prepare an international bill of rights which can be accepted by all the member nations as an integral part of their own systems of law, just as our Bill of Rights has been an integral part of our system of law." Enumerating the "Four Freedoms" stated by President Roosevelt, he pledged that the United States Government "will work actively and tirelessly, both for its own people, and—through the international organization—for peoples generally, toward protection and promotion of these rights and freedoms."[21] In his closing speech to the Conference, President Truman said that under the Charter "we have good reason to expect the framing of an international bill of rights, acceptable to all the nations involved. The bill of rights will be as much a part of the international life as our own Bill of Rights is a part of our Constitution."[22] When the Universal Declaration of Human Rights was before the General Assembly in 1948, Mrs. Eleanor Roosevelt stressed that it "was first and foremost a declaration of the basic principles to serve as a common standard for

[20] STATE DEPT., 1 FOREIGN RELATIONS OF THE UNITED STATES 25-26 (1942).
[21] 12 STATE DEPT. BULL. 928-29 (1945).
[22] 1 U.N.C.I.O. DOCS. 717 (1945).

all nations. Its proclamation by the General Assembly would be of importance comparable to the 1789 Proclamation of the Rights of Man or the Declaration of Independence of the United States of America, and similar declarations made in other countries."[23]

### 1.5.2 The United States Turns Inward

Despite this early interest and leadership, the United States withdrew from international human rights activism during the Eisenhower Administration. While personal attitudes of the President and Secretary of State toward human rights treaties contributed to the abandonment of leadership in the international community, much more damaging to America's leadership was the chilling effect of the so-called Bricker era.

Between 1952 and 1957, there were various efforts to amend the U.S. Constitution with respect to the making and effect of treaties and other international agreements. Although the wording of the proposals varied widely over the years, the several versions of the proposed Bricker Amendment had one common objective: to insulate the United States from international human rights conventions.[24]

Three events gave rise to fears that international standards of human rights might be imposed upon the United States. The first concern was the human rights Covenants then being drafted in the United Nations. The second source of concern was the decision of the California Court of Appeals in *Sei Fijii v. State,* which held that the human rights provisions of the U.N. Charter were binding treaty obligations which superseded inconsistent state legislation by virtue of the supremacy clause.[25] The third, and most ominous to some segments of the American legal and political establishment, was the brief filed in the "restrictive covenant" cases by the NAACP, citing the Universal Declaration of Human Rights as the source of a rule of international law invalidating racial restrictions on the ownership of property.[26]

[23] 3 U.N. GAOR (180th mtg.) at 862 (1948).

[24] *See* W. BISHOP, INTERNATIONAL LAW: CASES AND MATERIALS 110-112 (1971).

[25] Sei Fujii v. California, 217 P. 2d 481 (1950), *rehearing denied,* 218 P. 2d 595 (Cal. App. 1950), *aff'd on other grounds,* 38 Cal. 2d 718, 242 P. 2d 617 (1952).

[26] *See* Corrigan v. Buckley, 271 U.S. 323 (1926), Hansberry v. Lee, 311 U.S. 32 (1940, Shelly v. Kraemer, 344 U.S. 1 (1948), Barrows v. Jackson, 346 U.S. 249 (1953). *Cf.* Lockwood, *The United Nations Charter and United States Civil Rights Litigation: 1946-1955,* 69 IOWA L. REV. 901 (1984).

To avoid Senate enactment of the Bricker Amendment, Secretary of State Dulles assured the Senate that no human rights convention would be submitted for its advice and consent. Although Dulles did not formally withdraw the Genocide Convention, which had been submitted to the Senate in 1949 by President Truman, his pledge had the effect of withdrawing executive support for ratification of the Convention. Finally, the provisions of State Department Circular 175, which suggested a circumscribed treaty-making power, were quickly construed as a declaration of the illegitimacy of human rights treaties.[27]

### 1.5.3 Re-entering the Mainstream

The Dulles commitment was reversed by the Kennedy Administration, which submitted several international human rights conventions to the Senate. While the United States has yet to reclaim its earlier position of leadership in the international human rights movement, a disavowal of the Eisenhower-Dulles policy has been apparent in subsequent Republican and Democratic administrations.

In 1967, the United States joined in an overwhelming vote in the Economic and Social Council to authorize the Commission on Human Rights to study "situations which reveal a consistent pattern of violations of human rights, as exemplified by the policy of *apartheid.*" In 1970, the United States supported ECOSOC resolution 1503, which created a procedure for considering private communications which appear to reveal a "consistent pattern of gross and reliably attested violations of human rights and fundamental freedoms." President Nixon urged the Senate to give its advice and consent to the long-pending Genocide Convention.

Then, the Final Act of the Conference on Security and Cooperation in Europe was signed in Helsinki in 1975 by 33 Western and Eastern European States as well as the United States and Canada. While not a formal treaty, all of the signatories agreed to respect the human rights set forth in the document and to submit to a continuing review

[27] "Treaties should be designed to promote United States interests by securing action by foreign governments in a way deemed advantageous to the United States. Treaties are not to be used as a device for the purpose of effecting internal social changes, or to try to circumvent the constitutional procedures established in relation to what are essentially matters of domestic concern." 11 F.A.M. 700, 796 (State Dept. Circular No. 175).

process. The 1989 plenary review meeting in Vienna reaffirmed the commitment of the 35 signatories to respect human rights and, more specifically, to consider acceding to the two Covenants and the Optional Protocol. In order to monitor human rights and other developments within the Helsinki context, a joint executive-legislative U.S. Commission on Security and Cooperation in Europe was created in 1976.

During this period there also were bipartisan Congressional initiatives designed to elevate human rights to a more prominent position on the foreign policy agenda. Beginning in 1973, the House Foreign Affairs Subcommittee on International Organizations initiated a series of hearings and reports. The first round of hearings resulted in the release of a report with a number of recommendations, many of which (such as designation of human rights officers in each of the State Department's five geographic bureaus) were implemented early in 1974.[28] In mid-1975, the State Department responded to further recommendations by creating an Office of Humanitarian Affairs, appointing a special assistant on human rights in the Office of the Deputy Secretary, and designating an Assistant Legal Adviser for Human Rights in the Office of the Legal Adviser.

Several statutes created a linkage between U.S. bilateral assistance and a potential recipient's human rights record.[29] Section 32 of the Foreign Assistance Act of 1973[30] and Section 46 of the Foreign Assistance Act of 1974[31] expressed "the sense of the Congress" that the President should reduce or terminate economic, military or security assistance in cases of a "consistent pattern of gross violations of internationally recognized human rights." The International Development and Food Assistance Act of 1975 became the first human rights legislation to adopt mandatory language, prohibiting aid to human rights violators, although it did allow such aid despite human rights violations if "assistance will directly benefit the needy

[28] "Human Rights in the World Community: A Call for U.S. Leadership," Report of the Subcommittee on International Organizations and Movements, Committee on Foreign Affairs, 93rd Cong., 2d Sess. (1974).

[29] *See generally* Cohen, *Conditioning U.S. Security Assistance on Human Rights Practices,* 76 AJIL 246 (1982); International Human Rights Law Group, U.S. Legislation Relating Human Rights to U.S. Foreign Policy (4th ed. 1991).

[30] 87 Stat. 733 (1973).

[31] 88 Stat. 1815 (1974) (amending Sec. 502B of the Foreign Assistance Act of 1961).

people in such a country."[32] In 1976, the International Security Assistance and Arms Export Control Act further strengthened the prohibition on security assistance to human rights violators and, *inter alia,* directed the President "to formulate and conduct international security assistance programs of the United States in a manner which will promote and advance human rights."[33] Then, in 1977, Congress prohibited the United States from approving any World Bank or Inter-American Development Bank loans to countries exhibiting a "consistent pattern of gross violations of human rights," exempting only those loans aimed at "basic human needs."[34]

At the outset, the Carter Administration announced that human rights considerations would play an integral part in the formulation of foreign policy. This new policy, combined with legislation already in force which would deny or reduce military assistance and other foreign aid to governments that engaged in a "consistent pattern of gross violations of internationally recognized human rights," suggested that the United States would move further into the mainstream of the international human rights movement. Additional encouragement came with the Administration's announcement that it would ratify the human rights Covenants, as well as other conventions which had been pending for years. The Ford Administration had begun to support the strengthening of the Inter-American Commission on Human Rights in 1976; the Carter Administration pledged to increase this support both directly as an OAS member and indirectly through domestic human rights policy. Offending countries were put on notice that human rights violations would cost them something.[35] In 1977, President Carter signed the American Convention on Human Rights and the two Covenants. In 1979, he submitted the Covenants and two other treaties pertaining to human rights to the Senate for its advice and consent.[36]

The first international conference to review implementation of the Helsinki Final Act was held in Belgrade during the first year of the

[32] International Development and Food Assistance Act of 1975, Pub. L. No. 94-161, Sec. 310, 89 Stat. 860 (1975) (amending Sec. 116 of the Foreign Assistance Act of 1961).

[33] International Security Assistance and Arms Export Control Act of 1976, Pub. L. No. 94-329, Sec. 301(a), 90 Stat. 748 (1976) (amending Sec. 502B of the Foreign Assistance Act of 1961).

[34] International Financial Institutions Act of 1977, Sec. 701, 22 U.S.C. Sec. 262d, Pub. L. No. 95-118.

[35] *See,* e.g., President Carter's commencement address at the University of Notre Dame, State Dept. News Release, 22 May 1977.

[36] Message of the President, *supra* note 18.

Carter Administration. In signing the Final Act, the Soviet Union and the Eastern Bloc States had agreed to submit to procedures designed to review their respect for the human rights stipulated in the document, thereby abandoning the argument that external scrutiny was an improper interference in their domestic affairs. It was with that fact in mind, and in anticipation of the October 1977 conference, that Senator Robert Dole reminded the Senate that "human rights has become a cornerstone of American foreign policy with the full support of the Congress."[37]

If human rights considerations were to play an integral part in the formulation of foreign policy, an inadequate bureaucracy would have to be expanded. The Office of Humanitarian Affairs, as originally mandated, consisted of two people, the Coordinator and Deputy Coordinator of Human Rights. Under the Ford Administration, an additional foreign service officer was assigned to assist the Deputy Coordinator. In addition to the Office of Humanitarian Affairs, the Department of State had assigned a human rights officer to each geographical and functional bureau. In 1977 the rank of Coordinator was upgraded to that of Assistant Secretary, and the Department of State established a Bureau of Human Rights and Humanitarian Affairs.[38] The Bureau is charged with administering the legislative mandate, accomplishing the country's human rights policy goals, and coordinating the United States' efforts to fulfill its international human rights obligations.

Critical of the Carter Administration for allegedly pursuing a human rights policy which hectored those whom the United States could influence (its friends) and not those whose reaction should be feared (its adversaries), the Reagan Administration reinterpreted rather than eliminated the role of human rights considerations in American foreign policy.[39] The statutory guidelines for applying human rights considerations to foreign aid and financial assistance decisions remain in place, and the United States remains committed to "working to

[37] CONG. REC., 19 Sept. 1977, at 15188.

[38] Foreign Relations Authorization Act, Fiscal year 1978, Pub. L. No. 95-105, 91 Stat. 846, Sec. 7 (1977).

[39] The bipartisan rejection by the Senate Foreign Relations Committee of President Reagan's first nominee for the position of Assistant Secretary of State for Human Rights and Humanitarian Affairs, in part because the nominee had previously called for the repeal of all U.S. legislation linking human rights and foreign policy, underscored the continued commitment of Congress to the policies developed in the 1970s. *See Nomination of Ernest W. Lefever: Hearings before the Senate Comm. on Foreign Relations,* 97th Cong., 1st Sess. (1981).

move all countries to show greater respect for the internationally agreed standards of human rights."[40]

While the Reagan Administration eventually abandoned its flawed distinction between human rights in "totalitarian" and "authoritarian" regimes, one cannot ignore other fundamental differences between the Reagan and Carter policies concerning, for example, the relative importance of various rights or even the existence of economic, social and cultural rights.[41] In addition, U.S. withholding of assessed contributions from the United Nations and U.S. withdrawal from UNESCO and the compulsory jurisdiction of the International Court of Justice demonstrated a certain lack of support for multilateral institutions and, perhaps, international law.

Nevertheless, "[t]he advancement of human rights and the promotion of democracy have been a key tenet of the Reagan Administration's foreign policy."[42] The Reagan Administration supported ratification of the Genocide Convention and submitted the Convention against Torture to the Senate for its advice and consent,[43] although it maintained for eight years the ludicrous official position that ratification of the Covenants was "under review." Without executive branch support, the Senate Foreign Relations Committee took no action on the Covenants during the Reagan years.

Although President Bush generally followed the approach of his predecessor with respect to human rights policy, a more meaningful review of the Covenants and other human rights treaties was instituted mid-way through the Bush Administration's term of office.

[40] *U.S. Commitment to Human Rights: Hearings on Implementation of Congressionally Mandated Human Rights Provisions Before the Subcomm. on Human Rights and International Organizations of the House Comm. on Foreign Affairs,* 97th Cong., 1st Sess. (1981). (Statement of Walter J. Stoessel, Jr., Under Secretary for Political Affairs.)

[41] *Compare,* for example, the different approaches in the State Department's annual reports to Congress on human rights practices. The Carter Administration focused on the three basic categories of rights of the integrity of the person, the right to fulfillment of vital needs (such as food, shelter, health care, and education), and civil and political liberties. *See,* e.g., State Dept., *Report on Human Rights Practices in Countries Receiving U.S. Aid* (1979) at 2-3. The Reagan Administration substituted reporting on "political rights" (the right of citizens to change their government) for Carter's attention to economic rights, and the latter were discussed only in the context of the "economic, social and cultural situation" in each country surveyed. *See,* e.g., State Dept., *Country Reports on Human Rights Practices for 1983* (1984) at 1-2.

[42] "U.S. Human Rights Policy: An Overview," address by Paula Dobriansky, Deputy Assistant Secretary for Human Rights and Humanitarian Affairs, 3 June 1988, State Dept. Bureau of Public Affairs, Current Policy No. 1091, at 1.

[43] Message of the President Transmitting the Convention Against Torture and Other Cruel, Inhuman or Degrading Treatment or Punishment, S. Treaty Doc. No. 20, 100th Cong., 2d Sess. (1988).

In August 1991, the President requested the Foreign Relations Committee to renew its consideration of the Covenant on Civil and Political Rights, and the Committee held hearings in November 1991. The Committee unanimously recommended that the Senate give its advice and consent to the Covenant, including the new package of reservations, understandings, and declarations recommended by the Bush Administration. Following Senate approval, the United States formally ratified the CPR Covenant on 8 June 1992.

No similar interest has been expressed by the Bush Administration in ratification of the Covenant on Economic, Social and Cultural Rights, although other pending human rights treaties (including the Convention on the Elimination of All Forms of Racial Discrimination and the Convention on the Rights of the Child) were reportedly the subject of more serious consideration.

## 1.6 THE INHERENT LIMITATIONS OF UNILATERAL NATIONAL ADVOCACY

No matter how welcome and consistent with American values, there are inherent limitations to a one-nation advocacy of human rights. The place that international human rights should have within the context of a foreign policy whose basic imperative is the defense of national interest is problematic even for a government whose national interests most closely coincide with international human rights programs.[44] The domestic conditions in other countries cannot always be the sole or most important determinant of policy toward that State. Rather, United States policy must be determined by American interests, and priorities, strategies, and tactics must be altered over time and in differing circumstances. Furthermore, a vigorous application of human rights principles may not always be possible if other policy goals are to be attained. But if a national human rights policy can only be selectively applied, such a course will inevitably generate charges of hypocrisy by both proponents and opponents of national human rights initiatives.

Promoting human rights touches on the very foundations of a State's regime, on its sources and exercise of power, on its links to its

[44] *See,* for instance, Statement of Richard Schifter before the 38th United Nations Commission on Human Rights, 8 Mar. 1982.

citizens. It is a difficult issue that may give rise to the charge that the United States is seeking to impose values on other countries as it interferes in their internal affairs. Recent administrations have responded that the rights promoted by United States policy are not just American values but are standards which are derived from three decades of international consensus.

But, as Henkin has observed, the United States has not exactly been a pillar of the church in the formal acceptance of that international consensus. Instead, it has played the role of a flying buttress supporting it from the outside.[45] With the exception of a handful of minor human rights treaties, only the Universal Declaration of Human Rights could be cited as the embodiment of the international consensus as far as the United States was concerned prior to its belated ratification of the CPR Covenant in 1992. The credibility of the United States was impaired so long as it sought to invoke an international consensus and at the same time was unwilling to subject itself to the obligations embodied in that consensus.

It is curious that the United States, through its failure to ratify many important human rights treaties, has chosen to ignore the changes that have occurred in that international consensus since 1948.[46] Yet, in the same way that fundamental constitutional doctrines such as "due process" and "equal protection" required decades of legislative and judicial refinement before they acquired real meaning, the general standards of the Universal Declaration of Human Rights have been given greater definition through their codification in the Covenants and their interpretation by the Human Rights Committee and, eventually, by the Committee on Economic, Social and Cultural Rights.

The importance of the Covenants is not that they signify an end to the doctrinal struggle over the relative priority to be given to civil, political, economic, social, or cultural rights. Opinion in the world as to what constitutes the best form of society and government genuinely diverges. The Covenants do offer the opportunity to nudge the struggle away from purely political confrontations between national governments and toward the application of legal standards and international enforcement mechanisms.

[45] *See* HENKIN, *supra* note 5, at 33.

[46] It is true that the U.S. has accepted the political (not legal) obligations set forth in the Helsinki Final Act in 1975, but, in many respects, the Helsinki standards fall short of the international norms expressed in the Covenants.

In the end, there is no escape from the tedious job of negotiation to establish and maintain international mechanisms that will reinforce the general principles upon which there may be agreement. Human rights simply cannot be promoted without buttressing the principles with mechanisms for surveillance and implementation. This can only come through international accommodation, and that, in turn, depends on continuing consensus building—a more complex process than national advocacy and activism, essential as they may be.[47]

A final argument in favor of the multilateral promotion of human rights is that it may offer a more effective means of persuading States to change certain practices which violate international consensus, at least where those changes do not threaten the very existence of a government. Bilateral pressures, particularly when linked to foreign trade or assistance, may create resentment rather than a willingness to cooperate (particularly when those pressures come from a superpower, such as the United States). However, a State may be more willing to respond to less confrontational recommendations from regional or universal human rights bodies.

The availability of international implementation mechanisms is only the beginning of what promises to be a long and vitally important struggle over the content of the international consensus. It is clear that the human rights Covenants carry the imprint of American values. Indeed, it is unlikely that the United States could ever renegotiate documents as consonant with our traditions. But "universal acceptance of our ideas and even of our words is a dangerous compliment, for it threatens that others, not of our persuasion, will seek to distort them to other meanings and other ends. We will have to be alert to attempts to exploit the inevitable inadequacy of words to extend their peripheral ambiguities in order to erode the hard core of certainty; or to stretch exceptions (e.g. the needs of "national security") until they swallow the stated right."[48]

U.S. ratification of the CPR Covenant is to be warmly welcomed, although at least some of the reservations, understandings, and declarations which accompany the ratification may limit the Covenant's direct effect in the United States. The lack of U.S. government interest in ratification of the ESC Covenant remains inexplicable;

[47] *See* HUMAN DIGNITY: THE INTERNATIONALIZATION OF HUMAN RIGHTS 55-56 (A. Henkin ed. 1979).

[48] L. HENKIN, *supra* note 5, at 31.

perhaps the present volume will contribute to a better understanding within the United States of the content of economic, social, and cultural rights and their potential impact in U.S. law.

Nevertheless, the fact that the United States has now formally accepted one of the most fundamental statements of international human rights norms is extremely encouraging. The intitial U.S. report on compliance with the Covenant required under Article 40 will offer an opportunity for nongovernmental organizations to challenge alleged U.S. failures to protect human rights adequately. A U.S. expert on the Human Rights Committee may make useful contributions to the Committee's developing jurisprudence. Perhaps most importantly, U.S. ratification of the CPR Covenant (and the conventions on genocide and torture) may signal a commitment to international norms and international law which was rarely evidenced during the 1980s.

# PART II
# THE APPLICABLE LAW

# II
# THE APPLICABLE LAW

This chapter examines treaty law from both an international and a domestic perspective as background for the detailed discussion of the two Covenants in relation to United States' law in chapters III and IV. A brief review of the basic elements of the international law of treaties is followed by a more comprehensive treatment of the domestic law of treaties as developed in the United States.

## 2.1 INTERNATIONAL LAW

*Dinah Shelton*

Although there are special forms[1] and definitions[2] of "treaty" under international law, a treaty may be defined generically as a legally binding international agreement between two or more States which is governed by international law.

In 1969, the Vienna Conference completed work on the Vienna Convention on the Law of Treaties,[3] which consists of eighty-five

[1] Treaties may also be called protocols, conventions, covenants, charters, statutes, acts, declarations, concordats, exchanges of notes, agreed minutes, memoranda of agreement, *modi vivendi,* or *proces verbaux.* It is difficult to discern any consistency in the use of forms and titles for international agreements.

[2] See, e.g., J.G. CASTEL, INTERNATIONAL LAW, CHIEFLY AS INTERPRETED AND APPLIED IN CANADA (3d ed. 1976).

[3] Vienna Convention on the Law of Treaties, adopted 22 May 1969; *entered into force* 27 Jan. 1980, 1155 U.N.T.S. 331. Currently, 69 States are parties to the Convention. The United States signed the Convention in 1970 but has yet to ratify it.

articles and an annex. The Convention is not in force for the United States, yet a number of its provisions are essentially codifications of existing customary law.[4] Those provisions which are not constitute presumptive evidence of emerging rules.

The manner in which treaties are negotiated and brought into force does not affect their binding character. There are no substantive requirements of form, and in practice form is governed by usage. Though the Vienna Convention applies only to agreements in written form, Article 3 stipulates that this limitation is without prejudice to the legal force of agreements "not in written form."

The various steps in the creation of obligations by treaty are: negotiation; signature; ratification, accession, or adhesion; entry into force; registration and publication; and application and enforcement. The successful outcome of negotiation is the adoption and authentication of an agreed text. This is followed by signature, which has as one of its functions that of authenticating the text, but authentication may also be done in other ways.[5] Signature may qualify the signatory State to proceed to ratification, acceptance, or approval. While signature alone does not establish consent to be bound, it does create a good faith obligation to refrain from acts calculated to frustrate the object and purpose of the treaty.[6] It is generally agreed that signature does not create an obligation to ratify. Where the treaty is not subject to ratification, acceptance, or approval, signature can establish consent to be bound. Adherence and accession are procedures whereby a State becomes a party to a multilateral agreement which it has not signed and may occur before or after the treaty has entered into force.

Ratification for the United States involves two distinct procedural acts: the first is by the appropriate domestic organ, the Senate; the second is an international procedure which brings a treaty into force by a formal exchange or deposit of the instrument of ratification. The domestic action is a precondition to the international ratification. It is

[4] E.g., "The rules laid down by the Vienna Convention...concerning termination of a treaty relationship on account of breach (adopted without a dissenting vote) may in many respects be considered as a codification of existing customary law on the subject." Legal Consequences for States of the Continued Presence of South Africa in Namibia (South West Africa) Notwithstanding Security Council Resolution 276 (1970), 1971 I.C.J. Advisory Opinion 16.

[5] E.g., by incorporating the text in the final act of a conference, by initialing, or, more recently, by adoption in the U.N. General Assembly through a resolution.

[6] *See* Vienna Convention, *supra* note 3, art. 18; Upper Silesia (Germ. v. Pol.), 1925 P.C.I.J. (Ser. A) No. 7 at 30 (Aug. 25); A.D. McNair, Law of Treaties 119-205 (1961); I. Brownlie, Principles of Public International Law 606-07 (4th ed. 1990).

the intention of the parties reflected in the treaty or elsewhere which determines what acts are necessary to bring the treaty into force.[7]

The provisions of the treaty determine the manner in which and the date on which the treaty enters into force. After a treaty is concluded, the written instruments of ratification or accession, together with any reservations and other declarations, are placed in the custody of a depository, which may be one or more States or an international organization.[8]

### 2.1.1 Reservations

In the process of becoming party to a treaty, States may file reservations to their consent to be bound unless the treaty provides otherwise. The Vienna Convention defines a reservation as a "[u]nilateral statement, however phrased or named, made by a State, when signing, ratifying, accepting, approving or acceding to a treaty, whereby it purports to exclude or to modify the legal effect of certain provisions of the treaty in their application to that state."[9]

The validity of reservations is determined on a contractual and not on a unilateral basis. Prior to 1945, reservations were generally held to be valid only if the treaty concerned permitted reservations and if all other parties accepted the reservations. In essence the reservation constituted a counter-offer which required a new acceptance. This rule rested on the notion of the absolute integrity of the treaty as adopted.

While scattered support for this principle remains, practice in regard to multilateral treaties demonstrates considerable variation on the acceptability and effect of reservations. When questions arose on the admissibility of reservations to the Genocide Convention, a request was made for an advisory opinion from the International Court of Justice.[10] The Court in its opinion stressed the divergence of practice as well as the unique character of the Genocide Convention, including the intent of the drafters and parties that the Convention be universal in scope. Although its findings were expressly limited to the

[7] *See* Vienna Convention, *supra* note 3, art. 14.

[8] The function of the United Nations is important. *See* U.N. Charter, art. 102, and BROWNLIE, *supra* note 6, at 591.

[9] Vienna Convention, *supra* note 3, art. 2(d).

[10] Reservations to the Convention on the Prevention and Punishment of the Crime of Genocide, 1951 I.C.J. Advisory Opinion 15.

Genocide Convention, the Court's often-cited holding was that "a State which has made...a reservation which has been objected to by one or more of the parties to the Convention but not by others, can be regarded as being a party to the Convention if the reservation is compatible with the object and purpose of the Convention...."[11]

The compatibility test is incorporated in the Vienna Convention in Articles 19-21, which provide that where not prohibited or limited by the treaty in question, reservations are permitted, unless "the reservation is incompatible with the object and purpose of the treaty." Under the provisions of Article 20, States may file objections to the reservations submitted by other States, which may prevent entry into force of the treaty between the reserving and objecting State.

The effect of a reservation is to modify relations between the reserving State and other States Parties to the treaty to the extent of the reservations. This applies on a reciprocal basis, meaning that no State may invoke a provision to which it has reserved until the reservation is withdrawn. Reservations may be withdrawn at any time, as may objections to reservations.

State practice with regard to human rights treaties shows that reservations to substantive provisions have not been common. For example, with regard to the 1926 Slavery Convention,[12] only four States have filed reservations,[13] of which three concern the territorial application of the Convention.[14] No reservations have been filed to the Protocol to the Slavery Convention,[15] nor to the Supplementary Convention on Slavery.[16] With regard to the Genocide Convention,[17] every reservation filed concerns territorial application of the Convention to non-self-governing territories or dispute settlement and jurisdictional questions.[18] As of 1 September 1987, 43 of the 124

[11] *Id.*

[12] Slavery Convention, *signed* 25 Sept. 1926, *entered into force* 9 Mar. 1927, 182 U.S.T. 479, T.I.A.S. No. 3532, 60 L.N.T.S. 253.

[13] United Nations, Status of International Instruments, U.N. Doc. ST/HR/5, U.N. Sales No. E.87.XIV.2, at 200-02 (1987).

[14] *Id.* at 200-01.

[15] Protocol Amending the Slavery Convention, *signed* and *entered into force* 7 Dec. 1953, 7 U.S.T. 479, T.I.A.S. No. 3532, 182 U.N.T.S. 51.

[16] Supplementary Convention on the Abolition of Slavery, the Slave Trade, and Institutions and Practices Similar to Slavery, *signed* 7 Sept. 1956, *entered into force* 20 Apr. 1957, 18 U.S.T. 3201, T.I.A.S. No. 6418, 226 U.N.T.S. 3.

[17] Convention on the Prevention and Punishment of the Crime of Genocide, *opened for signature* 9 Dec. 1948, 78 U.N.T.S. 277 (ratified by U.S. Senate on 23 Feb. 1989). *See also* Genocide Convention Implementation Act of 1987, 18 U.S.C. 1091.

[18] Status of International Instruments, *supra* note 13, at 178.

States Parties to the U.N. Convention on the Elimination of Racial Discrimination had filed reservations, of which 29 related to Article 22 of the Convention (requiring submission of disputes arising from the Convention to the International Court of Justice).[19] Only five reservations concerned the anti-discrimination articles of the Convention. Of the 100 parties to the Convention on the Elimination of All Forms of Discrimination Against Women (CEDAW)[20] as of February 1990, 37 had filed reservations, of which 23 could be considered to be substantive.[21] With the unfortunate exception of CEDAW, reservations on dispute settlement mechanisms and those limiting application of human rights conventions in non-self-governing territories constitute the large majority of all reservations filed.

This practice has continued with respect to the Covenants. Neither Covenant expressly addresses the issue of reservations, so the question is one of compatibility with the object and purpose of the treaties.

In regard to the ESC Covenant, 18 States expressed reservations out of the 90 that had ratified as of the end of 1987.[22] The reservations of 17 of the 18 States concern substantive rights, but in many cases the reservations are postponements of application rather than permanent exemptions. Nearly half of the permanent reservations limit in some way the right to strike guaranteed in Article 8(1)(d); three States do not accept the requirement to pay for public holidays; five temporarily or permanently limit the right to education; and one provides regional preferences for workers.

In regard to the CPR Covenant, 25 out of 86 States Parties had made over 120 separate reservations or declarations as of the end of 1987.[23] Twelve states, primarily from the Soviet bloc, lodged objections (having no legal effect) to Article 48(1) as discriminatory. Thirteen States filed what could be termed substantive reservations. Ten of the reservations concern application of the Covenant to non-self-governing territories of the United Kingdom and The Netherlands. Another set of reservations has been filed by parties to the European Convention on Human Rights, giving priority to certain of

[19] *Id.*

[20] *Adopted* 18 Dec. 1979, *entered into force* 3 Sept. 1981, G.A. Res. 34/180, 34 U.N. GAOR, Supp. (No. 46) 193 (1979).

[21] *See* Cook, *Reservations to the Convention on the Elimination of all Forms of Discrimination Against Women,* 30 VA. J. INT'L L. 643 (1990).

[22] *See supra* note 13, at 4-24.

[23] *Id.* at 28-52.

its provisions over those of the Covenant. The remaining reservations made to the CPR Covenant are more varied in nature than those made to the ESC Covenant. More than half concern norms of criminal procedure contained in Articles 10 and 14.

An underlying feature of the majority of the reservations made to substantive provisions is that States wish to maintain some flexibility in their judicial and penal systems, without having procedures that may vary slightly from the Covenant criticized as violating the treaty's principles. For example, one of the most common reservations limits Article 10, paragraph 3, which requires the segregation of adult convicts from juvenile offenders.[24] As is stated in the Danish reservation, "considerable efforts are made to ensure appropriate age distribution of convicts..., but it is considered valuable to maintain possibilities of flexible arrangements."[25] Similarly, 35 reservations have been made to sub-paragraphs of Article 14. These relate to the appeal of minor offenses not involving imprisonment; the retrial of acquitted defendants in certain circumstances; the access of the press to trials and hearings; the publication of sentences; and the requirement of free legal assistance. The large number of separate reservations reflects the precision of reserving States, which frequently file separate reservations for each paragraph of an article, rather than reserving to the entire article.[26]

Finally, reservations have been made regarding restrictions on speech. Eleven States have taken issue with Article 20's ban on racist and war propaganda, finding it to contradict the guarantee of free speech set forth in Article 19. Procedural and territorial reservations concern application of the provisions of the treaty to non-self-governing territories and compatibility of obligations under the Covenant with those under other treaties. Both the Federal Republic of Germany and the United Kingdom have made reference in their reservations to their obligations under other treaties. In the latter case, this was done by reference to the United Kingdom's Charter obligations within the Trusteeship system:

> ...The United Kingdom declare their understanding that, by virtue of Article 103 of the Charter of the United Nations, in the event of any

[24] Twelve States have filed such a reservation as of 1987. *Id.* at 28-49.

[25] *Id.* at 33.

[26] For example, five States filed three separate reservations to particular provisions in art. 14.

conflict between their obligations under Article 1 of the Covenant and their obligations under the Charter (in particular, under Articles 1, 2 and 73 thereof) their obligations under the Charter shall prevail.[27]

Eight (Denmark, France, Iceland, Italy, Luxembourg, Norway, Spain, and Sweden) of those States which have adhered to the Optional Protocol have stated that the Human Rights Committee shall not consider any communication from an individual if the matter has been examined under another procedure of international investigation or settlement.[28]

In analyzing the reservations made to the Covenants and the Optional Protocol, it should be noted that none of the former Soviet bloc countries had filed reservations to any of the specific requirements detailed therein. However, no Soviet bloc country had recognized the competence of the Human Rights Committee to hear either State or individual claims. Throughout, the reservations made to the CPR Covenant suggest some dissatisfaction with the drafting of certain individual provisions, hence the more complicated and varied types of reservations presented. The desire to retain individual flexibility is emphasized, particularly in the area of criminal procedure.

Several countries with federal or provincial forms of government have ratified the Covenants, including Canada, Australia, and New Zealand. However, no State has made a reservation with regard to the problem of constitutionally enforcing delegated powers. The absence of such reservations may indicate that the contracting parties perceive no contradiction between their federal systems and their obligations under the Covenants, but, more likely, it stems from the view that, under Article 50 of the CPR Covenant, such reservations would be incompatible with the purposes of the treaty and thus not allowable.

Past United States practice is consistent with the generally limited use of reservations to human rights treaties. The United States submitted one reservation to the 1926 Slavery Convention, none to the Supplementary Convention on Slavery, and none to the two Conventions on the Political Rights of Women. All four treaties were unanimously approved by the Senate.

[27] STATUS OF INTERNATIONAL INSTRUMENTS, *supra* note 13, at 46.

[28] The Committee of Ministers of the Council of Europe specifically recommended this reservation to its member States.

### 2.1.2 Effect and Interpretation of Treaties

The principal rule governing treaty law is that every treaty in force is binding upon the parties to it and must be performed by them in good faith.[29] Further, a party may not invoke the provisions of its internal law as justification for failure to perform a treaty; internationally the treaty takes precedence.[30] Thus, although in the United States a subsequent statute is given effect over a prior treaty, the later statute could not be invoked in international forums to excuse breach of a treaty.[31]

Competence to interpret a treaty rests with the parties, or with institutions or organs on which such competence is conferred by the treaty itself. There are few rules of interpretation, although general principles are set out to aid in treaty interpretation. The most commonly cited principle, as stated in the Vienna Convention, is that "a treaty shall be interpreted in good faith in accordance with the ordinary meaning to be given to the terms of the treaty in their context and in light of its object and purpose."[32]

The textual approach of the Vienna Convention limits the use which can be given to "legislative history" or the *travaux préparatoires.* In a hierarchical approach, Article 32 provides that the preparatory work may be used as a "supplementary means of interpretation" only when a textual approach would leave the meaning ambiguous or obscure or would result in a manifestly absurd or unreasonable interpretation. Preparatory work may also be used to confirm the meaning reached through application of Article 31. The International Court of Justice and the Permanent Court of International Justice before it have refused to resort to preparatory work if the meaning is sufficiently clear in itself.[33]

Compliance and enforcement are generally matters to be undertaken by States Parties individually, although a treaty may give international bodies a supervisory role. In any case, primary responsibility for carrying out treaty obligations rests with States Parties. Disputes are generally resolved according to the procedures provided for in the agreement. In the case of the Covenants, there are several

[29] Vienna Convention, *supra* note 3, art. 26.
[30] *But see id.*, art. 46.
[31] *See* AMERICAN LAW INSTITUTE, 1 RESTATEMENT (THIRD) OF THE FOREIGN RELATIONS LAW OF THE UNITED STATES §115 (1987) (hereinafter cited as "RESTATEMENT").
[32] *Supra* note 3, art. 31(1).
[33] *See,* e.g., BROWNLIE, *supra* note 6, at 630.

different international procedures included in the texts which are discussed more fully below.[34]

## 2.2 UNITED STATES TREATY LAW

*Anne M. Williams*

The basis for United States law concerning treaties lies in the following Constitutional provisions:

*Article II, Section 2, cl. 2*

> He [the President] shall have power, by and with the Advice and Consent of the Senate to make Treaties, provided two thirds of the Senators present concur;....

*Article I, Section 10, cl. 1, 3*

> No [s]tate shall enter into any Treaty, Alliance, or Confederation;....
>
> No [s]tate shall, without the Consent of Congress...., enter into any Agreement or Compact with another [s]tate, or with a foreign Power,....

*Article VI, cl. 2*

> This Constitution, and the Laws of the United States which shall be made in Pursuant thereof; and all Treaties made, or which shall be made, under the Authority of the United States, shall be the supreme Law of the Land; and the Judges in every [s]tate shall be bound thereby, any Thing in the Constitution or Laws of any [s]tate to the Contrary notwithstanding.

It is from judicial interpretations of these provisions and practice developed during the past two hundred years that U.S. treaty law has evolved.

### 2.2.1 What is a Treaty?

Under international law, "treaty" is one name given to an international agreement.[35] International usage appears to sanction the use of the term "treaty" in a generic sense to comprehend all formal

[34] *See infra,* secs. 3.5 and 4.5.

[35] *See* Vienna Convention, *supra* note 3, art. 2; RESTATEMENT §301 comment a at 149. *See generally* M. WHITEMAN, 14 DIGEST OF INTERNATIONAL LAW (1970).

instruments of agreement, by whatever titles designated, between or among States, which create among them a relationship governed by international law.[36] Under United States law, however, the term "treaty" usually denotes only those international agreements concluded by the federal Government which are ratified by the President upon receiving the advice and consent of the Senate.[37]

International agreements brought into force with respect to the United States other than with the advice and consent of the Senate are normally referred to as executive agreements.[38] Both the Covenants have been submitted to the Senate for its advice and consent.[39]

### 2.2.2 Extent of the Treaty-Making Power

Although the Constitution does not explicitly limit the treaty-making power it gives to the President and Senate, it is generally agreed that limitations exist. The scope of some of these limitations has been clearly defined. Thus, for example, treaties may not contravene the Bill of Rights; Thirteenth, Fourteenth, and Fifteenth Amendments to the Constitution; or any other constitutional prohibitions. According to the Supreme Court:

> It would be manifestly contrary to the objective of those who created the Constitution, as well as those who were responsible for the Bill of Rights—let alone alien to our entire constitutional history and tradition—to construe

[36] McLaughlin, *The Scope of the Treaty Power in the United States,* 42 MINN. L. REV. 709, 710 (1958).

[37] In construing the term "treaty" in a congressional enactment the courts will look to the intent of Congress to determine whether the term refers specifically to an Article II international agreement. Rossi v. Brown, 467 F.Supp. 960 (D.C. Cir. 1979).

[38] *See generally,* RESTATEMENT §303 and comments. No one has clearly stated when an international agreement should be submitted to the Senate as a treaty and when it need not be, but the State Department has suggested the following guidelines:

> In determining a question as to the procedure which should be followed for any particular international agreement, due consideration is given to the following factors...:
>
> a. The extent to which the agreement involves the commitments or risks affecting the nation as a whole;
>
> b. Whether the agreement is intended to affect [s]tate laws;
>
> c. Whether the agreement can be given effect without the enactment of subsequent legislation by the Congress;
>
> d. Past United States practice with respect to similar agreements;
>
> e. The preference of Congress with respect to a particular type of agreement;
>
> f. The degree of formality desired for an agreement;
>
> g. The proposed duration of the agreement, the need for prompt conclusion of an agreement, and the desirability of concluding a routine or short-term agreement; and
>
> h. The general international practice with respect to similar agreements.

11 F.A.M. 700, 721.3 (commonly known as "Circular No. 175").

[39] Message of the President Transmitting Four Treaties Pertaining to Human Rights, S. Exec. Doc. No. 95-C, D, E & F, 95th Cong. 2d Sess. (1978).

> Article VI (the Supremacy Clause) as permitting the United States to exercise power under an international agreement without observing constitutional prohibitions. In effect, such construction would permit amendment of that document in a manner not sanctioned by Article V. The prohibitions of the Constitution were designed to apply to all branches of the National Government and they cannot be nullified by the Executive or by the Executive and the Senate combined.[40]

Although it has been argued that the subject matter of treaties is limited by the Tenth Amendment of the Constitution, the Supreme Court summarily disposed of this argument in *Missouri v. Holland*.[41] In that case a Migratory Bird Treaty and subsequent statute regulated the killing of migratory birds. An earlier statute, not in pursuance of a treaty, to regulate the killing of migratory birds had been ruled unconstitutional by lower courts as a violation of the Tenth Amendment. In *Holland,* the treaty and subsequent statute were challenged on the same ground, but were upheld as constitutional, on the ground that the treaty power is an expressly delegated power and that therefore the Tenth Amendment does not apply.

The significance of *Missouri v. Holland* has faded considerably as the powers of Congress have expanded under the Thirteenth and Fourteenth Amendments and the Commerce Clause. As noted by one commentator, "*Missouri v. Holland* will remain interred in the casebook and history tests—and properly so. What is unlikely is that it will find crucial new applications in the development of the American Constitution."[42]

> The treaty power, as expressed by the Constitution, is in terms unlimited except by those restraints which are found in that instrument against the action of the government or of its departments, *and those arising from the nature of the government itself and of that of the states.* It would not be contended that it extends so far as to authorize what the Constitution forbids, *or a change in the character of the government or in that of one of the states,* or a cession of any portion of the territory of the latter without its consent.[43]

Although no court has considered specific treaty provisions as interfering in the governmental activities of a state, a recent case suggests the scope of this prohibition. In *National League of Cities v. Usery*,[44] the Court considered the constitutional validity of the 1974 amendments to the Fair Labor Standards Act which extended the

[40] Reid v. Covert, 354 U.S. 1, 17 (1957).
[41] 252 U.S. 416 (1920).
[42] C.A. Lofgren, *Missouri v. Holland in Historical Perspective,* 1975 Sup. Ct. Rev. 77, 122 (1975). *See also* RESTATEMENT §302 comment d Reporter's Note 3.
[43] De Geofroy v. Riggs, 133 U.S. 258, 267 (1890) (emphasis added).
[44] 426 U.S. 833 (1976).

minimum wage and maximum hours provisions to employees of states and their political subdivisions. The Court held that in attempting to exercise its Commerce Clause authority to regulate wages and hours to be paid by the states,

> Congress has sought to wield its power in a fashion that would impair the [s]tates' "ability to function effectively in a federal system".... This exercise of congressional authority does not comport with the federal system of government embodied in the Constitution. We hold that insofar as the challenged amendments operate to directly displace the [s]tates' freedom to structure integral operations in areas of traditional governmental functions, they are not within the authority granted Congress by Art. I, S.8, c1.3.[45]

When read in conjunction with *dicta* such as that in *Geofroy v. Riggs, Usery* suggests that the treaty-making power is limited at least by those matters which would displace the states' freedom to structure integral operations in areas of traditional governmental functions.[46]

In other cases the assertion of additional constitutional limitations to the treaty-making power has failed. In *Edwards v. Carter,*[47] for example, the Court of Appeal found that the property clause in Art. IV, section 3, clause 2, did not give Congress exclusive jurisdiction over the disposition of property belonging to the United States. Therefore, the property clause does not prohibit the transfer of U.S. property through self-executing treaties.[48]

Beyond these constitutional limitations, the treaty-making power appears to be essentially unlimited.

Contrary to what was once suggested, the Constitution does not require that an international agreement deal only with "matters of international concern." "International law knows no limitations on the purpose or subject matter of international agreements, other than that they may not conflict with a preemptory norm of international law.... Thus, the United States may make an agreement on any subject suggested by its national interests in relations with other nations."[49]

[45] 426 U.S. 852. In a footnote the Court stated: "We express no view as to whether different results might obtain if Congress seeks to affect integral operations of state governments by exercising authority granted it under other sections of the Constitution such as the spending power, Art. 1, Sec. 8, c1.1., or Sec. 5 of the Fourteenth Amendment."

[46] *See* RESTATEMENT §302 Reporters Notes 1 and 3 at 155, 156-7.

[47] 580 F.2d 1055 (D.C. Cir. 1978), *cert. denied,* 435 U.S. 907 (1978).

[48] It is interesting to note that the Court assumed the Panama Canal treaties, the subject of the case, to be self-executing. The Court contrasted the property clause with the appropriation clause, which it considered to give exclusive power to Congress. Therefore, treaties requiring appropriations cannot be self-executing. It appears, then, that the real question in this case is not the constitutional validity of the treaties, but their self-executing nature.

[49] RESTATEMENT §302 comment c at 153-4; *also see* Reporters' Note 2 at 155-56.

Even if there were a requirement that an agreement be of "international concern," it is difficult to see how this could constitute a substantive limitation on the scope of the treaty power. Indeed, it could be persuasively argued that simply by making a matter the subject of an international agreement the requisite level of "international concern" had been attained (so long as the treaty was entered into in good faith and was not merely a sham for an essentially unilateral U.S. action).

In any event, human rights have been the subject of multilateral and bilateral international agreements at least since the 1648 Treaty of Westphalia. Despite the limited number of international human rights treaties which the United States has ratified, U.S. international treaty commitments nevertheless include obligations with respect to slavery, refugees, protection of combattants and civilians during armed conflict, women's rights, and workers' rights.

In summary, the Constitution grants broad treaty-making powers while imposing few limitations on these powers. A treaty may not violate express international norms, including the rights guaranteed in the Bill of Rights, or operate to destroy either the federal or a state's form of government. A treaty which violates the Constitution cannot operate as the law of the land and be enforced in the courts. However, there is no constitutional barrier to U.S. ratification of the Covenants or other international human rights instruments.

### 2.2.3 The Treaty-Making Process

#### *Advice and Consent*

Other than prescribing that the Senate must give its advice and consent to the ratification of a treaty, the Constitution is silent on the process of treaty making. It does not even state how or at what stage in that process the Senate should give its advice and consent.

Originally, it was thought that the Senate would participate with the President in negotiating a treaty, giving its advice and consent at every juncture.[50] However, when President Washington attempted to involve the Senate in negotiations with the Southern Indians, the

[50] One of the reasons for giving the Senate, rather than the House of Representatives, the advice and consent role was the small size of the Senate. It was felt that the secrecy necessary to most negotiations would be kept more readily by this smaller body. McLaughlin, *supra* note 36, at 736-39.

subsequent debate over documents so annoyed him that he reportedly said that "he would be damned if he ever went there again."[51] Since that time, the policy has been to solicit the advice of the Senate formally only after a treaty has been negotiated and signed.

Nevertheless, in an impressive number of instances, the Senate or its committees dealing with foreign affairs have participated in the negotiating process in advance of the conclusion of a treaty, lending at least advisory assistance but leaving the ultimate power of consent or non-consent to the formal senate vote. The House of Representatives has likewise participated in such an advisory role. Thus, in some instances, members of the Senate and House of Representatives have been members of the U.S. delegations to important international conferences at which treaties were formulated. An outstanding example is the United Nations Conference on International Organization at San Francisco at which the Charter of the United Nations was signed. On the U.S. delegation at that conference were the highest ranking Democratic and Republican members of the Senate Committee on Foreign Relations and the House Committee on Foreign Affairs. In other cases, due to the special importance of a contemplated treaty, the Executive Branch has sought and obtained the cooperation of the Senate.[52]

Once negotiations are complete, the President signs the treaty as an indication that the text represents the agreement reached by the parties.[53] At that stage, the President decides whether to submit the treaty to the Senate for its advice and consent to ratification.[54] If it is submitted to the Senate, the President usually sends an accompanying report explaining the treaty's provisions and the circumstances which make its ratification desirable.

Once the Senate receives the treaty, it is referred to the Committee on Foreign Relations. "The Committee's procedure on a treaty is the same as that on bills and resolutions. All proceedings, including the motion to report, are by majority vote. The Senate rules do not

[51] Id. at 738. *See also* L. HENKIN, FOREIGN AFFAIRS AND THE CONSTITUTION 130-32 (1972); Staff of Senate Comm. on Foreign Relations, 95th Cong., 1st Sess., *The Role of the Senate in Treaty Ratification* 33-42 (Comm. Print 1977).

[52] 30 WHITEMAN, *supra* note 35, at 53.

[53] Although not formally bound prior to ratification, after signature the United States also "is obliged to refrain from acts that would defeat the object and purpose of the agreement." RESTATEMENT §312(3) at 172; *also see* comment i at 174-75 and Reporters' Note 6 at 178.

[54] The Senate does not "ratify" a treaty. Rather it gives advice and consent to ratification. The President ratifies.

regulate that hearings be held or a written report filed, but this has become customary."[55]

The Committee may or may not decide to report the treaty to the full Senate for its advice and consent. Sometimes the Executive Branch may request that the Committee withhold or suspend action on the treaty. When the treaty is submitted to the full Senate, the advice and consent of the Senate must be given by a vote of two-thirds of the Senators present. Few treaties have been defeated in recent years by a direct vote, and non-action is the usual method of withholding consent to controversial treaties.

### *Reservations, Understandings and Declarations*

By the time a treaty is returned to the President for ratification, it may have been clarified, altered, or amended, either by the Executive Branch itself or by the Senate in the process of giving its advice and consent.[56] Whatever the process, the treaty ratified by the President will contain only those reservations and understandings attached by the Senate as conditions to its advice and consent to ratification.[57]

These conditions under which the United States agrees to be bound by a treaty may be formulated under a number of different names, although the legal effects depend not upon their label but upon their nature. As noted above in section 2.1, a reservation formally seeks to modify the international legal effect of certain provisions of a treaty and directly affects the bilateral or multilateral international obligations of the United States.

An *understanding* does not change the substance of a treaty provision. Instead, it is a unilateral attempt to clarify or explain the meaning of a treaty provision, primarily relevant to the treaty's meaning in domestic law. The President will normally communicate any understanding (and reservations) to the other parties to a treaty upon ratification, and U.S. courts appear to be bound to interpret a treaty subject to any such explicit understanding.[58]

[55] *Role of the Senate, supra* note 51, at 3.

[56] The power of the Senate to attach reservations to a treaty when giving its advice and consent was noted in Haver v. Yaker, 76 U.S. (9 Wall.) 32, 35 (1869).

[57] *See* RESTATEMENT §314 comment b at 187.

[58] *See* RESTATEMENT §314 at 186 comment d at 188. The Supreme Court recently suggested, in *dictum,* that even informal interpretations of a treaty as expressed in the Senate's pre-ratification debates and reports may be relevant to the treaty's meaning. *See* United States v. Stuart, No. 87-1064, slip op. at 12-14 (Sup. Ct. Feb. 28, 1989). Justice Scalia's concurrence, which rejects the use of such debates where the treaty itself is unambiguous and questions their use in any circumstances, is more persuasive than the majority opinion. "The question before us in a treaty case is what the two or more sovereigns agreed to, rather than what a single one of them, or the legislature of a single one of them, thought it agreed to." *Id.* at 4 (Scalia, J., concurring in the judgment). *Cf.*

The President and/or Senate also may include certain *declarations* regarding a treaty, which may be equivalent to understandings related to the meaning of a treaty provision or which may refer to purely domestic concerns not directly related to a treaty's meaning or the substance of the international obligations undertaken. Into this latter category would fall, for example, declarations regarding the non-self-executing nature of a treaty[59] or the declaration attached to the Genocide Convention, stating that the United States would not formally deposit its ratification until the adoption of domestic implementing legislation.

Often there is confusion in the use of a particular label or descriptive term, and in evaluating the legal effect of a particular statement. The effect of any statement necessarily depends upon its substance. It is the substance, and not what it is called, that determines whether a statement is a reservation or a declaration short of a reservation. Thus, an interpretation clearly in accord with the intent of the treaty negotiators may improperly be designated a reservation.[60]

Sometimes the Senate attaches conditions to its consent to a treaty which do not modify the international obligations it imposes, but which control its effect in the United States. For example, in an extended and unedifying controversy with several Presidents, the Senate has consented to the United States' adherence to general arbitration conventions only on condition that any specific submission to arbitration thereafter also obtain the consent of the Senate. The Senate has sometimes insisted that a treaty should not take effect, or that action not be taken under it by United States officials, without prior approval of Congress. There also are reservations requiring the President to perform some domestic act. On several occasions the Senate provided that nothing in a treaty could enhance the powers of the President; in a recent instance, the Senate also expressed its intent that nothing in the treaty add to, or subtract from, the powers of Congress.[61]

A condition imposed by the Senate that does not seek to modify the treaty is not part of the treaty and therefore not part of the "supreme

---

Rainbow Navigation, Inc. v. Dept. of Navy, 686 F.Supp. 354 (1988) (significance of Senate understanding of the Anti-Ballistic Missile Treaty at the time of its advice and consent to ratification); Rainbow Navigation, Inc. v. Dept. of Navy, 699 F.Supp. 339 (1988) (same).

[59] *See* discussion *infra,* Part 5.

[60] *See* WHITEMAN, *supra* note 35, at 137.

[61] L. HENKIN, *supra* note 51, at 134.

Law of the Land." Nevertheless, such a condition may constitute a legitimate exercise of the Senate's advice and consent role and thus have legal effect.[62]

### *Ratification*

After the Senate gives its advice and consent, a treaty is returned to the President for ratification. The President may either ratify the treaty as presented by the Senate, or, if he believes any Senate action taken is undesirable, the treaty may be returned to the Senate for further consideration. The President may also decide not to ratify the treaty.[63]

After a treaty is ratified, which is a domestic action, some form of international action must be taken to bring the treaty into force. Usually the treaty specifies this action as the exchange or deposit of a certain number of instruments of ratification.

After a treaty is ratified, the President issues a proclamation making the treaty public. There is disagreement over whether a treaty must be proclaimed before it takes effect domestically, for neither the Constitution nor statute requires proclamation. Nonetheless, the usual practice is to issue a proclamation.[64] The proclamation may be useful in determining the date of entry into force of the treaty.

[62] *See* RESTATEMENT §303 Reporters' Note 4 at 164.

[63] The procedure by which a treaty is ratified has been described as follows: "*Ratification.* Upon the supposition that the Senate, in accordance with recommendations made by the Committee on Foreign Relations, advises and consents to ratification of the treaty the original document will be returned to the Department of State with a resolution certifying to that effect. It then becomes necessary for an instrument of ratification to be prepared for the President's signature. This instrument will set forth all pertinent facts, including the title of the treaty, the date of signature, the countries involved, and the language or languages in which signed, with an indication that the original or the certified copy of the treaty is annexed thereto, followed by a specific statement as to the action taken by the Senate, with the text of any reservation or amendment which the Senate may have proposed, and a declaration by the President that he has seen and considered the said treaty, and that he does thereby 'in pursuance of the aforesaid advice and consent of the Senate, ratify and confirm the same and every article and clause thereof.' A duplicate of this ratification, the duplicate commonly being referred to as 'the exchange copy,' is prepared at the same time. It differs from the principal instrument in that the text of the treaty usually is set forth 'word for word' in the instrument of ratification, whereas the principal instrument annexes the original or the certified copy. The instrument of ratification and the exchange copy thereof then are sent to the White House where, if approved by the President, he will sign them and have them returned to the Department of State for further action." Whittington, *Treaties and Other International Agreements: Procedure, Formalities, and the Information Facilities of the Department of State,* STATE DEPT. BULL. No. 255, 13 May 1944, at 445, 452-453.

[64] WHITEMAN, *supra* note 35, at 113-117; HENKIN, *supra* note 51, at 158; RESTATEMENT §312 comment k at 175 Reporters' Note 4 at 177.

### *Enforcement of Treaties*

Under Article VI, clause 2, of the Constitution, treaties are the law of the land. Thus, in addition to creating international obligations, they automatically have force as domestic law and are to be enforced domestically as federal statutes.

Although Article VI does not specify the relationship between treaties and federal statutes, the courts have found them to be of equal status.

By the Constitution, a treaty is placed on the same footing as an act of legislation. Both are declared to be the supreme law of the land, and no superiority is given to either over the other. When the two relate to the same subject, the courts will always endeavor to construe them so as to give effect to both, if that can be done without violating the language of either; if the two are inconsistent, the one last in time will control the other, provided that the treaty on the subject is self-executing.[65]

With only one exception, cases in this area have involved a conflict between an earlier treaty and a later statute with the latter prevailing.[66] In *Diggs v. Shultz,* for example, the Court held valid a statute permitting the importation of chrome from Rhodesia and thereby overriding a treaty commitment to boycott trade with Rhodesia.[67]

The congressional power of abrogation does not extend beyond municipal law. Technically, Congress is not acting upon the treaty when it passes a subsequent inconsistent statute. Rather, it is merely exercising its basic legislative power. Thus congressional action does not vary a treaty's validity under international law; barring renunciation by a State involved, the treaty remains in full force internationally. Passage of an inconsistent statute does not *per se* constitute a breach of international obligations, but any affected state could seek relief by appropriate means.[68]

Article VI of the Constitution specifically addresses the relationship of treaties to state laws and constitutions: treaties prevail at all times

[65] Whitney v. Robertson, 124 U.S. 190, 194 (1888); *also see* The Chinese Exclusion Case, 130 U.S. 581, 600 (1889); RESTATEMENT §115 comment and Reporters' Notes at 63-69.

[66] "In contrast to the many instances of judicially sanctioned abrogation of treaties by statutes, the Supreme Court has explicitly ruled only once that a treaty provision voids an earlier statute." Cook v. United States, 208 U.S. 102 (1933). *Also see Congressional Power to Abrogate the Domestic Effect of a United Nations Treaty Commitment,* 13 COL. J. TRANS. L. 155, 158 (1974).

[67] 470 F.2d 461 (D.C. Cir. 1972), *cert. denied,* 411 U.S. 931 (1973).

[68] See RESTATEMENT §115(1)(b).

over state law and shall be applied by the state courts. This provision was designed to ensure that treaties were binding on the states, something which was not clear under the Articles of Confederation.[69] The leading case upholding the supremacy of treaties over state law is *Ware v. Hylton,* in which the British Peace Treaty of 1783 was held to override a Virginia statute sequestering British-owned debts.[70] Since that time:

> [O]ther cases have reserved state action against the treaty rights of aliens to inherit or acquire property or to engage in occupations, subject to "the normal scope of the police power." Treaty provisions have prevailed over state statutes of limitations, over probate court practice with respect to the powers of foreign consuls to administer the property of aliens, over state policy with respect to the limitation of tort liability, and even over state taxation.[71]

Responsibility for carrying out treaty obligations lies with the President. If a treaty requires implementing legislation it is the duty of the President to request congressional action. If a treaty is self-executing or has been implemented by Congress, the President has the duty, as with laws, to see that the treaty is faithfully implemented.

Often the Executive Branch alone can implement treaties just as it executes other laws. The Executive Branch can intervene in court cases which require the interpretation of treaties, and it can communicate with state governors and legislatures regarding the international obligations of the United States.[72]

At other times, the courts may be the implementing agents of treaties. Where a treaty grants private rights, individuals may seek redress in the courts for the violation of those rights.[73] If prosecuted or sued under a contrary state statute, individuals may use treaty rights as a defense. However, an individual seeking court relief must comply with all statutory and court-developed rules involved in bringing suit, including requirements for jurisdiction, case or controversy, justiciability, and standing.

[69] See, e.g., Evans, *Self-Executing Treaties in the United States of America,* 30 BRIT. Y.B. INT'L L. 179-80 (1953).

[70] 3 U.S. (3 Dall) 199 (1796).

[71] Hynning, *Treaty Law for the Private Practitioner,* 23 U. CHI. L. REV. 36, 43-44 (1955).

[72] *See* HENKIN, *supra* note 51, at 165.

[73] See, e.g., 2 RESTATEMENT, §907 comment and Reporters' Notes at 395-99; with respect to remedies in the United States for violations of the customary international human rights law, *see id.* §703 Reporters' Note 7 at 181.

In *Diggs v. Shultz*,[74] a major issue was the plaintiffs' standing to bring the action. Using the tests set out in *Association of Data Processing Service v. Camp*[75] and *Flast v. Cohen*,[76] the Court found that: the plaintiffs could show injury from the U.S. violation of the U.N. embargo on Rhodesia; they were within the zone of interest of the embargo; and there was a logical nexus between the challenged action, the Byrd Amendment, and the plaintiffs' claim. The Court stated, "Of course it is true that appellants' plight stems initially from acts done by Southern Rhodesia, and that their primary quarrel is with it. But this does not foreclose the existence of a judicially cognizable dispute between appellants, on the one hand, and appellees, on the other, who are said to be acting in derogation of the solemn treaty obligation of the United States to adhere to the embargo for so long as it is in being."[77]

In *Diggs v. Richardson,* the issue of standing was not addressed directly, but the Court held the case to be nonjusticiable because the Security Council Resolution on which it was based was non-self-executing.[78] Although the government raised issues of standing and political question, the Court chose not to address them.[79]

As *Diggs v. Richardson* illustrates, one of the major issues raised when litigation involves a treaty is whether or not the treaty is self-executing, i.e., capable of being applied or enforced directly by the courts:

> A treaty is, in its nature, a contract between two nations, not a legislative act. It does not generally effect, of itself, the object to be accomplished, especially so far as its operation is infra-territorial; but is carried into execution by the sovereign power of the respective parties to the instrument.
>
> In the United States, a different principle is established. Our Constitution declares a treaty to be the law of the land. It is, consequently, to be regarded in courts of justice as equivalent to an act of the legislature, whenever it operates of itself without the aid of any legislative provision. But when the terms of the stipulation import a contract, when either of the parties engages to perform a particular act, the treaty addresses itself to the political, not the

[74] *Supra* note 67.
[75] 397 U.S. 150 (1970).
[76] 392 U.S. 83 (1967).
[77] 470 F.2d at 465.
[78] 555 F.2d 848 (D.C. Cir. 1976).
[79] For court dicta on standing, political questions and ripeness *see* Goldwater et al. v. Carter, 617 F. 2nd 697 (D.C.Cir. 1979), *vacated and remanded with directions to dismiss,* 444 U.S. 996 (1979).

judicial department; and the legislature must execute the contract before it can become a rule for the Court.[80]

The *Restatement* treats non-self-executing treaties as exceptions to the general rule that U.S. courts are to give effect to international agreements and identifies an agreement as non-self-executing if the agreement itself "manifests an intention that it shall not become effective as domestic law without the enactment of implementing legislation,"[81] if the Senate requires implementing legislation in giving its consent to a treaty, or if implementing legislation is constitutionally required.[82]

There is much disagreement as to the criteria that should be considered in determining whether or not a treaty is self-executing, and the Fifth Circuit Court of Appeals has referred to the question of self-execution as "one of the most confounding in treaty law."[83] While most commentators would seem to agree that a treaty cannot be self-executing if it requires action that the Constitution reserves for the exclusive law-making power of Congress,[84] it has been observed that "[t]here is no definitive authority" for this proposition.[85]

One criterion frequently suggested is that of the intent of the parties:

> In order for a treaty provision to be operative without the aid of implementing legislation and to have the force and effect of a statute, it must appear that the framers of the treaty intended to prescribe a rule that, standing alone, would be enforced in the courts.[86]

Frequently, however, the intent of the parties is unclear, and neither the language of the treaty nor the legislative history provides guidance in determining the intent. Indeed, as the domestic effect of a treaty is obviously a matter of domestic concern and varies from

[80] Foster v. Nielson, 27 U.S. (2 Pet.) 253, 314 (1829).

[81] RESTATEMENT §111(4)(a) at 43.

[82] *See id.* §111(4) at 42-43 comments h and i Reporters' Notes 5 and 6 at 46-48, 53-57.

[83] United States v. Postal, 589 F.2d 862, 876 (5th Cir.), *cert. denied,* 444 U.S. 832 (1979). *See* Riesenfeld, *The Doctrine of Self-Executing Treaties and U.S. v. Postal: Win at Any Price?,* 74 AJIL 892 (1980); cf. Paust, *Self-Executing Treaties,* 82 AJIL 760 (1988) (arguing that all treaties should be presumed to be self-executing with very limited exceptions).

[84] *See The Over the Top,* 5 F.2d 838 (treaties cannot enact criminal law); Turner v. American Baptist Missionary Union, 24 Fed. Cas. 344, No. 14, 251 (C.C.D. Mich. 1852) (appropriations cannot be made directly by treaty); RESTATEMENT §111 comment i at 47-48.

[85] RESTATEMENT §111 Reporters' Note 6 at 56.

[86] Sei Fujii v. State, 38 Cal. 2d 718, 242 P.2d 617, 620 (1952).

country to country, any "intent" of the parties to a treaty is likely to be illusory or irrelevant.[87]

Where intent is unclear, a court can arrive at two opposing decisions concerning the same language in the same treaty, as it did in *Foster v. Neilson.*[88] There, the plaintiff relied in part on the Florida Purchase Treaty with Spain in his attempt to recover a tract of land in Louisiana. The court held that the treaty was non-self-executing because the language that the grants of land in the ceded territories "shall be ratified and confirmed to the persons in possession of the lands" implied future action by the legislature. Thus, implementing legislation was intended, and the plaintiff's claim could not be upheld without such legislation. Four years later, the same court found, upon examination of the Spanish text, that the same treaty provision was self-executing.[89]

Perhaps the best judicial examination of the question of self-executing treaties is found in *People of Saipan v. United States Dep't of Interior,*[90] which found that the U.S. trusteeship agreement with the United Nations creating the Trust Territory of the Pacific Islands was self-executing:

> The extent to which an international agreement establishes affirmative and judicially enforceable obligations without implementing legislation must be determined in each case by reference to many contextual factors: the purposes of the treaty and the objectives of its creators, the existence of domestic procedures and institutions appropriate for direct implementation, the availability and feasibility of alternative enforcement methods, and the immediate and long-range social consequences of self- or non-self-execution.[91]

In the context of human rights, the holdings by the California Supreme Court in *Sei Fujii* that the human rights clauses of the U.N. Charter are non-self-executing has been followed with little discussion or analysis by courts since 1952.[92] On the other hand, courts seem to have assumed *sub silentio* that the Protocol Relating to the

[87] This argument was used in U.S. v. Postal, *supra* note 83, at 878.
[88] *Supra* note 83.
[89] U.S. v. Percheman, 32 U.S. 51 (1833).
[90] 502 F.2d 90 (9th Cir. 1974), *cert. denied,* 420 U.S. 1003 (1975).
[91] *Id.* at 97.
[92] While many commentators would argue that the case might be decided differently today, no case to date has explicitly departed from the *Fujii* holding. *See,* e.g., Frolova v. U.S.S.R., 761 F.2d 370 (7th Cir. 1985) (clauses are non-self-executing and therefore "do not confer rights on individual citizens").

Status of Refugees is self-executing,[93] and bilateral "friendship" commerce, and navigation" treaties which confer rights on foreign individuals also are regularly deemed to be self-executing without discussion.[94]

President Carter suggested that a declaration be attached to the two Covenants (and other human rights treaties pending before the Senate) to the effect that they are non-self-executing. While there is controversy over the legal effect of such declarations, the more logical view is that the courts are the final decision-makers on this issue.[95]

Over the past 200 years a body of law has developed in the United States which determines the legal responsibility of both private persons and public officers under treaties. The few rules which have emerged from that body of law are sufficiently flexible to permit change and expansion in concepts as the nature of treaties changes. United States law and practice certainly permit the ratification of the Covenants, which are consistent with the centuries-old commitment of the United States to the protection of private rights through international law.

[93] *Cf.* I.N.S. v. Stevic, 467 U.S. 407 (1984) (finding that then-current U.S. law and practice were consistent with the Protocol).

[94] *See* RESTATEMENT §111 Reporters' Note 5 at 54-56.

[95] *See* Henkin, *The Domestic Legal Effect of Declarations that Treaty Provisions are not Self-Executing,* 57 TEX. L. REV. 233 (1979); responses to questions posed by Senator Jacob Javits in *International Human Rights Treaties,* Hearings before the Committee on Foreign Relations, United States Senate, 96 Cong., 1st Sess., at 275-316; RESTATEMENT §303 comment d at 160 Reporters' Note 4 at 164.

# PART III
# THE INTERNATIONAL COVENANT ON CIVIL AND POLITICAL RIGHTS AND THE OPTIONAL PROTOCOL

# III
# THE INTERNATIONAL COVENANT ON CIVIL AND POLITICAL RIGHTS AND THE OPTIONAL PROTOCOL

This chapter discusses the International Covenant on Civil and Political Rights (CPR Covenant) and the Optional Protocol appended thereto.[1] It is divided into five sections. Section 1 analyzes the obligations undertaken by the States Parties to the CPR Covenant, notably the obligations "to respect" and "to ensure" the rights protected. Section 2 deals with the principles of non-discrimination and equality before the law, which, in the system of the Covenant, have the status of general principles. In Section 3, the substantive rights set forth in the Covenant are analyzed with respect to their content and scope and their compatibility with United States law. Section 4 discussed the conditions under which a State Party is permitted to limit those rights or to derogate from them. Finally, Section 5 describes the implementation mechanisms provided for in both the CPR Covenant and the Optional Protocol.

[1] There are numerous books and articles which consider various aspects of the CPR Covenant. Among the most helpful in comparing the substantive norms of the Covenant with corresponding U.S. law and practice are M. Bossuyt, Guide to the TRAVAUX PREPARATOIRES OF THE INTERNATIONAL COVENANT ON CIVIL AND POLITICAL RIGHTS (1987); H. HANNUM, MATERIALS ON INTERNATIONAL HUMAN RIGHTS AND U.S. CRIMINAL LAW AND PROCEDURE (1989); H. HANNUM, MATERIALS ON INTERNATIONAL HUMAN RIGHTS AND U.S. CONSTITUTIONAL LAW (1985); P. SIEGHART, THE INTERNATIONAL LAW OF HUMAN RIGHTS (1983); THE INTERNATIONAL BILL OF RIGHTS: THE COVENANT ON CIVIL AND POLITICAL RIGHTS (L. Henkin ed. 1981).

## 3.1 OBLIGATIONS ARISING FROM THE INTERNATIONAL COVENANT ON CIVIL AND POLITICAL RIGHTS AND THE OPTIONAL PROTOCOL

*Oscar M. Garibaldi*[2]

The obligations established by the CPR covenant are of two kinds. Some are substantive obligations, that is they relate to the treatment to be given by a State Party to the individuals subject to its power. Others are procedural obligations, that is, they relate to the procedures established by the treaty for the international oversight of each State Party's compliance with the substantive obligations. The procedural obligations established by the CPR Covenant are discussed below in Section 5, together with the other obligations, also procedural in nature, that arise from the Optional Protocol.

The substantive obligations arising under the CPR Covenant can in turn be classified into two subcategories: those that derive from the general provisions of Article 2, and those that derive from the more specific provisions contained in Parts I and III. The subject of this section is the substantive obligations arising under Article 2.

Article 2 of the CPR Covenant imposes on State Parties the following (substantive) obligations: (i) "to respect and to ensure" the rights recognized in the Covenant (paragraph 1 of Article 2); and (iii) to ensure that any person who suffers a violation of any of those rights shall have an effective domestic remedy available to him, an appropriate determination of his right to such a remedy, and enforcement of the remedy when granted (paragraph 3 of Article 2).

### 3.1.1 The Obligation "To Respect and to Ensure" the Rights Set Forth in the CPR Covenant

Paragraph 1 of Article 2 of the CPR Covenant establishes the fundamental obligation undertaken by a State Party: "to respect and to

[2] This section and the others that I have contributed to this book were first written in 1979-1980 and were revised and updated several times while awaiting publication. While the original research was conducted in 1979, all reasonable efforts have been made to bring it up to date. I gratefully acknowledge the Editor's assistance in this process and assume full responsibility for any inadequacies that remain. I also acknowledge my debt to Professor William H. Allen, my former partner at Covington & Burling, for his comments to the manuscript and for many other things besides.

ensure to all individuals within its territory and subject to its jurisdiction the rights recognized in the present Covenant, without distinction of any kind, such as race, color, sex, language, religion, political or other opinion, national or social origin, property, birth or other status." This clause specifies the content of the obligation, the individuals who are the beneficiaries of that obligation, and the manner in which it is to be discharged.

The content of the obligation is "to respect and to ensure" the rights recognized in the CPR Covenant. "To respect" means, plainly, to fulfill the specific obligations that are the counterparts of those rights. Thus, for example, the obligation to respect the right defined in the first sentence of Article 7 consists in the obligation to refrain from subjecting a person to torture or to cruel, inhuman or degrading treatment or punishment.

By contrast, the obligation "to ensure" the rights defined in the treaty entails something more than mere fulfillment of those counterpart obligations. "To ensure" suggests the need to take action aimed at guaranteeing that the rights in question are in fact respected.[3] Although the term "to ensure" is not defined in the treaty, the *travaux preparatoires* show that it was meant to refer to the use by the State of its domestic legislative and enforcement apparatus.[4]

[3] Art. 1(1) of the American Convention on Human Rights imposes a similar obligation "to ensure...the free and full exercise" of the rights defined in that treaty. Interpreting this provision, the Inter-American Court of Human Rights has held that the obligation to guarantee (i.e., to ensure) those rights

> "implies the duty of the States Parties to organize the governmental apparatus and, in general, all the structures through which public power is exercised, so that they are capable of juridically ensuring the free and full enjoyment of human rights. As a consequence of this obligation, the States must prevent, investigate and punish any violation of the rights recognized by the Convention and, moreover, if possible attempt to restore the right violated and provide compensation as warranted for damages resulting from the violation."

Velázquez Rodríquez v. Honduras, Inter-Am. Court H.R., Judgment of July 29, 1988, 9 Hum. Rts. L. J. 212, at para. 166.

[4] In early drafts, the word "to ensure" was used as the operative verb of an 14:39:28 Mon 03-01-1993 introductory clause governing various paragraphs, each of which described internal implementation measures. See, e.g., U.N. Doc. E/800, Annex B, Art. 2. At the 1949 session of the Commission on Human Rights, the United States proposed an amendment that would have obligated State Parties "to ensure...the rights set forth in the Covenant," but would have left unspecified the internal arrangements to be adopted by the State for such purpose. The United States representative argued that "[t]he general agreement of the State was sufficient; it was not necessary to go into detail concerning the domestic machinery by which that agreement would be put into effect, all the more so because such enumeration might be incomplete." Statement by Mrs. Roosevelt (U.S.A.), U.N. Doc E/Cn.4/SR.125, at 6 (1949). The ensuing debate shows that the word "to ensure" was generally understood to refer to the use by the State of its domestic legislative and enforcement machinery. *Id.* at 2-19. In the end, the Commission adopted the United States proposal only as an amendment to the first

Consequently, the obligation "to ensure" the rights set forth in Covenant should be understood as an obligation to adopt a domestic legal system that guarantees those rights and to make that system generally effective.[5] The internal measures required to fulfill the obligation to ensure the rights set forth in the treaty include those that are specified in paragraphs 2 and 3 of Article 2.

Most (but not all) of the rights defined in the CPR Covenant have corresponding negative obligations, i.e., obligations that call for mere inaction on the part of the obligor. Consequently, the obligation "to respect" a right will be, in most cases, a negative obligation. By contrast, the obligation "to ensure" the rights set forth in the treaty is always a positive obligation, i.e., it can only be discharged by taking appropriate action, including the actions specified in paragraphs 2 and 3 of Article 2.

The obligation "to respect" and the obligation "to ensure" the rights set forth in the CPR Covenant are mutually independent; a State Party is required to establish a domestic system that effectively guarantees those rights even though it faithfully respects them, and is required to respect those rights even though it is not obligated to do so under its own domestic law. Using a previous example, a State is obliged to prohibit torture even though it never tortures, and it is required not to torture even in circumstances in which torture may not be prohibited by domestic law.[6]

The subjects of the rights, i.e., the individuals with respect to whom the State must discharge its obligation to respect and to ensure the rights set forth in the treaty, are all individuals who are (i) within the territory of the State and (ii) subject to its jurisdiction.[7] In the

---

paragraph of the draft article (which later became the present paragraph 1), and retained the second paragraph of the draft (which later became the present paragraphs 2 and 3). *Id.:* U.NM. Doc. E/1681, Annex, Art. 1.

[5] In the *Velázquez Rodríguez case, supra* note 3, at para. 167, the Inter-American Court of Human Rights observed that "[t]he obligation to guarantee the free and full exercise of human rights is not fulfilled by the existence of a legal system designed to make it possible to comply with this obligation—it also requires the government to conduct itself so as to effectively ensure the free and full exercise of human rights."

[6] *See* Velazquez Rodriguez v. Honduras, *supra* note 2, at paras. 169-188.

[7] It follows, *a contrario sensu,* that under the Covenant persons subject to the jurisdiction of a State but not physically present in its territory do not have rights in relation to that State. In particular, such persons do not have the right, set forth in art. 14(3)(d), not to be tried *in absentia.* It has been suggested that this conclusion runs counter to the spirit of the treaty and calls into question a literal reading of art. 2(1). Similarly, the Human Rights Committee has expressed the view that, notwithstanding the phrase "within its territory," a State Party is accountable under art. 2(1) for violations of rights committed by its agents in the territory of another State. *See* Burgos v. Uruguay, No. R.12/52, *Report of the Human Rights Committee,* U.N. GAOR, Supp. (No. 40) at 176, U.N. Doc. A/36/40; Celiberti de Casariego v. Uruguay, id. at 185. However appealing this

system of the Covenant only individual human beings may be the subjects of rights (other than the right of self-determination established in Article 1).[8] Thus, action by the State directed against a legal entity cannot violate the Covenant except to the extent that it violates the rights of the entity's individual members.

The class of beneficiaries of the rights embraces all individuals who are subject to the jurisdiction of the State and are present within its territories. These conditions may be satisfied not only by nationals but also by aliens, for under customary international law aliens are generally subject to the jurisdiction of the State in whose territory they are physically present. Thus the CPR Covenant was designed to protect both nationals, who until a few decades ago were generally excluded from international protection, and aliens, who are the beneficiaries of a parallel system of diplomatic protection under customary international law. For the purposes of defining the class of subjects of the rights, the term "territory" probably refers to areas within the State's effective control, whether or not such areas are part of a metropolitan territory or are within official and recognized boundaries. Therefore, if the United States ratifies the CPR Covenant, this treaty will apply, barring a reservation, not only to United States territory *stricto sensu* but also to all areas within United States control, including overseas territories and possessions.

The obligation to respect and to ensure the rights defined in the treaty must be discharged in relation to every individual falling in the category just described, "without distinction of any kind, such as race, colour, sex, language, religion, political or other opinion, national or social origin, property, birth or other status." The quoted phrase, an instance of the principle of non-discrimination, prescribes the manner in which that obligation is to be discharged. The principle of non-discrimination is discussed in detail in Section 2 of this chapter.

### 3.1.2 The Obligation to Take General Measures to Give Effect to the Rights Set Forth in the CPR Covenant

Paragraphs 2 and 3 of Article 2 of the CPR Covenant specify the scope of a State Party's obligation to give effect to the treaty within

view may be *de lege ferenda*, it is not correct *de lege lata*, for it ignores the clear test of art. 2(a) and what appears to be the intent of the drafters. See 18 U.N. GAOR C.3 (1257th-1259th mtgs.) at (1963), U.N. Doc. A/C.3/SR.1257-1259.

[8] *Also see* discussion of art. 1 (self-determination), *infra*.

the State's domestic legal system. Paragraph 2 prescribes that "[w]here not already provided for by existing legislative or other measures, each State Party...undertakes to take the necessary steps, in accordance with its constitutional processes and with the provisions of the present Covenant, to adopt such legislative or other measures as may be necessary to give effect to the rights recognized in the present Covenant." This provision sets forth a conditional obligation, i.e., an obligation that arises only to the extent that the State Party's national legal system does not already contain adequate measures to that effect.

Since this provision refers to "legislative or other measures," it is plain that the measures required to be adopted need not take the form of legislation. As we shall see, however, measures that consist of providing for effective remedies in individual cases are specifically contemplated in paragraph 3 of the same article. For this reason, paragraph 2 was probably meant to refer to measures of general application (whether in the form of legislation, administrative regulation, judicial rule-making, or otherwise), as distinguished from measures designed to give effect to the rights set forth in the treaty in individual cases.

There seems to have been a general understanding among the drafters that those measures referred to in paragraph 2 are to be addressed not only to all government officials, but also, in principle, to the general population, in order to make the rights set forth in the CPR Covenant effective against private individuals as well. This principle of generality is not to be understood, however, as a rigid requirement of absolute universality; in enacting general measures to give internal effect to a given right defined in the CPR Covenant, a State is not barred from carving out exceptions to protect other rights or the legitimate exercise of individual preferences.[9]

Neither Article 2 nor general international law requires the incorporation of the treaty into the State's domestic legal system.[10]

[9] For example, a State Party is not required to enact legislation that would obligate private individuals to observe the principle of non-discrimination in all circumstances of their lives. Likewise, under several provisions of the CPR Covenant, a State Party is authorized to adopt limitations on the respective rights "for the protection of the rights and freedoms of others."

[10] There is no rule of customary international law requiring a State to incorporate a treaty provision into its domestic legal system. Many States—the United States among them—have international rules that provide for the automatic incorporation of treaties into municipal law, subject to varying prerequisites and qualifications. For instance, the principle of automatic incorporation contained in the Supremacy Clause of Article VI of the U.S. Constitution has been restricted by judicial construction to treaty provisions that are "self-executing." *See* discussion *supra*, sec. 2.2. Other States (e.g., the United Kingdom) deal with internal compliance on a case-by-case basis, through ordinary legislation. See LORD MCNAIR, THE LAW OF TREATIES, Chapter IV (1961). This issue was expressly raised during the preparatory work. *See Annotations of*

Both the CPR Covenant and the general law of treaties leave the means of internal compliance and the domestic effects of the CPR Covenant to the discretion and each contracting State.[11] As a State Party to the Covenant, the United States is thus free to choose the method whereby it will fulfill its duty of internal implementation under Article 2 of the treaty. The United States could have done so by treating some or all provisions of the Covenant as self-executing (and hence as falling under the principle that such provisions are automatically incorporated into United States law), by incorporating them through legislation, by enacting legislation putting the Covenant into effect without reproducing its wording, or by any other appropriate legislative, administrative or judicial measures.[12] In fact, the United States has declared, at the time of ratification, that it considers the substantive provisions of the Covenant to be non-self-executing, and the Executive has indicated its intent to rely on existing domestic law as the means of fulfilling the United States' duty of internal implementation.[13] While that declaration has the effect of depriving the Covenant of internal legal effects in the United States, the Covenant remains (subject to the valid reservations, understandings and declarations made by the United States) the standard by which domestic law is internationally to be judged, and the United States will be accountable to the other States Parties for any failure to meet that standard.

### 3.1.3 The Obligation To Provide for Effective Remedies in Individual Cases

Paragraph 3 of Article 2 requires a State Party to fulfill the Covenant in individual cases, by providing for effective domestic remedies in cases of violation of the rights set forth in the treaty. To

*the text on the draft International Covenants on Human Rights, U.N. Doc. A/2929, at 18. para. 12 (1955)* (hereinafter cited as *U.N. Annotations*).

[11] The *travaux preparatoires* show that this was a deliberate choice. *See* Schachter, *The Obligation to Implement the Covenant in Domestic Law* in Henkin, *supra* note 1, at 311-31 and esp. at 313-15.

[12] For a fuller discussion *see* Garibaldi, *Supplementary Statement,* in *International Human Rights Treaties: Hearings Before the Committee on Foreign Relations, United States Senate,* 96th Cong., 1st Sess., pp. 298-300.

[13] 138 Cong. Rec.§4783-84 (daily ed. April 2, 1992); 28 *Weekly Compilation of Presidential Documents* 1008-09 (1992). The Executive explained in its submission to the Senate that "[t]he intent is to clarify that the Covenant will not create a private cause of action in U.S. courts," and added that "existing U.S. law generally complies with the Covenant; hence, implementing legislation is not contemplated." S. Exec. Rep. No. 102-23, 103d Cong., 2d Sess. 19 (9192).

continue using a previous example, a State Party is obligated not only to refrain from imposing torture and to forbid the infliction of torture by its agents and the population at large, but also to provide an effective remedy to victims of torture. The obligation arising from Article 2(3) is spelled out in three subparagraphs, dealing respectively with the creation of the remedy, the institutional arrangement that is to pass upon the claim, and the enforcement of a decision granting the remedy.

Subparagraph (a) states that a State Party must "ensure that any person whose rights or freedoms as...recognized [in the CPR Covenant] are violated shall have an effective remedy notwithstanding that the violation has been committed by persons acting in an official capacity." This provision indicates that, quite apart from the enforcement of measures taken under paragraph 2 by the action of public officials, the State must provide for enforcement by private action.[14] But the precise content of such a system, that is, the exact meaning of "effective remedy," is far from clear.[15] First, it is uncertain whether a State Party would fulfill its obligation merely by empowering the victim to set the criminal process in motion, or must also provide the victim with a civil action for monetary compensation.[16] Second, in cases of violations committed by individuals acting in an official capacity, it is uncertain whether providing for a civil action against the agent will suffice, or a civil action against the State is also required. In particular, it is not clear whether systems of total or partial State immunity from civil liability are consistent with this provision.[17] In any event, the wording of subparagraph (a) suggests that when the violation was committed by a person acting in an official capacity and the remedial action is directed against that person, a plea of higher orders it not a valid defense.

[14] The French and Spanish texts of the Covenant are quite clear in this respect. The expressions used—"*recours utile,*" "*recurso efectivo*"—have a definite procedural connotation.

[15] The kind of remedy envisaged by this section does not seem to have been discussed by the Commission on Human Rights or higher bodies during the drafting process. See M. BOSSUYT, *supra* note 1, at 64-66.

[16] The Inter-American Court of Human Rights has observed, in reference to the American Convention, that "[t]he State has a legal duty to take reasonable steps to prevent human rights violations and to use the means at its disposal to carry out a serious investigation of violations committed within its jurisdiction, to identify those responsible, impose the appropriate punishment, and ensure the victim adequate compensation." Velázquez Rodríguez v. Honduras, *supra* note 2, at para. 174.

[17] In the United States, several statutes, notably the Federal Tort Claims Act, have partially abolished State immunity from tort liability in relation to claims adjudicated by the courts. *See* 28 U.S.C. 1346 and related provisions. A person whose claims fall within the narrow area of state immunity preserved by these statutes may still, in theory, seek redress from Congress.

Under subparagraph (b), a State Party must ensure that any person seeking the remedy referred to in subparagraph (a) "shall have his right thereto determined by competent judicial, administrative or legislative authorities, or by any other competent authority provided for by the legal system of the State...." Accordingly, there must be at least one public authority, belonging to some branch of government, capable of being seized of the claim: if the courts refuse to take cognizance of certain cases—pursuant to principles of judicial abstention such as the "political question" doctrine of United States constitutional law—the State is still under an international obligation to provide an alternative mechanism (legislative, administrative, or otherwise) for the determination of the claim. Further, the State is obligated to "develop the possibilities of judicial remedy," a phrase that carries the implication that a State may not diminish existing judicial competence over the matters regulated by the CPR Covenant.

Finally, subparagraph (c) requires a State party "[to] ensure that the competent authorities shall enforce such remedies when granted." If subparagraph (a) requires a civil remedy against the State, it follows from subparagraph (c) that the State must not make itself immune from the resulting enforcement or execution.

### 3.1.4 Obligations Arising Under the Optional Protocol

The obligations arising under the Optional Protocol are all procedural, i.e., they concern the system of compliance with the CPR Covenant on the international plane, which is analyzed in detail in Section 5 of this chapter. Here it need only be noted that, under Article 4(2) of the Optional Protocol, a State Party charged with violating any provision of the CPR Covenant is under an obligation to submit to the Human Rights Committee, within six months, "written explanations or statements clarifying the matter and the remedy, if any, that may have been taken."

## 3.2 THE PRINCIPLES OF NON-DISCRIMINATION AND EQUALITY BEFORE THE LAW

*Oscar M. Garibaldi*

The ideas of equality and non-discrimination appear in several provisions of the CPR Covenant:

Article 2(1) requires a State Party to respect and to ensure to all individuals within its territory and subject to its jurisdiction the rights set forth in the Covenant, "without distinction of any kind, such as race, colour, sex, language, religion, political or other opinion, national or social origin, property, birth or other status."

Article 3 provides that States Parties "undertake to ensure the equal rights of men and women to the enjoyment of all civil and political rights set forth" in the treaty.

Article 25 defines certain political rights, which are to be enjoyed by every citizen "without any of the distinctions mentioned in Article 2."

Article 24(1) states that every child has a right to certain means of protection "without any discrimination as to race, colour, sex, language, religion, national or social origin, property or birth."

Article 4(1) authorizes a State Party to take certain measures in derogation of its obligations under the treaty, but only if those measures "do not involve discrimination solely on the ground of race, colour, sex, language, religion or social origin."

Article 14 provides that "[a]ll persons shall be equal before the courts and tribunals."

Article 26 states: "All persons are equal before the law and are entitled without any discrimination to equal protection of the law. In this respect the law shall prohibit any discrimination and guarantee to all persons equal and effective protection against discrimination on any ground such as race, colour, sex, language, religion, political or other opinion, national or social origin, property, birth or other status."

These provisions are the vehicles through which the principle of non-discrimination and that of equality before the law have been incorporated in the CPR Covenant.

The principle of equality before the law is one possible form of the principle of equality. Equality, in the sense relevant here, is the absence of unequal treatment. Unequal treatment occurs when rights are conferred or duties are imposed on some individuals and not on others, and the distinction between the two categories is made on the basis of criteria deemed improper. Equal or unequal treatment may take place in the creation of general laws, i.e., at the time of formulating the content of general legislation, or in the creation of individual norms, i.e., at the time of applying general legislation to individual cases. A requirement of equal treatment in the creation of general laws is often called the principle of equality *in* the law, while a requirement of equal treatment in the application of general laws to individual cases is generally known as the principle of equality *before* the law. The principle of equality before the law requires equal treatment in the application of general laws to individual cases by any governmental authority. A more specific requirement of equal treatment by the organs charged with administering justice is generally known as the principle of equality before the courts.

In the system of the Covenant, the principle of non-discrimination is fundamentally equivalent with the principle of equality. Consequently, depending on the context, the principle of non-discrimination may bar certain forms of unequal treatment in the creation of general laws (as does the principle of equality in the law) or in the application of general laws to individual cases (as does the principle of equality before the law) or it may apply simultaneously to both the creation and application of general laws.

### 3.2.1 The Principle of Non-Discrimination

The principle of non-discrimination contained in the CPR Covenant prohibits treating some individuals in a manner different from that in which other individuals are treated, if (i) the distinction between the two groups is made on the basis of criteria deemed illegitimate; (ii) the treatment constitutes discrimination; and (iii) the treatment consists in or results from the creation of certain kinds of laws. The legal effects of the principle of non-discrimination depend, therefore, on the illegitimate criteria, the concept of discrimination, and the normative scope of the principle.

### 3.2.2 Illegitimate Criteria

The differential treatment of individuals is prohibited by the principle of non-discrimination only if the distinction is based on certain grounds regarded as improper or illegitimate. Each non-discrimination clause of the Covenant contains a list of illegitimate criteria, and some of these clauses indicate that there are other illegitimate criteria left tacit.

The grounds listed in Article 2(1) and Article 26 are race, color, sex, language, religion, political opinion, any other kind of opinion, national or social origin, property, birth, and other status. In these provisions, the words "without distinction of any kind, such as..." and "discrimination on any ground such as..." clearly indicate that the enumeration was not meant to be limitative.[18] The *eiusdem generis* principle requires, however, that any other grounds considered to be included in this formula be similar to those expressly listed.

In contrast, under Articles 3, 4(1) and 24(1), only the listed criteria are considered illegitimate. Article 3 merely restates the fact that sex is an improper ground for distinction. Article 4(1) mentions only race, color, sex, language, religion or social origin, thus implying that, for purposes of derogations in times of emergency, "political or other opinion," "national origin," "property," "birth," and "other status" are not illegitimate criteria. Finally, the list contained in Article 24(1) omits "political or other opinion" and "other status," the former (presumably) because children are deemed not to have opinions of their own, and the latter because Article 24 itself provides for special measures of protection "required by [the] status [of] a minor."

We shall not attempt here a detailed analysis of each illegitimate criterion.[19] Suffice it to note that "national origin" was not used in a legal sense, as a synonym of "nationality," but in a sociological sense, to refer to the aggregate of characteristics identifying a national group.[20] The expression "birth or other status" results from two separate attempts to translate the Russian term soslovie, which was

[18] Accord, E. VIERDAG, THE CONCEPT OF DISCRIMINATION IN INTERNATIONAL LAW 108 (1973).

[19] *See generally* E. VIERDAG, *supra* note 18, at 86-106.

[20] "[T]he Sub-Commission wished to make it clear that the words 'national origin' should be interpreted by taking this conception, not in the sense of criteria of a State, but in the sense of national characteristics." Report of the Sub-Commission on Prevention of Discrimination and Protection of Minorities, U.N. Doc. E/CN.4/52, at 5 (1947).

explained in the course of the debate as conveying the ideas of "class," "caste," "status," "social status," and "social condition."[21]

In the document submitting to the Senate proposed reservations, understandings and declarations, the Executive observed that "the very broad antidiscrimination provisions" contained in Articles 2(1), 4(1) and 26 of the CPR Covenant "do not precisely comport with longstanding Supreme Court doctrine in the equal protection field."[22] It noted that the list of illegitimate criteria under the Covenant includes a reference to any "other status," and added:

> Current U.S. civil rights law is not so open-ended; discrimination is only prohibited for specific statuses, and there are exceptions which allow for discrimination. For example, under the age Discrimination Act of 1975, age may be taken into account in certain circumstances. In addition, U.S. laws permits additional distinctions, for example between citizens and non-citizens and between different categories of non-citizens, especially in the context of the immigration laws.[23]

To prevent any inconsistency between the anti-discrimination provisions of the Covenant and United States law, the Covenant was ratified by the United States subject to an understanding that, as we shall presently see, has the effect of considerably narrowing the concept of discrimination in the covenant as it applies to the obligations of the United States.

### 3.2.3 The Concept of Discrimination

Even if differential treatment is based on one or more of the illegitimate criteria just discussed, it does not violate the principle of non-discrimination of the Covenant unless it constitutes discrimination. A discrimination is an objectionable (or not justifiable) differentiation. The travaux preparatoires make clear that the drafters of the Covenant did not intend to prohibit all legal distinctions, nor even all distinctions based on illegitimate grounds, but only those considered "wrong."[24]

[21] *See* U.N. Docs. E/CN.4/SR.52, at 5 (1948), and 3 U.N. GAOR C.3 (100th-102nd mtgs.) at 125-51, U.N. Docs. A/C.3/SR.100-102 (1948).

[22] S. Exec. Rep. No. 102-23, 102d Cong., 2d Sess., 14 (1992)

[23] Id.

[24] *See* statement of Mr. Capotorti (Italy), 16 U.N. GAOR, C.3 (1099th mtg.) at para. 10 ("...discrimination, in the sense of unfavourable and odious distinctions which lacked any objective or reasonable basis"); statement by Mr. Karapandza (Yugoslavia), id. (1100th mtg.) at para. 10; statement by Mr. Szleper (Poland), id. (1101st mtg.) at para. 24; U.N. Doc. A/2929, at para. 179. The assertion made in the text applies not only to those provisions that contain the word 'discrimination' (art. 4(1), art. 24(1), art. 26), but also to art. 2(1) which refers to "distinction[s]." Although the debates are not clear, it seems that the drafters

The criteria to separate "bad" distinctions (discrimination) from "good" distinctions (not discrimination) have never been clearly formulated. Some drafters spoke of "unfavourable," "odious," or "invidious" distinctions, but, of course, every distinction is unfavorable, odious, or invidious to those who bear the burden imposed or are excluded from the privilege granted. It is also said that a discrimination is a distinction that lacks any "objective" basis. But it is far from clear in what sense, if any, some of the distinctions that many people consider "good" (such as progressive taxation) have a more "objective" basis than those that the same people consider "bad" (such as qualifications on the right to vote based on wealth).

What seems to be required is that the distinction be, in some sense, justifiable. The criterion of justification, i.e., the content and structure of the reasoning that would justify a distinction under the Covenant, has been left open, perhaps of necessity.[25] But the drafters did provide examples of what they regarded as justifiable distinctions: distinctions based on citizenship or nationality with regard to immigration, extradition, access to public office or acquisition of property; distinctions based on wealth for purposes of taxation; and limitations on the legal capacity of minors and persons of unsound mind. In the understanding of the drafters, such distinctions did not constitute discrimination.[26] The so-called "special measures of protection adopted for the benefit of backward population groups" have become the most contentious form of differential treatment based on illegitimate criteria. There is clear evidence in the travaux preparatoires that this type of differential treatment was considered justifiable and, hence, not discriminatory.[27] Because these "special measures" do not

---

preferred the word "distinction" on the ground that it was used in the U.N. Charter and the Universal Declaration of Human Rights. See 18 U.N. GAOR, C.3 (1257th to 1259th mtgs.) (1963); M. BOSSUYT, *supra* note 1, at 55; Ramcharan, *Equality and Nondiscrimination,* in Henkin, *supra* note 1, at 258-59.

[25] Thus, it is not quite justifiable to suggest—as Vierdag seems to do—that the "goodness" of a distinction depends solely on the relation between such distinction and a (valid?) governmental objective. See E. VIERDAG, *supra* note 19, at 63-64. This form of reasoning, which prevails in our own constitutional law, is only one of several possible criteria of justification. As shown in the text below, Vierdag's comment has become an accurate statement of the way the United States understands the concept of discrimination in the CPR Covenant.

[26] *See,* e.g., statements by Lady Tweedsmuir (United Kingdom), 16 U.N. GAOR, C.3 (1097th mtg.) at para. 28 (1961); Mrs. Tsimboukis (Greece), *id.* (1098th mtg.) at paras. 33-34; Mrs. Afnan (Iraq), *id.,* at para. 52; Mr. Beaufort (Netherlands), *id.* 1099th mtg.) at para. 6; Mrs. Refslund-Thomsen (Denmark), *id.,* at para. 20; Miss Hampton (New Zealand), *id.,* (1101th mtg.) at para. 7; Mr. Sapozhnikov (U.S.S.R.), *id.,* at para. 49.

[27] *See generally* 19 U.N. GAOR, C.3 (1257th to 1259th mtgs.) (1963). The Committee report states as follows: "It was expressly emphasized by several members of the Committee that special measures for the advancement of any socially and educationally backward sections of society

constitute discrimination, they are not prohibited by the principle of non-discrimination. Conversely, it is equally clear that the principle of non-discrimination does not require a State Party to adopt or to retain any such "special measures."[28]

In the United States, the equal-protection guarantee of the federal constitution serves as the counterpart of the principle of non-discrimination in the CPR Covenant. The United States Supreme Court has developed a multi-tiered set of criteria (or "levels of scrutiny," in the jargon of Supreme Court jurisprudence) to test whether distinctions are permissibly under the equal-protection guarantee. In very broad terms, the most permissive criterion (i.e., the lowest level of scrutiny) will uphold a given classification as long as the classification bears a rational relationship to a legitimate governmental objective. This criterion, which in practice is quite undemanding, is normally applied to distinctions made in economic and social-welfare legislation. The most stringent criterion (i.e., the strictest level of scrutiny) will justify a classification if it is necessary to promote a constitutionally compelling end. This criterion is applied to so-called "suspect" classifications, most prominently those based on race. In between these two tests there appears to be a series of ill-defined criteria, of intermediate levels of strictness, which generally sustain classifications bearing a substantial relationship to important governmental interests. These intermediate criteria are variously applied to classifications based on matters such as gender, alienage and illegitimacy.[29]

Against this background, the United States issued the following understanding as a condition to its ratification of the CPR Covenant:

---

should not be construed as 'distinction' within the meaning of article 2.... The Committee agreed that that interpretation, to which there was no objection, should be specially mentioned in the report." U.N. Doc. A/5655 (1963), at para. 20, quoted in M. BOSSUYT, *supra* note 1, at 55; *accord,* Ramcharan, in Henkin, *supra* note 1, at 259-61.

[28] Accord, E. VIERDAG, cit., *supra* note 19, at 136-137. But see a comment by the Human Rights Committee to the effect that art. 3 of the CPR Covenant requires "not only measures of protection but also affirmative action designed to ensure the positive enjoyment of rights." General Comment 4(13), *Report of the Human Rights Committee,* 36 U.N. GAOR, Supp. (No. 40) at 109, U.N. Doc. A/36/40 (1981). To the extent that this interpretation requires the adoption of "special measures," it is not warranted by the text or the preparatory work of the CPR Covenant. It has been claimed that the equal treatment of persons who should be treated differently (according to some criterion) also constitutes discrimination. See E. VIERDAG, *supra* note 19, at 69-74. This theory finds some support in a series of decisions by the Permanent Court of International Justice concerning the treatment of minorities. Those decisions, however, rested on the specific terms of the minority treaties adopted at the conclusion of the First World War, which required equality "in fact" as well as "in law". See id. There is no basis for this thesis in either the text or the *travaux preparatoires* of the CPR Covenant.

[29] *See generally,* e.g., 3 R.D. ROTUNDA AND J.E. NOWAK, TREATISE ON CONSTITUTIONAL LAW (West 1992), Ch. 18.

> The Constitution and laws of the United States guarantee all persons equal protection of the law and provide extensive protections against discrimination. The United States understands distinctions based upon race, colour, sex, language, religion, political or other opinion, national or social origin, property, birth of any other status—as those terms are used in Article 2, paragraph 1 and Article 26—to be permitted when such distinctions are, at minimum, rationally related to a legitimate governmental objective.[30]

The effect of this understanding is to classify as "good" distinctions (i.e., non-discrimination) those that are, at a minimum, rationally related to legitimate governmental objectives. This is, as noted, the least demanding of the various alternative criteria applied by the United States courts to test whether a distinction is justified under the equal-protection guarantee of the United States Constitution.[31] If this understanding is accepted by other States Parties, the United States will have engrafted into the system of the Covenant (as far as its own obligations and those of the accepting Parties are concerned) the most permissive criterion of discrimination allowed by its domestic law.[32]

### 3.2.4 The Normative Scope of the Principle

The various forms of the principle of non-discrimination contained in the Covenant differ also with regard to their normative scopes, i.e., the types of legal rules to which they apply. The normative scope of the principle of non-discrimination may vary, as it were, in two directions: (i) vertically, the principle may apply to the creation of general laws, or to the application of such laws to individual cases, or to both; and (ii) horizontally, the principle may apply to all laws or only to laws enacted to ensure the rights set forth in the Covenant.

The non-discrimination clause of Article 2(1) applies only to the rights defined in the CPR Covenant, but has the widest vertical scope: it prohibits discrimination not only in the creation but also in the

[30] S. Exec. Rep. No. 102-23, 102d Cong., 2d Sess. 22 (1922) (second sentence omitted).

[31] It should be noted that, given the United States' goal of ensuring that its obligations under the non-discrimination clauses of the CPR Covenant extend no further than the equal-protection doctrine, it was hardly feasible for the United States to frame the understanding in a different way. It is difficult to see how an understanding (or a reservation) could have been drafted to capture all the nuances and open texture of the equal-protection doctrine.

[32] On the effects of an understanding, *see generally* 1 RESTATEMENT (3d), FOREIGN RELATIONS LAW OF THE UNITED STATES §313 and Comment g (1986).

application of general laws.[33] The same can be said of Article 3, which merely restates a principle contained in Article 2(1). The non-discrimination clauses of Articles 4(1), 24(1), and 25 also apply to governmental action at all levels, but their horizontal reach is limited to the matters regulated in each of those provisions. By contrast, the non-discrimination clause of Article 26 has the widest horizontal scope (encompassing all laws), but it only refers to the application of general laws to particular cases.

In any of these forms, the principle of non-discrimination refers to the conduct of the State, particularly to the creation, application, or execution of general or particular norms. In the course of the drafting, some States—not known for their devotion to the cause of freedom—argued that discrimination by private individuals should also be covered by the principle, in the sense that States Parties should be obligated to forbid it.[34] A large number of States opposed this view, either on the ground that it would make the principle of non-discrimination *pro tanto* unenforceable, or on the ground that it would place unacceptable restrictions on personal freedom.[35] Because of this fundamental disagreement, it cannot be maintained that the principle of non-discrimination was also meant to reach the conduct of private individuals as well.[36]

### 3.2.5 The Principles of Equality Before the Law

The principle of equality before the law is set forth in Article 26 of the Covenant. This principle includes the more specific principle of equality before the courts, which is also expressly set forth in paragraph 1 of Article 14. The Covenant does not contain the principle of equality in the law, except to the extent that this principle coincides with the principle of non-discrimination discussed above.

[33] *See generally* 16 U.N. GAOR, C.3 (1097th to 1103rd mtgs.) (1961).

[34] *See,* e.g., statement by Mr. Sapozhnikov (U.S.S.R.), *id.,* (1098th mtg.) at para. 4.

[35] *See,* e.g., statements by Lady Tweedsmuir (United Kingdom), *id.* (1097th mtg.) at para. 28; Mrs. Tsimboukis (Greece), *id.* (1098th mtg.) at para. 33; Mr. Beaufort (Netherlands), *id.* (1099th mtg.) at para. 3; Mr. Baroody (Saudia Arabia), *id.,* at para. 18; Mrs. Refslund-Thomsen (Denmark), *id.,* at para. 19; Mr. Nutting (Canada), *id.,* at para. 26; Mr. Moid (Pakistan), *id.* (1102nd mtg.) at para. 4.

[36] *See,* however, the exchange between Mr. Tomuschat and Mr. Tarnopolsky at the Human Rights Committee, U.N. Doc. CCPR/C/SR. 170, at paras. 39 and 82 (1979). Mr. Tarnopolsky clearly misreads art. 26. *Contra* Ramcharan, *supra* note 24, at 261-63 (concluding that only personal and social relationships are beyond the reach of the Covenant).

Article 26 of the Covenant consists of the following two sentences:

> All persons are equal before the law and are entitled without any discrimination to equal protection of the law. In this respect the law shall prohibit any discrimination and guarantee to all persons equal and effective protection against discrimination on any ground such as race, colour, sex, language, religion, political or other opinion, national or social origin, property, birth or other status.

It should be noted that the second sentence is introduced by the phrase "in this respect." The *travaux préparatoires* conclusively show that the phrase "in this respect" was inserted to limit the scope of the second sentence and to turn it into an explanation of the first.[37] The phrase "and are entitled without any discrimination to equal protection of the law" was probably added to clarify the idea of equality before the law, and to being the text into conformity with Article 7 of the Universal Declaration of Human Rights.[38] It is quite clear that this phrase was not meant to expand the principle or to undo the effects of the restriction intended by the phrase "in this respect."

Therefore, in the final text of Article 26, the principle of equality before the law and the principle of non-discrimination contained in that provision are co-extensive in both content and normative scope. The concept of equality mentioned in the first sentence is clarified by the second sentence as the absence of differential treatment of the kind forbidden by the second sentence. Thus, an instance of differential application of the law will violate the principle of equality before the law if (i) it is based on one or more illegitimate criteria, and (ii) it constitutes discrimination in the sense already discussed.

The phrase "in this respect" also shows that the principle of non-discrimination in Article 26 has the same vertical scope as the principle of equality before the law: both principles refer only to the application of general laws to particular cases. Finally, both principles

[37] The phrase "in this respect" was added by the Third Committee of the General Assembly in 1961, after a long debate in which both proponents and opponents of the amendment showed full understanding of its intended effects. *See* 16 U.N. GAOR, C.3 (1097th to 1103rd mtgs.) (1961).

[38] *See id.* Several States took the position that a reference to "equal protection of the law" was unnecessary, for it was already implicit in the idea of equality before the law. Others saw the phrase as completing the principle of equality before the law or making it more specific. Brazil suggested that "equal protection" could be construed as absolute equality before the law (with no qualifications), an idea which found no support. Many States supported both the "equal protection" clause and the phrase "in this respect." There was no suggestion that these two clauses would have incompatible effects.

have an unrestricted horizontal scope; they apply to any governmental act consisting of the application, enforcement or execution of any general law, whether or not that general law guarantees a right defined in the CPR Covenant. It follows that general laws aimed at protecting individuals (not all laws are of this kind) must be applied, enforced, and executed in a non-discriminatory manner. The "equal protection" clause makes this last conclusion explicit.

## 3.3 THE SUBSTANTIVE RIGHTS AND UNITED STATES LAW

*David Filvaroff, Hurst Hannum, Virginia Leary, and Dinah Shelton*

The following section analyzes, article by article, the provisions of the CPR Covenant which establish specific human rights, explaining what each means and comparing each article with United States law and practice. Reference is made where appropriate to the reservations, understandings, and declarations proposed by President Bush and included in the U.S. instrument of ratification deposited in June 1992; the complete texts of these qualifying statements are included as an annex to the present volume. Most of the formulations are similar to those proposed by President Carter in 1978, although several have been somewhat more narrowly drawn and represent an improvement over the Carter package.

There will be some redundancy with the treatment of Article 2 and Article 26 in section 3. This is because the principle of non-discrimination is at the same time both one of the clauses of general application and, in the form of equality before the law (Article 26), a separate right. Likewise, even though Articles 4 and 5 are analyzed in detail in section 4 of this chapter, they are treated below briefly for the sake of continuity.

## ARTICLE 1—SELF-DETERMINATION*

1. All peoples have the right of self-determination. By virtue of that right they freely determine their political status and freely pursue their economic, social and cultural development.

2. All peoples may, for their own ends, freely dispose of their natural wealth and resources without prejudice to any obligations arising out of international economic co-operation, based upon the principle of mutual benefit, and international law. In no case may a people be deprived of its own means of subsistence.

3. The States Parties to the present Covenant, including those having responsibility for the administration of Non-Self-Governing and Trust Territories, shall promote the realization of the right of self-determination, and shall respect that right, in conformity with the provisions of the Charter of the United Nations.

The principle of self-determination acquired increasing political significance during the nineteenth century and was strongly espoused by President Wilson during and after World War I. A more explicit enunciation of the principle developed after the founding of the United Nations, and the "principle" of self-determination is referred to in Articles 1 and 55 of the United Nations Charter. By 1960, the "principle" had developed into a "right," which was proclaimed in the influential Declaration on the Granting of Independence to Colonial Countries and Peoples[39] and later in the Declaration on Principles of International Law Concerning Friendly Relations and Cooperation Among States.[40]

The inclusion of the "right" to self-determination in identical language in the first article of both the Covenant on Civil and Political Rights and the Covenant on Economic, Social and Cultural Rights further underscores its significance. Many commentators assert that self-determination is a prerequisite to the exercise of other human rights.[41]

*Since the language is identical in Article I of the CPR Covenant and the ESC Covenant, the following discussion applies to both treaties.

[39] G.A. Res. 1514(XV), 15 U.N. GAOR Supp. (No. 16) at 66, U.N. Doc. A/4684 (1960).

[40] G.A. Res. 2625(XXV), 25 U.N. GAOR Supp. (No. 28) at 121, U.N. Doc. A/8028 (1970).

[41] *See,* e.g., *U.N. Annotations, supra* note 10, at 13-14, para. 4; Cassese, *The Self-Determination of Peoples,* in Henkin, *supra* note 1, at 101.

The meaning and scope of this right is not entirely clear from the text of Article 1.[42] In particular, the meaning of the term "peoples" in the first paragraph is not evident from the text, and no precise definition of the term exists in international law.[43] Debates in the United Nations suggest that "people" denotes a social entity possessing a clear identity and its own characteristics. . .implies a relationship with a territory. . .and should not be confused with ethnic, religious or linguistic minorities."[44] Factors frequently mentioned as relevant in determining whether a group constitutes a "people" are the existence of a common religion; common linguistic, cultural, and ethnic characteristics; and the connection of the group with a specified territory.

In applying the concept of self-determination, U.N. organs have in practice limited its scope to situations of colonialism, racist regimes, and foreign occupation. This limitation has been criticized as not necessarily inherent in the Charter.[45] But whatever the situation as regards other instruments, the preparatory work of the Covenants suggests that the term "all peoples" was intended to apply to peoples of independent and sovereign States as well as to the peoples of dependent territories.[46] A scholar who has written extensively on self-determination concluded that, under the Covenants, self-determination extends to national components of multinational States which have a distinct legal status within the constitutional framework.[47] Thus, the Covenants may assign a meaning to "peoples" which, at the

[42] *See generally* M. BOSSUYT, *supra* note 1, at 19-48; L. BUCHHEIT, SECESSION (1978); H. HANNUM, AUTONOMY, SOVEREIGNTY, AND SELF-DETERMINATION (1990); M. POMERANCE, SELF-DETERMINATION IN LAW AND PRACTICE (1982); A. RIGO SUREDA, THE EVOLUTION OF THE RIGHT OF SELF-DETERMINATION (1973); D. RONEN, THE QUEST FOR SELF-DETERMINATION (1979); U. UMOZURIKE, SELF-DETERMINATION IN INTERNATIONAL LAW (1972); Cassese, *supra* note 41. The Human Rights Committee adopted a "general comment" on Article 1 in 1984, but it does nothing to clarify the meaning of "self-determination" or the scope of a State's obligations under Article 1. *See Report on the Human Rights Committee,* 39 U.N. GAOR Supp. (No. 40) at 142-43, U.N. Doc. A/39/40 (1984).

[43] *See* Cristescu, *The Right to Self-Determination, Historical and Current Development on the Basis of United Nations Instruments.* U.S. Doc. E/CN.4/Sub.2/404/Rev. (1981) at para. 269 *et seq.* Cristescu states that "...whenever in the course of history a people has become aware of being a people, all definitions have proved superfluous." *Id.,* para. 274.

[44] *Id.,* para. 279.

[45] *See* Arangio-Ruiz, *Human Rights and Non-Intervention in the Helsinki Final Act,* 157 HAGUE RECUEIL 195, 225-26 (No. IV. 1977).

[46] Cassese, *supra* note 41, at 94-95.

[47] *Id.*

time of their adoption, may not have been identical with the meaning of "peoples" in formulations of the concept in other instruments.[48]

One difficulty in defining "self-determination" arises from the fact that it has both an internal and an external aspect. The former reflects the right of every people (normally organized in the form of a State) to independent, democratic institutions which govern the State free from outside interference. The latter includes the right of a people to *form* a State, i.e., to become independent from a colonial power or, if a broad definition of "peoples" is adopted, to secede from an existing State. While there would seem to be little disagreement that all peoples possess the right of internal self-determination, there is much greater controversy over the criteria which must be met in order for a non-State people also to possess the right of external self-determination.[49]

It also appears clear from the preparatory work and the text of the CPR Covenant as a whole that Article 1 was not intended to apply to minorities (although the distinction between "minorities" and "peoples" is less than definitive). Fear was expressed during the drafting that recognition of a right of self-determination for minorities might lead to the break-up of existing states. This concern is reflected in the Declaration on Principles of International Law Concerning Friendly Relations and Cooperation Among States, which includes the statement that self-determination should not be construed as "authorizing or encouraging any action which would dismember or impair, totally or in part, the territorial integrity or political unity of sovereign and independent States conducting themselves in compliance with the principle of equal rights and self-determination of peoples."[50] In the CPR Covenant, the subject of minorities is dealt with separately in Article 27, which further suggests that Article 1 was not intended to apply to minorities.

In exercising its rights to self-determination, a people may opt for a variety of modes of political relationships. The important element is that it does so freely. The Declaration on Principles of International

[48] *See* art. 31(4) of the Vienna Convention on the Law of Treaties, which provides "A special meaning shall be given a term if it is established that the parties so intended."

[49] The Chairman of the Human Rights Committee has correctly noted that the right to self-determination is "one of the most awkward to define, since the abuse of that right could jeopardize international peace and security in giving States the impression that their territorial integrity was threatened." U.N. Doc. CCPR/C/SR.503 (1984) at 32. *See,* in particular, L. BUCCHEIT, *supra* note 42.

[50] *Supra* note 40.

Law Concerning Friendly Relations elaborates on the possible means of implementing the right of self-determination by stating that the "establishment of a sovereign and independent State, the free association or integration with an independent State or the emergence into any other political status freely determined by a people constitute modes of implementing the right of self-determination by that people."[51]

A United Nations Special Rapporteur on self-determination has emphasized the importance of free choice in connection with self-determination. He writes that "the right to self-determination, which is a *sine qua non* for the existence of human rights and freedoms, basically implies that peoples must be able to exercise their will freely and independently, without any kind of external influence and under a legal system which guarantees freedom of expression. Although every people possesses the right to choose its own political, economic, social and cultural status, this right must be recognized in such a way that it can be exercised in conditions of complete freedom."[52] Thus, as noted above, a people's right to self-determination may be denied if external influence prevents its free choice of social and economic systems.

While the CPR Covenant is primarily concerned with the rights of individuals, the right to self-determination recognized in Article 1 belongs to peoples. Thus, although individuals may be the ultimate beneficiary of this right, the Human Rights Committee has declined to consider allegations of violations of the right to self-determination in the context of individual communications filed under the Optional Protocol.[53]

Paragraph 2 of Article 1 proclaims the right of a people to control its own natural wealth and resources. The concept of sovereignty over natural resources as a right pertaining to States has been frequently reiterated in United Nations resolutions since 1952. Paragraph 2 encapsulates aspects of the Declaration on Permanent Sovereignty

[51] *Id. Also see* Principles which should guide Members in determining whether or not an obligation exists to transmit the information called for under Article 73e of the Charter, G.A. Res. 1541 (XV), 15 U.N. GAOR, Supp. (No. 16) at 29, U.N. Doc. A/4684 (1960).

[52] Gros Espiell, *The Right to Self-Determination, Implementation of United Nations Resolutions,* U.N. Doc. E/CN.4/Sub.2/405/Rev. 1, at para. 58 (1980).

[53] *See Report of the Human Rights Committee,* 42 U.N. GAOR, Supp. (No. 40) at 106 (1987), U.N. Doc. A/42/40.

over Natural Resources, which was adopted by the U.N. General Assembly in 1962, with the affirmative vote of the United States.[54]

Unlike some later resolutions, this Declaration and paragraph 2 of Article 1 of the Covenants refer to "obligations arising out of...international law." The United States has traditionally considered this phrase as recognizing that foreign investors are entitled to prompt, adequate, and effective compensation in the event of nationalization and that contractual obligations must be respected. The United States has consistently supported declarations or resolutions referring to sovereignty over natural resources when a phrase referring to obligations under international law has been included. Cassese has pointed out that, under paragraph 2:

> the free disposition of the natural wealth and resources must not impair or run counter to international treaties entered into by the central authorities with a view to promoting international economic cooperation, nor should it violate international customary rules protecting the rights of foreign investors. It is apparent from the preparatory work that this limitation on the right of free disposition over natural resources which was pressed upon the majority of States by the developed countries, was motivated by two considerations: the fear that outside economic cooperation, so important in developing countries, might be discouraged by a rule laying down the right over natural resources in absolute terms, and even more important, the intent to protect foreign investments from expropriation or nationalization without compensation.[55]

Paragraph 3 of Article 1 sets forth the affirmative obligation of States Parties to respect and promote self-determination. Although this provision might seem to be simply a reiteration of Charter provisions, its inclusion in the Covenant benefits from the implementation provisions of the latter instrument.

Self-determination issues affecting the United States have been and continue to be considered within the United Nations by several organs, including the General Assembly, the Security Council, and the Working Group on Indigenous Populations of the U.N. Sub-

[54] G.A. Res. 1803 (XVII), 16 U.N. GAOR, Supp. (No. 17A) at 15, U.N. Doc. A/5100 Add. 1 (1962).

[55] Cassese, *supra* note 41, at 103-104. Identical arts. 47 of the CPR Covenant and 25 of the ESC Covenant confuse the matter further by stating that "[n]othing in the present Covenant shall be interpreted as impairing the inherent right of all peoples to enjoy and utilize fully and freely their natural wealth and resources." *See id.*, at 105-06.

The appropriate standard of compensation for nationalized property remains a subject of considerable international disagreement. *See generally* 2 RESTATEMENT §712 at 196-97, comments c and d at 198-99, Reporters' Notes 1-3 at 202-09.

Commission on Prevention of Discrimination and Protection of Minorities. Even if the Covenants do not add further substantive obligations to those already binding upon the United States through the U.N. Charter, ratification of the Covenants would entail reporting to additional supervisory bodies on implementation of the right to self-determination to the extent it is applicable to U.S. territories or asserted by domestic groups. Thus, a review of the status of these territories and groups may provide a useful context in which to examine U.S. obligations to implement the right of self-determination after ratification of the Covenants.[56]

### *U.S. Territories*

The United States has regularly submitted information to the United Nations, pursuant to Article 73e of the U.N. Charter, on U.S. activities with respect to the non-self-governing territories of Guam, American Samoa, and the U.S. Virgin Islands. Since 1970, this information has been considered by the U.N. Special Committee on the Situation with Regard to the Implementation of the Declaration on the Granting of Independence to Colonial Countries and Peoples (better known as the "Committee of 24").[57] Resolutions recommended by the Committee of 24 are then considered by the General Assembly's Fourth Committee and the General Assembly itself. The United States participates fully in these meetings of the Committee of 24 and, naturally, in the General Assembly and its committees.

U.N. action, without objection from the United States, has consistently reaffirmed the "inalienable right" of the respective peoples of Guam, American Samoa, and the U.S. Virgin Islands to self-determination.[58] The United States has agreed to cooperate with U.N. missions to all three territories, in 1977 (U.S. Virgin Islands), 1979 (Guam), and 1981 (American Samoa). The United States had long accepted the right of these three territories to decide upon the nature of the relationship each wishes to have with the United States.

As of 1990, American Samoa remained an "unincorporated territory" of the United States; while it enjoys a degree of self-government and controls entry and land ownership, ultimate authority remains in

[56] *See generally* A. Leibowitz, Defining Status (1989).

[57] *See,* e.g., the Committee's 1989 report, U.N. Doc. A/44/23 (1989).

[58] *See,* the annual resolutions adopted by the U.N. General Assembly, e.g., G.A. Res. 43/42 (1988) (Guam), Res. 43/43 (1988) (American Samoa), and Res. 43/44 (1988) (U.S. Virgin Islands).

the hands of the U.S. Congress.[59] Guam also is governed by an "Organic Act" adopted by Congress, although it elects its own governor and legislature.[60] While a locally prepared draft Commonwealth Act was approved by Guam voters in 1987, Congress has yet to adopt the necessary implementing legislation to change Guam's present status.[61] The status of the U.S. Virgin Islands is similar to that of Guam, in that territorial government is based on a federal "Organic Act."[62]

Given the existing U.S. cooperation with U.N. bodies and its commitment to self-determination for the three territories, ratification of the Covenants would not conflict with present U.S. law or policy.

### *Trust Territory of the Pacific Islands*

The Trust Territory of the Pacific Islands is the only "strategic trust" created by the United Nations pursuant to Articles 82-84 of the Charter and has been under U.S. administration since 1947. It is primarily distinguished from other trusteeship arrangements by the fact that its operation is overseen by the U.N. Security Council (where the United States enjoys veto power) rather than the General Assembly. Otherwise, the goals of the trusteeship remain the same, i.e., *inter alia,* "to promote the political, economic, social, and educational advancement of the inhabitants of the trust territories, and their progressive development towards self-government or independence."[63]

Negotiations between the United States and various island groups led to division of the initially integrated territory into constituent parts: the Northern Marianas Islands, Marshall Islands, Palau, and the Federated States of Micronesia. A "Covenant" between the United States and the Northern Marianas creating commonwealth status for the latter largely came into force in 1978; somewhat similar arrangements were reached with respect to the Marshall Islands,

[59] 48 U.S.C. §1661(c) grants "all civil, judicial, and military powers of government in American Samoa" to the Secretary of the Interior. *See generally* 48 U.S.C. ch. 13.

[60] Codified at 48 U.S.C. §§1421 et seq. A draft constitution proposed by a Guam Constitutional Convention in 1977 was rejected by the voters in a subsequent referendum, largely on the grounds that creating a local government structure did not make sense until the U.S.-Guam relationship was better defined.

[61] Legislation to establish the Commonwealth of Guam introduced in 1988 would have recognized, *inter alia,* "the inalienable right of self-determination of the indigenous Chamorro people of Guam." H.R. 98, 101st Cong., 1st Sess. S.102(a) (1989).

[62] 48 U.S.C. §1541 et seq.

[63] U.N. Charter, art. 76b.

Federated States of Micronesia, and Palau in the mid-1980s. The United Nations observed the local referenda approving the agreements in all four territories, which were described by the United States as "sovereign act[s] of self-determination."[64]

In 1986, the United States unilaterally declared that the trusteeship was terminated with respect to the Northern Marianas, Marshall Islands, and the Federated States of Micronesia, and the various agreements between the United States and the territories entered into force.[65] While the voters of Palau had approved a compact with the United States in 1986, a conflict between the compact and the constitution of Palau regarding the transit and storage of nuclear weapons persists despite a series of referenda and judicial decisions in Palau. As a result, the United States has not considered the process of approving the compact to be completed in Palau and has stated that "the United States would continue to discharge its responsibilities in Palau as Administering Authority under the Trusteeship Agreement."[66] In 1990, the U.N. Security Council finally decided to terminate the trusteeships over the Federated States of Micronesia, the Marshall Islands, and the Northern Marianas Islands;[67] the trusteeship agreement with Palau remains in force.

Whatever the legal status of the Trust Territory of the Pacific Islands, ratification of the Covenants will not affect that status.

### *Puerto Rico*

Puerto Rico was acquired by the United States from Spain in 1899 and administered as an unincorporated territory until 1952. Following a series of referenda and a constitutional convention in Puerto Rico in 1952, a constitution was adopted and status as *estado libre asociado* (generally rendered in English as "commonwealth") chosen.[68] The U.N. General Assembly recognized that "the people of the Commonwealth of Puerto Rico have effectively exercised their right to self-

[64] Presidential Proclamation No. 5564, Nov. 3, 1986, 58 Fed. Reg. 40,399 (1986) *excerpted in* Leich, *Contemporary Practice of the United States Relating to International Law,* 81 AJIL 405 (1987).

[65] *Id. See* Leich, *supra* note 64, at 405-08 (1987). The validity of the U.S. action is questioned in Clark, *Letter to the Editor,* 81 AJIL 927 (1987).

[66] *See* Leich, *supra* note 64, at 408.

[67] S.C. Res. 683 (Dec. 22, 1990). Only Cuba dissented in the 14 to 1 vote.

[68] *See generally* W. REISMAN, PUERTO RICO AND THE INTERNATIONAL PROCESS—NEW ROLES IN ASSOCIATION (ASIL Studies in Transnational Legal Policy No. 6) (1975); Clark, *Self-Determination and Free Association—Should the United Nations Terminate the Pacific Islands Trust?,* 21 HARV. INT'L L. J. 1, 41-46 (1980).

determination" and agreed that it was appropriate to drop Puerto Rico from the list of non-self-governing territories.[69]

While questions have subsequently been raised about the legitimacy of Puerto Rico's "self-determination," attempts to reinstate Puerto Rico on the United Nations's list of non-self-governing territories have failed. A 1953 undertaking[70] by President Eisenhower to seek "immediately" Congressional approval of any resolution adopted by the Puerto Rico legislature in favor of independence remains U.S. policy. Under Puerto Rican law, a vote on Puerto Rico's status must be held whenever 10% of the voters request it.

In light of the consistent actions of the United Nations since 1953, U.S. ratification of the Covenants is not likely to alter the situation. However, if one adopts a broad definition of both "peoples" and their right to external self-determination, the people of Puerto Rico would certainly seem to fall within that definition. This would not appear to be inconsistent with current U.S. law or policy.

### *Native Americans*

United States policy toward Native Americans is more complex than the policy towards overseas territories because of the "dependent" status of Native Americans and their presence within the continental United States. Are Native Americans "peoples" for the purpose of right to self-determination? Each tribe is ethnically distinct and has a religion, language, and set of traditions and customs which have united it in the past and continue to unite it today. The Supreme Court has recognized that Native Americans remain a "separate people, with the power of regulating their internal and social relations."[71]

The original sovereignty of Native American nations also is beyond question. Feliz Cohen wrote, "The right of self-government is not something granted to the Indians by any act of Congress. It is rather an inherent and original right of the Indian tribes, recognized by the courts and legislators, a right of which the Indian tribes have never been deprived."[72] Support for this view is implicit in the principle of

[69] G.A. Res. 748, 8 U.N. GAOR Supp. (No. 17) at 25, U.N. Doc. A/2630 (1953).
[70] *See* 29 STATE DEPT. BULL. 841 (1953).
[71] U.S. v. Kagama, 118 U.S. 375, 381-872 (1886).
[72] Cohen, *Indian Rights,* 24 MINN. L. REV. 145, 147 (1940).

tribal self-government described by Chief Justice Marshall in a landmark case:

> The Indian nations had always been considered as distinct independent political communities. The very fact of repeated treaties with them recognized their right of self-government; and the settled doctrine of the law of nations is that a weaker power does not surrender its independence—its right to self-government—by associating with a stronger power and taking its protection.[73]

Both statutory and case law continue to recognize the distinct status of Indian lands and the authority of Indian tribes and their governments within those lands.[74]

However, it also is the United States' view that, by signing treaties which affirmed their allegiance to the United States and their desire for its protection, the Indian tribes surrendered certain aspects of sovereignty.

> Indian tribes are of course no longer possessed of the full attributes of sovereignty. Their incorporation within the territory of the United States, and their acceptance of its protection, necessarily divested them of some aspects of the sovereignty which they had previously exercised. By specific treaty provision they yielded up other sovereign powers; by statute, in the exercise of its plenary control, Congress has removed still others. In sum, Indian tribes still possess those aspects of sovereignty not withdrawn by treaty or statute or by implication as a necessary result of their dependent status.[75]

U.S. legislation has consistently eroded Indian authority and sovereignty. The 1830 Removal Act forced tribes to abandon ancestral lands; the Major Crimes Act in 1885 transferred jurisdiction over serious crimes committed on reservations from tribal to federal authorities; and the 1887 General Allotment Act effectively abolished Indian communal land holding and distributed "surplus" land to white settlers. The 1934 Indian Reorganization Act returned some powers to tribal governments, but only on condition that "modern" forms of democratic government were adopted.

Relations between the U.S. government and Indian tribes are considered to be within the "plenary powers" of the U.S. Congress. Indian governments have "sovereign" powers to legislate with respect

[73] Worcester v. Georgia, 31 U.S. 515 (1832).
[74] *See* 25 U.S.C. §§461-479; Fisher v. District Court, 424 U.S. 352 (1976).
[75] United States v. Wheeler, 435 U.S. 313, 323 (1978).

to their own territory, including powers of taxation, but only if there is no superseding federal legislation.[76] For example, Indian tribes have no criminal jurisdiction over non-Indians for acts committed on reservations.[77] The internal sovereignty of Indian tribes is generally exempt from the provisions of the U.S. Constitution, but Congress has imposed most of the provisions of the federal Bill of Rights upon the tribes.[78] Indians in the United States are full citizens and cannot be discriminated against by the states, and state and local governments have no jurisdiction over Indian tribes unless it is specifically granted by federal law.

Thus, the U.S. commitment to Native Americans would be more accurately described as promoting self-government rather than self-determination in the latter's classic formulation. One month before passage of the Indian Civil Rights Act, for example, President Johnson had urged its enactment as part of a legislative and administrative program with the overall goal of furthering "self-determination," "self-help," and "self-development" of Indian tribes.[79] In upholding the validity of the Act, the Supreme Court stated that the legislation manifested a congressional purpose to "protect tribal sovereignty from undue interference" and "to promote the well established federal policy of furthering Indian self-government."[80] In a message to Congress in 1970, President Nixon stated: "The time has come to create the conditions for a new era in which the Indian future is determined by Indian acts and Indian decisions."[81] On 4 January 1975, Congress enacted the Indian Self-Determination and Educational Assistance Act[82] which supports and encourages the tribes' right to govern their own affairs and administer their own programs and activities.

Particularly during the past decade, there has been a significant increase in international activity with respect to identifying and developing the rights of indigenous peoples.[83] The International

[76] *Cf.* Merrion v. Jicarilla Apache Tribe, 455 U.S. 130 (1982) (regarding tribal taxation of oil and gas leases).

[77] Oliphant v. Suquamish Indian Tribe, 435 U.S. 191 (1978).

[78] *See* Indian Civil Rights Act of 1968, 24 U.S.C. §1301 et seq.

[79] *See* 114 Cong. Rec. 5518, 5520 (1968).

[80] Santa Clara Pueblo v. Martinez, 436 U.S. 49, 63 (1977).

[81] 116 Cong. Rec. 23131 (1970).

[82] *Codified at* 25 U.S.C. §450a-n.

[83] *See generally*, e.g., Barsch, *Indigenous Peoples: An Emerging Object of International Law,* 80 AJIL 369 (1986); Hannum, *New Developments in Indigenous Rights,* 28 VA. J. INT'L L. 649 (1988).

Labour Organisation has revised the only international treaty concerning indigenous groups.[84] A Working Group on Indigenous Populations of the U.N. Sub-Commission on Prevention of Discrimination and Protection of Minorities was created in 1981, and it is currently in the process of drafting a declaration on indigenous rights. Issues related to indigenous self-determination are part of these discussions, and it is likely that any development of indigenous rights to self-determination will occur in this context rather than through interpretations of the Covenants or the activities of the Human Rights Committee.

Article 1 of the Covenants is certainly relevant to U.S. policy towards Native Americans. However, given the limited nature of the right to self-determination currently recognized by international law and State practice, that policy does not appear to be inconsistent with international norms.

## ARTICLE 2—EQUALITY OF TREATMENT

1. Each State Party to the present Covenant undertakes to respect and to ensure to all individuals within its territory and subject to its jurisdiction the rights recognized in the present Covenant, without distinction of any kind, such as race, colour, sex, language, religion, political or other opinion, national or social origin, property, birth or other status.

2. Where not already provided for by existing legislative or other measures, each State Party to the present Covenant undertakes to take the necessary steps, in accordance with its constitutional processes and with the provisions of the present Covenant, to adopt such legislative or other measures as may be necessary to give effect to the rights recognized in the present Covenant.

3. Each State Party to the present Covenant undertakes:

(a) To ensure that any person whose rights or freedoms as herein recognized are violated shall have an effective remedy notwithstanding that the violation has been committed by persons acting in an official capacity;

(b) To ensure that any person claiming such a remedy shall have his right thereto determined by competent judicial, administrative or legislative authorities, or by any other competent authority provided for by the legal system of the State, and to develop the possibilities of judicial remedy;

[84] Convention Concerning the Protection and Integration of Indigenous and Other Tribal and Semi-Tribal Populations in Independent Countries (I.L.O. No. 107), *signed* 26 June 1957, 328 U.N.T.S. 247, *revised by* Convention Concerning Indigenous and Tribal Peoples in Independent Countries (I.L.O. No. 169), *adopted* 27 June 1989, *entered into force* 5 Sept 1991.

(c) To ensure that the competent authorities shall enforce such remedies when granted.

Paragraph 1 of Article 2 declares the undertaking of each ratifying government "to respect and to ensure to all individuals within its territory and subject to its jurisdiction" all of the rights recognized in the Covenant without "distinction of any kind, such as race, colour, sex, language, religion, political or other opinion, national or social origin, property, birth or other status."[85] The Human Rights Committee's general comment on this article underscores the fact that "implementation does not depend solely on constitutional or legislative enactments, which in themselves are often not *per se* sufficient.... This aspect calls for specific activities by the States Parties to enable individuals to enjoy their rights."[86]

The list of grounds upon which discrimination is prohibited is, by its express terms, not exclusive and would include others of like nature.[87] At the same time, the provision is not open-ended. It was intended only to bar unjustified, invidious or improper distinctions; not all distinctions based on the specifically proscribed criteria are barred. The drafters clearly recognized the legitimacy of some differences of treatment, even those relying upon categories listed in paragraph 1. It should also be noted that the drafters intended that the article not be read to preclude the taking of "affirmative action" to benefit disadvantaged or minority groups; the position is one of neutrality on the issue, neither prohibiting nor requiring such steps.

Article 2's prohibition against invidious discrimination accords with American notions of fairness and with the general requirements of constitutional equal protection as applied to the federal government by the Fifth Amendment[88] and to the states by the express provisions of the Fourteenth Amendment. Like the Covenant, the Constitution does not bar all distinctions or discriminations, only those which are irrational, unjustified, or illegitimate. The Supreme Court has elaborated a standard for application of Equal Protection limitations

[85] Several other articles also prescribe equality of treatment and prohibit discrimination; *see* discussion *supra*, sec. 3.2.

[86] General Comment 3(13), *Report of the Human Rights Committee,* 36 U.N. GAOR Supp. (No. 40) at 109 (1982), U.N. Doc. A/36/40.

[87] The inclusion of the words "other status" at the end of the list of proscribed grounds of discrimination is apparently not intended to work a general expansion of the paragraph's coverage; instead, the phrase is to be read in conjunction with the word "birth" so as to refer more generally to the ideas of "class," "caste," etc.

[88] *See* Bolling v. Sharpe, 347 U.S. 497 (1954).

which requires "special scrutiny" of governmental classifications, drawing on distinctions based upon "suspect" classes or categories or which affect "fundamental rights." In such cases the government, in order to justify the differential treatment, must demonstrate the highest degree of rationality in support of its action and must show that it serves a "compelling state interest" not achievable by less intrusive means. In other instances, the degree of scrutiny and the strength of governmental justification may vary, depending upon the nature of the classification used or the private right or interest affected.[89] Though the full dimensions of constitutional equal protection doctrine may be somewhat uncertain, it seems clear that any distinctions based upon race, color, religion, political or other opinion, or national or social origin (most of the categories listed in Article 2 of the Covenant) would be considered as affecting a "suspect" class or fundamental rights, or both, and would thus be justifiable only under the most limited of circumstances. Similarly, it would be safe to conclude that governmental action which discriminated on the basis of any of the remaining enumerated categories—sex, language, property, or birth—would be subject to heightened scrutiny and would require substantial justification to be legitimate. While U.S. constitutional standards may not be the only ones which might be used to test the legitimacy of allegedly improper discriminations, both the methodology and the results produced would appear to be compatible with the non-discrimination requirements of paragraph 1 of the article.

Since the relatively broad standards in Article 2 do not comport precisely with U.S. constitutional law concerning equal protection,

[89] This description of the Supreme Court's elucidation and application of "equal protection" doctrine is an oversimplification of what has become a highly complex constitutional field. Decisions of the Burger Court have produced extensive commentary. *See, e.g.*, materials cited in G. GUNTHER, CONSTITUTIONAL LAW (10th ed., 1980) at 675, note 10; J. NOWAK, R. ROTUNDA & J. YOUNG, CONSTITUTIONAL LAW (2d ed. 1983) at 585-831. It has been suggested that the Warren Court's two-class or two-tier standard of review in Equal Protection cases has given way to a "multi-tiered" set of classifications for review. Justice Marshall has argued, for example, that the Court "has applied a spectrum of standards in reviewing discrimination allegedly violative of the Equal Protection Clause...a spectrum [which] clearly comprehends variations in the degree of care with which the Court will scrutinize particular classifications...depending on the constitutional and societal importance of the interest adversely affected and the recognized invidiousness of...the particular classification...." San Antonio Ind. School Dist. v. Rodriguez, 911 U.S. 1, 70, 98-99 (1973) (dissenting opinion). A variety of equal protection "models" or interpretive schemes have been proposed or read into modern cases. *See generally, e.g.*, L. TRIBE, AMERICAN CONSTITUTIONAL LAW, Ch. 16 (1978) and materials cited in GUNTHER, *supra*.

the United States attached an understanding to its ratification. This understanding declares that the United States will consider the distinctions identified in Article 2 (and Article 26) permissible "when such distinctions are, at minimum, rationally related to a legitimate governmental objective."

Additional protections against discrimination are contained in various domestic statutes, affecting both governmental and private conduct in a number of areas.[90] These, in particular, would help fulfill what some argue is an obligation of governments under the Covenant not only to recognize the rights specifically enumerated in the various articles and to prevent their denial by official action, but to protect them from private violation as well.[91] In like fashion, federal criminal statutes prohibiting official and private interference with the exercise of federal rights give added protection to rights guaranteed by the Covenant.[92] Even in the absence of such specific statutory provisions, however, a wide variety of common law doctrines, such as those which protect privacy, reputation, and the integrity of both person and property, as well as criminal prohibitions against threats or violence or other improper interference with person or property, afford substantial additional protection for those rights which might be subject to invasion by private action. This should constitute substantial fulfillment of the generalized obligation in Article 2 "to ensure to all individuals" the rights mentioned in the Covenant.

Consistent with the more generally stated obligations of States in paragraph 1, paragraph 2 requires that appropriate legislative or other action be taken "as may be necessary" to give effect to the rights enumerated in the Covenant. Whether and to what extent the United States would be required to take such steps depends upon the protections already afforded each of the specific rights recognized in the Covenant. (Each such right is separately considered in this

[90] *See,* e.g., 42 U.S.C. §§1981-1983, 1985-86, and the Civil Rights Act of 1964, 1965, and 1968. The Constitution itself generally protects only against governmental actions, not against private conduct.

[91] It has been suggested that the requirement of Article 2 that governments not only "respect" but also "ensure" the rights enumerated in the Covenant extends to protecting against private as well as official deprivations. *See* Henkin, *Constitutional Rights and Human Rights,* 13 HARV. CIV. PTS.-CIV. LIB. L. REV. 593 (1978). There is evidence, however, that this is not the case, at least insofar as the non-discrimination provisions of the Covenant are concerned. *Cf.* text accompanying notes 8-17, 34-36 *supra.*

[92] *See,* e.g., 18 U.S.C. §§241-55.

section.) In any event, there can be no doubt about the power of the Congress to enact any required legislation.[93]

Under the final paragraph of Article 2, each party to the Covenant undertakes to assure that any person whose rights are violated shall have an effective and enforceable remedy, preferably a judicial remedy. Rights without remedies are strongly disfavored in American law, and the cases in which a person can be denied a right and left with no recourse whatsoever are few. A wide, generally effective, range of remedies is available in state and federal courts for violation of individual rights. As already noted, a great body of general civil law—mainly tort law—allows injunctive or compensatory relief against both official and private parties for violation of private rights; particularly relevant in this context, for example, are actions for false imprisonment and malicious prosecution (Article 9), libel and slander (Article 17), physical abuse (Articles 7 and 17, among others), invasion of privacy and trespass (Article 17), and medical treatment without informed, voluntary consent (Article 7). In some instances, state and federal tort claims statutes work a waiver of sovereign immunity to allow direct recovery from governmental units.

For example, a long-standing federal statute[94] specifically provides for both equitable and injunctive relief in cases in which a state official violates civil rights granted by the Constitution or federal statute. Suits may be brought against most offending officials and against local governmental units, though not against a state.[95] Exercising its power under Section 5 of the Fourteenth Amendment, Congress also could make state governments liable for official violations of federal civil rights.[96]

Numerous other specific provisions protect certain civil rights against violation by either official or private action.[97] And, where necessary as the only effective remedy, the Supreme Court has shown

[93] Congress clearly has power to require all agencies of the federal government not to violate any rights protected by the Covenant. Similarly, acting pursuant to its authority under the Thirteenth, Fourteenth, and Fifteenth Amendments, as well as under the Commerce Clause, Congress could prohibit violation of Covenant rights by state or local government or by private conduct. Finally, Congress has general authority to implement the provisions of the Covenant as an adjunct of the treaty-making power. *See* Missouri V. Holland, 252 U.S. 416 (1920); *cf.* discussion *supra,* sec. 2.2.2.

[94] 42 U.S.C. §1983.

[95] *See* Monell v. Dept. of Social Services of New York, 98 S. Ct. 2018 (1978), and Quern v. Jordan, 99 S. Ct. 1139 (1979).

[96] *See* Fitzpatrick v. Bitzer, 427 U.S. 445 (1976).

[97] *See,* e.g., 42 U.S.C. §§1981, 1982, 1985; Civil Rights Acts of 1964, 1965 and 1968.

a willingness to imply a cause of action for damages against federal officials who violate constitutional rights.[98] Even where various immunities apply, some remedy is ordinarily available. If sovereign immunity or other limitations such as the Eleventh Amendment remain applicable to bar an action directly against a government unit, relief may often be obtained by suing the offending official.[99] If personal immunities or conditional or partial defenses preclude recovery of damages from an official,[100] injunctive relief will still ordinarily be obtainable to remedy continuing wrongs and prevent realistically threatened future ones. Even when the offending official is accorded absolute immunity from suit, as are judges and some prosecutorial officials,[101] there may be other avenues to relief, such as direct appeal or collateral review, to correct violations occurring in the course of criminal or other proceedings: suppression or exclusion of illegally obtained evidence; or personally suing the official carrying out the judicial order, rather than the judge.

In short, there is a broad, if complex, array of state and federal remedies available to enforce and protect the rights guaranteed by the Covenant. To the extent that there are gaps in the structure of domestic law which could, in certain circumstances, allow violation of a civil or even constitutional right to go without remedy, they are not so numerous as to preclude the United States from being in substantial compliance with the Covenant. In any event, such unjust and currently unremediable violations deserve early legislative attention and correction, wholly apart from any obligations under the Covenant.

## ARTICLE 3—SEX DISCRIMINATION

> The States Parties to the present Covenant undertake to ensure the equal rights of men and women to the enjoyment of all civil and political rights set forth in the present Covenant.

The Fifth and Fourteenth Amendments to the United States Constitution would appear to guarantee domestic compliance with

[98] *See* Bivens v. Six Unknown Named Agents of Fed. Bur. of Narcotics, 403 U.S. 388 (1977); Davis v. Passman, 442 U.S. 228 (1979).

[99] *See,* e.g., Ex Parte Young 209 U.S. 123 (1908).

[100] *See* Wood v. Strickland, 420 U.S. 308 (1975); Scheuer v. Rhodes, 416 U.S. 232 (1974) ("good faith" is a defense to damage claims against state and local officials).

[101] *See,* e.g., Stump v. Sparkman, 435 U.S. 349 (1978); Imblev v. Pachtman, 424 U.S. 409 (1976).

this Article, despite failure to adopt the Equal Rights Amendment.[102] Any official discrimination based on gender in implementing or recognizing the specific rights enumerated in the Covenant would presumably violate governmental obligations to afford equal protection of the laws. In a number of cases the Supreme Court has held that invidious and unjustified gender-based classifications could not withstand constitutional scrutiny.[103]

The Human Rights Committee has observed that this article "requires not only measures of protection but also affirmative action designed to ensure the positive enjoyment of rights."[104]

## ARTICLE 4—DEROGATION IN EMERGENCIES

1. In time of public emergency which threatens the life of the nation and the existence of which is officially proclaimed, the States Parties to the present Covenant may take measures derogating from their obligations under the present Covenant to the extent strictly required by the exigencies of the situation, provided that such measures are not inconsistent with their other obligations under international law and do not involve discrimination solely on the ground of race, colour, sex, language, religion or social origin.

2. No derogation from Articles 6, 7, 8 (paragraphs 1 and 2), 11, 15, 16, and 18 may be made under this provision.

3. Any State Party to the present Covenant availing itself of the right of derogation shall immediately inform the other States Parties to the present Covenant, through the intermediary of the Secretary-General of the United Nations, of the provisions from which it has derogated and of the reasons by

[102] The Equal Rights Amendment would require that "[e]quality of rights under the law shall not be denied or abridged by the United States or by any [s]tate on account of sex" and would empower Congress to enact appropriate implementing legislation. Ratification of the Amendment would make explicit the prohibition of discrimination on grounds of sex which the equal protection aspects of the Fifth and Fourteenth Amendments now reach only in a more general and probably less encompassing fashion. The issue in question here, however, is not whether men and women are in all respects treated equally under the law but, more narrowly, whether they are treated equally with respect to those rights which are set out in the CPR Covenant. In one area in which the issue of inequality might otherwise arise, that is, with respect to marital rights, the Covenant makes it clear that full and immediate equality between spouses it not required. *See* discussion of art. 23, *infra.*

[103] *See,* e.g., Reed v. Reed, 404 U.S. 71 (1971); Frontiero v. Richardson, 411 U.S. 677 (1973); Orr v. Orr, 440 U.S. 268 (1979), *but compare,* e.g., Schlesinger v. Ballard, 419 U.S. 498 (1975).

[104] General Comment 4 (13), *Report of the Human Rights Committee,* 36 U.N. GAOR Supp. (No. 40) at 109, U.N. Doc. A/36/40 (1982). The Convention on the Elimination of All Forms of Discrimination Against Women, which also is pending before the Senate for its advice and consent, requires parties to adopt "appropriate measures" to ensure equality between men and women, which may include "temporary special measures aimed at accelerating *de facto* equality."

> which it was actuated. A further communication shall be made, through the same intermediary, on the date on which it terminates such derogation.

This article permits parties to the Covenant to derogate from its provisions "[i]n time of public emergency which threatens the life of the nation." No derogation is permitted from Articles 6 (right to life), 7 (torture, cruel and inhuman punishment), 8 (slavery), 11 (imprisonment for debt), 15 (ex post facto laws), 16 (recognition before the law), and 18 (freedom of thought, conscience and religion). To the extent that these seven articles each deal with rights subject to constitutional guarantee, they are equally protected from violation by domestic law. Paragraph 1 of Article 4 prohibits emergency measures based "solely" on certain criteria. A U.S. understanding, recommended by President Bush, interprets this prohibition as allowing distinctions "that may have a disproportionate effect upon persons of a particular status." This interpretation does not appear to be inconsistent with the intent of the Covenant language.

The precise circumstances allowing derogations, the manner in which they are to be made, and other limits on their nature and effect are discussed in section 3.3.4, *infra.*

## ARTICLE 5—DESTRUCTION OR LIMITATION OF RIGHTS

> 1. Nothing in the present Covenant may be interpreted as implying for any State, group or person any right to engage in any activity or perform any act aimed at the destruction of any of the rights and freedoms recognized herein or at their limitation to a greater extent than is provided for in the present Covenant.
>
> 2. There shall be no restriction upon or derogation from any of the fundamental human rights recognized or existing in any State Party to the present Covenant pursuant to law, conventions, regulations or custom on the pretext that the present Covenant does not recognize such rights or that it recognizes them to a lesser extent.

On its face, this provision seems no more than a simple rule of interpretation disclaiming any reading on the Covenant affirmatively to create, under any interpretation, a right to act to destroy or, except as otherwise expressly provided, to limit its guarantees. So read, it is a useful provision which, other than as a simple guide to construction of the Covenant's content, has no operative domestic effect. The Carter Administration appeared to see in it, however, at least an implication of a potential for inhibiting the exercise of free speech rights under the First and Fourteenth Amendments and, accordingly, proposed a reservation to the paragraph.[105] Though this concern may be overdrawn, there is no reason not to protect against the possibility, as is necessary with respect to Article 20's conflict with constitutional guarantees of freedom of speech.

The second paragraph of Article 5 is, in effect, a "savings clause" which merely bars use of the Covenant itself as a basis for restricting more expansive conceptions of rights already existing under U.S. law or practice.[106]

## ARTICLE 6—RIGHT TO LIFE

> 1. Every human being has the inherent right to life. This right shall be protected by law. No one shall be arbitrarily deprived of his life.
>
> 2. In countries which have not abolished the death penalty, sentence of death may be imposed only for the most serious crimes in accordance with the law in force at the time of the commission of the crime and not contrary to the provisions of the present Covenant and to the Convention on the Prevention and Punishment of the Crime of Genocide. This penalty can only be carried out pursuant to a final judgment rendered by a competent court.
>
> 3. When deprivation of life constitutes the crime of genocide, it is understood that nothing in this article shall authorize anyway State Party to the present Covenant to derogate in any way from any obligation assumed under the provisions of the Convention on the Prevention and Punishment of the Crime of Genocide.
>
> 4. Anyone sentenced to death shall have the right to seek pardon or commutation of the sentence. Amnesty, pardon or commutation of the sentence of death may be granted in all cases.
>
> 5. Sentence of death shall not be imposed for crimes committed by persons below eighteen years of age and shall not be carried out on pregnant women.

[105] *See* Message of the President Transmitting Four Treaties Pertaining to Human Rights, S. Exec. Doc. No. 95-C, D, E & F, 95th Cong., 2d Sess., at xi-xii (1978). The Administration's view is not without support. *See* Williams, *The European Convention on Human Rights: A New Use?* 12 Tex. Int'l L. J. 279 (1977), which discusses both realized and potential readings given parallel language in the European Convention.

[106] The right to property, for example, is not guaranteed in the CPR Covenant. It is clear from this article that the Covenant is not intended to reduce rights already protected under national law, and, since the Fifth Amendment to the U.S. Constitution protects the right to property, the Covenant cannot affect the protection of the right to property under U.S. law.

6. Nothing in this article shall be invoked to delay or to prevent the abolition of capital punishment by any State Party to the present Covenant.

Article 6 concerns the most fundamental of all human rights, the right to life. Paragraph 1 declares generally the right of each human being to life, requires its protection by law, and prohibits arbitrary deprivation of life. In so doing, it confirms basic human values reflected in American culture and law.

Although Article 6 is not one of the articles from which derogation is permitted in time of public emergency, it does not outlaw war.[107] Nor does it outlaw capital punishment, but it does establish limits on the manner and circumstances in which the death penalty may be imposed and carried out. These limitations are generally consistent with domestic law and practice.[108]

The first paragraph imposes a positive obligation on States Parties to adopt laws punishing intentional deprivation of life by public authorities and private persons and to provide adequate procedures for the prosecution of persons committing homicide.[109]

Although Article 6 does not expressly define "the right to life," analysis of the drafting history and a comparison with other international instruments makes it clear that it was not intended to deal with the issue of abortion.[110] An attempt to amend the draft article to add the phrase "from the moment of conception" at the end of the first sentence was defeated.[111] States which have already ratified

[107] The humanitarian law established by the 1949 Geneva Conventions and Protocols thereto (rather than these Covenants) would apply to the conduct of armed conflict. *But see also* art. 4 of the CPR Covenant.

[108] *But see* discussion of art. 7, *infra.*

[109] *U.N. Annotations, supra* note 10, at 30, para. 4.

[110] The Human Rights Committee has not directly addressed the issue of abortion, but questions have arisen in the context of regional human rights treaties. In no cases has the relevant international norm been used to overturn domestic law, and the cases generally adopt a moderate position of guaranteeing a woman's right to choose while also recognizing a legitimate governmental interest in protecting fetal rights to some extent. *See* Paton v. U.K., App. No. 8416/78, Eur. Comm'n Human Rts. dec. on admissibility of 13 May 1980, 19 Dec. & Rep. 244; Bruggemann & Scheuten v. Fed. Rep. of Germany, App. No. 6959/75, Eur. Comm'n Human Rts. Report of 12 July 1977, 10 Dec. & Rep. 100; Case 2141 (United States), Inter-Am. Comm'n Human Rts. Res. No. 23/81 of 6 Mar. 1981, *reprinted in Annual Report 1980-81,* at 25, O.A.S. Off. Rec. OEA/Ser.L/V/11.54, doc. 9 rev. 1 (1981).

[111] The addition was opposed on the grounds, *inter alia,* that it was impossible for the State to determine the moment of conception and hence undertake to protect life from that moment; that it involved the question of the rights and duties of the medical profession; and that legislation on the subject was based on different principles in different countries, and it was, therefore, inappropriate to include such a provision in an international instrument. *Report of the Third Committee* (12th session), U.N. Doc. A/3764 and Add. 1, at para. 112 (1957).

the CPR. Covenant have widely differing laws on abortion, and none has perceived a need to make a reservation to the article in this regard. The article neither condemns nor condones laws on abortion; in the absence of an international consensus, it simply does not deal with the subject.[112]

Article 6 does not forbid every taking of life but only those deprivations which are arbitrary. Although not expressly stated, it may be assumed from the drafting history that killing in self-defense, in making a lawful arrest or preventing the escape of a person lawfully detained, or in quelling a riot, would not be forbidden, if excessive force were not used. Such exceptions are specifically listed in the comparable article of the European Convention on Human Rights. An enumeration of exceptions was not included in the Covenant because it was believed that any enumeration would necessarily be incomplete and would convey the impression that greater importance was being given to the exceptions than to the right.[113]

During the drafting of Article 6, some objections were raised to the use of the term "arbitrarily." It was argued that it was ambiguous and that the word "intentionally" would be preferable. The term was retained, however, since it had been used in other articles of the Covenant [Article 9(1), Article 12(4), Article 17(1)], and it may be considered to include the concepts of "illegally" and "unjustly."[114]

As already indicated, Article 6 does not bar capital punishment, but paragraphs 2-6 do place some limits on its use.[115] The death penalty is

[112] Insofar as the U.S. Constitution limits governmental power to restrict abortions, contrary international undertakings, by treaty or otherwise, would be invalid.

[113] *See U.N. Annotations, supra* note 10, at 29-30, para. 2. There are other issues concerning the right to life—such as waiver of the right of life, the necessity for the use of extraordinary means to continue life, and the moment at which death occurs—with respect to which art. 6 provides no guidance.

[114] *See U.N. Annotations, supra* note 10, at 30, para. 3. "The importance of the distinction is highlighted by the fact that if 'arbitrary' means 'illegal,' all despotic acts and oppressive laws of a government would be unassailable so long as these legislative enactments were in accordance with municipal laws. If 'arbitrary' is synonymous with 'unjust,' then governments would have to respond to a higher standard." Parvez, *The International Covenants on Human Rights: An Approach to Interpretation,* 19 BUFFALO L. REV. 35-37 (1968-69). *Cf.* UNITED NATIONS, STUDY OF THE RIGHT OF EVERYONE TO BE FREE FROM ARBITRARY ARREST, DETENTION AND EXILE 5-7 (1964); Dinstein, *The Right to Life, Physical Integrity, and Liberty,* in Henkin, *supra* note 1, at 130-31.

[115] Paragraph 2 applies to "countries which have not abolished the death penalty," and paragraph 6 provides that nothing in the article should "be invoked to delay or prevent the abolition of capital punishment." It has been suggested that the phraseology of paragraph 2 could be interpreted to mean that capital punishment, once abolished in a country, could not be reinstated, as provided in the American Convention on Human Rights. However, neither the drafting history nor the express language of Article 6 require such an interpretation. The Human Rights Committee has observed that abolition is desirable and that the death penalty "should be a quite exceptional measure," but it has not addressed the question of

restricted to the "most serious crimes"[116] and may be imposed only in accordance with the law in force at the time of commission of the offense. The penalty must be carried out pursuant to a final judgment of a competent court and there must be a right to seek pardon or commutation. The article further provides that the death sentence shall not be imposed for crimes committed by persons below 18 years of age and shall not be carried out on pregnant women.

Current decisional law in the United States permits both the federal government and the states to choose whether or not to use the death penalty; at the same time, the Constitution imposes substantive and procedural restrictions parallel to a number of those contained in the Covenant.

Consistent with Article 6 of the Covenant, the Constitution prohibits arbitrary imposition of the death penalty,[117] limits its use to only the most serious crimes,[118] and even then precludes inflexible, automatic or mandatory sentencing in capital cases. "[F]undamental respect for humanity," the Supreme Court has declared, "requires consideration of the character and record of the individual offender and the circumstances of the particular offense as a constitutionally indispensable part of the process of inflicting the penalty of death."[119]

The Ex Post Facto and Due Process clauses of the Constitution should assume compliance with those provisions of paragraph 2 of Article 6 which prohibit retroactive sentences of death and require that the penalty be carried out only pursuant to a final judgment of a competent court. The right to seek pardon or commutation of a death sentence, as set out in paragraph 4 of Article 6, also seems to be consistent with domestic practice.[120]

---

reinstatement. *See* General Comment 14 (23), *Report on the Human Rights Committee,* 40 U.N. GAOR Supp. (No. 40) at 162 (1985), U.N. Doc. A/40/40.

[116] It was recognized during the drafting that the term "most serious crimes" lacked precision since the concept might differ from country to country. *See U.N. Annotations, supra* note 10, at 30, para. 6.

[117] *See* Furman v. Georgia, 408 U.S. 238 (1972).

[118] *See* Coker v. Georgia, 433 U.S. 584 (1977). In *Coker,* the Supreme Court held that a sentence of death for the crime of rape of an adult woman was grossly disproportionate and excessive punishment forbidden by the Eighth Amendment.

[119] Woodson v. North Carolina, 428 U.S. 280, 304 (1976).

[120] "Each state in the United States that allows capital punishment also has a provision for pardon." Weissbrodt, *United States Ratification of the Human Rights Covenants,* 63 MINN. L. REV. 35, 72-73, no. 210 (1978). There may be a constitutional right to petition for a pardon or commutation of sentence, and the power to grant such a request would seem to be an inherent aspect of governmental authority, though its exercise may be assigned by law to a specific agency (usually the head of the executive branch). Thus, for example, the U.S. Constitution specifically grants the President the power to "grant reprieves and pardons for offenses against the United States."

Paragraph 5 of Article 6 bars imposition of the death penalty on persons below 18 years of age at the time of their offense and prohibits execution of pregnant women. While the Constitution contains no such specific limits, these requirements are wholly reasonable and reflect a decent, if minimum, respect for human life. Execution of pregnant women was barred by common law,[121] and at least several states prohibit it by statute.[122] There can be little, if any, justification for refusing merely to delay execution of a pregnant woman until after the birth of her child.

Although the execution of juvenile offenders is relatively rare, the constitutionality of the practice was challenged in several cases which reached the Supreme Court in the 1980s. In June 1988, four justices held that the execution of persons who were under sixteen years old at the time of their offense violated the Eighth Amendment; Justice O'Connor agreed that execution was impermissible on the facts of the particular case.[123] However, the execution of juvenile offenders was upheld when the Court was presented with the issue more directly the following term.[124]

Both the Carter and Bush Administrations recommended reservations to Article 6. While the latter did accept the prohibition against the execution of pregnant women, the prohibition against juvenile executions was explicitly rejected.[125] With the exception of pregnant women, the reservation permits the United States to execute any person "duly convicted under existing or future laws permitting the imposition of capital punishment."

[121] *See* W. BLACKSTONE, 4 COMMENTARIES 394-95 (G. Starswood ed. 1859); *see also* Union Pacific Ry. Co. v. Botsford, 141 U.S. 250, 253 (1891).

[122] *See* e.g., Cal. Penal Code §§3705-06 (West 1970); N.Y. Correction Law §§658-660 (McKinney 1978). As of 1978, at least 15 other states had similar legislation. *See* Weissbrodt, *supra* note 120.

[123] Thompson v. Oklahoma, 487 U.S. 815 (1988).

[124] *See* Stanford v. Kentucky, 109 S.Ct. 2969 (1989). For an opposing view, based on international norms, *see* Hartman, *"Unusual" Punishment: The Domestic Effects of International Norms Restricting the Application of the Death Penalty,* 52 U. CIN. L. REV. 655 (1983). The failure of the U.S. to establish national minimum standards for the execution of juvenile offenders was found by the Inter-American Commission on Human Rights to violate the principles of the American Declaration on the Rights and Duties of Man. *See* Case 9647 (United States), *Annual Report of the Inter-American Commission on Human Rights 1986-1987* (1987) at 147. *Cf.* discussion of art. 7's relevance to capital punishment, *infra.*

[125] *See* International Covenant on Civil and Political Rights, S. EXEC. DOC. No. 102-23, 102d Cong. 2d Sess. 11 (1992).

Mention might be made here of the Second Optional Protocol to the CPR Covenant, which was adopted in 1989.[126] The Protocol abolishes capital punishment under all circumstances, but, as its name indicates, acceptance by States Parties to the CPR Covenant is entirely discretionary. Unsurprisingly, the United States has indicated no intention of ratifying the Second Optional Protocol.

## ARTICLE 7—TORTURE, CRUEL AND INHUMAN TREATMENT

> No one shall be subjected to torture or to cruel, inhuman or degrading treatment or punishment. In particular, no one shall be subjected without his free consent to medical or scientific experimentation.

In its prohibition of torture and "cruel, inhuman or degrading treatment or punishment," Article 7, like Article 9, reflects not only the content of other international human rights instruments,[127] but also the values expressed in our own Constitution. The international consensus on this prohibition was reflected in unanimous adoption by the U.N. General Assembly of a Declaration against Torture[128] in 1975 and the adoption in 1984 of the Convention against Torture and Other Cruel, Inhuman or Degrading Treatment or Punishment.[129] The Senate gave its consent to U.S. ratification of the Convention against Torture in November 1990. However, as of mid-1992, the necessary implementing legislation had not yet been adopted by Congress and the United States has therefore not yet formally ratified the Torture Convention.

The Eighth Amendment, which expressly bars "cruel and unusual punishments," certainly prohibits "torture"[130] and other forms of

[126] Second Optional Protocol to the International Covenant on Civil and Political Rights, aiming at the abolition of the death penalty, *adopted* 15 Dec. 1989, *entered into force* 11 July 1991, G.A. Res. 44/128, 44 Un GAOR, Supp. (No. 49), UN Doc. A/44/49, at 206 (1989).

[127] Nearly identical provisions are found in the Universal Declaration of Human Rights (art. 5), the European Convention on Human Rights (art. 3), and the American Convention on Human Rights (art. 5(2)).

[128] GA Res. 3452 (XXX), 30 U.N. GAOR, Supp. (No. 34) at 91, U.N. Doc. A/10034 (1975).

[129] *Adopted* 10 Dec. 1984, *entered into force* 28 June 1987, G.A. Res. 39/46, 39 U.N. GAOR, Supp. (No. 51) at 197, U.N. Doc. A/39/51 (1984).

[130] The 1984 Convention Against Torture, *supra* note 129, defines torture as:

> any act by which severe pain or suffering, whether physical or mental, is intentionally inflicted on a person for such purposes as obtaining from him or a third person information or a confession, punishing him for an act he or a third person has committed or is suspected of having committed, or intimidating or coercing him or a third person, or for any reason based on discrimination of any kind, when such pain or suffering is inflicted by or at the instigation of or with the consent or acquiescence of a public official or other person acting in an official capacity. It does not include pain or suffering arising only from, inherent in, or incidental to, lawful sanctions.

cruel or inhuman punishment. The use in Article 7 of the word "degrading" may go beyond the phrasing of the Eighth Amendment, but the underlying concepts would seem to be parallel in those cases where both apply.[131] As Chief Justice Warren said in *Trop v. Dulles,*"The basic concept underlying the Eighth Amendment is nothing less than the dignity of man. While the State has the power to punish, the Amendment stands to assure that this power be exercised within the limits of civilized standards."[132]

Torture and other cruel, inhuman treatment inflicted by the government for purposes other than punishment would run afoul not only of the Eighth Amendment but of the Due Process Clause of the Fifth and Fourteenth Amendments. These provisions require, as Justice Frankfurter declared for the Supreme Court in *Rochin v. California,* that law enforcement not use methods which "offend the community's sense of fair play and decency" and that the State must "respect certain decencies of civilized conduct."[133]

Use of the word "treatment" reflects a broader scope than simply "punishment," although the concept of "degrading treatment" is not intended to include "situations which might be due to economic and social factors."[134] However, in interpreting the similar prohibition against "inhuman or degrading treatment or punishment" found in the European Convention on Human Rights, the European Court of Human Rights found that the very long period of time spent on death row in Virginia could constitute "a real risk of treatment going beyond the threshold" of the European Convention.[135]

---

Art. 2 reiterates that "[n]o exceptional circumstances whatsoever, whether a state of war or threat of war, internal political instability or any other public emergency, may be invoked as a justification of torture" and that the defense of superior orders similarly cannot justify torture.

The European Court of Human Rights has defined torture as "deliberate inhuman treatment causing very serious and cruel suffering." Ireland v. U.K., Eur. Ct. of Human Rts., Judgment of 18 Jan. 1978, Ser. A. No. 25.

131 The Eighth Amendment has been held to be applicable only in the criminal justice context. *See* Ingraham v. Wright, 430 U.S. 651 (1977), in which the Court ruled that the Amendment's strictures did not reach corporal punishment of children in the public schools; in so holding, however, the Court emphasized that traditional available tort remedies that had been used on the child would be unreasonable, 430 U.S. at 670.

132 356 U.S. 86, 100 (1958).

133 342 U.S. 165, 173 (1952).

134 *U.N. Annotations, supra* note 10, para. 13, at 31.

135 Soering v. U.K., Eur. Ct. Human Rts. Judgment of 7 July 1989, Ser. A No. 161. The Court's decision was narrowly based on the facts of the case, which arose in the context of a challenge to the accused's extradition from the U.K. to the U.S. and the expressed intention of the Virginia authorities to seek the death penalty. The relevant "personal circumstances" of the accused included, *inter alia,* his youth and mental state at the time of the crime, as well as the fact that, as a German citizen, he could be extradited and tried in the Federal Republic of Germany. The Court specifically noted that "[t]he democratic character of the Virginia legal system in general and the positive features of Virginia trial, sentencing and appeal procedures in particular

In part as a direct reaction to this decision, the Bush Administration recommended a new reservation to Article 7, substantively identical to a reservation the United States intends to file when it formally ratifies the Convention against Torture. The reservation limits U.S. obligations under Article 7 to those prohibited by the Fifth, Eighth and/or Fourteenth Amendments to the Constitution, thus denying to U.S. citizens the broader protection set forth in the CPR Covenant. It is one of the most unfortunate and inappropriate conditions attached to U.S. ratification of the Covenant, and it should be withdrawn at the earliest opportunity.

In general, the kind of "cruel, inhuman or degrading treatment" that would violate Article 7 is the same as that which would violate the Eighth Amendment, if it could be considered to be criminal punishment, and, if not, then the Due Process Clause.[136]

Article 7 also bars medical or scientific experimentation upon an individual without free consent.[137] This principle is unexceptionable and comports with both constitutional and common law norms.[138]

## ARTICLE 8—SLAVERY AND FORCED LABOR

1. No one shall be held in slavery; slavery and the slave-trade in all their forms shall be prohibited.

---

are beyond doubt." *Id.* at para. 111. The Virginia prosecutor subsequently agreed not to seek the death penalty in the case, and Soering was extradited to the U.S. *Cf.* Kirkwood v. U.K., App. No. 10479/83, Eur. Comm'n Human Rts. dec. on admissibility of 12 Mar. 1984 (under particular circumstances of case, "death row phenomenon" found not to violate prohibition against degrading treatment or to bar extradition from U.K. to California).

[136] Thus, in *Ireland v. U.K., supra* note 130, the European Court of Human Rights treated the following interrogation techniques as "inhuman or degrading" treatment rather than as "torture," because they did not produce serious or cruel enough suffering: hooding of detainees together with enforced wall standing for long periods, deprivation of sleep, a diet of bread and water, and subjection to continuous noise. Such methods would presumably also contravene the Eighth Amendment if imposed as punishment. And, if used for other purposes, they would presumably violate the Due Process Clause of the Fifth and Fourteenth Amendments. *See,* e.g., Rochin v. California, *supra* note 133, holding it to be a violation of Due Process for authorities to compel a suspect to undergo involuntary "stomach-pumping."

[137] This requirement, contained in the second sentence of art. 7, was intended to prohibit the type of excesses which occurred in National Socialist Germany during and before World War II. Although it was considered that outlawing of such medical experimentation was encompassed within the general prohibitions of the first sentence of art. 7, it was felt important enough to require a separate and specific reference. *U.N. Annotations, supra* note 10, at 31, para. 14.

[138] Consent is a prerequisite in American law even in ordinary medical treatment; without it, there is a battery. Where experimental remedies or procedures are involved, the more recently developed concept of "informed consent" would seem particularly applicable. *See generally* PROSSER, LAW OF TORTS 101-108, 165-66 (1971). And where the treatment or experimentation is done by or at the behest of government, the Due Process Clause would be implicated.

2. No one shall be held in servitude.

3. (a) No one shall be required to perform forced or compulsory labor;

(b) Paragraph 3(a) shall not be held to preclude, in countries where imprisonment with hard labour may be imposed as a punishment for a crime, the performance of hard labour in pursuance of a sentence to such punishment by a competent court;

(c) For the purpose of this paragraph the term "forced or compulsory labour" shall not include:

(i) Any work or service not referred to in sub-paragraph (b), normally required of a person who is under detention in consequence of a lawful order of a court, or of a person during conditional release from such detention;

(ii) Any service of a military character and, in countries where conscientious objection is recognized, any national service required by law of conscientious objectors;

(iii) Any service exacted in cases of emergency or calamity threatening the life or well-being of the community;

(iv) Any work or service which forms part of normal civil obligations.

Article 8 prohibits slavery and involuntary servitude, as does our own Thirteenth Amendment;[139] it permits imprisonment with hard labor as punishment for a crime, as does the Thirteenth Amendment, and, in addition, contains appropriate exceptions to cover compulsory military and other public or civil service.

The United States is a party to the 1926 Slavery Convention and its Protocol[140] and the 1956 Supplementary Convention on the Abolition of Slavery.[141] The concept of forced labor has been examined in the context of two ILO Conventions,[142] although the U.S. is not a

[139] The Thirteenth Amendment applies to both governmental and private action. In addition, the holding of another in slavery, peonage or involuntary servitude is made criminal under federal law, 18 U.S.C. §§1551-88.

[140] *Signed* 25 Sept. 1926, *entered into force* 9 Mar. 1927, 46 Stat. 2183, T.S. No. 778, 60 L.N.T.S. 253 (*entered into force for U.S.* 21 Mar. 1929); Protocol Amending the Slavery Convention, *signed and entered into force* 7 Dec. 1953, 7 U.S.T. 479, T.I.A.S. No. 3532, 182 U.N.T.S. 51 (*entered into force for U.S.* 7 Mar. 1956).

[141] *Signed* 7 Sept. 1956, *entered into force* 30 Apr. 1957, 18 U.S.T. 3201, T.I.A.S. No. 6418, 266 U.N.T.S. 3 (*entered into force* for U.S. 6 Dec. 1967).

[142] Convention Concerning Forced or Compulsory Labour (ILO No. 29), *adopted* 28 June 1930, *entered into force* 1 May 1932, 39 U.N.T.S. 55; Convention on the Abolition of Forced Labour (ILO No. 105), *adopted* 25 June 1957, *entered into force* 17 Jan. 1959, 320 U.N.T.S. 291. *See generally* I.L.O. Committee of Experts on the Application of Conventions and Recommendations, *Abolition of Forced Labour* (Report III [Part 4 B], 1979) and the Committee's annual reports to the International Labour Conference, which include comments on the application of Conventions Nos. 29 and 105.

party to either convention, and in some of the cases considered under the European Convention on Human Rights.[143]

Ratification of this article presents no constitutional or practical difficulties for the United States, and no reservation, declaration, or understanding to Article 13 was proposed by either President Carter or President Bush.

## ARTICLE 9—RIGHT TO LIBERTY AND SECURITY

1. Everyone has the right to liberty and security of person. No one shall be subjected to arbitrary arrest or detention. No one shall be deprived of his liberty except on such grounds and in accordance with such procedures as are established by law.

2. Anyone who is arrested shall be informed, at the time of arrest, of the reasons for his arrest and shall be promptly informed of any charges against him.

3. Anyone arrested or detained on a criminal charge shall be brought promptly before a judge or other officer authorized by law to exercise judicial power and shall be entitled to trial within a reasonable time or to release. It shall not be the general rule that persons awaiting trial shall be detained in custody, but release may be subject to guarantees to appear for trial, at any other stage of the judicial proceedings, and, should occasion arise, for execution of the judgement.

4. Anyone who is deprived of his liberty by arrest or detention shall be entitled to take proceedings before a court, in order that that court may decide without delay on the lawfulness of his detention and order his release if the detention is not lawful.

5. Anyone who has been the victim of unlawful arrest or detention shall have an enforceable right to compensation.

Paragraph 1 declares a general right to liberty and security, bans "arbitrary" arrest or detention, and requires that any deprivation of liberty be in substantive and procedural conformity with law. Except where otherwise specified, the article applies to all deprivations of liberty and not just to criminal cases.[144] As in the case of the use of the word "arbitrarily" in Article 6, the term here means more than simply "illegal." Thus, the fact that arrest and detention were in accordance with national law would not guarantee conformity with this article if such arrest or detention was otherwise unjust or unreasonable.[145] Both

[143] *See* COUNCIL OF EUROPE, 1 DIGEST OF STRASBOURG CASE-LAW RELATING TO THE EUROPEAN CONVENTION ON HUMAN RIGHTS 237-69 (6 vols. 1984-85).

[144] *See* General Comment 8 (16), *Report of the Human Rights Committee,* 37 U.N. GAOR Supp. (No. 40) at 95 (1982), U.N. Doc. A/37/40.

[145] The draftsmen considered that "[A]n arbitrary act was any act which violated justice, reason or legislation, or was done according to someone's will or discretion, or which was capricious, despotic, imperious, tyrannical or uncontrolled." *Report of the Third Committee,* 13

the Fifth Amendment, applicable to the federal government, and the Fourteenth Amendment, applicable to the states, prohibit deprivations of liberty without due process of law, and the Fourth Amendment, which applies directly to the federal government and, through the Fourteenth, to the states, protects against arbitrary or unreasonable arrest.

It was understood at the time of drafting Article 9 that the right to liberty and security might be subject to restrictions, but it was decided not to include any reference to possible grounds on which such deprivation might be justified.[146] However, certain procedural guarantees in the event of arrest or detention are included.[147] Paragraphs 2 and 3 thus require that a person be informed of the reason for his or her arrest, the nature of any charges, and that he or she be brought promptly before a judicial official. Paragraph 3 also requires trial within a "reasonable time" and declares that pre-trial detention shall not be the general practice; release on bond or subject to such other guarantees (to appear for trial and for execution of judgment) as may be appropriate is permitted. These provisions are also consistent with U.S. law and practice and are in general constitutionally mandated.[148]

---

GAOR, Annexes, Agenda Item 32, at 7, para. 49, U.N. Doc. A/4045 (1958-59). *See also* H. HANNUM (1989), *supra* note 1, at 17-18; STUDY OF THE RIGHT OF EVERYONE TO BE FREE FROM ARBITRARY ARREST, DETENTION AND EXILE, *supra* note 114; Hassan, *The International Covenants on Human Rights: An Approach To Interpretation, 19 BUFFALO L. REV. 35 (1969-70)*. The Restatement identifies the prohibition against "prolonged arbitrary detention" as part of the customary international law of human rights and therefore binding on the U.S. 2 RESTATEMENT §702 comment h, Reporters' Note 6 at 161, 164-65, 171-72.

[146] *See U.N. Annotations, supra* note 10, at 35, para. 27.

[147] The complicated and often arcane norms of criminal procedure have been the subject of extensive international and domestic jurisprudence that cannot be adequately summarized within the constraints of the present work. With respect to the international norms, *see generally*, e.g., J. FAWCETT, THE APPLICATION OF THE EUROPEAN CONVENTION ON HUMAN RIGHTS 68-199 (2d ed. 1987); H. HANNUM (1989), *supra* note 1; P. SIEGHART, *supra* note 1, at 268-305; Dinstein, *supra* note 114.

[148] The Sixth Amendment, applicable to the states through the Fourteenth, requires that "[i]n all criminal prosecutions, the accused shall enjoy the right to a speedy...trial...and to be informed of the nature and cause of the accusation...." Release on bail or other security in appropriate cases is implicitly guaranteed by the Eighth Amendment and is generally available in domestic practice. Prompt appearance before a judicial official is a right generally accorded in the United States to those who are arrested and is a requirement under federal practice. *See* Mallory v. United States, 354 U.S. 449 (1957), McNabb v. United States, 318 U.S. 332 (1942). The *McNabb-Mallory* rule has been modified somewhat by subsequent legislation, e.g., 18 U.S.C. §3501(c). And, although the rule in its precise requirements has not been held to be constitutionally required, it is probable that the Constitution would bar any "unreasonable" delay in bringing an accused before a judicial official.

Paragraph 4 requires that there be a procedure under which a person arrested or detained may obtain a prompt judicial determination of the legality of the arrest or detention, an essential process constitutionally guaranteed by the Great Writ, our own habeas corpus, and generally available under one name or another in state courts.

Paragraph 5 of Article 9 sets out the rule that "[a]nyone who has been the victim of 'unlawful' arrest or detention shall have an enforceable right to compensation." The principle is fair and equitable, but, unhappily, American law is not fully in compliance with it. For a variety of reasons, including the lack of complete congruence among common law, statutory, and constitutional remedies, and various defenses and immunities available to individual officials or agencies, a person illegally arrested or detained in this country may not, in some cases, have an enforceable right to compensation.[149] There is little if any justification for this anomaly and, whether or not required by the Covenant, it would be desirable to adopt legislation which would provide compensatory damages whenever a person is unjustly deprived of personal liberty by illegal arrest or detention. The reluctance of the Carter Administration to recognize the principle of fair compensation in all such cases, as is the vague U.S. understanding that compensation "may be subject to the reasonable requirements of domestic law."

## ARTICLE 10—TREATMENT OF PRISONERS

> 1. All persons deprived of their liberty shall be treated with humanity and with respect for the inherent dignity of the human person.
>
> 2. (a) Accused persons shall, save in exceptional circumstances, be segregated from convicted persons and shall be subject to separate treatment appropriate to their status as unconvicted persons;

[149] An arrest could be "unlawful" either because it violates statutory or common law rules or constitutional standards, or both. The availability of a remedy, if any, under federal or state law would turn on the nature of the violation. In addition, police and other law enforcement officials have certain personal defenses or immunities in suits for damages resulting from their official actions, even though such actions may be "illegal." *See,* for example, as to federal civil rights law, Peirson v. Ray, 386 U.S. 547 (1967) (judicial officials); Scheuer v. Rhodes, 416 U.S. 232 (1974) (executive officials); Imbler v. Pachtman, 424 U.S. 409 (1976) (prosecutors); Bivens v. Six Unknown Named Agents, 456 F.2d 1339 (2d Cir. 1972) (on remand) (police and like officials). Some governmental units may be insulated from monetary liability under federal or state law by doctrines of sovereign immunity or by limitations on the scope of statutory provisions or legislative waivers. *See generally* discussion of remedies in connection with art. 2, *supra.*

(b) Accused juvenile persons shall be separated from adults and brought as speedily as possible for adjudication.

3. The penitentiary system shall comprise treatment of prisoners the essential aim of which shall be their reformation and social rehabilitation. Juvenile offenders shall be segregated from adults and be accorded treatment appropriate to their age and legal status.

Article 10 deals with the treatment to be accorded persons who are incarcerated. It requires that all such persons be treated "with humanity and with respect for [their]...inherent dignity"; that juveniles be separated from adults and be accorded appropriate treatment; that, "save in exceptional circumstances," those accused be segregated from those who have been convicted and be treated in accord with their status;[150] and that prison systems have as their purpose, treatment aimed at "reformation and social rehabilitation" of offenders. The objectives of this article are worthy indeed,[151] but domestic practice unfortunately is not yet up to the standards it sets out. Thus, President Carter, while not disclaiming either the desirability or applicability of the article, recommended adoption of a "statement" which would consider the specific rights enumerated in its second and third paragraphs (relating to the separation of inmates and juveniles and to the nature and aims of the penitentiary system) as "goals to be achieved progressively rather than through immediate implementation."[152] The Senate, following President Bush's recommendation, ultimately adopted an understanding concerning para-

[150] It was pointed out during the drafting of this article that segregation of accused from convicted persons could be achieved even though all prisoners were in the same building. The terminology "in separate quarters" was rejected since it might have required construction of new prisons. The drafting history does not provide examples of the "exceptional circumstances" which might justify failure to segregate. The phrase was, however, adopted in preference to the word "normally" which had been suggested by some representatives who doubted that such segregation was practical. *See* Noor Muhammed, *Due Process of Law for Persons Accused of Crimes*, in Henkin, *supra* note 1, at 114-65. Reference should also be made in this context to other internationally adopted standards relating to the treatment of prisoners, including the Standard Minimum Rules for the Treatment of Prisoners, *adopted* in E.S.C. Res. 663C, 24 UN ESCOR, Supp. (No. 1) at 11, U.N. Doc. E/3048 (1957), *extended,* E.S.C. Res. 2976 (LXIII), 62 U.N. ESCOR, Supp. (No. 1) at 35 (1977), and the presently adopted Body of Principles for the Protection of All Persons Subject to Any Form of Detention, G.A. Res. 43/173, 43 U.N. GAOR, Supp. (No. 49), at 297, U.N. Doc. A/43/49 (1988).

[151] Both the U.S. Department of Justice "Federal Standards for Corrections" (proposed in 1978) and the American Correctional Association's Commission on Accreditation for Corrections, in its "Manual of Standards for Adult Local Detention Facilities" (published in 1977), provide for the segregation of convicted and unconvicted persons and of juveniles. *See* "Federal Standards" at 48; "Manual" at 71.

[152] Message of the President, *supra* note 105, at xii.

graph 2(a) of Article 10 which partially defines "exceptional circumstances" to include situations where imprisonment of an accused person with convicted persons "is appropriate in light of an individual's overall dangerousness."

Although desirable in principle, the required segregation of prisoners depends for its implementation on the facilities and resources of each community. Insofar as this country's jails and penal institutions are not adequate at present to meet these standards, and could not immediately be made so, a reservation may be an appropriately candid expression of realistic possibilities. The reservation adopted states that U.S. practice is "generally in compliance" with the Covenant's provisions on this issue but reserves the right, "in exceptional circumstances to treat juveniles as adults." Several European and other governments have entered similar reservations with regard to the segregation of adults and juveniles.[153]

Paragraph 3 of Article 10 was apparently not intended to convey that the sole purpose of the penitentiary system should be reformation and social rehabilitation. The phraseology used was not intended to disregard the views of those who considered the deterrent aspect of punishment as important.[154] Nonetheless, it would appear reasonable to make this clear, and the understanding adopted by the Bush Administration and the Senate states that the goal of rehabilitation "does not diminish the goals of punishment, deterrence, and incapacitation as additional legitimate purposes for a penitentiary system."

## ARTICLE 11—IMPRISONMENT FOR DEBT

> No one shall be imprisoned merely on the ground of inability to fulfill a contractual obligation.

Consistent with American law and practice,[155] this Article forbids the imprisonment of a person "merely on the ground of inability to fulfill a contractual obligation." There may be no derogation from this article.

[153] *See* UNITED NATIONS, STATUS OF INTERNATIONAL INSTRUMENTS (1987), Sales No. E.87.XIV.2, at 28-49.

[154] *See* Report of the Third Committee, 13 U.N. GAOR, Annexes, Agenda Item 32, at para. 81, U.N. Doc. A/4045 (1958); Noor Muhammed, *supra* note 150.

[155] Most of the state constitutions contain provisions which prohibit imprisonment for debt. In Tate v. Short, 401 U.S. 395 (1971), the Supreme Court held that it was a violation of the Fourteenth Amendment's Equal Protection Clause for a state to imprison an indigent person who was unable to pay a fine, the only penalty prescribed by the law he was convicted of violating.

This article covers contractual obligations but "does not cover crimes committed through the non-fulfillment of obligations of public interest, which were imposed by statute or court order, such as the payment of maintenance allowance."[156] Thus, there is no prohibition against imprisonment for contempt or for failure to make court-ordered support payments. In addition, because of the clause "merely on the ground of inability," the article does not protect one who has the means to fulfill his obligation but refuses to do so.[157]

## ARTICLE 12—FREEDOM OF MOVEMENT

1. Everyone lawfully within the territory of a State shall, within that territory, have the right to liberty of movement and freedom to choose his residence.

2. Everyone shall be free to leave any country, including his own.

3. The above-mentioned rights shall not be subject to any restrictions except those which are provided by law, are necessary to protect national security, public order (*ordre public*), public health or morals or the rights and freedoms of others, and are consistent with the other rights recognized in the present Covenant.

4. No one shall be arbitrarily deprived of the right to enter his own country.

This article guarantees to everyone lawfully within the country the right of freedom of movement and residence, as well as the right to travel, emigrate, and not to be "arbitrarily" deprived of the right to enter his own country.[158]

These provisions are obviously part of American tradition and practice. "[F]reedom to travel throughout the United States has long been recognized as a basic right under the Constitution,"[159] and "the right to travel abroad is 'an important aspect'" of the "liberty"

[156] *U.N. Annotations, supra* note 10, at 37, para. 45.

[157] *Id.* at para. 47.

[158] In connection with this article, *see generally* H. HANNUM, THE RIGHT TO LEAVE AND RETURN IN INTERNATIONAL LAW AND PRACTICE (1987); *Analysis of the current trends and developments regarding the right to leave any country, including one's own, and to return to one's own country, and some other rights or considerations arising therefrom,* (C. Mubanga-Chipoya, Special Rapporteur), U.N. Doc. E/CN.4/Sub.2/1988/35 & Add. 1 (1988); *Study of Discrimination in Respect of the Right of Everyone to Leave Any Country, Including His Own, and to Return to His Country* (J. Ingles, Special Rapporteur), U.N. Sales No. 64.XIV.2 (1963).

[159] United States v. Guest, 383 U.S. 745, 758 (1966). The Privileges and Immunities Clause (in art. IV, §2, and as applied through the Fourteenth Amendment) and the Commerce Clause have variously been identified as the source of this right. *See* Shapiro v. Thompson, 394 U.S. 618, 630 n. 8 (1969).

guaranteed by the Due Process Clause of the Fifth Amendment.[160] As the Supreme Court declared in *Kent v. Dulles:*

> The right to travel is part of the "liberty" of which the citizen cannot be deprived without due process of law under the Fifth Amendment.... Freedom of movement across frontiers in either direction, and inside frontiers as well, was a part of our heritage.... Freedom of movement is basic in our scheme of values.[161]

The Human Rights Committee has focused particularly on the right to leave one's country and has raised questions concerning restrictions on this right, particularly in some Eastern European countries.[162]

The provision in paragraph 4 of the Article that "[N]o one shall be arbitrarily deprived of the right to enter his own country"[163] also comports with fundamental U.S. principles. The citizen's right to return to the United States has been recognized by the courts.[164] A Human Rights Committee addressed the right to return in several cases brought under the Optional Protocol, concerning Uruguayan citizens whose passports were revoked or denied by the military government then in power. The Committee noted that even those citizens resident outside Uruguay had a right to a passport, at least where the government offered no justification for its refusal to issue a passport.[165]

[160] Aptheker v. Secretary of State, 378 U.S. 500, 505 (1964).

[161] However, the right of foreign travel may be somewhat less absolute in the United States than the right of domestic or interstate travel. *Compare*, e.g., Aptheker v. Secretary of State, *supra* note 160, and Kent v. Dulles, 356 U.S. 116 (1958), *with* Regan v. Wald, 468 U.S. 222 (1984), and Haig v. Agee, 453 U.S. 380 (1981).

[162] Reference was made by one member of the Committee to the relationship of this article to the right to family life guaranteed in art. 23, since restrictions on freedom to leave might have adverse effects on family life. *See* Fischer, *Reporting Under the Covenant on Civil and Political Rights: The First Five Years of the Human Rights Committee,* 76 AJIL 142 (1982).

[163] For treatment of the meaning of the word "arbitrarily," see discussion in connection with art. 6 and art. 9, *supra.*

[164] "We think it is inherent in the concept of citizenship that the citizen, when absent from the country to which he owes allegiance, has a right to return, again to set foot on its soil. It is not to be wondered that the occasions for declaring this principle have been few. In United States v. Ju Toy, 198 U.S. 253,...it was assumed that to deny entrance of a citizen into the United States was a deprivation of a liberty secured by the Fifth Amendment. In the dissenting opinion in that case it was said that it is no crime for a citizen to come back to his native land. 198 U.S. 253, 269,...." Worthy v. United States, 328 F.2d 386, 394 (5th Cir. 1964).

[165] *See,* e.g., Lichtensztejn v. Uruguay, Communication No. 77/1980, *Report of the Human Rights Committee,* 38 U.N. GAOR, Supp. (No. 40) at 166, U.N. Doc. A/38/40 (1982); Vidal Martins v. Uruguay, Communication No. R.13/57, *Report of the Human Rights Committee,* 37 U.N. GAOR, Supp. (No. 40) at 157, U.N. Doc. A/37/40 (1981).

The rights referred to in paragraphs 1-3 (but not paragraph 4) are subject to such restrictions, provided by law, as may be necessary to protect national security, public order, health or morals, or the rights and freedoms of others;[166] any such restrictions must also be consistent with the other rights recognized in the Covenant.[167]

## ARTICLE 13—RIGHTS OF ALIENS

An alien lawfully in the territory of a State Party to the present Covenant may be expelled therefrom only in pursuance of a decision reached in accordance with law and shall, except where compelling reasons of national security otherwise require, be allowed to submit the reasons against his expulsion and to have his case reviewed by, and be represented for the purpose before, the competent authority or a person or persons especially designated by the competent authority.

Article 13 provides that an alien lawfully within the country may be expelled only in accordance with law and that, "except where compelling reasons of national security otherwise require," such an alien be permitted to submit reasons against expulsion, to have his case reviewed by "competent authority," and to be represented for that purpose. The U.S. Constitution requires at least as much. It is well settled that the Due Process Clause applies to lawfully resident aliens and that they may not be expelled "without allowing a fair opportunity to be heard."[168] The article does not specifically require either a full-dress hearing or judicial review, nor does it speak to or limit the reasons for expulsion. Its protections do not extend to those who are not lawfully within the country.

## ARTICLE 14—FAIR TRIAL; CRIMINAL PROCEDURE

1. All persons shall be equal before the courts and tribunals. In the determination of any criminal charge against him, or of his rights and

[166] During the drafting of the article, representatives suggested that such restrictions might be permissible in a national emergency, in an epidemic, for the control of prostitution, on immigrants as a temporary measure, on migrant workers in some cases, and on indigenous populations in certain circumstances for their own protection. *U.N. Annotations, supra* note 10, at 38-39, para. 53. As regards the right to leave one's country, "[I]t was agreed that the right...could not be claimed in order to escape legal proceedings or to avoid such obligations as the payment of fines, taxes or maintenance allowances." *Id.* The term "public order/*ordre public*" is used in a number of articles of the Covenant and is discussed *infra* at note 171.

[167] The requirement that any limitations be consistent with other rights in the Covenant was included because otherwise the article "could be interpreted as authorizing States to impose any limitations they wished," so long as "provided by law." *U.N. Annotations, supra* note 10, at 39, para. 54.

[168] See Kwong Hai Chew v. Colding 344 U.S. 590, 598 (1953). *See generally,* L. HENKIN, FOREIGN AFFAIRS AND THE CONSTITUTION 355-57 (1972).

obligations in a suit at law, everyone shall be entitled to a fair and public hearing by a competent, independent and impartial tribunal established by law. The press and the public may be excluded from all or part of a trial for reasons of morals, public order (*ordre public*) or national security in a democratic society, or when the interest of the private lives of the parties so requires, or to the extent strictly necessary in the opinion of the court in special circumstances where publicity would prejudice the interests of justice; but any judgement rendered in a criminal case or in a suit at law shall be made public except where the interest of juvenile persons otherwise requires or the proceedings concern matrimonial disputes or the guardianship of children.

2. Everyone charged with a criminal offense shall have the right to be presumed innocent until proved guilty according to law.

3. In the determination of any criminal charge against him, everyone shall be entitled to the following minimum guarantees, in full equality:

(a) To be informed promptly and in detail in a language which he understands of the nature and cause of the charge against him;

(b) To have adequate time and facilities for the preparation of his defense and to communicate with counsel of his own choosing;

(c) To be tried without undue delay;

(d) To be tried in his presence, and to defend himself in person or through legal assistance of his own choosing; to be informed, if he does not have legal assistance, of this right; and to have legal assistance assigned to him, in any case where the interests of justice so require, and without payment by him in any such case if he does not have sufficient means to pay for it;

(e) To examine, or have examined, the witness against him and to obtain the attendance and examination of witnesses on his behalf under the same conditions as witnesses against him;

(f) To have the free assistance of an interpreter if he cannot understand or speak the language used in court;

(g) Not to be compelled to testify against himself or to confess guilt.

4. In the case of juvenile persons, the procedure shall be such as will take account of their age and desirability of promoting their rehabilitation.

5. Everyone convicted of a crime shall have the right to his conviction and sentence being reviewed by a higher tribunal according to law.

6. When a person has by a final decision been convicted of a criminal offence and when subsequently his conviction has been reversed or he has been pardoned on the ground that a new or newly discovered fact shows

conclusively that there has been a miscarriage of justice, the person who has suffered punishment as a result of such conviction shall be compensated according to law, unless it is proved that the non-disclosure of the unknown fact in time is wholly or partly attributable to him.

7. No one shall be liable to be tried or punished again for an offence for which he has already been finally convicted or acquitted in accordance with the law and penal procedure of each country.

The first paragraph of Article 14 guarantees a right of fair trial in both civil and criminal cases. The remainder of the article (paragraphs 2-7) establishes certain procedural standards applicable only in criminal cases.[169]

Paragraph 1 provides that all persons shall be equal before the courts and that in all cases—civil as well as criminal—"everyone shall be entitled to a fair and public hearing by a competent, independent and impartial tribunal established by law."[170] It does, however, allow exclusion of the press and public from all or part of a trial for reasons of morals, public order (*ordre public*),[171] or national security in a

[169] The Human Rights Committee has adopted a detailed commentary on this article, General Comment 13 (21), *Report of the Human Rights Committee,* 39 U.N. GAOR Supp. (No. 40) at 143 (1984), U.N. Doc. A/39/40. *Also see generally* H. HANNUM (1989), *supra* note 1.

[170] "The use of the word 'competent' before 'independent and impartial tribunal' in paragraph 1 was intended to ensure that all persons should be tried in courts whose jurisdiction had been previously established by law, and arbitrary action so avoided." *U.N. Annotations, supra* note 10, at 42, para. 77.

[171] The language "public order (*ordre public*)" is used in a number of the articles of the Covenant (12, 14, 19, 21, and 22). The *U.N. Annotations* on art. 18 of the Covenant (where the term "Public...order" only is used) states:

> [T]he English expression 'public order' was not equivalent to—and indeed was substantially different from—the French expression *l'ordre public* (or the Spanish expression orden publico). In civil law countries the concept of *l'ordre public* is a legal concept used principally as a basis for negating or restricting private agreements, the exercise of police power, or the application of foreign law. In common law countries, the expression "public order" is ordinarily used to mean the absence of public disorder. The common law counterpart of *l'ordre public* is "public policy" rather than "public order." The use of the expression "public order" or *l'ordre public* in the limitations clauses would create uncertainty and might constitute a basis for far-reaching derogations from the rights guaranteed. *U.N. Annotations, supra* note 10, at 48-49, para. 113.

In the Third Committee of the General Assembly the difference in the meaning of the two terms was pointed out, and the Committee decided to insert in art. 14 the French term after the English term. *See* Noor Muhammad, *supra* note 150. *See also* Kiss, *Permissible Limitations on Rights,* in Henkin, *supra* note 1; van der Meersch, *Does the [European] Convention [On Human Rights] Have the Force of Ordre Public in Municipal Law,* in HUMAN RIGHTS IN NATIONAL AND INTERNATIONAL LAW 97, (A. Robertson ed., 1968). In the course of the examination of a government report by the Human Rights Committee, a member of the Committee commented with regard to art. 14 that "public order" must be interpreted very narrowly if it was to be compatible with the spirit of the Covenant and art. 14. U.N. Doc. CCPR/SR.109 (1978). The meaning of the terms "public order" and "*l'ordre public*" are further discussed at text accompanying note 272 et seq. In any event, it appears that the civil law term generally has a broader and more inclusive meaning than the English "public order."

democratic society, or when the interests of the private lives of the parties so requires, or to the extent strictly necessary in the opinion of the court in special circumstances where publicity would prejudice the interests of justice.[172] Judgments rendered in such cases are nonetheless required to be made public "except where the interest of juveniles otherwise require or the proceedings concern matrimonial disputes or the guardianship of children."

The Due Process Clauses of the Fifth and Fourteenth Amendments, of course, require at a minimum that all trials be "fair" and be conducted before competent, independent and impartial tribunals according to law. The Sixth Amendment, which applies only to criminal proceedings, expressly guarantees defendants a "public trial"[173] by an "impartial jury,"[174] although the extent to which a defendant may waive the right to a public trial and permit the court to exclude press and public in the interest of fairness is not entirely clear.[175] The requirement that, except in specified cases, judgments rendered in secret trials must be made public seems unexceptionable.

Paragraph 2 of Article 14 declares that a person charged with a criminal offense shall be presumed innocent until convicted, a basic premise of American justice. Paragraph 3 provides that every criminal defendant is entitled to the following minimum guarantees: to be informed of the charges against him in a language he understands; to have adequate time and facilities to prepare his defense; to be tried without undue delay in his presence; to defend himself in person or through legal assistance of his own choosing and to be informed of this right; to have legal assistance assigned to him in any case where the interests of justice so require and without payment by him if he

[172] E.g., in litigation concerning secret industrial processes or to protect "the special position of legally incapable persons and first offenders." *See U.N. Annotations, supra* note 10, at 43, para. 80.

[173] Closure of any judicial proceedings is rare in this country. Though the Sixth Amendment, by its terms, is applicable only to criminal cases, it would seem that similar strictures, drawn perhaps in part from the First Amendment (as well as the Fifth and Fourteenth), would limit exclusion of press and public from civil proceedings also. *See* Richmond Newspapers, Inc. v. Virginia, 448 U.S. 555 (1980).

[174] It might be noted that neither the CPR Covenant nor other international human rights instruments require trial by jury. This omission cannot, of course, diminish the fundamental constitutional right to a jury trial guaranteed in the Sixth Amendment.

[175] *See* Gannett Co., Inc. v. De Pasquale, 443 U.S. 368 (1979), upholding the closing of pretrial proceedings; Richmond Newspapers, Inc. v. Virginia, *supra* note 173, reversing an order closing a state court criminal trial to press and public. Recent cases have tended to uphold the right of public access to trials and related proceedings. *See,* e.g., Press Enterprise Co. v. Superior Court (Press Enterprise II), 478 U.S. 1 (1986); Press Enterprise Co. v. Superior Court (Press Enterprise I), 464 U.S. 501 (1984); Globe Newspaper Co. v. Superior Court, 475 U.S. 596 (1982).

does not have sufficient means to pay for it; to examine or have examined the witnesses against him and to obtain the attendance and examination of witnesses on his behalf under the same conditions as witnesses against him; to have the free assistance of an interpreter if necessary; and not be compelled to testify against himself or confess guilt.[176]

All these rights are guaranteed by the U.S. Constitution under the Fifth and Sixth Amendments and the Due Process Clause of the Fourteenth Amendment. The Sixth Amendment includes a concise declaration of most of them:

> In all criminal prosecutions, the accused shall enjoy the right to a speedy and public trial, by an impartial jury..., and to be informed of the nature and cause of the accusation; to be confronted with the witnesses against him; to have compulsory process for obtaining witnesses in his favor, and to have the Assistance of Counsel for his defense.

The Supreme Court has said:

> Because these rights are basic to our adversary system of criminal justice, they are part of the "due process of law" that is guaranteed by the Fourteenth Amendment to defendants in the criminal courts of the [s]tates. The rights to notice, confrontation, and compulsory process, when taken together, guarantee that a criminal charge may be answered in a manner now considered fundamental to the fair administration of American justice—through the calling and interrogation of favorable witnesses, the cross-examination of adverse witnesses, and the orderly introduction of evidence. In short, the Amendment constitutionalizes the right in an adversary criminal trial to make a defense as we know it.[177]

The right to be present at trial,[178] the right to represent oneself,[179] the right of indigents to free counsel when imprisonment is imposed,[180]

[176] A proposal made during the drafting that this language be followed by the phrase "or be induced to make such a confession by a promise of reward of immunity" was rejected. *See U.N. Annotations, supra* note 10, at 43, para. 88.

[177] Faretta v. California, 422 U.S. 806, 818 (1975). Of course, notice of the charges must be made in a language the defendant understands and the right to counsel, if it is to be "effective" counsel as constitutionally required, includes time and opportunity to prepare a defense. Similarly, an interpreter would be essential to assure a fair trial where the defendant understood no English.

[178] "One of the most basic rights guaranteed by the Confrontation Clause [of the Sixth Amendment] is the accused's right to be present in the courtroom at every stage of his trial." Illinois v. Allen, 397 U.S. 337, 338 (1970); however, the right can be lost by disruptive behavior in the courtroom. *Id.*

[179] *See* Faretta v. California, *supra* note 176.

[180] *See* Gideon v. Wainwright, 372 U.S. 335 (1963); Argersinger v. Hamlin, 407 U.S. 25 (1972). The constitutional right to appointed counsel does not extend to cases in which imprisonment is not imposed. Scott v. Illinois, 99 S. Ct. 1158 (1979).

and the right to be informed of one's constitutional rights,[181] and the privilege against self-incrimination[182] have also been held to be constitutionally required in both federal and state proceedings.

Paragraph 4 of Article 14 provides that, in the case of juveniles, the procedure shall be such as to take into account their age and the desirability of promoting their rehabilitation. These directives are clearly consistent with the objectives of our juvenile courts and related systems. Paragraph 5 declares that "[e]veryone convicted of a crime shall have the right to his conviction and sentence being reviewed by a higher tribunal according to law." While the U.S. Constitution apparently does not guarantee a right of appeal, review of federal claims is generally available by way of federal habeas corpus and direct appeal, if necessary, from state courts to the U.S. Supreme Court. In addition, direct appeal, other post-conviction review, or both is generally granted at the state and federal levels.[183] Review of sentences is much less common.

Paragraph 6 provides for compensation "according to law" to those persons who have "suffered punishment" as a result of "final" convictions which are subsequently reversed or who are pardoned on the ground of "new or newly discovered" evidence which shows "conclusively that there has been a miscarriage of justice." U.S. law does not generally require such compensation. In certain cases in which a conviction was obtained or punishment imposed in violation of the Constitution, however, there may be a right to sue for damages.[184] In most cases, though, compensation would have to be obtained through enactment of a private bill at the state or federal level as appropriate. As noted above in the discussion of Article 9, the U.S. ratification of the Covenant included an understanding with respect to the issue of compensation:

[181] *See* Miranda v. Arizona, 384 U.S. 436 (1966).

[182] *See* Malloy v. Hogan, 378 U.S. 1 (1964). Because art. 14 limits application of its guarantee against compulsory testimony and confession of guilt to situations involving "determination of any criminal charges" against the defendant, it, like the Fifth Amendment's Self-Incrimination Clause, presumably permits appropriate immunity statutes, *see* Kastigar v. United States, 406 U.S. 441 (1972).

[183] Appointed counsel is not required for higher discretionary appeals, Ross v. Moffitt, 417 U.S. 600 (1974), although the Supreme Court has invalidated on equal protection grounds the practice of a state appellate court of refusing to appoint counsel where it deemed such an appointment "of no value to either the defendant or the court." Douglas v. California, 372 U.S. 353 (1963).

[184] *See* 42 U.S.C. §1983; Bivens v. Six Unknown Named Agents, *supra* note 98.

> [T]he United States understands the right to compensation . . . to require the provision of effective and enforceable mechanisms by which a victim of an unlawful arrest or detention or a miscarriage of justice may seek and, where justified, obtain compensation from either the responsible individual or the appropriate governmental entity. Entitlement to compensation may be subject to the reasonable requirements of domestic law.[185]

Paragraph 7 prohibits double jeopardy.[186] This provision is consistent with the Fifth Amendment, except insofar as the latter has been held not to bar successive state and federal prosecutions.[187] In one respect, paragraph 7 does not go as far as U.S. constitutional limits, for it does not bar another prosecution until after there has been a final conviction or appeal. Under domestic law, "jeopardy" attaches much earlier in the trial process, usually when the jury is empaneled and sworn.[188]

Both the Carter and Bush Administrations recommended understandings with respect to aspects of Article 14, although President Carter acknowledged that it "is possible to read all the requirements contained in Article 14 as consistent with United States law, policy and practice."[189] The understanding adopted reads as follows:

> [T]he United States understands that subparagraphs 3(b) and (d) of Article 14 do not require the provision of a criminal defendant's counsel of choice when the defendant is provided with court-appointed counsel on grounds of indigence, when the defendant is financially able to retain alternative counsel, or when imprisonment is not imposed. The United States further understands that paragraph 3(e) does not prohibit a requirement that the defendant make a showing that any witness whose attendance he seeks to compel is necessary for his defense. The United States understands the prohibition upon double jeopardy in paragraph 7 to apply only when the judgment of acquittal has been rendered by a court of the same governmental unit, whether the Federal Government or a constituent unit, as is seeking a new trial for the same cause.

185 President Carter proposed an understanding which simply declared that the "United States considers that provisions of United States law currently in force constitute compliance with paragraph 6." Message of the President, *supra* note 105, at xiii.

186 It has been suggested that the concluding phrase "in accordance with the law and penal procedure of each country" limits the scope and effectiveness of the guarantee. However, the limiting phrase in paragraph 7 appears to refer not to the scope or nature of the guarantee but rather to the propriety under domestic law of the prior conviction or acquittal. Thus, the narrow reading of the provision seems unlikely here.

187 *See* Bartkus v. Illinois, 358 U.S. 121 (1959); Abbate v. United States, 359 U.S. 187 (1959). The Double Jeopardy Clause is applicable to the states through the Fourteenth Amendment. Benton v. Maryland, 395 U.S. 784 (1969).

188 *See* Serfass v. United States, 420 U.S. 377, 388 (1975).

189 Message of the President, *supra* note 105, at xiii.

While several other governments have made reservations to the detailed provisions of this article,[190] the U.S. understandings are largely unnecessary. The right to free counsel in Article 14 is expressly conditioned upon the defendant's financial ability to pay; moreover, though it is true that the constitutional right to counsel does not generally extend to cases in which no imprisonment is imposed, paragraph 3(d) requires free counsel for indigents only in cases in which "the interests of justice so require," a limitation which would appear broad enough to be consistent with domestic law and practice. The "understanding" relating to compulsory attendance of defense witnesses is superfluous, as paragraph 3(e) surely does not require compulsory attendance of unnecessary or irrelevant witnesses. As indicated above, domestic law and practice may already conform to the provision in paragraph 6 for compensation of those who are unjustly punished. To the extent that present U.S. law and practice might not be wholly compatible, there can be little doubt about the justice and propriety of affording relief in the classes of cases described.

The "understanding" relating to the double jeopardy provision of paragraph 7 goes to an issue of more substance. As noted, the Fifth Amendment does not preclude successive prosecutions by state and federal authorities, a practice which paragraph 7 could well be read to prohibit. While the ability of the federal government to initiate a prosecution after the defendant has been tried in a state court has proved useful in at least certain kinds of cases (for example, those involving civil rights violations by public officers), the practice has been limited; the right to be free from successive prosecutions for the same act is an important protection against governmental abuse and the understanding is unfortunate.

## ARTICLE 15—PROHIBITION OF RETROACTIVE APPLICATION OF CRIMINAL LAW

> 1. No one shall be held guilty of any criminal offense on account of any act or omission which did not constitute a criminal offense, under national or international law, at the time when it was committed. Nor shall a heavier penalty be imposed than the one that was applicable at the time when the

[190] Among the governments which have filed reservations to Art. 14 are Australia, Austria, Barbados, Belgium, Denmark, Finland, France, Gambia, Germany, Guyana, Iceland, Italy, Luxembourg, Netherlands, New Zealand, Norway, Sweden, Trinidad and Tobago, and the United Kingdom. *See* STATUS OF INTERNATIONAL INSTRUMENTS, *supra* note 153. at 29-49.

criminal offense was committed. If, subsequent to the commission of the offence, provision is made by law for the imposition of a lighter penalty, the offender shall benefit thereby.

2. Nothing in this article shall prejudice the trial and punishment of any person for any act or omission which, at the time when it was committed, was criminal according to the general principles of law recognized by the community of nations.

Article 15 is designed to preclude retroactive application of criminal sanctions[191] and parallels the Ex Post Facto Clause of the U.S. Constitution except in one respect. The article provides that offenders shall receive the benefit of any lessening of penalty which occurs as a result of changes in law subsequent to commission of the crime. Although this right is often granted in practice, it is not currently required under U.S. law, and both the Carter and Bush Administrations recommended a reservation to this paragraph. Such a reservation was included in the U.S. ratification. A better case could be made that U.S. law should be changed so as to conform with this provision, as once society has determined that the penalty for a given class of crimes should be decreased, the reduced penalty should be applicable to all persons who have committed the offense.

## ARTICLE 16—RECOGNITION BEFORE THE LAW

Everyone shall have the right to recognition everywhere as a person before the law.

Article 16 reproduces verbatim Article 6 of the Universal Declaration of Human Rights, setting forth a plainly unexceptionable proposition which is wholly consistent with United States law. This provision emphasizes the prohibition against slavery and would prohibit legislation in certain countries which refused married women recognition as independent persons before the law. It was also intended to emphasize that foreigners should be recognized as "persons before the law," e.g., capable of contracting, marrying, and having recourse to the courts.

[191] Paragraph 1 requires that the offense charged must have been criminal "under national or international law" at the time committed. The reference to international law was intended to assure that "no one shall escape punishment for a criminal offense under international law by pleading that his act was legal under his own national law." *U.N. Annotations, supra* note 10, at 45, para. 94.

## ARTICLE 17—PROTECTION OF PRIVACY AND REPUTATION

> 1. No one shall be subjected to arbitrary or unlawful interference with his privacy, family, home or correspondence, nor to unlawful attacks on his honour and reputation.
>
> 2. Everyone has the right to the protection of the law against such interference or attacks.

This article similarly declares a set of basic tenets: freedom from arbitrary or unlawful interference with privacy, family, home, and correspondence, and freedom from "unlawful attacks"[192] on honor and reputation. These interests are to be protected against both governmental and private action.[193] The U.S. Constitution bars improper governmental intrusion into the home and into areas of personal and family privacy; the Fourth Amendment expressly preserves the "right of the people to be secure in their persons, houses, papers and effects, against unreasonable searches and seizures." Interpreting this and other provisions, the Supreme Court has identified a constitutionally protected zone of family and personal privacy.[194]

Paragraph 2 imposes a positive obligation on States Parties. While some felt that this language might be interpreted to require prior censorship, it is clear that such an interpretation would be inconsistent with the provisions on freedom of opinion and expression in Article 19 of the Covenant. Common law actions for invasion of privacy and for libel and slander by officials and private parties[195] would meet the requirements of this article.

[192] The word "unlawful" before "attacks" was intended to meet an objection that the clause, unless qualified, might be construed in such a way as to limit free expression of public opinion. It was thought "that the law could protect the individual only against 'unlawful' or 'abusive' or 'unwarranted' attacks on his honour and reputation and that fair comments or truthful statements which might affect an individual's honour or reputation should not be considered as 'attacks on his honour and reputation.'" *U.N. Annotations, supra* note 10, at 47, para. 103.

[193] *See* General Comment 16 (32), *Report of the Human Rights Committee,* 43 U.N. GAOR Supp. (No. 40) at 181, U.N. Doc. A/43/40 (1988).

[194] *See,* e.g., Roe v. Wade, 410 U.S. 113 (1973); Griswold v. Connecticut, 381 U.S. 479 (1965).

[195] When concern was voiced that art. 17 as drafted might be construed as requiring changes to be made in existing rules of private law, particularly for countries with Anglo-Saxon legal traditions, "it was pointed out that the article, which was couched in general terms, merely enunciated principles, leaving each State free to decide how those principles were to be put into effect." *U.N. Annotations, supra* note 10, at 46, para. 10. In any event, Congress could not, by ratification of a treaty or other legislation, eliminate those aspects of defamation law founded on the Constitution.

## ARTICLE 18—FREEDOM OF THOUGHT, CONSCIENCE AND RELIGION

1. Everyone shall have the right to freedom of thought, conscience and religion. This right shall include freedom to have or to adopt a religion or belief of his choice, and freedom, either individually or in community with others and in public or private, to manifest his religion or belief in worship, observance, practice and teaching.

2. No one shall be subject to coercion which would impair his freedom to have or to adopt a religion or belief of his choice.

3. Freedom to manifest one's religion or beliefs may be subject only to such limitations as are prescribed by law and are necessary to protect public safety, order, health, or morals or the fundamental rights and freedoms of others.

4. The States Parties to the present Covenant undertake to have respect for the liberty of parents and, when applicable, legal guardians to ensure the religious and moral education of their children in conformity with their own convictions.

This article provides that everyone shall have the right to freedom of thought, conscience and religion. The right includes freedom to have or adopt a religion or belief of choice, free of coercion,[196] and to manifest this belief, individually or in community, in worship, observance, practice, and teaching. It provides that freedom to manifest one's religion or beliefs may be subject "only to such limitations as are prescribed by law and are necessary to protect public safety, order, health or morals or the fundamental rights and freedoms of others."[197] These provisions are all consistent with the First Amendment.

The special interest of parents in the religious and moral education of their children, for which the final paragraph of Article 18 requires respect,[198] is also constitutionally guaranteed. In *Wisconsin v. Yoder,*[199] the Supreme Court upheld the religious claims of Amish parents to

[196] "It was understood that the word 'coercion' in this context should not be construed as applying to moral or intellectual persuasion, or to any legitimate limitation of freedom to manifest one's religion or belief." *U.N. Annotations, supra* note 10, at 48, para. 110.

[197] "It is surely significant...that art. 18(3) permits limitation only to protect public safety, order, health or morals. Presumably 'public' modified 'order' as well as 'safety,' but here it is used without the interpretative addition of the French term *ordre public*.... That clearly suggests that limitations on freedom to manifest one's religion cannot be imposed to protect *ordre public* with its general connotations of national public policy, but only where necessary to protect public order narrowly construed, i.e., to prevent public disorder." Partsch, *Freedom of Conscience and Expression, and Political Freedoms,* in Henkin, *supra* note 1, at 212.

[198] *See also* art. 13(3) of the ESC Covenant.

[199] 406 U.S. 205 (1972).

remove their children from the secularizing influences of compulsory attendance in public schools, thereby giving renewed emphasis to its earlier ruling that the Constitution protects "the liberty of parents and guardians to direct the upbringing and education of children under their control."[200] Like our own Constitution, Article 18 does not require governments to provide the kind of education desired by parents, but only to respect their freedom to arrange for it themselves.[201]

## ARTICLE 19—FREEDOM OF OPINION AND EXPRESSION

1. Everyone shall have the right to hold opinions without interference.

2. Everyone shall have the right to freedom of expression; this right shall include freedom to seek, receive and impart information and ideas of all kinds, regardless of frontiers, either orally, in writing or in print, in the form of art, or through any other media of his choice.

3. The exercise of the rights provided for in paragraph 2 of this article carries with it special duties and responsibilities. It may therefore be subject to certain restrictions, but these shall only be such as are provided by law and are necessary:

(a) For respect of the rights or reputations of others;

(b) For the protection of national security or of public order (*ordre public*), or of public health or morals.

Article 19 protects the rights of freedom of opinion and expression, which are among the most fundamental to the U.S. constitutional system. In fact, the restrictions referred to in paragraph 3 may go beyond those which would be permissible under current U.S. constitutional standards. As noted in section 2.2 of Part II, above, ratification of an international treaty cannot diminish the rights guaranteed under the U.S. Constitution, and the fact that the United States might not avail itself of all of the permissible restrictions mentioned in paragraph 3 requires no formal declaration or understanding.

Restrictions on freedom of opinion and expression are unfortunately common in many parts of the world. Even in light of the "special duties and responsibilities" referred to in paragraph 3, the Human Rights Committee has noted that limitations on freedom of expres-

[200] Pierce v. Society of Sisters, 268 U.S. 510, 534-35 (1925).
[201] *See* Partsch, *supra* note 197, at 213.

sion may not jeopardize the right itself and that a country may have to take "effective measures" to prevent unwarranted control of the mass media in ways that would impermissibly inhibit real freedom of expression.[202]

## ARTICLE 20—PROPAGANDA FOR WAR, RACIAL HATRED

1. Any propaganda for war shall be prohibited by law.

2. Any advocacy of national, racial or religious hatred that constitutes incitement to discrimination, hostility or violence shall be prohibited by law.

Unless construed to apply only to advocacy inciting violence or other illegal action,[203] this provision is one of the few to be in plain conflict with the strictures of the U.S. Constitution. As several other countries have done,[204] the United States included a reservation to this article in order to preserve an expansive view of freedom of speech:

> Article 20 does not authorize or require legislation or other action by the United States that would restrict the right of free speech and association protected by the Constitution and laws of the United States.[205]

A reservation or understanding is appropriate in this instance, in order to clarify internationally the fact that U.S. obligations under this article are subject to the mandate of the First Amendment.

## ARTICLE 21—RIGHT OF PEACEFUL ASSEMBLY

> The right of peaceful assembly shall be recognized. No restrictions may be placed on the exercise of this right other than those imposed in conformity with the law and which are necessary in a democratic society in the interests

[202] *See* General Comment 10 (19), *Report of the Human Rights Committee,* 38 U.N. GAOR Supp. (No. 40) at 109 (1983), U.N. Doc. A/38/40. *See generally* the various commentaries prepared since 1986 by ARTICLE 19, a London-based nongovernmental organization, on the periodic reports submitted to the Human Rights Committee under art. 40 of the Covenant.

[203] *See,* e.g., Brandenburg v. Ohio, 395 U.S. 444 (1969). The Human Rights Committee has observed that the prohibition of this article extends to propaganda "that constitutes incitement to discrimination, hostility or violence." General Comment 11 (19), *Report of the Human Rights Committee,* 38 U.N. GAOR, Supp. (No. 40) at 109, U.N. Doc. A/38/40 (1983).

[204] Australia, Belgium, Denmark, Finland, Iceland, Luxembourg, Netherlands, and the United Kingdom have filed reservations or declarations expressing their concern that art. 20 not be interpreted in such a manner so as to unjustifiably limit the right to freedom of expression guaranteed in art. 19. *See* STATUS OF INTERNATIONAL INSTRUMENTS, *supra* note 153, at 28-49.

[205] This formulation is a welcome narrowing of the language proposed by the Carter Administration, which referred to the "Constitution, laws, and practice" of the United States. *See* Message of the President, *supra* note 105, at xi-xii.

> of national security or public safety, public order (*ordre public*), the protection of public health or morals or the protection of the rights and freedoms of others.

Peaceful assembly also is a basic U.S. constitutional right, although Article 21 may go beyond U.S. constitutional requirements in that the right must be protected from both private and public interference.[206] Nevertheless, while the First and Fourteenth Amendments may only protect against governmental or official interference, they also may imply an obligation to protect those exercising First Amendment rights from violence or other illegal interference by a hostile audience.[207] In any event, traditional tort and criminal law remedies are available in the United States to protect against illegal interference by private individuals with constitutional rights.

There is no doubt that the "time, place, and manner" limitations permissible under U.S. constitutional law are compatible with the permissible restrictions enumerated in the second sentence of Article 21.

## ARTICLE 22—FREEDOM OF ASSOCIATION

> 1. Everyone shall have the right to freedom of association with others, including the right to form and join trade unions for the protection of his interests.
>
> 2. No restrictions may be placed on the exercise of this right other than those which are prescribed by law and which are necessary in a democratic society in the interests of national security or public safety, public order (*ordre public*), the protection of public health or morals or the protection of the rights and freedoms of others. This article shall not prevent the imposition of lawful restrictions on members of the armed forces or the police in their exercise of this right.
>
> 3. Nothing in this article shall authorize States Parties to the International Labour Organization Convention of 1948 concerning Freedom of Association and Protection of the Right to Organize to take legislative measures which would prejudice, or to apply the law in such a manner as to prejudice, the guarantees provided for in that Convention.

[206] "Although a suggestion was made that freedom of assembly should be protected only against 'governmental interference,' it was generally understood that the individual should be protected against all kinds of interference in the exercise of this right." *U.N. Annotations, supra* note 10 at 54, para. 139.

[207] *Cf.* National Socialist Party v. Skokie, 432 U.S. 43 (1977); Gregory v. Chicago, 394 U.S. 111 (1969); Edwards v. South Carolina, 372 U.S. 229 (1964); Terminiello v. Chicago, 337 U.S. 1 (1949). *But compare* Feiner v. New York, 340 U.S. 315 (1951).

The right of freedom of association, including the right to form and join a trade union, is protected by Article 22.[208] Restrictions on the right are permitted by law as necessary for national security, public safety, order, health or morals, or to protect the rights and freedoms of others; specific allowance is made for lawful restrictions on associational activities of the military and the police.[209]

The First and Fourteenth Amendments guarantee the right of association,[210] and union organization and activities are included within this protection. The government is constitutionally prohibited from improper interference with the right of workers "individually or collectively to voice their views to their employers."[211] Perhaps more significantly, federal and state labor laws offer the vast majority of American workers specific protection for their right to organize and to join unions.

## ARTICLE 23—PROTECTION OF THE FAMILY

1. The family is the natural and fundamental group unit of society and is entitled to protection by society and the State.

2. The right of men and women of marriageable age to marry and to found a family shall be recognized.

3. No marriage shall be entered into without the free and full consent of the intending spouses.

4. States Parties to the present Covenant shall take appropriate steps to ensure equality of rights and responsibilities of spouses as to marriage, during marriage and at its dissolution. In the case of dissolution, provision shall be made for the necessary protection of any children.

Article 23 declares the family to be "the natural and fundamental group unit of society" and, as such, entitled to protection; it also protects marriage and requires "free and full" consent of the intending spouses.[212] Governments are required to "take appropriate steps to

[208] Trade union rights are also dealt with in greater detail in art. 8 of the ESC Covenant, discussed *infra,* Part IV, sec. 4.3. Although art. 8 of the ESC Covenant was drafted before art. 22 of the CPR Covenant, it was decided that trade unions should be mentioned in the latter as well, because failure to do so "could lead to an erroneous interpretation that these rights were not civil rights as well as economic and social rights." *U.N. Annotations, supra* note 10, at 56, para. 148.

[209] Art. 8 of the ESC Covenant specifically refers to "lawful restrictions" on the union activities of those engaged in "the administration of the State," as well as of the military and the police. The difference in wording is apparently unintentional, and it is assumed that art. 22 would also be read to permit limitations with respect to government employees.

[210] *See* e.g., N.A.A.C.P. v. Alabama, 357 U.S. 449 (1958).

[211] Babbitt v. United Farm Workers, 99 S. Ct. 230 (1979).

[212] These rights are also protected under art. 10 of the ESC Covenant; *see* discussion *infra,* Part IV, sec. 4.3.

ensure equality of rights and responsibilities of spouses"[213] and to protect children in the event of divorce or other dissolution of a marriage.

Consistent with the Covenant, the Constitution has long been deemed to include within its protected liberties the right "to marry, establish a home and bring up children,"[214] a right described by the Supreme Court as "one of the basic rights of man."[215] Equality between spouses and parents has also become an element of constitutional protection,[216] and concern for the welfare of minor children is a traditional concern of domestic law.

## ARTICLE 24—PROTECTION OF CHILDREN

> 1. Every child shall have, without any discrimination as to race, colour, sex, language, religion, national or social origin, property or birth, the right to such measures of protection as are required by his status as a minor, on the part of his family, society and the State.
>
> 2. Every child shall be registered immediately after birth and shall have a name.
>
> 3. Every child has the right to acquire a nationality.

Paragraph 1 of Article 24 provides that every child shall have "without any discrimination as to race, colour, sex, language, religion, national or social origin, property or birth, the right to such measures of protection as required by his status as a minor." Although it was suggested by some representatives during the drafting that differences in matters of inheritance between children in wedlock and those born out of wedlock were necessary to safeguard the family, the Human Rights Committee has called for the abolition of all discrimination between children born in and out of wedlock, including in the field of inheritance.[217]

[213] This language does not require immediate implementation of equality between spouses and resembles the obligations of gradual implementation imposed under the ESC Covenant. The reasons for this approach are evident from the discussions during the drafting: "Any attempt to put into effect immediately the principle of equal rights for spouses would require radical changes in the civil laws and customs of most countries." *U.N. Annotations, supra* note 10, at 48, para. 156.

[214] Meyer v. Nebraska, 262 U.S. 390, 399 (1923).

[215] Skinner v. Oklahoma, 316 U.S. 535, 541 (1942).

[216] *See,* e.g., Weinberger v. Wiesenfeld, 420 U.S. 636 (1975); Stanley v. Illinois, 405 U.S. 645 (1975).

[217] General comment 17 (35), U.N. Doc. E/1989/57 (1989) at 3. *See* debates reprinted in M. BOSSUYT, *supra* note 1, at 462-63. Art. 2 of the Convention on the Rights of the Child, *adopted* 20 Nov. 1989 *entered into force* 2 Sept 1990, G.A. Res. 44/25, 44 U.N. GAOR, Supp. (No. 49) at 166, U.N. Doc. A/44/49 (1989), prohibits discrimination "of any kind, irrespective of the

The declaration of the right to acquire a nationality represents an attempt to eliminate statelessness among children insofar as possible. However, this "does not necessarily make it an obligation for States to give their nationality to every child born in their territory."[218]

There is no definition of "child" in either covenant, and neither of the covenants nor any other international instrument directly addresses the issue of when life begins or the rights, if any, of the fetus.[219] In the context of regional human rights treaties in Europe and the Americas, international bodies faced with the issue of abortion have recognized the lack of consensus on the issue and have generally found that the rights of neither the mother nor the fetus are absolute; reasonable governmental regulations which do not unduly interfere with a mother's right of privacy have been upheld.[220]

Of course, children also benefit from all the other rights set forth in the CPR Covenant, unless their rights may be legitimately restricted on one of the permitted grounds. In addition, a more extensive provision regarding the protection of children is found in Article 10 of the ESC Covenant, which is discussed below in Part IV.

Thirty years after the Declaration on the Rights of the Child,[221] the U.N. General Assembly adopted a new Convention on the Rights of the Child,[222] which entered into force in 1990.

## ARTICLE 25—POLITICAL PARTICIPATION

> Every citizen shall have the right and the opportunity, without any of the distinctions mentioned in Article 2 and without unreasonable restrictions:
>
> (a) To take part in the conduct of public affairs, directly or through freely chosen representatives;

---

child's...birth or other status." This apparently prohibits distinctions between legitimate and out-of-wedlock children.

[218] General comment 17 (35), *supra* note 217, at 4; *see* M. Bossuyt, *supra* note 1, at 463-67. It might be noted that the Covenant contains no general right to a nationality.

[219] *Cf.* discussion of art. 6, *supra.*

[220] *See* Paton v. U.K., Eur. Comm'n Human Rts. dec. on admissibility of 13 May 1980, 19 Decisions and Reports 244; Bruggemann & Scheuten v. Fed. Rep. of Germany, Eur. Comm'n Human Rts. Report of 12 July 1977, 10 Decisions and Reports 100; Case 2141 (United States), Inter-Am. Comm'n Human Rts. Res. No. 23/81 of 6 Mar. 1981, reprinted in INTER-AM COMM'N HUMAN RTS., ANNUAL REPORT 1980-81, at 25, O.A.S. Off. Rec. OEA/Ser.L/V/II.54, doc. 9 rev. 1 (1981). *Cf.* discussion in H. HANNUM (1985), *supra* note 1, at 95-100.

[221] G.A. Res. 1386 (XIV), 14 U.N. GAOR, Supp. (No. 16) at 19, U.N. Doc. A/4354 (1959).

[222] *Supra* note 217.

(b) To vote and to be elected at genuine periodic elections which shall be by universal and equal suffrage and shall be held by secret ballot, guaranteeing the free expression of the will of the electors;

(c) To have access, on general terms of equality, to public service in his country.

Article 25 sets forth the basic democratic rights of every citizen to participate in public affairs, to vote and to stand for office in free elections (by secret ballot and with universal and equal suffrage),[223] and to seek government service, all without invidious discrimination or "unreasonable" restriction.[224] These rights are protected both by the Constitution and by federal statute.

As the Supreme Court said in *Reynolds v. Simms,*[225] "Undeniably the Constitution of the United States protects the right of all qualified citizens to vote, in state as well as in federal elections.... The right to vote freely for the candidate of one's choice is of the essence of a democratic society...."[226] Impairment of the right on grounds of race or sex is specifically barred by the Fifteenth and Nineteenth Amendments, respectively,[227] and invidious discrimination in suffrage, public service, and elective policies is broadly prohibited by the Equal Protection Clause of the Fourteenth Amendment and the Due Process Clause of the Fifth Amendment.[228] Various provisions of

[223] The term "universal and equal suffrage" means that each vote cast has the same effect but "does not imply that each voter should be guaranteed identical weight by means of some kind of proportional representation in the electoral system." 16 U.N. GAOR C.3 (1096th mtg.) at paras. 8-9, U.N. Doc. A/C.3/SR. 1096 (1961). American constitutional law goes at least as far. *See,* e.g., the early reapportionment cases, Baker v. Carr, 369 U.S. 186 (1962); Gray v. Sanders, 372 U.S. 368 (1963); Reynolds v. Sims, 377 U.S. 533 (1964), establishing the "one man—one vote" rule.

[224] The clause "without unreasonable restrictions" qualifies the exercise of all the rights in the article. It has been pointed out that many countries deny the vote to certain persons, such as minors and mental incompetents, and that such restrictions on the rights guaranteed by this article are justifiable. *See* Partsch, *supra* note 197, at 242-43. The constitutional requirement that the President must be a "natural-born" citizen is presumably a "reasonable" restriction within the meaning of art. 25.

[225] 377 U.S. 533, 555-556 (1964).

[226] "The right to vote, as distinguished from a right not to be denied the vote for improper reasons, does not appear on the face of our Constitution, though the Supreme Court has viewed the right as though it were. *See* Harper v. Virginia Bd. of Elections, 383 U.S. 663 (1966); Reynolds v. Sims, 377 U.S. 533 (1964)." Henkin, *Constitutional Rights and Human Rights,* 13 HARV. CIV. RTS.—CIV. LIB. L. REV. 593, 610, n.61 (1978).

[227] In addition, the Twenty-Fourth Amendment outlaws the poll-tax, and the Twenty-Sixth Amendment guarantees the voting rights of those 18 years of age and older.

[228] Article VI of the Constitution also bars the use of any "religious test" as a qualification for office.

federal statutory law provide additional protection for citizens in the exercise of the rights mentioned in Article 25.[229]

## ARTICLE 26—EQUAL PROTECTION OF THE LAW

> All persons are equal before the law and are entitled without any discrimination to the equal protection of the law. In this respect, the law shall prohibit any discrimination and guarantee to all persons equal and effective protection against discrimination on any ground such as race, colour, sex, language, religion, political or other opinion, national or social origin, property, birth or other status.

Article 26 contains an independent and general guarantee of "equal protection of the law." The phrase is an American one and reflects the content of our own Fifth and Fifteenth Amendments.[230]

The second sentence was included in the article despite the general principle contained in Article 2 providing for non-discrimination in the application of all Covenant rights. Article 26 does not depend for its application upon invocation or violation of another substantive right under the Covenant; freedom from discrimination, it was believed, should be considered as a right in itself.[231] The article does not either require or prohibit affirmative action on behalf of minorities.[232]

[229] *See, e.g.*, Civil Rights Act of 1964 and Voting Rights Act of 1965 (implementing the right to vote); 18 U.S.C. §§241-243, 245 (criminal provisions protecting against violation of federal rights in general and, in particular, the rights to serve on juries, to vote or stand for office or to seek or enjoy federal employment); 42 U.S.C. §§1983-85 (providing civil remedies for violation of such rights by state officials and others).

[230] The first sentence, which declares all persons "equal before the law" and entitled "without discrimination to equal protection of the law," is identical to the first sentence of art. 7 of the Universal Declaration of Human Rights. It was presumably included to preclude a ranking of legal rights according to a caste system or on the basis of titles of nobility or other status. Compare Article I, §9, of the U.S. Constitution, which prohibits the granting of any title of nobility by the United States and bars the acceptance by federal officials of any foreign title, unless with consent of Congress. The Fourteenth Amendment provision defining as full citizens "all persons born or naturalized in the United States" was intended to grant former slaves equal legal status. Also noteworthy is the federal legislation implementing the Thirteenth Amendment by guaranteeing the same rights as are "enjoyed by white citizens," 42 U.S.C. §§1981-82.

[231] *U.N. Annotations, supra* note 10, at 61, para. 181.

[232] *But see* discussion of art. 27, *infra*. *Cf.* art. 1(4) of the Convention on the Elimination of Racial Discrimination, which provides that affirmative action ("special measures") to secure adequate advancement of certain racial or ethnic groups shall not be deemed racial discrimination provided that such measures do not lead to "the maintenance of separate rights for different racial groups and that they shall not be continued after the objectives for which they were taken have been achieved."

Given its derivation and purposes, this article can be expected to parallel the meaning and effect of our own constitutional guarantees, which bar invidious discrimination by federal, state, and local government.[233] As noted in the discussion of Article 2, the U.S. undertanding regarding discrimination also applies to Article 26.

## ARTICLE 27—RIGHTS OF PERSONS BELONGING TO MINORITIES

> In those States in which ethnic, religious or linguistic minorities exist, persons belonging to such minorities shall not be denied the right, in community with the other members of their group, to enjoy their own culture, to profess and practice their own religion, or to use their own language.

Despite unfortunate instances of social and other discrimination during our country's history, the guarantee of cultural, religious, and linguistic rights is a fundamental component of U.S. constitutional jurisprudence.[234] No reservations or understandings concerning this article were suggested in President Carter's message transmitting the CPR Covenant to the Senate for its advice and consent, and there is no doubt that U.S. law meets the minimal requirements of protection set forth in Article 27.

Unfortunately, neither the country reports filed with the Human Rights Committee under Article 40 of the CPR Covenant, the discussion of those reports by the Committee, nor its consideration of individual complaints filed under the Optional Protocol to the Covenant are of much help in defining the precise content of minority rights under Article 27 of the Covenant. Thus far, the Committee has been unable to agree on formulation of a "general comment" with respect to Article 27.

[233] The Fifth and Fourteenth Amendments reach only conduct involving "state action." Art. 26 would seem to be similarly limited, both by the express language of its first sentence and by the use of the phrase "in this respect," prefacing the second. Congress, of course, has the power to prohibit discrimination by non-governmental actors and, indeed, has done so in a number of key areas. *See,* e.g., Civil Rights Act of 1964 (public accommodations and employment); Civil Rights Act of 1968 (housing). Many state and local governments have adopted similar legislation.

[234] *See,* e.g., Wisconsin v. Yoder, 406 U.S. 205 (1972) (education, religion, "way of life"); Meyer v. Nebraska, 262 U.S. 390 (1923) (language); Pierce v. Society of Sisters, 218 U.S. 510 (1925) (education, religion). *Cf.* Lau v. Nichols, 414 U.S. 563 (1974) (recognition of rights of linguistic and ethnic minority under federal statute).

Article 27's reference to the right "to profess and practise their own religion" has probably been subsumed for all practical purposes into the guarantees of religious freedom included in Article 18 of the Covenant and other human rights instruments. This right is certainly protected under the First Amendment to the Constitution.

The meaning of the right to enjoy one's own culture is somewhat less clear. One leading commentator concludes that this "includes the right to have schools and cultural institutions,"[235] but the extent of protection for other cultural manifestations is rather murky. Certainly Article 27 permits restrictions on cultural and/or religious practices that offend fundamental community beliefs (e.g., polygamy, divorce, use of alcohol) or which are deemed to be outweighed by health or safety concerns (e.g., a requirement that motorcyclists wear helmets or the provision of medical treatment to minors despite the religious objections of their parents).[236]

Use of language is one of the most divisive issues in minority-majority relations, although the right to use one's own language is one of the most widely guaranteed minority rights in international law. Restrictions on the private use of language would seem to be clearly unjustifiable under Article 27, but positive recognition of language rights for other purposes (e.g., bilingual education) is not required.

There is disagreement as to whether Article 27 implies a positive obligation on States to intervene on behalf of or provide support to minorities, as well as the negative obligation not to deny them the right to enjoy their own culture.[237] The most important study done under U.N. auspices concluded that there is such a positive obligation,[238] while another authority observes that this interpretation "is logical, but has not as yet become part of any subsequent instrument, nor does it command universal assent."[239]

Finally, it should be noted that Article 27 does not recognize group rights per se; rather, the rights of "persons belonging to such

[235] Sohn, *The Rights of Minorities,* in Henkin, *supra* note 1, at 284.

[236] *See generally* T. FRANCK, 1 HUMAN RIGHTS IN THIRD WORLD PERSPECTIVE AT 455-510 (1982); J. NOWAK, R. ROTUNDA AND J. YOUNG, CONSTITUTIONAL LAW at 1053-81 (2d ed. 1983); S. POULTER, ENGLISH LAW AND ETHNIC MINORITY CUSTOMS (1986); P. SIEGHART, *supra* note 1, at 321-26.

[237] A proposal that "the State shall ensure" minority rights was rejected by the Commission on Human Rights. *See* M. Bossuyt, *supra* note 1, at 496; cf. Sohn, *supra* note 235, at 284-85.

[238] *See* F. Capotorti, *Study on the Rights of Persons Belonging to Ethnic, Religious and Linguistic Minorities,* U.N. Sales No. E.78.XIV.1, at 36-37 (1979).

[239] Thornberry, *Minorities and Human Rights Law* at 7 (Minority Rights Group Report No. 73, 1987), at 7.

minorities" are protected. In addition, Article 27's introductory reference to "those States in which ethnic, religious or linguistic minorities exist" is intended to protect "well-defined and long-established" minorities and not to grant special rights to immigrants.[240]

## 3.4 THE LIMITATION AND DEROGATION CLAUSES

*Oscar M. Garibaldi*

The obligations undertaken by the State Parties to the CPR Covenant are a function of the rights defined in the treaty. In this respect, certain provisions of the Covenant limit the scope of the defined rights, and other provisions authorize each State Party to restrict the scope of defined rights under specified conditions. When the conditions under which a State Party is permitted under the CPR Covenant to restrict a given right reflect ordinary circumstances, we normally refer to the resulting restrictions as limitations; when such conditions reflect events or states of affairs that are out of the ordinary, the CPR Covenant refers to the restrictions as derogations. Thus, the extent of a State Party's obligations under the CPR Covenant is determined, ultimately, not by the rights as defined in the instrument, but by those rights as restricted—i.e., limited or derogated from—by or pursuant to the treaty.

### 3.4.1 Limitations

The limitations permitted by the CPR Covenant can be classified as direct and indirect. Direct limitations are those that are imposed by the Covenant itself, and they may be viewed as a component of the definitions of the rights to which they apply. Indirect limitations, on the other hand, are those that a State Party is authorized to impose under certain conditions specified in the Covenant. Most of the limitations provided by the CPR Covenant are of the latter kind.

[240] *See* M. BOSSUYT, *supra* note 1, at 494-96; Sohn, *supra* note 235, at 279, 281.

In the CPR Covenant, as well as in other human rights treaties and declarations, the rights defined in the instrument are limited (or may be limited by the State) pursuant to two types of provisions: general limitation clauses, which refer to all the rights so defined, and specific limitation clauses, which refer to some right or rights in particular. The CPR Covenant contains a general limitation clause in Article 5(1), and specific limitation clauses in nearly every article of Part III. Among the specific limitation clauses, those in Article 12(3), 14(1), 18(3), 19(3), 21, and 22(2) are so similar in structure and wording that it is appropriate to study them as a group, together with the general limitation clause of Article 5(1).

It so happens that, in the system of the CPR Covenant, the two classifications just mentioned roughly coincide: the general limitation clause of paragraph 1 of Article 5 lays down direct limitations while the specific limitation clauses of Article 12(3), 14(1), 18(3), 19(3), 21 and 22(2) (and most of the other specific limitation clauses of Part III) impose limitations only indirectly, by specifying the circumstances in which State-created limitations are permissible.

### *(1) Direct Limitations*

Article 5(1) of the CPR Covenant states, in part:

> Nothing in the Covenant may be interpreted as implying for any group or person any right to engage in any activity or perform any act aimed at the destruction of any rights and freedoms recognized [in the Covenant]....

It follows from the quoted text that none of the rights set forth in the treaty includes the right to engage in any activity or to perform any act aimed at the destruction of any of those rights. Since the acts and activities in question are not protected as rights under the treaty, a State Party is permitted to prohibit or to suppress them.

Being permitted to prohibit or to suppress those acts and activities does not mean being required to do so. A State Party is free to prohibit or suppress those acts or activities, to leave them unregulated, or even to guarantee them as rights. This conclusion is particularly important for the United States, because some of the acts or activities in question may be protected by the United States Constitution.[241] The United

[241] For example, United States courts have held unconstitutional a municipal ordinance which effectively barred members of the National Socialist Party of America from conducting a demonstration in the Village of Skokie, Illinois. Collin v. Smith, 578 F. 2d 1197 (7th Cir.), *affirming,* 447 F.Supp. 676, *cert. denied,* 439 U.S. 916 (1978). *See also,* Village of Skokie v. National Socialist Party of America, 373 N.E. 2d 21 (Sup. Ct. Ill. 1978), *aff'g in part and rev'g in part,* 366 N.E. 2d 347 (App. Ct. Ill. 1977). One may assume that, as indicated by the ideological pronouncements of the N.S.P.A. (*see* 578 F. 2d at 1199), the demonstration probably had the ultimate aim of destroying rights that are among those protected by the Covenant. Consequently,

States may continue to enforce such constitutional rights without fear of violating the principle of article 5(1) of the Covenant.

Article 5(1) limits the rights set forth in the CPR Covenant only to the extent that their exercise constitutes acts or activities "aimed at the destruction of any right recognized" in the Covenant. This phrase was meant to include not only those acts and activities which aim at the destruction of any of those rights, but also those that consist in such destruction.[242] It was also suggested that in the course of the drafting that the words "acts" and "activities" do not embrace mere expressions of opinion.[243]

An individual who performs an act or engages in an activity aimed at the destruction of any of the rights defined in the treaty is not placed beyond the protection of the Covenant; he does not forfeit the non-restricted portions of the rights in question nor does he forfeit his other rights. For example, even though a person may have no right under the Covenant to associate with others for purposes of terrorism or to work for the establishment of a totalitarian State, a person who engages in such activities may not be deprived of the right to a fair trial.[244]

### (2) Indirect Limitations

The six specific limitation clauses studied in this section—Articles 12(3), 14(1), 18(3), 19(3), 21, and 22(2)—specify the conditions under which a State Party may impose limitations on the rights to

---

the activity in question would be excluded, by virtue of art. 5, from the scope of the freedom of assembly defined in art. 21 of the Covenant. The same activity was held by United States courts to be guaranteed by a constitutional right.

[242] *See* statement by Mr. Malik (Lebanon), U.N. Doc. E/CN.4/AC.1/SR.28, at 5 (1948); statement by Mr. Dehousse (Belgium), 3 U.N. GAOR, C.3 (155th mtg.) at 667; Mr. Carrera Andrade (Ecuador), *id.;* Mr. Jimenez de Arechaga (Uruguay), *id.* (156th mtg.) at 674; Mr. Grumbach (France), *id.* at 673. An Ecuadorian proposal to substitute "which might destroy" for "aimed at the destruction of" was rejected, perhaps because it was too vague, but the drafters clearly intended to refer not only to preparatory acts but also to the destructive activity itself.

[243] *See* statement by Mr. Jimenez de Arechaga, *id.* (155th mtg.) at 667.

[244] *See, e.g.*, decisions by the European Commission and Court of Human Rights interpreting the similar provision in art. 17 of the European Convention on Human Rights: Lawless v. Ireland, Eur. Ct. Human Rts. Judgment of 1 July 1961, Ser. A No. 3 (detention of member of Irish Republican Army); X v. Italy, App. No. 6741/74, Eur. Comm'n Human Rts. Dec. on Admissibility, 5 Decisions & Reports 83 (1976) (ban on reorganization of Italian Fascist Party); X v. Austria, App. No. 1747/62, Eur. Comm'n Human Rts. Dec. on Admissibility, 6 Y.B. EUR. CONV. ON HUMAN RTS. 424 (1963) (punishment for national-socialist activities); German Communist Party v. F.R.G., App. No. 250/57, Eur. Comm'n Human Rts. Dec. on Admissibility, 1 Y.B. EUR. CONV. ON HUMAN RTS. 222 (1957) (outlawing of German Communist Party). *Cf. Symposium: Limitation and Derogation Provisions in the International Covenant on Civil and Political Rights,* 7 HUMAN RTS. Q. 1 (1985), at 38-40.

which those clauses apply. For example, paragraph 2 of Article 22 provides:

> No restrictions may be placed on the exercise of this right other than those prescribed by law and which are necessary in a democratic society in the interests of national security or public safety, public order (*ordre public*), the protection of public health or morals or the protection of the rights and freedoms of others....

Under this provision, a State Party is authorized to impose limitations on the right in question, as long as the limitations meet the conditions specified in the clause. Any limitation that does not meet those conditions will be in breach of the treaty.

To belabor the obvious, a State is permitted, but not required, to adopt indirect limitations. At the time of ratifying the CPR Covenant, the United States declared its view "that States Party to the Covenant should wherever possible refrain from imposing any restrictions or limitations on the exercise of the rights recognized and protected by the Covenant, even when such restrictions and limitations are permissible under the terms of the Covenant."[245]

Under each of the limitation clauses of articles 12(3), 18(3), 19(3), 21 and 22(2), the validity of a limitation is subject to three conditions. The first, which may be called the principle of legality, is that the limitation take the form of or be based on domestic substantive law, and that such law fulfill certain minimum requirements of generality and certainty. The second condition is that the limitation maintain a certain specified relationship to one or more specified governmental interests. The third condition, which may be referred to as the principle of non-destruction, is that the limitation should not consist in or aim at the destruction of the affected right. In Article 21 and 22(2) a fourth condition is added: that the limitation be consistent with the principles of a democratic society, a condition that may be referred to as the principle of democratic content. Finally, only the second, third and fourth conditions are required in the limitation clause set forth in the second sentence of Article 14(1).

[245] S. Exec Rep. No. 102-23, 102d Cong., 2d Sess. 23 (1992).

*(i) The Principle of Legality.*[246]

The first condition for the validity of a limitation under articles 12(3), 18(3), 19(3), 21 and 22(2) is that it observe a certain specified connection with domestic law. Articles 12(3) and 19(3) require that the limitation be "provided by law;" articles 18(3) and 22(2) require that it be "prescribed by law;" and article 21 that it be imposed "in conformity with the law." This requirement, which I have called the principle of legality, serves the purpose of ensuring that any limitation imposed by the State be consistent with its own law and be in the form of a general and reasonably precise substantive norm, so as to bring into play, as a first system of control, any domestic safeguards against arbitrary legislation or the arbitrary application of domestic laws. To take an extreme example, the principle of legality is designed to guarantee that limitations will not be imposed in violation of the State's own legal system, or at the whim of public officials, or by ad hoc decrees aimed at one particular person or group, or by rules so open-ended that the persons subject to them cannot know the limits placed upon their rights.

The preparatory work makes clear that the "law" referred to in the various formulae listed above is domestic substantive law.[247] Thus, it is not enough that the limitation be imposed by an authority sufficiently empowered therefor by mere rules of competence. It is also necessary that the content of the limitation be established by substantive law or, in the case of limitations imposed in individual cases, that it be based on substantive law.

The *travaux préparatoires* also indicate that the laws by which limitations are imposed or on which limitations are based must be general laws.[248] A general law is one that applies to a generality of individuals and to a generality of occasions. Although no criteria of generality (either in respect of the subjects of the limitation or the occasions on which it applies) have been made explicit in the Covenant, it is safe to say that, at a minimum, a limitation law will be insufficiently general if it affects only a person or group in violation of the principle of non-discrimination.[249]

[246] *See generally* Garibaldi, *General Limitations on Human Rights: The Principle of Legality*, 17 HARV. INT'L L.J. 503-57 (1976).

[247] *See* Garibaldi, *id.* at 552-56.

[248] *See* Garibaldi, *id.* at 542-46; *accord*, *Symposium*, *supra* note 244, at 5, 18.

[249] As already noted, the principle of legality is not among the requirements of the second sentence of Article 14(I), which governs limitations to a right to a public trial. The drafters of the Covenant apparently felt that an order to close a trial to the public was so dependent on the circumstances of each case that the validity of such order should not depend on its conformity with a pre-existing substantive general law.

In order to satisfy the principle of legality, a limitation law must have a reasonable degree of certainty, in the sense that its consequences must be reasonably foreseeable by the subjects.[250] The certainty of a limitation law is inversely proportional to the vagueness of its wording and the degree of discretion that it confers on public officials. In this respect, there is evidence in the drafting history that the various formulae used to express the principle of legality were not meant to be synonymous: "in conformity with the law" was probably meant to convey a requirement of moderate certainty, while "prescribed by law," and "provided by law" probably indicate that the limitation laws must be highly certain.[251] At least the highest of these two standards excludes ex post facto laws.

In the course of the drafting, some State representatives argued that "law" should be understood to refer exclusively to statutes enacted by the legislature.[252] This view was rejected by other delegates as too narrow.[253] The understanding that appeared to prevail was that the term "law" refers to all forms of substantive law, including statutes, regulations, custom and judicial precedent.[254] It follows that, in a common-law system, a limitation will not be in violation of the CPR Covenant just because it derives from the common law.

The constitutional law of the United States contains principles that are functionally similar to (but not co-extensive with) the principle of legality of the CPR Covenant. Some form of generality is required by

[250] *See* Garibaldi, *supra* note 246, at 542-46. Interpreting a similar expression, the European Court of Human Rights has held that "a norm cannot be regarded as a 'law' unless it is formulated with sufficient precision to enable the citizen to regulate his conduct: he must be able—if need be with appropriate advice—to foresee, to a degree that is reasonable in the circumstances, the consequences which a given action may entail." Sunday Times v. United Kingdom, Eur. Ct. Human Rts., Judgment of 26 April 1979, Ser. A No. 30, at para. 49. The imprecision of a statute may be remedied by consistent case law. *See* Case of Markt intern Verlag GmbH and Klaus Beerman, Eur. Ct. Human Rts., Judgment of 20 November 1989, Ser. A No. 165, at para. 30.

[251] *See* Garibaldi, *supra* note 246, at 551-56; *contra, Symposium, supra* note 244, at 18.

[252] *See,* e.g., statements by the representatives of Chile and Guatemala, U.N. Doc. E/CN.4/SR.236, at 10 (1951).

[253] *See,* e.g., U.N. Doc. E/CN.4/AC.1/4, at 7 (1937); statement by the French representative, U.N. Doc. E/CN.4/SR.236, at 9 (1951). Also, by analogy, *see* Malone v. U.K., Eur. Ct. Human Rts., Judgment of Aug. 2, 1984, Ser. A No. 82 (purely administrative authorization of wiretaps not sufficiently clear to control exercise of discretion and therefore violative of right to privacy); Sunday Times v. U.K., *supra* note 249 (English common law of contempt of court sufficiently precise to be foreseeable, although use of contempt proceedings on facts of case unjustifiable).

[254] In the Sunday Times case, the European Court of Human Rights observed that the word "law" in the expression "prescribed by law" as used in the European Conventions "covers not only statute but unwritten law" and declined to attach importance to the fact that the limitation at issue in the case "is a creature of common law and not of legislation." Sunday Times v. United Kingdom, *supra* note 250, at para. 47.

the Equal Protection Clause of the Fourteenth Amendment and by the Bill of Attainder Clause of Article I, Section 9, of the Constitution.[255] In interpreting these clauses, however, the courts have moved away from the idea of generality and have focused instead on the relationship between the challenged legislation and a legitimate governmental purpose.[256] The idea of certainty is represented in the constitutional law of the United States by the Ex Post Facto Law Clause of Article I, Section 9, of the Constitution, the "void for vagueness" doctrine and the doctrine of procedural overbreadth.[257] It is not entirely clear whether the degree of certainty required by these doctrines will satisfy the requirement of certainty in the CPR Covenant.

### *(ii) The Limitation and the Legitimate Interests.*

Under each of the limitation clauses here analyzed, a limitation is required to bear a specified relationship with one or more specified governmental interests, which the Covenant accepts as legitimate.

The required relationship is denoted in Articles 12(3) and 18(3) by the phrase "necessary to protect;" in Article 14(1) by the words "for reasons of" and in a subsequent clause by the expression "strictly necessary;" in Article 19(3) by the phrases "necessary for" and "[necessary] for the protection of" and in Article 21 and 22(2) by the words "necessary...in the interest of." These formulae can be analyzed into two components: a first component, represented by the words "to protect," "for reasons of," "for," "for the protection of" and "in the interests of," and a second component, consisting of the word "necessary."

The first component suggests a means-ends relationship or, more precisely, that the limitation, as a means, must be reasonably sufficient condition to attain a legitimate interest, as an end.[258] The word "necessary," on the other hand, clearly conveys the idea that the

[255] *See* U.S. v. Brown, 381 U.S. 437 (1965); U.S. v. Lovett, 328 U.S. 303 (1946).

[256] *See* Nixon v. Administrator of Gen. Services Adm'n, 433 U.S. 425 (1977).

[257] *See* Broadrick v. Oklahoma, 413 U.S. 601 (1973); Papchristou v. City of Jacksonville, 405 U.S. 156 (1971); NAACP v. Button, 371 U.S. 415 (1963); Calder v. Bull, 3 U.S. (3 Dall.) 386 (1798).

[258] The phrases "in the interest of" and "for the protection of" suggest a means-end relation. The phrase "for reasons of" should be construed as equivalent with "in the interest of," as shown by the fact that it was rendered as "*dans l'interet de*" in the French text of art. 14(1) of the Covenant. *See generally* U.N. Docs. E/CN.4/SR.165, at 18, and SR.166 at 6-7 (1950).

limitation must be a necessary condition for the fulfillment of the legitimate interest, i.e., that such interest would not be fulfilled in the absence of such limitation.[259] The concept of a necessary condition conveyed by the word "necessary" implies what has been called the principle of proportionality: a limitation is invalid to the extent that the same legitimate governmental objective could have been achieved by means of a less restrictive alternative. Indeed, anything in excess of the least restrictive limitation that attains the goal is, by definition, not necessary.

The concepts of necessary condition and sufficient condition rest on causation. Because causation in a social context is very difficult to establish with certainty, the judgments of sufficiency and necessity required by the limitation clauses must be understood as reasonable judgments to be made on the basis of the best information available. In other words, the relationships of sufficiency and necessity required by the limitation clauses should be understood as generally qualified by a standard of reasonableness. As an exception, the phrase "strictly necessary" in Article 14(1) suggests the need for a more rigorous proof of the necessity of a limitation.[260]

The presence of both components in a given formula indicates that the limitation must be both reasonably sufficient and reasonably necessary to fulfill a legitimate interest. For example, Article 22(2), which governs restrictions on the right to freedom of association, requires that a limitation be "necessary...in the interests of...the protection of public health." Under this clause, no limitation on freedom of association can be imposed to prevent the spread of AIDS (an application of the concept of protection of public health) unless, to the best of current medical knowledge (and other things being equal), AIDS can reasonably be expected not to spread further if the limitation is imposed and can reasonably be expected to spread further if it is not.

[259] This conclusion is based on the ordinary meaning of "necessary" and the syntactic function of this word in the limitation clauses. *See Vienna Convention on the Law of Treaties, adopted* 22 May 1969, *entered into force* 27 Jan. 1980, 1155 U.N.T.S. 331, art. 31(1). *See also* statements by Mr. Simsarian (U.S.), U.N. Doc. E/CN.4/SR.321, at 8 (1952); statement by Mr. Malik (Lebanon), U.N. Doc. E/CN.4/SR.119, at 11 (1949). The European Court of Human Rights has stated that the notion of "necessary" implies a "pressing social need," which must be assessed in light of a certain margin of appreciation enjoyed by the State. E.g., Case of the Observer and Guardian v. the United Kingdom, Judgment of 26 November 1991, Ser. A No. 216, at para. 59.

[260] *See* Handyside v. U.K., Eur. Ct. Human Rights, Judgment of 7 Dec. 1976, Ser. A, No. 24, at para. 48 (interpreting the European Convention).

United States law also contains a multi-tiered system of controls on legislation, based on its relationship with legitimate ends. Since early times, the "necessary and proper" clause of Article I, Section 8, of the Constitution has been construed in a very permissive fashion, validating virtually all means of pursuing valid governmental aims, save those expressly prohibited by the Constitution.[261] Under the current interpretation of the equal-protection and due-process guarantees, all that is generally required is that the legislation be rationally related to a legitimate governmental end.[262] As exception to this principle, in cases involving certain invidious classifications or the infringement of fundamental rights (i.e., cases subject to "strict scrutiny"), the legislation must be necessary to achieve a compelling state interest; in cases involving distinctions based on gender, alienage or illegitimacy the legislation is normally required to bear a substantial relationship to an important governmental objective; and in First Amendment cases the legislation is generally required to represent the least restrictive alternative.[263] The relationship that is required by Supreme Court precedents in cases of strict scrutiny and in First Amendment cases is not unlike the relationship denoted by the word "necessary" in the limitation clauses of the CPR Covenant.

The legitimate interests referred to in Articles 12(3), 14(1), 18(3), 19(3), 21 and 22(2) of the CPR Covenant are (leaving aside some of very narrow application): "the rights and freedoms of others," "public health," "morals," "public morals," "national security," "public safety," and "public order (*ordre public*)." A limitation governed by any of those six clauses is invalid unless it serves at least one of the interests listed in the same clause. But even if the limitation does serve one of those interests, if it in addition has the aim of destroying the right in question (or any of the other rights set forth in the CPR Covenant), then it is invalidated by paragraph 1 of Article 5.

The phrase "the rights and freedoms of others" can refer to any of the rights that are set forth in the CPR Covenant or in any other

[261] *See* McCulloch v. Maryland, 17 U.S. (4 Wheat.) 316 (1819).

[262] *See,* e.g., City of New Orleans v. Duke, 427 U.S. 297 (1976); Dandridge v. Williams, 397 U.S. 471 (1970); Renaldi v. Yeager, 384 U.S. 305 (1966); Williamson v. Lee Optical, 348 U.S. 483 (1955); U.S. v. Carolene Products, 304 U.S. 144 (1938), Lindsley v. Natural Carbonic Gas Co., 320 U.S. 61 (1911).

[263] *See,* e.g., Craig v. Boren, 429 U.S. 190 (1976); Washington v. Davis, 426 U.S. 229 (1976); Roe v. Wade, *supra* note 194; Broadrick v. Oklahoma, *supra* note 257; U.S. v. Robel, 389 U.S. 258 (1967); Griswold v. Connecticut, 381 U.S. 470 (1965); NAACP v. Button, *supra* note 257; Shelton v. Tucker, 364 U.S. 479 (1960); Thornhill v. Alabama, 310 U.S. 88 (1940); U.S. v. Carolene Products, *supra* note 262, at 152-53 n.4.

international instrument, or that arise under domestic law. The effect of this provision is to permit the limitation of a given right for the sake of other rights (of the same or different kind) of other persons. This permission gives rise to potential conflicts between the rights subject to the limitation clause and other rights of the same kind, between those rights and other rights guaranteed by the CPR Covenant, and between the first set of rights and other rights (of similar or different nature) derived from other international instruments or domestic law. The Covenant contains no criterion for the resolution of any such conflict. Therefore, a State Party must be considered free to adopt its own balancing or ranking of rights, as long as it satisfies the other conditions for the validity of the limitations that it chooses to impose.[264]

"Public health" is a relatively clear concept; it refers, for example, to the control of disease or the prevention of epidemics.[265] "Public morals" has a more uncertain scope; it may refer to norms of positive morality (the morals of the public) or to moral norms governing public (as distinguished from private) conduct.[266] In Article 14(1), the term "morals" is unqualified, a fact suggesting that the right to a public trial may be restricted for reasons related to an individual's private conduct.

National security and public safety are closely related concepts. "National security" may be interpreted as referring to the security of

[264] *See generally Symposium, supra* note 244, at 76-84. The European Commission of Human Rights has applied the concept of protection of the "rights and freedom of others" to justify limitations imposed on a variety of cases, including the following: a conviction for activities aimed at the reintroduction of National Socialism; a prosecution for distributing materials to servicemen seeking to persuade them to disobey their orders; the prohibition of homosexual acts between male persons under 21; the eviction of a person from his home under a housing control law aimed at preventing over-population which would be harmful to the economy; failure to give a husband a right to be consulted on, or to seize the authorities of, the question of a proposed termination of pregnancy by his wife; a compulsory medical test to determine paternity; etc. *See* P. SIEGHART, *supra* note 1, at 97-98.

[265] *See* Kiss, *supra* note 171, at 290-310. The European Commission on Human Rights has relied on the phrase "the protection of health" to justify, *inter alia,* limitations on religious freedom aimed at preventing bovine tuberculosis (X v. Netherlands, App. No. 1068/61, Eur. Comm's Human Rts. Dec. on Admissibility of 14 Dec. 1962, 5 Y.B. EUR. CONV. ON HUMAN RIGHTS 278 (1962)) or at protecting motorcyclists by requiring them to wear helmets (X v. U.K., App. No. 7992/77, Eur. Comm'n Human Rts. Dec. on Admissibility of 12 July 1978, 14 Decisions & Reports 234 (1978)).

[266] *See* Kiss, *supra* note 171, at 303-04. In the *Handyside* case, the European Commission of Human Rights justified the suppression of a book that provided sexual information and advice to children and adolescents. The Court concluded that "the competent English judges were entitled, in the exercise of their discretion, to think at the relevant time that the book would have pernicious effects on the morals of many of the children and adolescents who would read it." Handyside v. U.K., Eur. Ct. Human Rts. Judgment of 7 Dec. 1976, Ser. A No. 24, at para. 52.

the nation as a whole in the face of external threats, such as threats to its territorial integrity or political independence.[267] Public safety appears to be the safety of the community in the face of internal threats, such as violent crime.[268]

Public health, safety and morals are the three traditional components of the concept of police power in American law. This concept has now come to embrace the notion of general welfare,[269] used first to refer to the economic needs of the community and more recently to the public good in general. This expanded concept of police power is often put forth as encompassing the sum of governmental objectives regarded as legitimate at any particular time.[270]

The concept of public order (*ordre public*) has given rise to much controversy.[271] It is clear that "public order" is used in the CPR Covenant not in the sense of "absence of public disorder," but in a wider sense akin to the civil-law concept conveyed in French by the expression "*ordre public.*" This is true not only of the clauses that include the French formula in the English text but probably also of those that do not. It is not easy, however, to determine the meaning of "*ordre public*" in French law or that of its counterparts in other civil-law systems. These terms have a variety of functions, some of which

[267] *See* Kiss, *supra* note 171, at 295-97; *Symposium, supra* note 244, at 70-74. The European Commission on Human Rights expressed the view that "desertion of soldiers can, even in peacetime, create a threat to 'national security' in that it tends to weaken the army's role as an instrument destined in a democratic society to protect it from internal or external threats." Arrowsmith v. U.K., Eur. Comm'n Human Rts. report of 12 Oct. 1978, 19 Dec. & Rep. 5, at para. 85. *See also* X v. Austria, App. No. 5321/71, Eur. Comm'n Human Rts. dec. on admissibility, 42 Collection of Decisions 105 (1972); X v. U.K. App. No. 5459/72, Eur. Comm'n Human Rts. dec. on admissibility, 40 Collection of Decisions 75 (1972); X v. Austria, App. No. 1747/62, Eur. Comm'n Human Rts. dec. on admissibility, 6 Y.B. EUR. CONV. ON HUMAN RTS. 424 (1963).

[268] *See,* e.g., Klass v. F.R.G., Eur. Ct. Human Rts. Judgment of 6 Sept. 1978, Ser. A No. 28 (wiretapping); X v. U.K., App. No. 5229/71, Eur. Comm'n Human Rts. dec. on admissibility, 42 Collection of Decisions 140 (1972) (refusal to allow a convict to attend his mother's funeral); X v. F.R.G., App. No. 1307/61, Eur. Comm'n Human Rts. dec. on admissibility, 5 Y.B. EUR. CONV. ON HUMAN RTS. 230 (1962) (maintenance of records of past criminal cases).

[269] "General welfare" is a term frequently used to describe the powers and functions of government in general. In the U.N. debates, however, it was apparently used in a narrower sense, embracing only the economic well-being of the community as a whole. *See,* e.g., statement by Mr. Cassin (France) 3 U.N. GAOR, C.3 (154th mtg.) at 653. Indeed, the supposedly restricted meaning of "general welfare" (more exactly, of the French equivalent "*bien-etre general*") was offered as an argument for including the concept of *ordre public* in art. 29 of the Universal Declaration. *Id.*

[270] *See,* e.g., Ex Parte Kazas, 70 P.2d 962 (Cal. 1937). *See also* Ghaster Properties, Inc. v. Preston, 200 N.E. 2d 328 (Ohio 1964); Wisconsin Lutheran High School Conference v. Sinar, 65 N.W.2d 43 (Wis. 1954); Anthony v. City of Atlanta, 18 S.E.2d 81 (Ga. 1941); Gin S. Chow v. City of Santa Barbara, 22 P.2d 5 (Cal. 1933); Standard Oil Co. v. City of Bowling Green, 50 S.W.2d 960 (Ky. 1932).

[271] *See* Kiss, *supra* note 171, at 297-302; *Symposium, supra* note 244, at 19-20, 56-63.

roughly coincide with some of the functions of "public policy" and "police power" in Anglo-American law.

In civil-law systems, the concept of *ordre public* is used as an overriding principle to justify restrictions on individual rights based on the acknowledged powers of the government to act in the general interest. The area of application of this principle has increased as a result of the historical growth of government functions. Once limited to order, safety and sanitation, this principle is now said to include within its scope aesthetic, moral, economic and political aspects. The concept of *ordre public* is also used in civil law to invalidate private agreements that transgress principles or values regarded as fundamental, and in conflict-of-laws to prevent the application of any foreign law that is contrary to certain basic principles or values of the forum. Civil-law scholars often group these functions together and characterize *ordre public* as a concept that embraces the fundamental principles accepted by a community at any particular time.[272]

It has been argued that the *ordre public* clauses of the Covenants incorporate the concept just described.[273] This interpretation is subject, however, to a serious objection. The object and purpose of these treaties is the establishment of *international* standards for the protection of human rights. If the principles embodied in the concept of *ordre public* were to vary unrestrictedly from country to country and from time to time, the very *raison d'être* of the Covenants would be substantially impaired.[274]

Unsatisfactory though this theory may be, the alternative interpretations do not fare better. One conceivable approach would be to use the *ordre public* of one country at one time (for instance, that of France at the time the CPR Covenant was drafted) as the general international standard. Such a standard would be fairly precise, but, of course, highly arbitrary. A second conceivable approach would be to draw a composite idea of *ordre public* from the laws of several, or all, civil-law

[272] See P. BERNARD, LA NOTION D'ORDRE PUBLIC EN DROIT ADMINISTRATIF (1962); J. COSTA, LIBERTE, ORDRE PUBLIC ET JUSTICE EN FRANCE (1966-67).

[273] See, e.g., statement by Mr. Ruda (Argentina) 14 U.N. GAOR (956th mtg.) at para. 29 (1959); statement by Mr. Vidal Gabas (Spain), id., at para. 35.

[274] It would be incorrect to maintain, however, that under such construction the Covenant would be totally deprived of its *raison dêtre.* Even if "*ordre public*" were equivalent with "any value whatever," a limitation enacted for the protection of "*ordre public*" would still have to satisfy the principle of legality, the principle of non-destruction, the required relationship with the value in question, and, if applicable, the principle of democratic content. It is easy to see, however, that this interpretation would virtually eliminate one of the conditions for the validity of indirect limitations and would substantially weaken the system established by the Covenant.

countries. This method would be less objectionable than the first, though it would still be arbitrary to disregard the basic principles of the excluded countries.

If ours were a truly homogeneous world, surely the best approach would be to develop a universal concept of *ordre public* by drawing from all the legal systems of the world those common fundamental principles that constitute the basic fabric of social organization. Quite apart from the immensity of the task and the practical obstacles that it would encounter, the basic premise of this approach is at odds with reality. Leaving aside "technical" legal principles, such as the limitation of actions or *lex posterior derogat priori,* it cannot be maintained, at the present stage of civilization, that all States share a single set of fundamental political principles and the basic values embodied in them. Thus, the likely result of such an endeavor would be a set of principles so general and so basic, so far removed from the conflict of values inherent in the real-life limitation of specific rights, that they would have little relevance as standards for the validity of those limitations. This kind of approach is both feasible and appropriate in the case of a relatively small community of like-minded States, such as that formed by the parties to the European Convention on Human Rights. It does not (yet) carry conviction when transposed to the universal plane.[275]

In sum, none of the competing theories offers a satisfactory solution to the problem of *ordre public.* Until a better legal theory is found, the application of this open-ended concept will depend on extra-legal considerations, a discussion of which would exceed the scope of this essay.

### *(iii) The Principle of Non-Destruction*

A third condition for the validity of an indirect limitation under the CPR Covenant is that the limitation should not consist in or aim at

[275] I wrote these words in 1980 at the height of the Cold War. In the twelve years since elapsed, the world had undergone epochal changes. The Soviet Union, which had been the greatest obstacle to the development of an ideological consensus at the time the CPR Covenant was drafted, is now lying in the graveyard of history. Its state ideology, Communism, has suffered a near-worldwide collapse, and vast areas of the world have made long strides toward political and economic freedom. While we are far from a state of uniform openness and freedom (and we may never reach that stage, for history has no necessary direction), we are fast approaching the point at which it will be meaningful to attempt to construct a true international concept of *ordre public.* When that point is reached, I shall be the first to celebrate the obsolescence of the judgment made in the text.

the destruction of any of the rights set forth in the same treaty. This requirement, which may be called the "principle of non-destruction," is a corollary of paragraph 1 of Article 5:

> Nothing in the Covenant may be interpreted as implying for any State any right to engage in any activity or perform any act aimed at the destruction of any of the rights and freedoms recognized [in the Covenant] or at their limitation to a greater extent than is provided for in the Covenant.

This provision restricts the scope of the State's right to impose limitations pursuant to the limitation clauses, and the concluding phrase of the quoted text makes clear that no limitations may be imposed other than those expressly provided for in the Covenant.

The principle of non-destruction in the Covenant is functionally similar to the constitutional doctrine of substantive due process in United States law, which was also designed to protect the core of certain constitutional rights from governmental interference. The extent to which this doctrine retains validity in American constitutional law is a matter of controversy.[276]

### *(iv) The Principle of Democratic Content*[277]

Three of the six specific limitation clauses here discussed contain the phrase "in a democratic society." In Article 14(1), this expression follows a partial list of legitimate interests, while in Articles 21 and 22(2) it is placed immediately after the word "necessary." These textual differences have given rise to two opposing theories: one, that "in a democratic society" qualifies the legitimate interests, requiring that they be consistent with democratic principles; the other, that "in a democratic society" qualifies the relation that must exist between the limitation and the legitimate interests, turning the relation denoted by the term "necessary" into something more akin to political justification than to the notion of proportionality.[278]

[276] See, e.g., 2 R.D. ROTUNDA 7 J.E. NOWAK, *op. cit., supra* note 29, Chap. 15.4.

[277] *See* Garibaldi, *On the Ideological Content of Human Rights Instruments: The Clause "In a Democratic Society"* in CONTEMPORARY ISSUES IN INTERNATIONAL LAW, ESSAYS IN HONOR OF LOUIS B. SOHN (T. Buergenthal ed. 1984) at 23-68.

[278] *See* Garibaldi, *id.,* at 29-39. The first theory is based on some remarks made by French representatives during the drafting of the Universal Declaration and the Covenants. *See especially,* statement by Mr. Ordonneau (France), U.N. Doc. E/CN.4/SR.74, at 12 (1948); statement by Mr. Cassin (France), U.N. Doc. E/CN.4/SR.166, at 8 (1950). The second theory is based on the English text of Articles 8 through 11 of the European Commission on Human Rights, as well as on some decisions of the European organs. *See* Klass v. F.R.G., Eur. Ct. Human Rts. Judgment of 6 Sept. 1978, Ser. A No. 28, at para. 46.

Neither of these theories, however, can account for the function of the clause "in a democratic society" in all places in which it appears in the CPR Covenant and other human-rights instruments. For this reason, each of these theories leads to the dubious conclusion that the clause "in a democratic society" was meant to have two radically different functions in the same instrument—a conclusion for which there is no evidence whatsoever in the drafting history of the clause.

On the contrary, the *travaux préparatoires* clearly indicate that the overall purpose of this clause was to add a standard of political legitimacy to the conditions that a limitation must fulfill in order to be valid under the Covenant. This purpose is best served by interpreting the clause "in a democratic society" as a qualification applicable to the limitation itself, and, therefore, as an independent condition for the validity of the limitations to which the clause applies.[279]

Thus, the clause "in a democratic society" should be construed as requiring that the content of the limitation be consistent with those principles that define a democratic society. Just what "democratic society" means is a more difficult question. The preparatory work suggests that the concept of "democracy" advocated by what was then the Soviet bloc did not prevail, and that the phrase "democratic society" must consequently be understood to refer to some set of substantive political principles drawn from the Western tradition.[280] It

[279] *See* Garibaldi, *supra* note 277, at 39-42. This interpretation expresses the basic ideas conveyed by the two theories mentioned above in a simpler and more comprehensive manner. It also finds support in the French text of arts. 8 through 11 of the European Convention, as well as some statements made in the preparatory work of the Universal Declaration and the Covenants. *See* statement by Mr. Watt (Australia), 3 U.N. GAOR, C.3 (154th mtg.) at 657 (1948); statement by Mr. Ciasullo (Uruguay), U.N. Doc. E/CN.4/SR.235, at 9 (1951). *Accord, Symposium, supra* note 244, at 5, 49.

[280] *See* Garibaldi, *supra* note 277, at 53-63. During the preparatory work on art. 29 of the Universal Declaration, the Soviet bloc advocated the phrase "democratic State," while Western countries, divided at first, eventually joined in supporting the expression "democratic society." These two formulae became code words for two opposing conceptions of democracy, only one of which was embodied in the final text. *See* debates in 3 U.N. GAOR, C.3 (153rd and 154th mtgs.). A similar controversy took place during the drafting of the Covenants: the Soviet bloc sought to add the phrase "in the interest of democracy" as a general qualification to the definition of several rights, and the Western States opposed it. A new war of symbols ensued, and the Soviet proposals were categorically rejected. *See* debates in U.N. Doc. E/CN.4/SR.120, 121 (1949); SR.320, 322 (1952). It has been suggested that "democratic society" in the Universal Declaration means a society in which the rights set forth in the Declaration are recognized and respected. *See, e.g.*, E.I. DAES, THE INDIVIDUAL'S DUTIES TO THE COMMUNITY AND THE LIMITATIONS ON HUMAN RIGHTS AND FREEDOMS UNDER ARTICLE 29 OF THE UNIVERSAL DECLARATION OF HUMAN RIGHTS, U.N. Sales No. E.82.XIV.1 (1983), at 127-28; *Symposium, supra* note 244, at 5. In view of the fact that such recognition and respect are a function of the limitations validly imposed under the Declaration, and that such valid limitations are a function of the concept of democratic society,

remains indeterminate, however, which one of the Western versions of democracy constitutes the proper interpretation of this clause.

### 3.4.2 Derogations

Article 4 of the CPR Covenant provides that a State Party may validly derogate from its obligation under the Covenant if all the following conditions are satisfied: (i) there must be a "public emergency which threatens the life of the nation and the existence of which is officially proclaimed"; (ii) the measures taken must not exceed "the extent strictly required by the exigencies of the situation"; (iii) those measures must not be inconsistent with the other obligations of the State under international law; (iv) the measures must "not involve discrimination solely on the ground of race, colour, sex, language, religion or social origin"; (v) the measures must not derogate from Articles 6, 7, 8 (paragraphs 1 and 2), 11, 15, 16 and 18 of the CPR Covenant; and (vi) the State must immediately inform the other States Parties, through the Secretary-General of the United Nations, "of the provisions from which it has derogated and of the reasons by which it was actuated."[281] In addition, the State Party is obligated to communicate to the other States Parties the termination of the derogation.

In the United States, the functional counterpart of Article 4 is the judicially-developed doctrine of emergency. Broadly characterized, this doctrine justifies certain restrictions on individual rights by reference to emergency conditions. To the extent that a comparison is possible—the elements of this doctrine must be gathered from fragmentary precedents, which often stress the need for case-by-case adjudication—the doctrine of emergency appears to be considerably more permissive than Article 4 of the Covenant. This discrepancy does not mean, however, that Article 4 of the Covenant would place an intolerable burden on the United States. However permissive the

the proposed definition is hopelessly circular. The function of the "democratic society" clause presupposes a substantive concept of democracy, i.e., democracy understood as a system of substantive political principles, not a concept of democracy based on the method by which the rulers accede to power. For a full discussion of this point, *see* Garibaldi, *supra* note 277, at 42-49.

[281] *See generally* M. BOSSUYT, *supra* note 1, at 81-103; United Nations, *Study of the implications for human rights of recent developments concerning situations known as states of siege or emergency* (N. Questiaux, Special Rapporteur), U.N. Doc. E/CN.4/Sub.2/1982 (1982); *Symposium, supra* note 244, at 23-34, 89-131.

doctrine of emergency may seem to be, the history of restrictions actually imposed in the United States suggests that the United States should not find it impossible to comply with Article 4.[282]

### *(1) The Public Emergency*

For a derogation to be valid under the CPR Covenant, the state of affairs on which it is premised must be a public emergency. War, the archetype of a public emergency, is expressly mentioned in Article 15 of the European Convention on Human Rights, which served as a model for Article 4 of the Covenant. The drafters of the Covenant preferred not to refer to war, on the unconvincing ground that the possibility of war should not be alluded to in a United Nations document.[283] In spite of this symbolic gesture, war would clearly constitute a public emergency in the sense of Article 4, as would serious internal disturbances and civil strife. It is less clear whether the concept of "public emergency" includes natural disasters and economic crises.[284]

The public emergency must be of sufficient magnitude to threaten the life of the nation. The *travaux prêparatoires* suggest that the threat must be to the nation as a whole.[285] This is not a reference to the territorial boundaries to which the threat is confined, but to the magnitude or seriousness of the threat. Decisions of the organs of the European Convention, interpreting a virtually identical text, suggest that the public emergency threatens the life of the nation when it is actual or imminent, affects the whole population (or the whole nation), threatens the continuance of the organized life of the community, and is exceptional, in the sense that the regime of limitation authorized by the Covenant is plainly inadequate to meet the threat.[286]

[282] The restrictions imposed in the United States in post-Civil War emergencies have been mild in comparison with restrictions regularly imposed in other countries under states of siege or emergency, martial law, suspension of *habeas corpus,* or other emergency doctrines and procedures. A notorious exception—illustrative of the dangers of an unlimited or all-too-flexible doctrine of emergency—was the internment of persons of Japanese ancestry during the Second World War. *See* Korematsu v. U.S., 323 U.S. 214 (1944).

[283] *U.N. Annotations, supra* note 10, at 23.

[284] *See,* e.g., *Symposium, supra* note 244, at 91-98.

[285] *Id.*

[286] *See* Ireland v. U.K., Eur. Ct. Human Rts. *supra* note 130; Lawless v. Ireland, Eur. Ct. Human Rts. Judgments of 14 Nov. 1960 (preliminary objections) and 1 July 1961 (merits), Ser. A Nos. 1 and 3; "Greek Case," Eur. Comm'n Human Rts. Report of 5 Nov. 1969, 12 Y.B. EUR. CONV. HUMAN RTS. (1969).

Finally, the existence of the public emergency must be officially proclaimed. The preparatory work makes clear that such a proclamation need not be legal (i.e., authorized) under municipal law; it is sufficient that it be made by an organ with apparent authority to promulgate "official" acts.[287] On the other hand, the word "proclaimed" seems to imply that the announcement must be made public.

The concept of emergency just described seems to be considerably narrower than its counterpart in United States law. Although in the United States declarations of emergency have chiefly referred to war or to the Great Depression, the potential scope of such declarations is much wider. The deferential attitude of American courts on this matter indicates that there are no clear limits, if any, to the power of legislature to characterize a situation as an "emergency."

*(2) Relation Between the Derogation and the Public Emergency*

The second condition for the validity of a derogation is that the measures taken be strictly required by the exigencies of the situation," a formulation that entails both the notion of necessity and that of proportionality.[288] Under U.S. law, by contrast, emergency legislation must be "reasonable and appropriate" (or rationally related) to a legitimate end, the severity of the emergency being one of the circumstances that bears on the question of reasonableness.[289] If, however, the measure involves a racial classification, United States law requires that it bear a "definite and close relationship" to a pressing public necessity.[290] Only when the measure consists in the imposition of military rule do the cases suggest that it is limited strictly to the needs of the emergency.[291] With this exception, the forms of nexus that are required under U.S. law are considerably weaker than the relationship required by the Covenant.

*(3) Relation Between the Derogation and the State's Other Obligations Under International Law*

A derogation is valid under Article 4 only if it is consistent with the State's other obligations under international law, including obligations

[287] Report of the Third Committee, 18 U.N. GAOR, Annexes, Agenda Item 48, U.N. Doc. A/5655 (1954) at para. 49.

[288] *See Symposium, supra* note 244, at 105-12.

[289] *See* Woods v. Cloyd W. Miller Co., 333 U.S. 138 (1948); Veix v. Sixth Ward Building and Loan Assn., 310 U.S. 32 (1940); Home Building and Loan Assn. v. Blaisdell, 290 U.S. 398 (1934); Levy Leasing Co. v. Siegel, 258 U.S. 242 (1922); Block v. Hirsch, 256 U.S. 135 (1921); Hamilton v. Kentucky Distilleries and Warehouse Co., 251 U.S. 146 (1919).

[290] *See* Korematsu v. U.S., *supra* note 282.

[291] *See* Ex Parte Milligan, 71 U.S. (4 Wall.) 2 (1886), Luther v. Borden, 48 U.S. (7 How.) 1 (1849).

arising under customary international law and under treaties to which the State is a party. Some treaties (for example, those that codify the humanitarian law of war) are specifically designed to apply in times of emergency. These or other applicable treaties may contain no derogation clause or clauses that are stricter than Article 4 of the CPR Covenant. Thus, for example, if the United States should ratify the American Convention on Human Rights, any derogation that the United States may wish to make under the Covenant would have to be consistent, by virtue of the Covenant itself, with the stricter standards of the American Convention.[292]

*(4) The Principle of Non-discrimination*

A derogation is invalid under Article 4 of the CPR Covenant if it involves discrimination "solely on the grounds of race, colour, sex, language, religion or social origin." This is another application of the principle of non-discrimination, which has been analyzed in section 3.2 of this chapter.

It should be noted that a derogation is in violation of this principle only if it applies to a class of individuals identified exclusively by means of one or more of the impermissible criteria listed above. If, on the contrary, that class of individuals is determined by a different criterion (e.g., physical presence in the area affected by the emergency), the derogation will not violate the principle of non-discrimination, even though it may solely or disproportionately affect individuals who happen to fall within a class determined by an impermissible criterion. The same interpretation was adopted by the United States in the following understanding made at the time of ratification:

> The United States...understands the prohibition in paragraph 1 of Article 4 upon discrimination, in time of public emergency, based "solely" on the status of race, colour, sex, language, religion or social origin not to bar distinctions that may have a disproportionate effect upon persons of a particular status.[293]

The equal-protection guarantee of the United States Constitution—the counterpart of the principle of non-discrimination in the Covenant—applies both to ordinary and emergency situations. Never-

[292] *Compare* art. 4 of the CPR Covenant with art. 27 of the American Convention on Human Rights. Some rights which may be subject to derogations under the Covenant are not so subject under the American Convention.

[293] S. Exec. Rep. No. 102-23, 102d Cong., 2d Sess. 22 (1992)

theless, the forced relocation of persons of Japanese ancestry during the Second World War, which involved a form of discrimination that would almost certainly be unconstitutional in normal times, was adjudged lawful in the context of the emergency.[294] A similar measure would probably be invalid under Article 4(1) of the Covenant.

### *(5) Rights Not Subject to Derogation*

Emergency measures are invalid under paragraph 2 of Article 4 of the CPR Covenant if they derogate from one or more of the following provisions of the treaty: Article 6 (right to life), Article 7 (prohibition of torture), Article 8, paragraphs 1 and 2 (prohibition of slavery and servitude), Article 11 (prohibition of imprisonment for non-fulfillment of contractual obligations), Article 15 (principle of non-retroactivity of criminal laws and penalties), Article 16 (right to be recognized as a person before the law), and Article 18 (freedom of thought, conscience and religion).

### *(6) Notice of Derogation*

The sixth condition for the validity of a derogation is procedural: a State Party must give notice of the derogation to the other States Parties. Paragraph 3 of Article 4 regulates the content and the timing of the notice and the mechanism for its transmittal. The notice must specify the provisions of the Covenant affected by the derogation and the "reasons by which [the State] was actuated." In general, the required information is that which would enable the other States Parties to form an opinion on the validity of the derogation under Article 4.[295] The notice must be given "immediately" and through the intermediary of the Secretary-General of the United Nations.

Paragraph 3 establishes an additional obligation, to notify the other States Parties of the termination of the derogation. This requirement is obviously not a condition for the validity of the derogation: if the derogation has been terminated, a failure to give notice of such termination is a separate violation of the treaty, but this violation does not render the derogation retroactively invalid. Different is the case of a State that fails to terminate a derogation even though the emergency conditions on which the latter was based have ceased to exist. In this

[294] *See* Korematsu v. U.S., *supra* note 282.

[295] *See* Buergenthal, *To Respect and to Ensure: State Obligations and Permissible Derogations,* in Henkin, *supra* note 1, at 84-86.

case, the derogation itself becomes invalid under the CPR Covenant from the time the emergency ended, because thenceforth it can no longer be said that the derogation meets the "public emergency" requirement of Article 4(1).

### 3.4.3 The Minimum-Standard Clause

Article 5(2) of the CPR Covenant provides:

> There shall be no restriction upon or derogation from any of the fundamental rights recognized or existing in any State Party of the present Covenant pursuant to law, conventions, regulations or custom on the pretext that the present Covenant does not recognize such rights or that it recognizes them to a lesser extent.

This provision makes clear that the Covenant lays down only minimum standards: if domestic law contains a higher standard—i.e., one more favorable to the individual than those contained in the CPR Covenant—the Covenant may not be relied upon as a ground for lowering such domestic standard. For instance, the fact that the rights protected by the Covenant do not include a right to private property cannot serve as a ground for restricting the right to private property guaranteed by United States law.[296]

It should be noted that Article 5(2) does not require a State Party to maintain its adherence to any existing standard that is higher than the one required by the Covenant; it merely prohibits the State from invoking the CPR Covenant as a pretext for lowering that standard. A State is therefore free to lower its domestic standards, as long as it does so on *bona fide* grounds other than a comparison with the standards of the Covenant, and as long as it maintains the minimum level of protection required by the treaty.

[296] The right to private property is a "fundamental right" in the sense of art. 5(1) because, *inter alia,* it is recognized as such in Article 17 of the Universal Declaration of Human Rights. The Universal Declaration provided the context within which the Covenants were drafted.

## 3.5 COMPLIANCE MECHANISMS

*Dinah Shelton*

Each State Party has primary responsibility for implementing the Covenant through appropriate legislative, administrative, or other measures. Article 2(1) obliges each State Party "to respect and to ensure to all individuals within its territory and subject to its jurisdiction the rights recognized" in the Covenant. How this basic commitment is to be realized is not specified. It is left to each State Party to choose "in accordance with its constitutional processes," those measures "as may be necessary to give effect to the rights recognized in the present Covenant," to the extent that such rights are not already provided for. Choice of the means of implementation, and whether action should be taken at the state or national level in a federal system, are matters for domestic determination.[297] The fundamental obligation is to respect and ensure rights, an obligation of result. In some cases legislation may be required; in others it may not be enough, and "other measures" may be necessary.

Because the Covenant is a treaty, the conformity of domestic practices to its requirements is not left solely to the State in question. The Covenant provides three main avenues of international implementation to ensure effective protection for the rights recognized in the Covenant. First, States Parties must report periodically on measures taken to give effect to civil and political rights. In addition to the reporting requirement, two optional implementation procedures are available. These consist of an interstate complaint mechanism provided for in the text of the Covenant (Article 41) and a procedure for individual communications contained in a separate Optional Protocol. States Parties also may have recourse to other bilateral and multilateral procedures for settling disputes and implementing human rights obligations.

The Covenant created a new international supervisory organ, the Human Rights Committee. It is composed of eighteen members

[297] Paragraph 3 of art. 2 adds the more specific obligation that an effective remedy must be provided to any person whose rights are violated, including developing the possibility of judicial remedy. *See supra* sec. 3.1.3.

serving in their individual capacities, not as governmental representatives.[298] These persons are nominated and elected by the States Parties, of which they must be nationals, with no more than one national to be elected from a single State. The Committee has authority to review State reports, comment upon them, and transmit both reports and comments to the States Parties and to ECOSOC.[299] The Committee also serves as a factfinding and conciliation body, under the optional inter-State procedure of Article 41, and it receives individual communications arising under the Optional Protocol.

The independence of members of the Human Rights Committee is emphasized in various provisions: they must be persons of high moral character and recognized competence in the field of human rights; consideration must be given to the usefulness of participation by persons having legal experience; the members are elected by secret ballot by the States Parties; they receive salaries from the United Nations; they are to serve in their personal capacity; and they must expressly declare their impartiality. Staff and facilities are provided by the United Nations. Finally, the rules of procedure of the Committee require that, in case of the resignation of a member of the Committee, he or she must notify the chairman or the Secretary-General in writing.[300] Governments may not present the resignation of a Committee member, nor give instructions on any matters before the Committee.

The persons thus far elected to the Human Rights Committee have been among the most qualified and dedicated found in any international human rights oversight body, and their individual personalities have done much to shape the form and content of the Committee's work.[301] While consensus has eluded the Committee on many important issues, such as the scope of "general comments" under Article 40, most members have fully utilized their independence to participate actively in the Committee's work and to question government representatives with a degree of directness uncommon in

[298] Part IV of the Covenant, arts. 28-45, concerns the composition and activities of the Committee.

[299] There has been considerable disagreement about the Committee's authority under Article 40(4) of the Covenant. *See* Fischer, *Reporting under the Covenant on Civil and Political Rights: The First Years of the Human Rights Committee,* 76 AJIL 141 (1982).

[300] Rules of Procedure, Rule 16.

[301] *See,* e.g., Shelton, *Supervising Implementation of the Covenants: The First Ten Years of the Human Rights Committee,* ASIL *Proceedings* (1980) at 413, 414-15.

diplomatic settings.[302] While there have certainly been ideological differences among Committee members, their deliberations have not been marred by the overtly political polemics found in many other international bodies.

The Committee's rules of procedure provide, *inter alia,* that the reports, formal decisions, and all other official documents of the Committee and its subsidiary bodies should be documents of general distribution, that is, public, unless the Committee decides otherwise in a particular case. Periodic reports by States and additional information submitted by them are also given general distribution. Only documents and decisions relating to inter-State complaints and individual communications remain confidential. Even in this regard, the Committee has in practice identified the States concerning which communications have been received for consideration and published its decisions on individual cases in the form of "Final Views."[303]

Article 39 of the Covenant establishes that twelve members of the Committee constitute a quorum and that decisions be made by a majority of members present. When drafting the rules of procedure, some members argued in favor of adopting decisions by consensus, in conformity with a trend toward this method of decision-making in many international organizations. It was decided not to adopt such a rule, since it might restrict the Committee's ability to act and would be inconsistent with the explicit provision of Article 39 that decisions shall be taken by majority vote. As a result, rule 51 provides for a simple majority vote, but, in a footnote, the Committee has indicated that "the method of work normally should allow for attempts to reach decisions by consensus before voting."

### *Periodic Reports*

Under Article 40 of the Covenant, States Parties are to file reports on (1) measures they have adopted, including legislative or judicial action, which give effect to the rights recognized within the Covenant; (2) the progress made in the enjoyment of those rights; and (3) the factors and difficulties encountered in giving them effect. The

[302] *See* Shelton, *supra* note 301; *cf.* Coliver, *International Reporting Procedures,* in GUIDE TO INTERNATIONAL HUMAN RIGHTS PRACTICE (168-173) (H.Hannum ed., 2d. 1992).

[303] See, e.g., *Report of the Human Rights Committee,* 40 UN GAOR, Supp (No. 40), UN Doc. A/43/40 (1988) at 150-59; HUMAN RIGHTS COMMITTEE, SELECTED DECISIONS UNDER THE OPTIONAL PROTOCOL, UN Sales No. E.84.XIV.2 (1985); *id.,* U.N. Sales No. E.89 XIV.1 (vol. 2, 1990).

reports are due within one year of the entry into force of the Covenant for each State Party and are filed with the U.N. Secretary-General, who transmits them to the Human Rights Committee for consideration and comment. Following its consideration, the Committee may transmit the reports and its comments to the States Parties and to ECOSOC. States Parties are permitted to make observations on any comments made by the Committee.

Rules 67-71 of the Committee's rules of procedure govern the Committee's consideration of reports. The Committee may inform States of its wishes as regards the form and content of their reports; representatives of the States Parties may be present when their reports are examined; and such representative "should be able to answer questions which may be put to him by the Committee and make statements on reports already submitted by his State and also submit additional information." These latter rules follow the practice of the Committee on the Elimination of Racial Discrimination (CERD) and were instituted in spite of the objection by one member of the Committee that it amounted to an "investigatory procedure."[304] To date, no report has been examined by the Committee without the presence of a representative of the State concerned.

At its second session, the Committee drafted guidelines for States Parties regarding the form and content of their initial reports.[305] During the 13th session, the Committee adopted guidelines for subsequent reports.[306] The guidelines for the initial reports are in two parts. The first part concerns the domestic effect of the Covenant. The State is asked to describe the general legal framework within which civil and political rights are protected. Among the important points to be specifically covered are the manner in which the provisions are incorporated into national law, if at all, and whether the individual may invoke provisions of the Covenant before domestic courts or administrative authorities. Subsequent reports are to include information on, *inter alia,* progress made or difficulties remaining in implementing the Covenant, any changes made in laws or practices

[304] *See* ICJ REVIEW at 25 (No. 20, 1978).

[305] *See Report of the Human Rights Committee,* 32 UN GAOR, Supp. (No. 44), U.N. Doc. A/32/44 (1977) at 69-70.

[306] *Report of the Human Rights Committee,* 36 UN GAOR, Supp. (No. 40), U.N. Doc. A/36/40 (1981) at 102-03.

involving the Covenant, and additional information requested by the Committee during consideration of the initial report.[307]

In the second part of the guidelines, the Committee has asked that three sets of information be provided: (1) the legislative, administrative or other measures in force in regard to each right; (2) any restriction or limitations imposed by law or practice on the enjoyment of each right; and (3) any other factors or difficulties affecting the enjoyment of the rights. The intent of the reports is to develop a "constructive dialogue" with each State Party in regard to the implementation of the Covenant.

There is no explicit provision in the Covenant for consideration of outside information by the Committee in reviewing State reports, which has resulted in some dispute within the Committee on the role of specialized agencies and non-governmental organizations. In practice, the specialized agencies have been invited to attend public meetings of the Committee where State reports are considered and to address the Committee on any matter on which it might require information. In addition, the Committee has agreed in rule 67 of its rules of procedure to have the Secretary-General transmit relevant parts of reports to the specialized agencies. It should be noted, however, that the specialized agencies have no right under the Covenant to comment on State reports and may do so only if specifically requested by the Committee. The Committee has not formalized any procedure by which the specialized agencies may present information on their practice in relation to the application of provisions similar to those of the Covenant.

Although specialized agencies have not presented formal reports, the Committee has made use of the work of other organs of the United Nations. In the case of Chile, it took official notice of General Assembly resolutions and the work of the United Nations' Ad Hoc Working Group on Chile.[308] The result was a request of Chile to file a new report, based on the view that the first report did not reflect the realities of the human rights situation in that country.

There is no provision in either the Covenant or the rules of procedure which would permit formal presentation of information to the Committee by non-governmental organizations (NGOs). This

[307] *Id.* at 102.

[308] *Report of the Human Rights Committee,* 34 UN GAOR, Supp. (No. 40) at 17-27, UN DOC. A/34/40 (1979).

does not prevent NGOs from supplying information to members of the Committee individually, but use of such information was questioned by at least one State in the Committee's early deliberations. Now, however, Committee members have frequently referred directly to information provided by NGOs, such as Amnesty International and Article 19.

The power of the Committee is limited in respect to making recommendations. The Committee's mandate is to "study" the reports submitted and then to "transmit its reports" on them, together with such "general comments" that it considers appropriate. These comments are also transmitted to the States Parties and may be sent to the Economic and Social Council. States Parties may submit to the Committee their observations on the latter's comments on their reports. The only publication requirement is that the Committee submit an annual report on its activities through ECOSOC to the General Assembly.

Committee members have not been able to agree fully on the scope of the "general comments" it is permitted to make under article 40(4) of the Covenant. While the Committee has adopted a number of comments on the substantive content of particular rights or procedural matters to guide reporting states,[309] it has not directly addressed the issue of any specific State's compliance or non-compliance with its obligations. However, several individual members have adopted the practice of offering their own opinions on the adequacy of a State's report or its guarantee of Covenant rights as part of their final comments during consideration of Article 40 reports. These comments are reflected in the Committee's summary records and also are summarized in the Committee's annual report to the General Assembly.[310]

In general, although it appears that some States have been delinquent in presenting their reports, compliance with the reporting requirement has been extensive. Most reports contain detailed information on measures taken to implement the Covenant, and every

[309] The Committee had adopted 17 "general comments" through April 1989, most of which consist of short commentaries on specific articles or rights. *See* General Comments, UN Doc. CCPR/C21/Rev.1 (1989). *Cf.* Shelton, *supra* note 301, at 416-18.

[310] *See, e.g.*, the brief summaries of members' comments contained in *Report of the Human Rights Committee,* 43 UN GAOR, Supp. (No. 40), UN Doc. A/43/40 (1988) at 22 (Trinidad and Tobago), 46 (Denmark), 57-58 (Rwanda), 63 (Guinea), 70 (Central African Republic), 81 (Ecuador), 94 (France), 128 (Colombia), 135-36 (Barbados), 148 (Japan).

State has sent a representative to the proceedings to introduce the State report and answer questions. The Committee has begun to develop links with specialized agencies and other bodies, as well as informal contacts from NGOs, from whom independent information can be obtained.

Thus, while State reporting as an effective measure of implementation has been criticized, the Committee appears to be making reasonably full use of its authority to assess impartially the efforts of States Parties to implement the Covenant. When such critical appraisal is permitted and made, including obtaining supplemental information, using outside sources, and commenting on inadequate or inaccurate reporting, a reporting mechanism can be an effective, if limited, enforcement measure.

### *Inter-State Communications*

Article 41 of the Covenant permits (but does not require) a State to file a declaration that it "recognized the competence of the Committee to receive and consider communications to the effect that a State Party claims that another State Party is not fulfilling its obligations under the present Covenant." As of mid-1992, over thirty States had made such declarations, including the United States.

There are several points of immediate interest. First, the declaration is a separate action by a State Party in addition to the act of ratification. Second, the term "communication" is used, rather than complaint or petition, indicating a deliberate avoidance of judicial terminology. Third, the procedure concerns all obligations under the Covenant and not only violations of human rights. Thus, it would appear that communications may be filed by a State against another State Party in reference to the reporting or financial obligations contained within the Covenant. Finally, provided that the proper declarations have been made by the two concerned States, it is not necessary that a State allege that its own rights or the rights of its nationals have been violated. The complainant State is acting on behalf of all States Parties to the Covenant in enforcing treaty obligations allegedly violated.

There are several prerequisites to the filing of an inter-State communication, the foremost of which is a requirement of standing, based upon the principle of reciprocity. Only States which themselves have filed declarations accepting the Committee's jurisdiction may file communications against another State Party. Thus, the United States can only complain against violations by other States which have accepted the jurisdiction of the Committee.

In addition to reciprocity, domestic remedies for alleged violations of human rights must have been exhausted, and the parties must first attempt to settle the matter bilaterally. Reference to the Human Rights Committee must be preceded by a communication which the State initiating the procedure sends to the State which allegedly is not giving effect to the provisions of the Covenant. The receiving State is allowed three months to return to the sending State "an explanation or any other statement in writing clarifying the matter," including, "to the extent possible and pertinent, reference to domestic procedures and remedies taken, pending or available in the matter." If there is no solution within six months, whether due to non-cooperation on the part of the receiving State or lack of agreement between the parties, the Committee may take up the matter.

The Committee has no authority to express an opinion as to whether there has been a violation of the Covenant. The Committee may, after submission of the communication, hold a closed meeting in which it may call for all relevant information from State representatives, who may make both oral and written submissions. The Committee is obliged to make available its good offices with a view toward friendly settlement of the matter, based upon respect for human rights. If such a settlement is not achieved, the Committee is required to submit a report, which is to be confined to a brief statement of the facts. Thus, the function of the Committee is limited to fact-finding and friendly settlement, though, in practice, the Committee's finding of fact may be tantamount to finding a violation.

If a dispute is not resolved after Committee consideration of the matter, the States involved may agree to appointment by the Committee of an *ad hoc* conciliation commission, which will again attempt a settlement. The commission is to consist of five members who are nationals of States which have accepted Article 41 but not of the States Parties to the dispute. The procedure of the *ad hoc* commission is discussed in detail in Article 42 of the Covenant.

When the ad hoc commission has completed its work, it makes its own report to the States and Committee. If a solution is found, the report contains a brief statement of the facts and the settlement reached. If no solution is reached, the report will contain a full statement of the facts and the Commission's views on the possibilities of an amicable solution of the matter. The latter phrase should be taken to mean its suggestions for a solution of the matter, although, as no precedent exists, a more limited interpretation may be adopted.

The inter-State procedure of the Covenant went into effect in March 1979, but no communications had been filed as of the time of writing. This experience reflects that of other international organizations, in which the politically charged possibility of filing an inter-State complaint is rarely invoked.

### *Individual Communications*

States which become parties to the Optional Protocol recognize the competence of the Human Rights Committee to receive and consider communications from individuals who claim that rights recognized in the Covenant have been violated.[311] The composition of the Committee remains the same for this as for its other functions.

An individual submitting a communication must be "subject to the State's jurisdiction," that is, within its physical control, or be its national.[312] In addition, the right of individual communication applies only to victims; neither non-governmental organizations nor other interested parties have standing to file communications directly. However, the individual victim may act through a duly appointed representative or by a person with the authority to act on behalf of the victim, especially where the victim is unable to submit the communication.[313]

Communications are channeled through the Secretary-General of the United Nations, who prepares a list of communications received and a brief summary of their contents for circulation to the members of the Committee. A register of communications is kept. The Secretary-General may request additional information or clarification, particularly as regards exhaustion of domestic remedies. The Secretary-General also distinguishes among all communications received those which are intended for the Human Rights Committee under the terms of the Optional Protocol. In case of doubt, he must consult the

[311] As of 1 Mar. 1990, 49 of the 90 parties to the CPR Covenant had accepted the Optional Protocol. For a comparison with other procedures which permit the filing of complaints by individuals in international forums, *see generally* Hannum, *supra* note 302.

[312] The Covenant requires each State to guarantee rights to individuals "within its territory and subject to its jurisdiction." The question has been raised as to whether an individual could allege a violation by the State of nationality occurring outside its territory.

[313] *See* Human Rights Committee, Rules of Procedure, Rule 90(b).

author of the communication; if there is still doubt, he must seize the Committee of the matter.

The Committee's work under the Optional Protocol is divided into two main stages, concerned respectively with consideration of the admissibility of a communication and its consideration on its merits.[314]

The Protocol provides certain grounds of inadmissibility in Article 3, including anonymity, abusiveness, or incompatibility with the provisions of the Covenant. If the Committee finds that any of these grounds exist, it simply informs the author of the communication of its decision. The grounds listed also appear in substance in Article 27 of the European Convention on Human Rights, and a substantial body of jurisprudence has developed in the European Commission on the meaning of these terms.

No time limit is included in the provisions of the Protocol; however, the Committee has declared communications inadmissible if the events complained of took place prior to the entry into force of the Covenant and the Optional Protocol. However, if the author claims a continuing violation or that the effects of prior events currently constitute a violation, the prior events may be considered as essential to the merits of the communication.

Under rule 91(2) of the Committee's rules of procedure, a communication may not be declared admissible unless the State Party concerned has been given an opportunity to submit information or observations on the question of admissibility. On the basis of this information and that contained in the communication, two further conditions must be met. Under Article 5 of the Optional Protocol the Committee must ascertain that the same matter is not being examined under another procedure of international investigation or settlement and that the individual has exhausted all available domestic remedies.[315] The Committee has decided that the procedures referred to in

[314] A description of the Committee's procedures and a selection of many of its decisions may be found in the two volumes of *Selected Decisions under the Optional Protocol, supra* note 303.

[315] This criterion raises the problem of the coexistence of regional and universal mechanisms for the protection of human rights, a problem which has received considerable attention within the context of the Council of Europe. Two reports were prepared for the Committee of Ministers of the Council by its Committee of Experts on Human Rights, in 1968 and 1970. In regard to individual applications or communications, it was agreed that the governing consideration should be the desire to secure the most effective protection of individuals rights. Consequently, the individual applicant should be free to choose from available forums and thus to apply either to the European Commission or to the Human Rights Committee, in accordance with his or her own judgment about the likelihood of success of his application. Nevertheless, once a decision had been made and an application filed, the individual should not be permitted to invoke the other forum. The text of the European

Article 5(2) of the Protocol refer only to individual communications. Thus, the procedure set forth in ECOSOC Resolution 1503 "does not constitute a procedure of international investigation or settlement within the meaning of Article 5(2a) of the Optional Protocol, since it is concerned with the examination of situations which appear to reveal a consistent pattern of gross violations of human rights and a situation is not 'the same matter' as an individual complaint."[316]

In regard to the rule that communications may not be considered unless the individual has exhausted all available domestic remedies, the Committee "considers that this provision should be interpreted and applied in accordance with the generally accepted principles of international law with regard to the exhaustion of domestic remedies as applied in the field of human rights."[317] Thus, once the allegations of exhaustion have been made by the author of a communication, the burden is upon the State to prove non-exhaustion, through producing details of available remedies not utilized by the alleged victim. A statement of generally available procedures is insufficient in this regard.

In practice, the stage of admissibility is often crucial: for example, more than 95 per cent of the applications registered with the European Commission are declared inadmissible.[318]

If all conditions of admissibility are met, the Committee brings the communication to the attention of the State alleged to be violating a right recognized in the Covenant. The State has six months to submit to the Committee written explanations or statements clarifying the matter and the domestic remedy, if any, that might have been taken. Once this information has been received or the six months have elapsed, the Committee may proceed to a consideration of the merits of the communication.

---

Convention prevents this possibility, but the provisions of the Optional Protocol permit application to it after other procedures have been terminated. The Committee has expressly stated that it will consider communications previously considered under another procedure. The Committee of Ministers of the Council of Europe therefore recommended to member Governments that they include a declaration or reservation to ratification of the Optional Protocol to the effect that Article 5(2) includes as inadmissible matters which are being examined or have been examined under another international procedure. Contracting parties to the European Convention which have ratified the Covenant have for the most part made such a declaration or reservation.

[316] *Report of the Human Rights Committee,* 33 UN GAOR, Supp. (No. 40), U.N. Doc. A/33/40 (1978) at 100.

[317] *Id.* at 101.

[318] European Commission on Human Rights, *Stock-taking on the European Convention on Human Rights* (1987, Supp. 1988) at 84.

The procedure is not adversarial, in the sense of permitting arguments of counsel or the examination of witnesses. Article 5(1) states that the proceedings shall be based on "all written information made available...by the individual and the State Party concerned," which would appear to exclude oral hearings and information from other sources. Nevertheless, supplemental information submitted by the individual and government, each commenting on the submissions of the other, would in most cases seem not only permissible, but necessary.

In considering communications, the Committee must hold closed meetings. The procedure concludes with the Committee forwarding its views to the State Party concerned and to the individual. Its "views on the matter" is a wider term than that used in regard to inter-State communications and requires the Committee to forward its views on the entire complex of facts and questions of law which have been presented to it, including its findings on violations.

There are two important rules of procedure for actual consideration of a communication. The first permits the Committee to appoint a working group of not more than five members to consider the communications and make recommendations to the Committee (Rule 89). The second (paragraph 3 of Rule 94) in effect permits dissenting opinions. This provision provoked a good deal of discussion in the Committee when the rules were being drafted, since it appeared to strengthen the quasi-judicial function of the Committee.

As noted above, both State-to-State complaints and individual communications are optional. No State Party has yet made a complaint under Article 41. As of the Committee's thirty-ninth session in 1990, 418 individual communications had been filed under the Optional Protocol. Of this number, the Committee adopted "views" in 110 cases; 33 cases had been declared admissible and were still pending; 172 cases were declared inadmissible or otherwise discontinued; and 103 cases were pending at the pre-admissibility stage.[319] The Committee concluded that violations had occurred in 85 of the first 100 cases in which views were adopted.[320]

[319] *Report of the Human Rights Committee,* 45 UN GAOR, Supp. (No. 40) at 131, U.N. Doc. A/45/40 (1990).

[320] *Id.* at 144.

# PART IV
# THE INTERNATIONAL COVENANT ON ECONOMIC, SOCIAL AND CULTURAL RIGHTS

# IV
# THE INTERNATIONAL COVENANT ON ECONOMIC, SOCIAL AND CULTURAL RIGHTS

This Chapter, the subject of which is the Covenant on Economic Social and Cultural Rights (ESC Covenant), is organized in the same manner as Chapter III. The obligations imposed by the ESC Covenant are discussed in section 1. The principle of non-discrimination is considered in section 2. In section 3, each of the substantive rights (Articles 6 to 15) of the Covenant is analyzed in terms of its meaning in the treaty and its implications for United States law. The permissible limitations on the rights specified in the treaty are analyzed in section 4. The compliance mechanism provided for in the treaty is described in section 5.

## 4.1 OBLIGATIONS ARISING FROM THE INTERNATIONAL COVENANT ON ECONOMIC, SOCIAL AND CULTURAL RIGHTS

*Oscar M. Garibaldi*

The substantive obligations undertaken by a State Party to the ESC Covenant are set forth in Article 2 as well as in various provisions of Parts I and III. Article 2 lays down the principle of progressive implementation of the rights defined in the treaty and the principle of non-discrimination in the enjoyment of those rights. Article 1 (in Part I) and several provisions in Part III establish additional substantive obligations, which are not subject to the principle of progressive implementation and hence must be formed immediately and in full.

The substantive obligations imposed by the ESC Covenant are the subject of this section; the procedural obligations of Part IV, which are related to a system of international monitoring of compliance with the treaty, are discussed below in section 5.

### 4.1.1 The Obligation of Progressive Implementation

Under Article 2(1) of the ESC Covenant, each State Party:

> undertakes to take steps, individually and through international assistance and cooperation especially economic and technical, to the maximum of its available resources, with a view to achieving progressively the full realization of the rights recognized in the. . . Covenant by all appropriate means, including particularly the adoption of legislative measures.

The principle contained in this provision is usually referred to as the principle of progressive implementation. Subject to a few exceptions noted below, this principle defines the obligations of a State Party in respect of the rights set forth in the Covenant. Accordingly, those rights are not the counterparts of duties to be performed in full and at once; they are rather, goals to be achieved progressively. The legal obligation undertaken by a State Party in that respect is limited to "tak[ing] steps. . . to the maximum of its available resources. . .[and] by all appropriate means" towards the full realization of those rights.

The reason for this approach, which is in stark contrast with that of the CPR Covenant, is that (for the most part) the rights set forth in the ESC Covenant are positive rights, that is, they are the counterpart of obligations that can only be discharged by positive governmental action. Positive action requires the expenditure of scarce resources, the availability of which must affect the degree to which a State Party is able at any given time to approximate the goals established by the treaty. Because the obligations created by the ESC Covenant are a function of the availability of resources (as recognized by the phrase "to the maximum of its available resources"), the unidirectional movement implied by the word "progressively" can only be part of the goal to be striven for, rather than a rigid characterization of the path to be taken. In other words, the degree of realization of rights subject to this principle need not always increase progressively; rather, the extent to which a State Party is required to realize those rights at any given time depends on what its economy can afford.

The effects of the reference to "international assistance and co-operation" are not altogether clear. This clause was probably added as a recognition of the special needs of less developed countries (which affect their available resources, and, hence, their obligations under the treaty), as well as to indicate that the "available resources" of a State include any assistance that it might receive from abroad.[1] It is clear, though, that this clause does not obligate developed State Parties to provide assistance to their less developed counterparts.

### 4.1.2 The Obligation to Guarantee Non-Discrimination

Articles 2(2) and 3 of the ESC Covenant prohibit discrimination on the basis of certain criteria deemed improper. Under the first of these provisions, a State Party undertakes to guarantee that the rights set forth in the ESC Covenant will be enjoyed without discrimination on the basis of race, color, sex, religion, political or other opinion, national or social origin, property, birth or other status. Article 3 reiterates a principle that is already contained in the more general formula of Article 2(2): a State Party is obligated to ensure the equal right of men and women to the enjoyment of the rights set forth in the treaty.

These two provisions represent different versions (one more general, the other more specific) of the principle of non-discrimination, which is discussed in section 4.2 below. Here it must be noted that the obligation to guarantee non-discrimination is not subject to the principle of progressive implementation. It was made clear during the preparatory work of the ESC Covenant that at every step in the progression toward the goals enunciated in the treaty, the benefits thus conferred should be enjoyed without any of the prohibited forms of discrimination.[2]

[1] *See Annotation on the text of the draft International Covenants on Human Rights,* U.N. Doc. A/2929, at 20, para. 24 (1955) (hereinafter cited as *U.N. Annotations*).

[2] *See id.* para. 27.

### 4.1.3 The Specific Obligations of Parts I and III

Under Article 1, paragraph 3, of the ESC Covenant, States Parties undertake the obligation to "promote the realization of the right of self-determination" and to "respect that right, in conformity with the provisions of the United Nations Charter." These obligations are identical with those established by Article 1 of the CPR Covenant, which has been analyzed in section 3.3.

The provisions of Part III of the Covenant are of three types: some provisions "recognize" a certain right (e.g., Article 6(1), 7, 9, 10, 11, 13(1), 13(2), 15(1)) others specify the steps to be taken towards the full realization of a right (Articles 6(2), 12(2), 15(2)); and in other States Parties "undertaken to ensure" a certain right (Article 8) or "undertake" to perform or to refrain from performing certain actions (Articles 13(3), 14, 15(3)).

The first two types of provisions merely complement Article 2. The rights "recognized" in the treaty are the rights that, under Article 2, must be realized progressively, and the steps specified are the steps to be taken, pursuant to the same article, towards the full realization of those rights. By contrast, the provisions of the third type impose independent legal obligations not subject to the principle of progressive implementation of Article 2. The *travaux préparatories* make it abundantly clear that by using the phrases "undertaken to ensure" and "undertake" instead of "recognize," the drafters intended to create independent legal obligations to be discharged in full and at once.[3] It should be noted that, except for Article 14 (which lays down a positive obligation to prepare and to adopt a plan of action for the progressive achievement of free compulsory education) and Article 8 (which requires the enactment of legislative measures to ensure trade-union rights), the other obligations excluded from the principle of progressive realization are all negative, i.e., they may be discharged by mere inaction.

[3] *See U.N. Annotations, supra* note 1, at 20, para. 22. More specifically, *see* debates in U.N. Docs. E/CN.4/Sr.271 at 4; SR.272, at 4, 8, 9, 13; SR.273, at 8-9; SR.274, at 4, 11; SR.275, at 5-6.

## 4.2 THE PRINCIPLE OF NON-DISCRIMINATION

*Oscar M. Garibaldi*

The system of the ESC Covenant also contains a principle of non-discrimination. According to paragraph 2 of Article 2:

> The State Parties to the present Covenant undertake to guarantee that the rights enunciated in the present Covenant will be exercised without discrimination of any kind as to race, colour, sex, religion, political or other opinion, national or social origin, property, birth or other status.

Paragraph 3 of Article 2 subjects this principle to an important exception, to be discussed below. The State Parties also undertake, under Article 3, "to ensure the equal right of men and women to the enjoyment of all economic, social and cultural rights" set forth in the treaty. In contrast with the CPR Covenant, the ESC Covenant does not contain a separate principle of equality before the law.

The principle of non-discrimination established by these provisions is conceptually identical with its counterpart in the CPR Covenant, analyzed in section 3.2. For this reason, only the basic elements of the principle need be discussed here.

As in the case of the CPR Covenant, an instance of differential treatment is prohibited by the principle of non-discrimination if (i) it is based on one or more illegitimate criteria, (ii) it constitutes discrimination, and (iii) it consists in or results from the creation of a law that is subject to the principle.

The illegitimate criteria, i.e., the grounds listed in Article 2(2) of the ESC Covenant, are the same criteria deemed illegitimate under the CPR Covenant. The phrase "of any kind as to" in Article 2(2) indicates that the enumeration of illegitimate criteria must be regarded as limitative. A case of differential treatment constitutes discrimination only if it is unjustifiable, but, save for the exception contained in Article 2(3), the criteria that would justify differential treatment and hence render it non-discriminatory have been left unstated. Article 2(3) authorizes "[d]eveloping countries," "with due regard to human rights and their national economy", to determine "to what extent they would guarantee the economic rights recognized in the Covenant to non-nationals."

The principle of non-discrimination in the ESC Covenant has the widest vertical scope: it applies to governmental action at all levels, that is, to the enactment of general laws and the application of such laws to individual cases. On the other hand, this principle has a restricted horizontal scope: it applies only to laws that guarantee or ensure the rights set forth in the ESC Covenant. It is important to point out that these laws are subject to the principle of non-discrimination regardless of the degree to which they realize those rights; as noted, the non-discrimination clauses of the ESC Covenant are not among the provisions of the treaty that are governed by the principle of progressive implementation.

## 4.3 THE SUBSTANTIVE RIGHTS AND UNITED STATES LAW*

*Burns H. Weston*

The purposes of this section are to help clarify the meaning of Articles 6-15 of the ESC Covenant and to comment broadly on the implications of these provisions in relation to United States law.[4] Before proceeding, it is useful to make several preliminary observations.

First, it should be noted that the concept of economic, social, and cultural "rights" was rejected altogether during the years of the Reagan Administration,[5] although, after seven years during which a

* The first draft of this section was prepared by Burns H. Weston, in special cooperation with Clyde W. Summers (arts. 6-11), Frank P. Grad (art. 12), Mark G. Yudof (arts. 13-14), and Paul Laskin (art. 15), and with the general assistance of Nina Shea. The final draft was revised by Joseph P. Grodin (arts. 6-11), Frank P. Grad, with the assistance of Ilise Levy Feitshans, (art. 12), Mark G. Yudof (arts. 13-14), and Stephen P. Marks, with the assistance of Sofia Grushkin, (art. 15), and edited by Hurst Hannum.

4 Art. 1 in the ESC Covenant is identical to art. 1 of the CPR Covenant and is discussed *supra*, sec. 3.3.

5 For example, the instructions to U.S. embassies regarding preparation of the annual "country reports" on human rights observed that inclusion of economic and social data "tended to blur the distinction which it has long been U.S. policy to maintain between fundamental political and civil rights on the one hand and so called 'economic and social rights' on the other. The USG [U.S. Government] has consistently taken the view that economic and social 'rights' are aspirations rather than present obligations and as such are not included in our understanding of the meaning of the term 'internationally recognized human rights'." Cable from the Secretary of State to all diplomatic and consular posts, State 282859 (Nov. 1986), *quoted in Status of U.S. Human Rights Policy, 1987, Hearing before the House Subcomm. on Human Rights and International Organizations,* 100th Cong., 2d Sess. 38-39 (Feb. 19, 1987).

policy might have been formulated, the Assistant Secretary of State for Human Rights and Humanitarian Affairs continued formally to assert that the ESC Covenant remained "under study."[6] Nevertheless, the ESC Covenant remains pending before the Senate for its advice and consent, and no position was ever taken by the Bush Administration on its ratification. Thus, the detailed examination undertaken in the present section seems even more appropriate than it might have been several years ago.

The ESC Covenant, unlike its companion Covenant on Civil and Political Rights, is not geared, with modest exception, to immediate implementation in the sense of instantaneously enforceable or justiciable rights.[7] As provided in Article 2(1), the States Parties undertake only "to take steps...with a view to achieving *progressively* the full realization of the rights recognized in the present Covenant," and then only to the extent of "the maximum of (their) *available* resources."[8] To use the late C. Wilfred Jenks' felicitous phrase, the Covenant is essentially a "promotional convention,"[9] stipulating objectives more than standards, requiring implementation over time rather than all at once. The legal obligation assumed by the States Parties, is, in short, rather like the legal obligation assumed by American society following the Supreme Court's mandate in the 1950s to desegregate "with all deliberate speed."

Despite the promotional character of much of the ESC Covenant, the Carter Administration nevertheless proposed the following "statement of understanding" when submitting the Covenant to the Senate:

> The United States understands paragraph (1) of Article 2 as establishing that the provisions of Articles 1 through 15 of this Covenant describe goals to be achieved progressively rather than through immediate implementation.[10]

[6] *The International Covenants on Human Rights: Prospects on U.S. Ratification, Hearing before the Commission on Security and Cooperation in Europe,* 100th Cong., 2d Sess. 10 (Mar. 29, 1988) (statement of Richard Schifter). Secretary Schifter later clarified that "the under study category means that at this particular point this administration has no position, one way or the other," on either Covenant. *Id.* at 13.

[7] Among the exceptions to this rule in the ESC Covenant are arts. 2(2), 3, and 8, and probably arts. 13(3) and 15(3).

[8] Emphasis added.

[9] Jenks, *The Application of International Labour Conventions by Means of Collective Agreements,* 19 ZEITSCHRIFT FUR AUSLANDISCHES OFFENTLICHES RECHT UND VOLKERRECHT 203 (1958).

[10] *See* Message of the President Transmitting Four Treaties Pertaining to Human Rights, S. Exec. Doc. No. 95-C, D, E & F, 95th Cong., 2d Sess., at ix (1978).

This statement initially appears innocently superfluous in relation to Article 2(1), and, therefore, more or less harmless. However, a closer examination suggests more serious consequences. Having potentially the same practical effect as a "reservation" stricto sensu, it risks contradicting the essential character of certain key Covenant provisions which call for immediate implementation (notably Articles 2(2), 3, and 8; also Articles 13(3) and 15(3)). It also raises the possibility that the obligation "to take steps" would itself become a goal to be realized progressively (i.e., gradually), and as a result it threatens to vitiate the object and purposes of the Covenant as a whole. Such an "understanding" is tantamount to a "reservation" which would be deemed impermissible under Article 19 of the Vienna Convention on the Law of Treaties.[11]

The ESC Covenant has been criticized for not recognizing the right to property proclaimed in Article 17 of the 1948 Universal Declaration of Human Rights. As a matter of legal principle, treaties do not regulate that about which they are silent, so it would be wrong to conclude, as has the Executive Branch, that the right to property is prejudiced by Article 2(3),[12] which authorizes developing countries to determine to what extent they would guarantee to non-nationals the economic rights "recognized in the present Covenant." Moreover, because it is proclaimed a fundamental human right in the Universal Declaration and elsewhere, the right to property is safeguarded by the non-derogation language of Article 5(2). Nevertheless, the Covenant's preparatory history does reveal a divergence of opinion that prevented the adoption of an article on the right to property in the course of drafting.[13] Article 1(2), which affirms the right of all peoples "freely [to] dispose of their natural wealth and resources without prejudice to any obligation arising out of international economic co-operation," and Article 25, which states that "[n]othing in the present Covenant shall be interpreted as impairing the inherent right of all peoples to enjoy and utilize fully and freely their natural wealth and resources," are susceptible of biased interpretation.

[11] *Adopted* 22 May 1969, *entered into force* 27 Jan. 1980, 1155 U.N.T.S. 331. While the Vienna Convention has not yet been ratified by the United States, it is generally accepted as restating customary international law governing international agreements. *See* AMERICAN LAW INSTITUTE, RESTATEMENT (THIRD) OF THE FOREIGN RELATIONS LAW OF THE UNITED STATES (2 vols. 1987) (hereinafter cited as "Restatement") Introductory Note at 144-46, §313 [reservations] at 170-80.

[12] *See* Message of the President, *supra* note 10, at ix.

[13] *See U.N. Annotations, supra* note 1 at 20, para. 24.

Accordingly, given the centrality of private property in American political theory and practice, a qualification concerning the right of property along the lines of the "declaration" and "understanding" proposed by the Executive Branch would seem appropriate.[14] A more accurate statement, as follows, is recommended:

> The United States understands that nothing in the Covenant derogates from the equal obligation of all States to fulfill their responsibilities under international law relative to foreign-owned property, including the obligation to provide just compensation and to ensure that no one shall be otherwise arbitrarily deprived of their property.

This revision would preserve the U.S. position without offending the sensibilities of the other States Parties.

It should be noted that all the economic, social, and cultural rights provided for in the ESC Covenant have been variously recognized not only in the Universal Declaration, but also in several other widely accepted international instruments, such as the 1948 American Declaration on the Rights and Duties of Man (hereinafter "American Declaration"),[15] the 1961 European Social Charter,[16] the 1967 Protocol to the Charter of the Organization of American States (hereinafter "OAS Charter"),[17] and the 1969 American Convention on Human Rights (hereinafter "American Convention").[18]

Finally, the rights provided for in the ESC Covenant span a very broad range of societal concerns and, as a result, they do not lend themselves easily to analysis from the perspective of one legal discipline only. Therefore, the present section reflects the efforts of a number of legal specialists and follows a different format than the section on the substantive rights in the CPR Covenant.

[14] The Executive Branch proposal reads as follows:

> The United States declares that nothing in the Covenant derogates from the equal obligation of all States to fulfill their responsibilities under international law. The United States understands that under the Covenant everyone has the right to own property alone as well as in association with others, and that no one shall be arbitrarily deprived of his property.

Message of the President, *supra* note 10, at ix.

[15] *Signed* 2 May 1948, O.A.S. Off. Rec. OEA/Ser.L/V/II.23, doc. 21, rev. 6 (English 1979).

[16] Signed 18 Oct. 1961, *entered into force* Feb. 26, 1965, 529 U.N.T.S. 89, (1965) Gr. Brit. T.S. No. 38 (Cmd. 2643).

[17] Protocol of Buenos Aires, *signed* 27 Feb. 1967, *entered into force* 27 Feb. 1970, 21 U.S.T. 607, T.I.A.S. No. 6847 (*entered into force for U.S.* 27 Feb. 1970).

[18] *Signed* 22 Nov. 1969, O.A.S.T.S. No. 36, at 1, O.A.S. Off. Rec. OEA/Ser.L/V/II.23, doc. 21, rev. 6 (English 1969).

## ARTICLE 6—RIGHT TO WORK

*Clyde W. Summers, as revised by Joseph P. Grodin*

> 1. The States Parties to the present Covenant recognize the right to work, which includes the right of everyone to the opportunity to gain his living by work which he freely chooses or accepts, and will take appropriate steps to safeguard this right.
>
> 2. The steps to be taken by a State Party to the present Covenant to achieve full realization of this right shall include technical and vocational guidance and training programmes, policies and techniques to achieve steady economic, social and cultural development and full and productive employment under conditions safegarding fundamental political and economic freedoms to the individual.

Under Article 6, the States Parties "recognize" the right to work proclaimed earlier in Article 23 of the Universal Declaration (also in the American Declaration,[19] the European Social Charter,[20] and the revised OAS Charter[21]). Additionally, they commit themselves to "take appropriate steps to safeguard this right," expressly agreeing to specific implementing measures beyond those provided in Article 2, thereby underscoring the importance of the right in question.

### *Analysis of Article 6*

Paragraph 1 stipulates that the right to work "includes," and therefore is not limited to, "the right of everyone to the opportunity to gain his living by work which he freely chooses or accepts." Several definitional inferences follow from this key language: first, that the right to work, being defined in non-exclusive terms, is not limited to remunerative employment; second, that "work" covers all manner of lawful activities which contribute to individual and societal development (a point corroborated by paragraph 2); third, that despite the sex-biased pronouns utilized, access to at least gainful employment is assured without discrimination based on personal identity, opinion, class, or other status in keeping with Articles 2 and 3; and fourth, that,

[19] *Supra* note 15, art. 14.
[20] *Supra* note 16, art. 1.
[21] *Supra* note 17, arts. 31(g), 43(b).

by virtue of the phrase "freely chooses or accepts," the right is intended not to embrace or sanction forced or compulsory labor, an inference which is entirely consistent with Article 8(3) of the CPR Covenant and the International Labour Organisation (ILO) conventions on forced and compulsory labor.[22] Each of these interpretations, supported by the preparatory history of Article 6,[23] can be asserted with confidence.

Somewhat less clear is the extent to which Article 6, in the absence of prohibited discrimination, is meant to guarantee "the right of everyone to the opportunity to gain his living by work which he freely chooses or accepts." Does it mean that every person must be assured a job, the right not to be unemployed? Does it mean that every person must be provided with employment of her or his choice? Does it mean that every person is entitled to work (or to work of one's choice) irrespective of merit and similar qualifications? Does it mean, as the expression "right to work" has evolved politically in the United States, a right to employment completely free of union restraint? Neither the text of Article 6 nor its preparatory history resolves these questions unequivocally, a principal reason being that the drafters consciously left the detailing of Article 6 to the ILO. However, considering the promotional character of the Covenant and judging from the pertinent practice of the ILO (which has been designed more to maximize the opportunities for employment than to guarantee jobs *per se,* let alone jobs of choice and altogether free of restrictions or restraint),[24] the answer to all these questions must be in the negative.

Common sense suggests the same conclusion. Few societies, if any, are so positioned that they can prevent, or even want to prevent, unemployment altogether. None can find it possible, not to mention practicable, to fulfill every vocational desire. Merit and other job

[22] *See* Convention Concerning Forced or Compulsory Labour, (I.L.O. No. 29), *adopted* 28 June 1930, *entered into force* 1 May 1932, 39 U.N.T.S. 55; Convention on the Abolition of Forced Labour, (I.L.O. No. 105), adopted 25 June 1957, *entered into force* 17 Jan. 1959, 320 U.N.T.S. 291.

[23] See *U.N. Annotations, supra* note 1, at 103, paras. 1-3; Report of the Third Committee, 11 UN GAOR Annexes (Agenda Item 31) 2, at 3 (1957), U.N. Doc. A/3525.

[24] *See,* e.g., Fee-Charging Employment Agencies Convention, 1933 (No. 34), ILO, CONVENTIONS AND RECOMMENDATIONS 1919-1966, at 201 (1966); Employment Service Recommendation, 1948 (No. 83), id. at 674; Employment Service Convention, 1948 (No. 88), *id.* at 668; Vocational Guidance Recommendation, 1949 (No. 87), *id.* at 770; Vocational Rehabilitation (Disabled) Recommendation, 1955 (No. 99), *id.* at 858; Vocational Training Recommendation, 1962 (No. 117), *id.* at 1033; Social Policy (Basic Aims and Standards) Convention, 1962 (No. 117), *id.* at 1015; Employment Policy Convention (No. 122) and Recommendation (No. 122), 1964, *id.* at 1097, 1100; Human Resources Development Convention (No. 142) and Recommendation (No. 150), 1975, 58 ILO, OFF. BULL., Ser. A, No. 1, at 32 (1975).

qualifications are routinely approved in licensing laws and equivalent codes to guard against incompetence and abuse. Finally, the right of trade unions to function freely in pursuit of legitimate economic and social interests, as provided for in Article 8, inevitably makes for some, even if at times only minimal, union restraint on employment. In sum, one would err to construe Article 6 too liberally.

Not to be slighted is the overriding purpose of Article 6, which is to commit the States Parties to a course of full and productive employment for all their people to the maximum possible. This promotional objective, which is particularly reflected in paragraph 2, is a logical extension of Article 55(a) of the U.N. Charter, which requires the United Nations to "promote...higher standards of living, full employment, and conditions of economic and social progress and development."[25] Also, it squares completely with the ILO's comprehensive Employment Policy Convention (No. 122) of 1964,[26] which calls upon the parties to declare and pursue an active policy designed to promote full, productive, and freely chosen employment.[27] At the same time, it contrasts sharply with a proposal made during the drafting of the Covenant by the Commission on Human Rights, to wit, "that the right to work should be guaranteed with the object of creating conditions precluding the threat of death from hunger or inanition...."[28] The proposal was rejected for representing too low a standard.[29]

In other words, the essential meaning of Article 6, and therefore the right to work as expressed therein, is that the States Parties must pursue progressively nothing less than the goal of full employment. As stated by the ILO in a report submitted pursuant to Article 18 of the Covenant, referring with approval to the full employment policies and measures detailed in its Employment Policy Convention, "the successful implementation of an active [full] employment policy would lead to the effective safeguarding of [the right to work]."[30]

[25] For an account of the history of the goal of full employment in the United Nations, *see* ASHER, et al., THE UNITED NATIONS AND PROMOTION OF THE GENERAL WELFARE (Brookings Institution, 1957).

[26] *Supra* note 24.

[27] The ILO Governing Body expressed this policy at its 115th, 118th, and 120th sessions and officially communicated its views to the United Nations; *see* U.N. Doc. A/2907/Add.2 (1955).

[28] *See U.N. Annotations, supra* note 1, at 103, paras. 1-3.

[29] *Id.*

[30] Second Report by the Committee of Experts on the Application of Conventions and Recommendations of the International Labour Organisation on Progress in Achieving Observance of the Provisions of Articles 6 to 9 of the International Covenant on Economic, Social and Cultural Rights, U.N. Doc. E/1979/33, at 7 (1979). [Hereinafter cited as "Second

The ILO added, "the degree of realization of the right to work must be judged by examining the policies and measures pursued, and the results achieved."[31]

### *Domestic Implications*

Neither U.S. law nor the U.S. economic system guarantees the right to work in the sense of work for all who are available for and seeking work. Even the traditionally accepted rate of 5% to 9% unemployment in time of "full employment" assumes that substantial numbers of people who want to work will be unable to find work; this would be even more true if the right to work were interpreted to mean the right to a job of one's choice. However, significant steps have been taken toward "achieving progressively" (per Article 2) the full realization of the right to work in the sense of employment for all who desire to work. The Full Employment Act of 1946, for example, declared it to be "the continuing policy and responsibility of the federal government...to coordinate and utilize all its plans, functions, and resources for the purpose of creating and maintaining...conditions under which there will be afforded useful employment opportunities...for those able, willing, and seeking to work...."[32] Similarly, in Section 102 of the Full Employment and Balanced Growth Act of 1978, in yet stronger language, Congress further declared and established "*as a national goal* the fulfillment of *the right* to full opportunities for useful paid employment at fair rates of compensation of all individuals able, willing, and seeking to work."[33] Other more limited governmental policies and programs, including fiscal and monetary ones, echo the same full employment theme (full employment being defined as less than 4% unemployment, so as to account for workers in job transition and those temporarily handicapped).

In view of these legislative and related initiatives to limit unemployment and provide work for the unemployed, including (per paragraph 2) "technical and vocational guidance and training programmes, policies and techniques" such as the several CETA

ILO Report."] *Cf.*, Alston, *The United Nations Specialized Agencies and Implementation of the International Covenant on Economic, Social and Cultural Rights,* 18 COLUM. J. TRANSNAT'L L. 79 (1979).

[31] Second ILO Report, *supra* note 30, at 7.

[32] 15 U.S.C. §1021 (1976).

[33] 15 U.S.C. §1021b (Supp. II, 1978); emphasis added.

programs,[34] it might have been said that, at least until the early 1980s, the United States had been taking steps toward "achieving progressively" the goal of full and productive employment. Since this goal is dependent mainly on the maintenance of a high-level free-market demand for goods and services, one may dispute whether these efforts are correctly designed, whether they are sufficient, and whether any real long-term progress is being made. Much of the safeguarding of the right to work in the United States, particularly in relation to minorities, has been slow and halting, even negative. The priority of the goal tends frequently to be disputed, and there is no denying that, even though almost all countries have come to accept substantial chronic unemployment as virtually inescapable, the guarantee of employment is less secure in the United States than it is in many of the other industrialized countries of the world.[35] Increasing unemployment rates in recent years also undermine U.S. compliance with the full compensation goals and requirements of Article 6.

However, the U.S. record improves when the right to work is considered from the standpoint of deliberate or purposeful limitations on employment. There are, for example, relatively few statutory limitations on employment in the United States. Children under a certain age may be barred from employment generally or from particular kinds of work, but these laws commonly are restricted to persons under 16-18 years of age, and ordinarily they are seen to fulfill the protective goals articulated in Article 10(3). Numerous occupations, trades, and professions require licenses which in turn necessitate apprenticeships and/or schooling, but, for the most part, these licenses and their requirements concern qualifications relevant to competency. In any event, they affect only a small percentage of the work force. While there is no federal statutory protection against discrimination based on political or other opinion, the U.S. Constitution provides such protection for public employees,[36] and some states provide protection for private employees through state constitutions or statutes.[37] The federal Civil Rights Act of 1964 prohibits discrimination in employment because of race, creed, national origin, or sex.[38]

[34] *See generally* Comprehensive Employment and Training Act, 29 U.S.C. §801 et seq. (Supp. II, 1978).

[35] *See generally* M. GANJI, THE REALIZATION OF ECONOMIC, SOCIAL AND CULTURAL RIGHTS: PROBLEMS, POLICIES, PROGRESS 10-14, 207-209, U.N. Sales No. E.75.XIV.2 (1975).

[36] *See, e.g.*, Pickering v. Board of Education, 391 U.S. 563 (1968).

[37] *See, e.g.*, California Labor Code §1101.

[38] *See* 42 U.S.C. §2000e-2(e) (1976).

Much the same can be said about international limitations on employment. Monopolistic restraints on entry into particular occupations, for example, except for licensing requirements, are believed to be few in number. The federal Labor Management Relations Act prohibits unions from requiring membership as a condition of initial employment (the "closed shop"). Only a requirement of membership after the thirtieth day of employment is permitted (the "union shop"), and even then a union may not deny membership to anyone willing to pay uniform initiation fees and dues which are required for performance of the union's collective bargaining role.[39] Workers who object to the use of their dues money for unrelated (e.g., political) purposes may obtain a proportional rebate.[40] In some states, under so-called "right to work" laws, even the union shop is prohibited.[41]

Thus, at least as regards deliberate or purposeful limitations on employment, the right to work probably is more fully secured in the United States than it is in most other countries, including countries which have ratified the Covenant. Overall, even though there exists much room for improvement, U.S. employment policies and programs might be considered to be generally consistent with the intent and spirit of Article 6.

### *Article 6 With or Without Qualification?*

In light of the foregoing, no statement of understanding, declaration, or reservation would seem needed. The gradualist language of Article 2(1) probably affords adequate legal protection against deficiencies in U.S. law and practice, although consistent and continued policies which do not have the goal of achieving full employment would raise serious questions.

[39] *See* 29 U.S.C. §158(a)(3).

[40] *See,* e.g., Chicago Teachers Union, Local No. 1 v. Hudson, 475 U.S. 292 (1986).

[41] *See,* e.g., Retail Clerks v. Scuermesnovym 383 U.S. 746 (1963).

# ARTICLE 7—RIGHT TO JUST AND FAVORABLE CONDITIONS OF WORK

*Clyde W. Summers, as revised by Joseph P. Grodin*

The States Parties to the present Covenant recognize the right of everyone to the enjoyment of just and favourable conditions of work, which ensure, in particular:

(a) Remuneration which provides all workers, as a minimum with:

(i) fair wages and equal remuneration for work of equal value without distinction of any kind, in particular women being guaranteed conditions of work not inferior to those enjoyed by men, with equal pay for equal work;

(ii) a decent living for themselves and their families in accordance with the provisions of the present Covenant;

(b) Safe and healthy working conditions;

(c) Equal opportunity for everyone to be promoted in his employment to an appropriate higher level, subject to no consideration other than those of seniority and competence;

(d) Rest, leisure and reasonable limitation of working hours and periodic holidays with pay, as well as remuneration for public holidays.

Under Article 7, the States Parties "recognize" the right to the enjoyment of just and favorable conditions of work, proclaimed earlier in Articles 23-25 of the Universal Declaration (also in the American Declaration,[42] the European Social Charter,[43] and the revised OAS Charter[44]). In so doing, they commit themselves to a cluster of constituent or subsidiary rights which separately and together imply more a general than a fixed standard: (1) fair wages and equal remuneration for equal work; (2) a decent standard of living for self and family; (3) safe and healthy working conditions; (4) equal opportunity for promotion without discrimination except for seniority and competence; and (5) time for rest and leisure, including periodic holidays with pay.

[42] *Supra* note 20, arts. 14, 15.
[43] *Supra* note 21, arts. 2-4, 7, 8.
[44] *Supra* note 22, arts. 31(g), 43(b).

### *Analysis of Article 7*

Like Article 6, this article is worded generally, although the ILO has established detailed standards relative to conditions of employment through numerous international instruments. For example, while the term "remuneration" is defined simply in terms of "a minimum" of "[f]air wages" and "[a] decent living," it is more fully explained in a number of ILO conventions on the subject, all of which encourage increased real earnings and income.[45] Similarly, while use of the term "workers" in paragraph (a) signals the possibility that Article 7 is meant to refer only to wage earners as distinct from working persons of all sorts, ILO practice makes clear that the drafters had an inclusive rather than narrow definition in mind. Further, a large number of ILO conventions and recommendations have given consistently progressive meaning, from the standpoint of the individual worker, to the words "[s]afe and healthy working conditions,"[46] as per paragraph (b), and the words "[r]est, leisure and reasonable limitation of working hours and periodic holidays with pay,"[47] as per

[45] See, e.g., Minimum Wage-Fixing Machinery Convention, 1928 (No. 26), ILO CONVENTIONS AND RECOMMENDATIONS 1919-1966, at 129 (1966); Minimum Wage-Fixing Machinery (Agriculture) Convention (No. 99) and Recommendation (No. 89), 1951, *id.* at 789, 793; Labour Clauses (Public Contracts) Convention (No. 94) and Recommendation (No. 84), 1949, *id.* at 722, 728; Protection of Wages Convention (No. 95) and Recommendation (No. 85), 1949 *id.* at 729, 735; Minimum Wage-Fixing Convention (No. 131) and Recommendation (No. 135), 1970, 53 ILO OFF. BULL. No. 3, at 260, 269 (1970).

[46] *See, e.g.*, Anthrax Prevention Recommendation, 1919 (No. 3), ILO CONVENTIONS AND RECOMMENDATIONS 1919-1966, at 18 (1966); Lead Poisoning (Women and Children) Recommendation, 1919 (No. 4), *id.* at 19; White Lead (Painting) Convention, 1921 (No. 13), *id.* at 57; Marking of Weight (Packages Transported by Vessels) Convention, 1929 (No. 27), *id.* at 141; Protection against Accidents (Dockers) Convention, 1929 (No. 28), *id.* at 144; Prevention of Industrial Accidents Recommendation, 1929 (No. 31), *id.* at 135; Protection against Accidents (Dockers) Convention (Revised), 1932 (No. 32), *id.* at 183; Safety Provisions (Building) Convention (No. 62) and Recommendation (N. 53), 1937, *id.* at 377 and 383; Protection of Workers' Health Recommendation, 1953 (No. 97), *id.* at 846; Occupational Health Services Recommendation, 1959 (No. 112), *id.* at 987; Radiation Protection Convention (No. 115) and Recommendation (No. 114), 1960, *id.* at 995, 999; Guarding of Machinery Convention (No. 119) and Recommendation (No. 118), 1963, *id.* at 1051, 1057; Hygiene (Commerce and Offices) Convention (No. 120) and Recommendation (No. 120), 1964, *id.* at 1065, 1069; Maximum Weight Convention (No. 127) and Recommendation (No. 128), 1967, 50 ILO OFF. BULL., No. 3, Supp. 1, at 1, 25 (1967); Benzene Convention (No. 136) and Recommendation (No. 144), 1971, 54 ILO OFF. BULL., No. 3, at 246, 255 (1971); Dock Work Convention (No. 137) and Recommendation (No. 145), 1973 56 ILO OFF. BULL., No. 1, at 17, 27 (1973); Occupational Cancer Convention (No. 139) and Recommendation (No. 147), 1974, 57 ILO OFF. BULL., No. 1, at 15, 22 (1974).

[47] *See, e.g.*, Hours of Work (Industry) Convention, 1919 (No. 1), ILO CONVENTIONS AND RECOMMENDATIONS 1919-1966, at 1 (1966); Weekly Rest (Industry) Convention, 1921 (No. 14), *id.* at 60; Night Work (Bakeries) Convention, 1925 (No. 20), *id.* at 95; Hours of Work (Commerce and Offices) Convention, 1930 (No. 30), *id.* at 168; Sheet-Glass Works Convention, 1934 (No. 43), *id.* at 264; Hours of Work (Coal Mines) Convention (Revised) 1935 (No. 46); *id.* at 277; Forty-Hour Week Convention, 1935 (No. 47), *id.* at 283; Reduction of Hours of Work

paragraph (d). In the latter connection, for example, except in respect of agriculture and the maritime fishing and transport industries, the ILO has pressed for a worldwide "social standard" of a 40-hour work week.[48] As noted in the second ILO report under Article 18 of the Covenant, these provisions "imply not a fixed standard of protection, but continuing action for the mobilization of available resources within balanced programmes of social and economic development."[49]

Article 7 is not to be understood only by reference to the work of the ILO. Also helpful is the preparatory work leading up to its adoption, and, in particular, the work of the Commission on Human Rights. Four observations may be made.[50]

First, the phrase "as a minimum" in paragraph (a) is not to be interpreted to mean that efforts relative to the improvement of wage standards may or should stop at some low level. The phrase was inserted to guarantee the peoples of underdeveloped countries at least a minimum.

Second, the explicit guarantee in paragraph (a)(i) of equal conditions of work between men and women is not to be read so as to weaken the protections afforded women elsewhere in the Covenant. The explicit guarantee was inserted at the special request of the Commission on the Status of Women to give added weight to the principle of equal pay for equal work which, it was reported, is not observed faithfully in all countries.[51] Doubts were expressed among the drafters regarding the possibility of the principle's immediate implementation in situations where it is not already operative. Also, the principle was seen not to apply in respect of "family responsibilities." A proposal that "due allowance" be made for "family responsibilities" in applying the principle was discussed but withdrawn.

---

(Glass-Bottle Works) Convention, 1935 (No. 49), *id.* at 292; Reduction of Hours of Work (Public Works) Convention, 1936 (No. 51), *id.* at 310; Holidays with Pay Convention, 1936 (No. 52), *id.* at 314; Reduction of Hours of Work (Textiles) Convention, 1937 (No. 61), *id.* at 371; Hours of Work and Rest Periods (Road Transport) Convention, 1939 (No. 67), *id.* at 449; Holidays with Pay (Agriculture) Convention (No. 101) and Recommendation (No. 93), 1952, *id.* at 805, 810; Holidays with Pay Recommendation, 1954 (No. 98), *id.* at 851; Weekly Rest (Commerce and Offices) Convention (No. 106) and Recommendation (No. 103), 1957, *id.* at 894, 899; Reduction of Hours of Work Recommendation, 1962 (No. 116), *id.* at 1028; Holidays with Pay Convention (Revised), 1970 (No. 132), 53 ILO OFF. BULL., No. 3, at 264 (1970); Paid Educational Leave Convention (No. 140) and Recommendation (No. 148), 1974, 57 ILO OFF. BULL., No. 1, at 18, 27 (1974).

[48] *See,* e.g., Reduction of Hours of Work Recommendation, 1962 (No. 116), ILO CONVENTIONS AND RECOMMENDATIONS 1919-1966, at 1028 (1966).

[49] Second ILO Report, *supra* note 30, at 11.

[50] *See U.N. Annotations, supra* note 1, at 104-105.

[51] Report of the Third Committee, *supra* note 23, at 6.

Third, the phrase "without distinction of any kind" in paragraph (a)(i) means that the principle of equal pay for equal work is not limited to men and women workers only. The principle is meant to apply to cases other than those involving women, including cases involving different races and cases involving nationals and non-nationals.

Fourth, Article 7—in particular, paragraph (a)—does not embrace the right of workers to share in profits or to have their wages fixed in relation to increases in the cost of living. Proposals to this effect were deliberately omitted from Article 7.

Finally, in the unlikely possibility that, despite Article 2(1), any part of Article 7 could be construed to involve individually enforceable rights, the correlative obligations would be the obligations of the employer rather than the State Party (unless, of course, the State Party were also the employer). The obligations of the States Parties are limited to adopting the legislation needed to cause employers to provide just and favorable conditions of work.

### *Domestic Implications*

In light of the foregoing, it would appear that the United States is, generally speaking, in compliance with Article 7. Over the years, there has been a determined, if not always successful, effort to promote just and favorable conditions of work. There exist, however, some shortcomings which merit attention.

#### *Fair Wages*

In general, except for minimum wage legislation, wages in the United States are determined by market forces. Whether the market mechanism itself is fair is a matter of dispute, although generally it is accepted as appropriate among many of the countries which have ratified the Covenant. Of more immediate relevance is one consequence of the market for determining wages in the United States: the collective (unionized) market represents about 15% of the private work force, and the individualized (non-unionized) market represents approximately 85% of the private work force. This results in a substantial wage inequality between unionized workers and workers who are without the benefit of collective bargaining arrangements.[52] This state of affairs probably does not of itself constitute a violation of Article 7, but the unhappy fate of the Labor Law Reform Act of 1978,[53] which was designed to extend the process and benefits of collective bargaining, suggests at least a present inability and possibly even an unwillingness to guarantee absolutely the principle of "equal remuneration for work of equal value without distinction of any kind" as set forth in Article 7. On the other hand, as evidenced by the Equal Pay Act of 1963,[54] as well as by a variety of anti-discrimination laws at the federal, state and local levels, the United States does appear to be committed to equal pay for equal work for men and women and people of different races, nationalities, and the like. Of course, it must be recognized that women and other minorities earn, on the average, less than white males. Problems of interpretation and enforcement do exist. But the basic principle of equal pay for equal work is now fully accepted.

### *A Decent Living*

In keeping with paragraph (a) of Article 7, which requires the States Parties to ensure all workers "as a minimum, with...[a] decent living for themselves and their families...," the Fair Labor Standards Act of 1938 now provides for a minimum wage of $4.25 per hour,[55] an increase of $4.00 since the Act first entered into force. It is possible, however, that this legislation is not adequate to the purposes of paragraph (a). In the first place, while there is some measurable progress toward achieving complete coverage, not all workers are covered by the Act. Agricultural employees, for example, are specifically exempt; because the law extends only to employees engaged in interstate commerce, it is not applicable to small employers engaged in purely local business and does not reach domestic or household workers. More problematic, however, is the level of the minimum wage. The present federal minimum provides a full-time worker with an annual income of approximately $8,600, but the federal government's own data indicate that 166% of this amount is

[52] Even more significantly, many of those who are legally protected do not have collective bargaining because of employer opposition, ineffective law enforcement, social attitudes, and other reasons.

[53] The Labor Law Reform Act of 1978 died in Senate debate.

[54] *See* 29 U.S.C. §206(d) (1976).

[55] *See* 29 U.S.C. §206.

substantially less than what is required for a minimum standard of living for a family of four in an urban area. By its own definition of "a decent living," thus, the United States may be out of step with Article 7. If the United States ratified the Covenant it might arguably be obliged to increase the minimum wage at a rate faster than the increase in the cost of living. On the other hand, real average hourly earnings in the United States have increased substantially over the last decade and employers, especially in recent years, have added significantly to total compensation by substantially increasing contributions to social insurance, pensions, benefits, and the like. On balance, therefore, even while admitting to certain deficiencies, it is possible to contend that United States law and policy basically comport with the "decent living" goals of Article 7.

### *Safe and Healthy Working Conditions*

The general legal principle that employers are obliged to provide safe and healthy working conditions is accepted in the United States. The principle has long been given expression in a web of statutes, particularly at the state level, and in 1970, via the Occupational Safety and Health Act (OSHA), Congress sought "to assure so far as possible every working man and woman in the Nation [with] safe and healthy working conditions....[56] This goal, as might be expected, has yet to be achieved. Enforcement still is not adequate. But it can fairly be said that the United States is "achieving progressively" (per Article 2) the purposes of paragraph (b).

### *Equal Opportunity for Promotion*

Federal laws which prohibit discrimination in employment on various grounds—such as race, sex, religion, national origin, handicap, and union membership or activity—apply to promotional decisions. The federal Constitution and some state constitutions limit the extent to which promotion may be denied on the basis of political affiliation or activity. And, some state laws protect against other forms of status discrimination, such as marital status or sexual preference. Such laws further the general objective of paragraph (c), but none go so far as to exclude all considerations other than seniority and competence.

[56] *See* 29 U.S.C. §651(b) (1976).

exclude all considerations other than seniority and competence. Federal and state civil service laws do protect that general principle, but they apply only to certain categories of public employees. Collective agreements under the NLRA also typically provide the general protection contemplated by paragraph (c), but they are applicable to less than 15% of the private work force.

*Rest, Leisure, etc.*

The United States legal system is virtually silent in respect of the rights mentioned in paragraph (d). While there are miscellaneous provisions, mainly at the state level, limiting work hours and requiring rest periods in certain occupations (such as in mining and in common carrier operations), there is no general acceptance of the principle that the law should limit the number of hours in a day, week, month, or year which an employee can be required to work. Thus, the so-called "maximum hour" provisions of the Fair Labor Standards Act of 1938[57] and other statutes are misnamed. Rather than limit work hours, they require only that hours in excess of the maximum be paid at a higher—usually "time and a half"—rate, with the result that employers are free to demand any number of hours of work subject only to overtime rates. It is true that the rights mentioned in paragraph (d) are commonly protected in collective bargaining agreements and that limited work hours and periodic rest periods, including paid vacations, are increasingly a part of the fabric of American life. Nevertheless, collective agreements reach only 15% of the private work force, as indicated, and there has been no substantial discussion or even suggestion that the law should otherwise extend limitations on work hours or that it should otherwise require vacations with pay. In these respects, the United States is well behind other free market economies which have legally guaranteed these rights.

### *Article 7 With or Without Qualification?*

Despite the shortcomings noted, the gradualist language of Article 2(1) affords adequate legal protection against any deficiencies in United States law and practice.

[57] *See* 29 U.S.C. §207 (1976).

## ARTICLE 8—TRADE UNION RIGHTS

*Clyde W. Summers, as revised by Joseph P. Grodin*

1. The States Parties to the present Covenant undertake to ensure:

(a) The right of everyone to form trade unions and join the trade union of his choice, subject only to the rules of the organization concerned, for the promotion and protection of his economic and social interests. No restrictions may be placed on the exercise of this right other than those prescribed by law and which are necessary in a democratic society in the interests of national security or public order or for the protection of the rights and freedoms of others;

(b) The right of trade unions to establish national federations of confederations and the right of the latter to form or join international trade-union organizations;

(c) The right of trade unions to function freely subject to no limitations other than those prescribed by law and which are necessary in a democratic society in the interests of national security or public order or for the protection of the rights and freedoms of others;

(d) The right to strike, provided that it is exercised in conformity with the laws of the particular country.

2. This article shall not prevent the imposition of lawful restrictions on the exercise of these rights by members of the armed forces or of the police or of the administration of the State.

3. Nothing in this article shall authorize States Parties to the International Labour Organisation Convention of 1948 concerning Freedom of Association and Protection of the Right to Organize to take legislative measures which would prejudice, or apply the law in such a manner as would prejudice, the guarantees provided for in that Convention.

Under Article 8, the States Parties "undertake to ensure" the right to form trade unions and to engage in trade union activity, proclaimed earlier in Article 23(4) of the Universal Declaration (also in the American Declaration,[58] the European Social Charter,[59] the revised

[58] *Supra* note 15, art. 22.
[59] *Supra* note 16, arts. 4, 5, 6.

OAS Charter,[60] and the American Convention[61]). The specific provisions of Article 8, which detail both individual and collective trade union rights, also are embraced by the more general language of Article 22 of the CPR Covenant concerning the right to freedom of association.

### *Analysis of Article 8*

As with the rights set forth in the two preceding articles, the trade union rights enumerated in Article 8 have been of fundamental and continuing concern to the ILO. One important illustration is the ILO's 1948 Convention Concerning Freedom of Association and Protection of the Right to Organize (No. 87),[62] to which express reference is made in paragraph 3. Another is the ILO's Right to Organize and Collective Bargaining Convention (No. 98) of 1949.[63] It is to these two conventions (both of which effect the exercise of the rights set out in Article 8), as well as to other relevant ILO conventions[64] and to the preparatory history leading up to Article 8, that one looks to clarify the meaning of Article 8.

In contrast to the other rights advanced by the Covenant, those embraced by Article 8 were intended by the drafters to be implemented immediately rather than "progressively." The view prevailed that the States Parties need only "ensure" (as opposed to "recognize") the free exercise of the right to form and join trade unions; no action, only non-interference with trade unions, was needed from States to guarantee the right.[65] "The recognition and realization of these rights is not dependent on availability of resources, but should represent an important contribution to the harnessing of the energies and support of the productive forces in society to the development process."[66] Thus, the "statement of understanding" proposed by President Carter

[60] *Supra* note 17, art. 43(c).

[61] *Supra* note 18, art. 16.

[62] *Adopted* 9 July 1948, *entered into force* 4 July 1950, 68 U.N.T.S. 17.

[63] *Adopted* 1 July 1949, *entered into force* 11 July 1951, 96 U.N.T.S. 257.

[64] *See,* in addition, Right of Association (Agriculture) Convention, 1921 (No. 11), ILO, CONVENTIONS AND RECOMMENDATIONS 1919-1966, at 52 (1966); Right of Association (Non-Metropolitan Territories) Convention, 1947 (No. 84), Id. at 649. Also: Workers' Representatives Convention (No. 135) and Recommendation (No. 143), 1971, 54 ILO OFF. BULL., No. 3, at 243, 251 (1971); Rural Workers' Organisations Convention (No. 141) and Recommendation (No. 149), 1975, 58 ILO OFF. BULL., Ser. A, No. 1, at 28, 43 (1975).

[65] *See U.N. Annotations, supra* note 1, at 106; Report of the Third Committee, *supra* note 23, at 69.

[66] Second ILO report, *supra* note 30, at 12.

relative to the implementation of the Covenant and discussed briefly at the beginning of this section conflicts directly with Article 8; it should be discarded or amended.[67]

Second, the word "everyone" at the outset of paragraph 1(a), which is subject to possible restriction via the second sentence of the same provision and the terms of paragraph 2, is probably to be interpreted liberally so as to include employers as well as employees. The matter is not altogether clear. According to the preparatory work of the Commission on Human Rights, Article 8 was not intended to govern the rights of employers,[68] and the Third Committee drafters could not agree on the meaning of the term.[69] The standard-setting practice of the ILO, however, indicates that an inclusive definition is proper. Both the 1948 ILO Convention No. 87 and the 1949 ILO Convention No. 98 refer to employers and employees, and, according to paragraph 3, Article 8 is not to be interpreted or applied in any way prejudicial to ILO Convention No. 87.

Next, regarding the phrase "of his choice," also in the first sentence of paragraph 1(a), some of the drafters from the Commission on Human Rights feared a limitation on the rights of unions to control their internal organization, particularly in relation to qualifications for membership.[70] However, judging from the first sentence in its entirety and from ILO practice relative to Conventions No. 87 and No. 98, the fear was unfounded. Under Article 8, trade unions are expected to have broad competence to manage their internal affairs—subject, however, to the requirements of a "democratic society" as per the second sentence of paragraph 1(a).

The above leads to the further observation that paragraphs (a) and (c) of paragraph 1—but not paragraph (b)—authorize general welfare and public order limitations upon the free exercise of the trade unionist rights provided for therein, and in so doing supplement the equivalent but more general language of Article 4 qualifying the entire Covenant (presumably to promote the Covenant among countries hesitant about trade union activity). Also to be noted is that

[67] It is, moreover, questionable how much would be gained by the "statement of understanding," given that art. 22 of the CPR Covenant, which addresses immediately enforceable rights, protects the right to freedom of association (including "the right to form and join trade unions") in any event.

[68] *See U.N. Annotations, supra* note 1, at 106.

[69] Report of the Third Committee, *supra* note 23, at 10-11.

[70] *See U.N. Annotations, supra* note 1, at 106.

these paragraphs partially parallel the terms of Article 22(2) of the CPR Covenant relative to the right to freedom of association. Whereas Article 22(2) expressly authorizes limitations for "the protection of public health or morals," Article 8 does not. The question therefore arises whether a State could properly invoke the broader language of Article 22(2) in an effort to limit trade union activity. The answer is probably no. According to the preparatory history bearing upon the two provisions, Article 22 is concerned with the right of peaceful assembly (as well as with the right to form and join trade unions), whereas Article 8 is not, and the "public health and morals" language was seen to deal with the former right.[71] This conclusion would be consistent with the expansive social purposes of Article 8.

Paragraph 2 of Article 8 also allows limitations on trade union rights, authorizing lawful restrictions on the exercise of such rights "by members of the armed forces or of the police or of the administration of the State." Article 8(2) is entirely compatible with ILO Convention No. 83 in respect of the first two categories of persons mentioned, since, under Article 9 of Convention No. 83, members of the armed forces and the police may be barred from forming and joining trade unions. In the case of members of government civil service, however, the Covenant and the ILO Convention are at odds, the former potentially curtailing and the latter guaranteeing the enjoyment of trade unionist rights among civil servants and other such governmental employees. Of course, as is made clear by paragraph 3, the restrictions permitted by ESC Covenant Article 8(2) cannot affect the obligation under ILO Convention No. 87 to guarantee trade unionist rights to members of the public administration. For States which have not ratified Convention No. 87, however, the opportunity to curb trade unionist rights is obviously broadened, a criticism raised by some of the drafters in the Third Committee who viewed Article 8(2) as prejudicial to the development of trade union rights in countries where large numbers of people are employed in State enterprises.[72]

[71] Report of the Third Committee, *supra* note 23, at 10.

[72] *Id.* It was argued that restrictions upon trade union rights should not be imposed according to labor classifications, but according to the degree of danger that trade union activity might pose for society. According to the Swedish delegate to the Third Committee, for example, a strike by power station engineers could be more threatening than a strike by police. However, there appears to be no uniform practice on these matters.

The drafters saw the right to strike (paragraph 1(d)) as vital for the protection of the economic and social interests of workers, to counterbalance the power of the State and the relatively more advantageous position usually occupied by employers.[73] However, the exercise of the right to strike was seen as only one among many options through which trade union interests might be defended, with stress being placed upon the strike as one of last resort, to be invoked only after all conciliatory procedures had failed.[74] Also, as implied by the provisional language of paragraph 1(d), the drafters thought it permissible to limit the right to strike in the case of public emergency or essential services.[75] However, such limitations would necessarily have to be narrowly drawn and temporary in character; no general or permanent prohibition of strikes could be tolerated without running afoul of the intent, if not the actual letter, of the Covenant and of ILO Convention No. 87.[76]

In sum, Article 8 requires States Parties to extend the maximum deference possible, consistent with the interests of national security and public order in a democratic society, to individuals and to trade unions choosing to participate in national and international trade union activity. This participation, in addition, must be consistent with the rights and freedoms of others.

### *Domestic Implications*

The law in the United States, both federal and state, probably can be viewed as conforming fully with the terms of Article 8. The nature of this congruity may be observed in respect of each of the four rights articulated.

#### *The Right to Form and Join Trade Unions*

The First Amendment constitutionally protects the right to form and join trade unions as an exercise of freedom of expression and of assembly. Except for members of the armed forces (whose trade union rights are uncertain but who would be subject to restriction under Article 8(2) in any event), all workers, both public and private and including police, are entitled to form and join trade unions.[77]

[73] Report of the Third Committee, *supra* note 23, at 10.

[74] *See U.N. Annotations, supra* note 1, at 106, para. 15.

[75] *See id.*

[76] *See* Second ILO Report, *supra* note 30, at 14-15.

[77] *See,* e.g., 29 U.S.C. §§151, 157 and 185(a)(1) (1976); O'Brien v. Leidinger, 452 F.Supp. 720 (1978); Johnson v. City of Albany, Ga., 413 F.Supp. 782 (1976); Lontine v. Van Cleave, 483 F.2d

However, this constitutional right to form and join trade unions does not necessarily carry with it the right to take action "for the promotion and protection of [one's] economic interests" as per Article 8(1). Such is the case, for example, in respect of public employees, who have no federal constitutional right to engage in collective bargaining, to make and enforce collective agreements, or to engage in strikes; and in most states, as well as under federal law, they actually are barred from striking.[78] However, this is permissible under Article 8(2).

The right to form and join trade unions is not only constitutionally protected against governmental restraint in the United States, it is protected by statute against employer restraints as well. The 1935 National Labor Relations Act[79] and the 1947 Labor Management Relations Act[80] provide protection for all workers reached under the Commerce Clause who wish to organize into trade unions and guarantee the right of such unions to bargain with their employers. Parallel state acts in a number of states protect workers not covered by these and other federal statutes. A later federal law is the Labor-Management Reporting and Disclosure Act of 1959,[81] under which certain basic rights are guaranteed to trade union members, including the right to nominate candidates for union leadership, to vote in elections or referendums of the labor organization, and to attend membership meetings. Somewhat lesser protection of these rights is given under the common law in most states.

It should be acknowledged that the legal protection afforded to union membership and activity by American law is often of limited efficacy. The law permits employers to voice opposition to unions, so long as they refrain from "threat, restraint, or coercion," and the remedies which the law provides against unlawful activity may be insufficient to deter an employer who is determined to avoid unionization. Many scholars believe that employer opposition, including illegal activity, accounts for much of the decline in union organization in the last decades.

---

966 (1973); United Federation of Postal Clerks v. Blount, 325 F.Supp. 879 (D.C.D.C. 1971), *affirmed without opinion,* 404 U.S. 802 (1971).

[78] Strikes by federal employees are prohibited by statute 5 U.S.C. §7311. For discussion of constitutional issues, *see* United Federation of Postal Clerks v. Blount, *supra* note 83. State law or constitutions may permit public employee strikes in some situations. *See,* e.g., Long Beach City Employees Association v. City of Long Beach, 719 P.2d 660 (Cal. Sup. Ct. 1986).

[79] *See* 29 U.S.C. §151 et seq. (1976).

[80] *See* 29 U.S.C. §141 et seq. (1976).

[81] *See* 29 U.S.C. §§153, 158-160, 164, 186-187, 401 et seq. (1976).

It should also be acknowledged that the whole collective bargaining system as legally constituted in the United States might be viewed by some as violating the right of an individual to join the trade union "of his choice," as provided in paragraph 1(a). Under the various federal and state labor relations statutes, a union selected by a majority of the employees of a given bargaining unit becomes the exclusive representative of all employees in that unit, and this means that some employees are legally compelled to be represented by a union they did not choose. To be sure, an employee is not always required to join the majority union, nor is the employee prohibited from retaining membership in a minority union. Strictly speaking, he or she thus may retain the right to join the union of choice. Nevertheless, the employee does not have free choice of the union which is to promote and protect his or her economic and social interests, and under certain circumstances an employee may even be compelled to pay union dues to the majority union. But, on final analysis, this manner of limiting the rights of the individual in favor of the rights of the collectivity probably is a restriction "prescribed by law" which would be deemed, per paragraph 1(a), "necessary in a democratic society...for the protection of the rights and freedoms of others," and therefore within the scope of Article 8. It may also be noted that, though the exclusive representation rule is unique to the United States, most Western European countries have legal regimes with some parallel or analogous legal consequences.[82]

### *The Right of Trade Unions to Confederate*

There are no legal limitations in the United States on the right of trade unions to establish national federations or confederations, or to form or join international trade union organizations. This right is, in fact, freely exercised, with control entirely in the hands of the trade union movement.[83]

[82] *But cf.* Young, James & Webster v. U.K., Eur. Ct. Human Rts. Judgment of 13 Aug. 1981, Ser. A No. 44 (finding contrary to the European Convention of Human Rights a "closed shop" arrangement which required existing non-union employees to join a specified union).

[83] One arguable exception is the provision in §9(c) of the National Labor Relations Act, which prohibits the National Labor Relations Board from certifying as the majority representative of employees who work as guards, any union which is affiliated directly or indirectly with an organization which admits employees other than guards. *See* 292 U.S.C. §159(c) (1976). Thus, a union of guards affiliated with the American Federation of Labor could not be certified by the N.L.R.B. as the statutory representative. Such a union could continue to exist and bargain collectively, but it would lose important legal and practical advantages which come from N.L.R.B. certification.

### *The Right of Trade Unions to Function Freely*

The Labor-Management Reporting and Disclosure Act of 1959,[84] which has no equivalent in any of the major industrial countries, is the principal legislation governing trade union operations in the United States. Pursuant to this law, unions are required to make financial reports; the use of union funds is restricted to union purposes; the timing and conducting of union elections is subjected to extensive regulation; the imposition of trusteeships on local unions is limited; and the right of union members to basic democratic rights within the union is guaranteed. These limitations and restrictions do narrow the field within which trade unions may "function freely," but they do so in order to guarantee minimum democratic procedures in union decision-making and to ensure that unions are responsive to the will of their members. Within these limitations, unions remain free to design their own internal organization, to fix their own dues, to determine how their monies shall be spent, to choose their own officers (except from among persons convicted of crimes), and to make their own substantive decisions concerning collective bargaining, social policy, and political action.[85] The 1959 Act appears to fit clearly within the restrictions which would be deemed, per paragraph 1(c), "necessary in a democratic society...for the protection of the rights and freedoms of others."

### *The Right to Strike*

There are numerous limitations on the right to strike in the United States. As noted, strikes by public employees are banned by federal law and in most states. The Labor Management Relations Act prohibits certain kinds of strikes, such as "secondary" strikes (a strike against a "neutral" employer to force it to cease doing business with an employer in dispute with the union) and "jurisdictional" strikes (designed to force an employer to assign particular work to members

[84] 29 U.S.C. §§153, 158-160, 164, 186-187, 401 et seq.

[85] Except insofar as it limits the use of union dues for political purposes, U.S. law imposes no legal limitations on union political activity that it does not impose on corporations. The Corrupt Practices Act of 1925, 18 U.S.C. §610 (1976), prohibits unions from using union dues to support the election of any candidate for federal office, and laws in some states put similar limitations on expenditures in state elections. But since equivalent limitations are placed on political contributions by business corporations, this restriction would seem to fall within the area of permissible restrictions authorized by para. 1(c).

of one union rather than another).[86] It also prohibits strikes to enforce demands not related to wages and working conditions, e.g., to achieve wider "political" objectives,[87] and strikes in breach of no-strike provisions contained or implied in most collective bargaining agreements.[88] The Act also permits the federal Executive Branch to seek an 80-day "cooling off" injunction against a strike deemed to "imperil the national health and safety."[89] Of course, even where a strike is legally permitted, strikers run the risk of losing their jobs through permanent replacement.[90]

Subject to these legal and practical limitations, however, workers in the private sector retain the right to strike for higher wages or better working conditions upon the expiration of an agreement, and public employees may have access to some alternative means (such as binding arbitration) of resolving their labor disputes. These limitations certainly fall within the almost illusory guarantee in Article 8(1)(d) of the right to strike, "provided that it is exercised in conformity with the laws of the particular country."

### *Article 8 With or Without Qualification?*

The statement of understanding proposed by the Executive Branch relative to the implementation of the Covenant conflicts directly with Article 8, and for this and other reasons it should be eliminated. No statement of understanding, declaration, or reservation is needed to protect United States interests that cannot be handled by the general welfare and public order limitations already included in Article 8.

## ARTICLE 9—RIGHT TO SOCIAL SECURITY

*Clyde W. Summers, as revised by Joseph P. Grodin*

The States Parties to the present Covenant recognize the right of everyone to social security, including social insurance.

[86] 29 U.S.C. §158(b)(4).
[87] 29 U.S.C. §158(b)(3).
[88] *See* Local 174, Teamsters v. Lucas Flour Co., 369 U.S. 95 (1962).
[89] 29 U.S.C. §183.
[90] *See,* e.g., N.L.R.B. v. Mackay Radio & Telegraph Co., 304 U.S. 333 (1938).

Under Article 9, the shortest and most general article in the Covenant, the States Parties "recognize" the right to social security, more or less proclaimed earlier in Articles 23(3) and 25(1) of the Universal Declaration (also in the American Declaration,[91] the European Social Charter,[92] and the revised OAS Charter).[93] By using the Universal Declaration as a preliminary guide, the drafters appear to have committed themselves to the progressive realization (per Article 2) of some form of security in the event of unemployment, sickness, disability, widowhood, old age, "or other lack of livelihood in circumstances beyond [one's] control."

### *Analysis of Article 9*

The drafters' discussions of Article 9 centered on whether and how to define "social security" and on the issue of the optimum cost distribution of social security schemes. Much of the discussion of the matter of definition turned on whether it was desirable to elaborate various aspects of social security. It was debated, for instance, whether "social security" was as wide in scope as "social welfare" and whether it included "social insurance."[94] Various texts were proposed, and, at one point, the term "social security" was interpreted broadly so as to include not only social insurance but also family allowances and other means of social protection.[95] In the end, however, the majority of the drafters, with support from the ILO, determined that to elaborate the various aspects of social security would be undesirable, if not impossible. It was generally felt that, because of differences in State practice, there could be no agreement on the risks to be covered; that to be explicit or exhaustive might deny States freedom to approach the problem as they see fit which, in turn, could have a chilling effect; and that the concept of social security is continually developing and therefore to be understood in broad terms. Also, the drafters were aware of the definitional problems that had been encountered in the drafting of the 1952 ILO Convention (No. 102) on Social Security (Minimum Standards) which, together with other ILO social security conventions and recommendations,[96] now serve as a guide to

[91] *Supra* note 15, at 16.
[92] *Supra* note 16, art. 12, 13.
[93] *Supra* note 17, art. 43(a) and (h).
[94] *See U.N. Annotations, supra* note 1, at 107.
[95] *Id.*
[96] *See,* e.g., Workmen's Compensation (Agriculture) Convention, 1921 (No. 12), ILO, CONVENTIONS AND RECOMMENDATIONS 1919-1966, at 54 (1966); Workmen's Compensation (Accidents) Convention, 1925 (No. 17), *id.* at 81; Workmen's Compensation (Occupational Diseases) Convention, 1925 (No. 18) *id.* at 88; Equality of Treatment (Accident Compensation) Convention, 1925 (No. 19), *id.* at 92; Sickness Insurance (Industry) Convention, 1927 (no. 24), *id.*

achievement for the range of risks for which protection is deemed appropriate and the kind and level of benefits which are considered desirable.[97]

On the other hand, the drafters were very clear about who, as a matter of right, should be entitled to social security. The word "everyone" is to be taken literally. This wording was preferred to an alternative formulation which spoke of the right to social security not for everyone but, more specifically, of workers and salaried employees.[98]

Methods of financing social security were debated at length in both the Commission on Human Rights and the Third Committee. A proposal put forward by the Soviet Union, according to which the cost would be borne by the State or the employer or both without contribution by the person benefitted, was rejected, on the grounds that it ignored the diversity of systems prevailing in different countries.[99] Accordingly, the issue of financing was left to the discretion of each State party. The substantial experience of the ILO provides a rich, though not necessarily determinative, precedent for developing policies and programs.[100]

### *Domestic Implications*

The United States complies with Article 9 in an adequate, if unfulfilled, fashion. Considering the general terms of the provision and the liberal options afforded by its preparatory history, it would be difficult to contend otherwise. By most Western European standards, the social security and social insurance system of the United States is

at 117; Sickness Insurance (Agriculture) Convention, 1927 (No. 25), *id.* at 121; Old-Age Insurance (Industry, etc.) Convention, 1933 (No. 35), *id.* at 207; Old-Age Insurance (Agriculture) Convention, 933 (No. 36), *id.* at 214; Invalidity Insurance (Industry, etc.) Convention, 1933 (No. 37), *id.* at 220; Invalidity Insurance (Agricultural) Convention, 1933 (No. 38), *id.* at 227; Survivors' Insurance (Industry, etc.) Convention, 1933 (No. 39), *id.* at 234; Survivors' Insurance (Agriculture) Convention, 1933 (No. 40), *id.* at 242; Unemployment Provision Convention, 1934 (No. 44), *id.* at 267; Equality of Treatment (Social Security) Convention, 1962 (No. 118), *id.* at 1022; Employment Injury Benefits Convention, 1964 (No. 121), *id.* at 1080; Invalidity, Old-Age and Survivors' Benefits Convention, 1967 (No. 128), 50 ILO OFF. BULL., No. 3, Supp. 1, at 4 (1967); Medical Care and Sickness Benefits Convention, 1969 (No. 130), 52 ILO OFF. BULL., No. 3, at 234 (1969).

[97] The definitional hurdles were perhaps a bit exaggerated. *Cf.* European Code of Social Security (with Annex and Addenda), *opened for signature,* 16 Apr. 1968, Parts II-X, 648 U.N.T.S. 235, 242-272, wherein "social security" is interpreted to include sickness, maternity, invalidity, survivor, unemployment, and family benefits, as well as old-age assistance.

[98] *See U.N. Annotations, supra* note 1, at 107.

[99] *See id. See also* Report of the Third Committee, *supra* note 23, at 12.

[100] *See* e.g., the ILO conventions cited *supra* note 96.

seriously deficient. It is inequitable both in giving unequal benefits and in applying irrational qualification requirements. It is inadequate in not guaranteeing even bare sustenance to certain groups, and it is incomplete because some individuals are unable to qualify for certain needed benefits. Nevertheless, in offering an array of cash benefits and other assistance to individuals and families from before-the-cradle to after-the-grave—for low-income, unemployment, sickness, disability, widowhood, old age, and like conditions—the United States is likely to meet the very general requirements of Article 9.[101]

### *Article 9 With or Without Qualification?*

Despite the inadequacies of the United States social security system, no statement of understanding, declaration, or reservation would seem needed. Upon ratification of the Covenant, the United States would commit itself only to some relatively undefined kind of social security system for all. Moreover, the gradualist language of Article 2(1) affords protection against current deficiencies in United States law and practice.

## ARTICLE 10—RIGHTS RELATING TO PROTECTION OF THE FAMILY

*Clyde W. Summers, as revised by Joseph P. Grodin*

The States Parties to the present Covenant recognize that:

1. The widest possible protection and assistance should be accorded to the family, which is the natural and fundamental group unit of society, particularly for its establishment and while it is responsible for the care and education of dependent children. Marriage must be entered into with the free consent of the intending spouses.

2. Special protection should be accorded to mothers during a reasonable period before and after childbirth. During such period working mothers should be accorded paid leave or leave with adequate social security benefits.

[101] *Accord,* COMM'N ON SECURITY AND COOPERATION IN EUROPE, FULFILLING OUR PROMISES: THE UNITED STATES AND THE HELSINKI FINAL ACT—A STATUS REPORT 95-97, 117 (November 1979).

> 3. Special measures of protection and assistance should be taken on behalf of all children and young persons without any discrimination for reasons of parentage or other conditions. Children and young persons should be protected from economic and social exploitation. Their employment in work harmful to their morals or health or dangerous to life or likely to hamper their normal development should be punishable by law. States should also set age limits below which the paid employment of child labour should be prohibited and punishable by law.

Under Article 10, the States Parties "recognize" that the family ("the natural and fundamental group unit of society") and the related statuses of marriage, motherhood, and childhood deserve special protection and assistance. There are counterparts in Articles 16 and 25 of the Universal Declaration as well as in the American Declaration,[102] the European Social Charter,[103] and the American Convention.[104] Many of its themes are embraced also by Articles 23 and 24 of the CPR Covenant, thus attesting to the article's importance as an expression of global social policy.

### *Analysis of Article 10*

A proper understanding of Article 10 must begin with the observation that it speaks in hortatory—not mandatory—language. Thus, protection and assistance "should be" accorded to the family, to mothers, and to children and young persons. The words "shall" and "will" are conspicuously absent, as is the word "right." The legal commitments assumed by the States Parties may be seen as only minimal, particularly in light of the gradualist language of Article 2(1).

The substantive generality of the text does little or nothing to offset this conclusion. By and large, the exhortations which comprise the article leave a great deal to interpretation. But looking beyond the text, it is possible to discern at least the basic policies and programs which Article 10 is intended to serve. For example, numerous ILO conventions and recommendations pertaining to the employment of women, children, and young persons provided a valuable guide to the community expectations which inform paragraphs 2 and 3.[105]

[102] *Supra* note 15, arts. 5-7.

[103] *Supra* note 16, arts. 7, 8, 16, and 17.

[104] *Supra* note 18, arts. 17, 19.

[105] *See*,e.g., Maternity Protection Convention, 1919 (No. 3), ILO, CONVENTIONS AND RECOMMENDATIONS 1919-1966, at 12 (1966); Night Work (Women) Convention, 1919 (No. 4), *id.* at 15; Minimum Age (Industry) Convention, 1919 (No. 5), *id.* at 22; Night Work of Young Persons (Industry) Convention, 1919 (No. 6), *id.* at 25; Minimum Age (Agriculture) Convention, 1921 (No. 10), *id.* at 47; Minimum Age (Non-Industrial Employment) Convention (No. 33) and Recommendation, 1932 (No. 41), *id.* at 193, 198; Night Work (Women) Convention (Revised),

Helpful, too, is the preparatory work of the Commission on Human Rights and the Third Committee, particularly as regards the key terms "family," "mothers," and "children and young persons."

Because paragraph 1, which addresses the protection of the family, evinces concern for the institution of marriage, one naturally might suppose that the word "family" refers to a marital unit. This is not the case. According to the drafters, to be entitled to protection and assistance, the family need not be "based on marriage." The Third Committee deleted this phrase from the Draft Covenant to protect children born out of wedlock (an intent made explicit in paragraph 3).[106]

The term "mothers" was adopted by the Third Committee in lieu of the term "motherhood." Among the drafters from the Commission on Human Rights, the latter term had come to signify maternal responsibility for the development of a child during its early years.[107] By adopting the term "mothers," the Third Committee saw the Covenant as guaranteeing a more limited "special protection," i.e., one restricted to the period of pregnancy and nursing.[108] This "special protection" was considered to be without prejudice to a mother's working or non-working status. However, it should be noted that

---

1934 (No. 41), *id.* at 257; Underground Work (Women) Convention, 1935 (No. 45), *id.* at 275; Minimum Age (Industry) Convention (Revised), 1937 (No. 59), *id.* at 353; Minimum Age (Non-Industrial Employment) Convention (Revised), 1937 (No. 60), *id.* at 365; Medical Examination of Young Persons (Industry) Convention, 1946 (No. 77), *id.* at 585; Medical Examination of Young Persons (Non-Industrial Occupations) Convention, 1946 (No. 78), *id.* at 590; Medical Examination of Young Persons Recommendation, 1946 (No. 79), *id.* at 595; Night Work of Young Persons (Non-Industrial Occupations) Convention (No. 79) and Recommendation (No. 80), 1946, *id.* at 599, 604; Night Work (Women) Convention (Revised), 1948 (No. 89), *id.* at 679; Night Work of Young Persons (Industry) Convention (Revised), 1948 (No. 90), *id.* at 683; Equal Remuneration Convention (No. 100) and Recommendation (No. 90), 1951, *id.* at 795; 799; Maternity Protection Convention (Revised) (No. 103) and Recommendation (No. 95), 1952, *id.* at 835, 841; Discrimination (Employment and Occupation) Convention (No. 111) and Recommendation (No. 111), 1958, *id.* at 969, 973; Minimum Age (Underground Work) Convention (No. 123) and Recommendation (No. 124), 1965 *id.* at 1117, 1120; Employment (Women with Family Responsibilities) Recommendation, 1965 (No. 123), *id.* at 1113; Medical Examination of Young Persons (Underground Work) Convention, 1965 (No. 124), *id.* at 1122; Conditions of Employment of Young Persons (Underground Work) Recommendation, 1965 (No. 125), *id.* at 1126; Minimum Age Convention (No. 138) and Recommendation (No. 146), 1973, 56 ILO OFF. BULL., No. 1, at 21, 34 (1973).

[106] *See U.N. Annotations, supra* note 1, at 108. *Cf.* Marckx v. Belgium, Eur. Ct. Human Rts. Judgment of 13 June 1979, Ser. A No. 31 (striking down certain inheritance laws which discriminated between legitimate and illegitimate children).

[107] *See U.N. Annotations, supra* note 1, at 108.

[108] Report of the Third Committee, *supra* note 23, at 14-15.

paragraph 2 does recommend paid maternity leave and social security benefits specifically to working mothers before and after childbirth.[109]

In choosing the term "children and young persons," the drafters consciously avoided the term "minors"—i.e., persons under 18 or 21 years of age—so as to avoid the specific legal ages which ordinarily attach to that term and thereby to encourage the special protection of dependent youth irrespective of age.[110] The choice was consistent with their concern, evidenced in paragraph 3 by the phrase "without any discrimination for reasons of parentage or other conditions," to encourage the protection not only of children born out of wedlock, but also orphans and destitute or handicapped children.[111] The phrase "work harmful to their morals" would appear to prohibit employment detrimental to the spiritual well-being of children and young persons.[112]

### *Domestic Implications*

The law in the United States gives substantial protection and assistance to the family and to children and young persons. However, it gives only minimal protection to mothers *per se,* and to this extent it compares unfavorably with the aims of Article 10. On the other hand, mothers in the United States do benefit from family protection, and it would seem inaccurate to conclude that the United States is not in compliance with the minimal requirements of Article 10.

#### *Protection of the Family*

Many aspects of U.S. social welfare law are directed toward protecting and assisting the family as a fundamental unit of American society.[113] Indeed, most welfare benefits are designated as family assistance and calculated on the basis of the family unit. Furthermore,

[109] The Soviet delegation to the Third Committee proposed that such benefits be made "at the expense of the State or employer." This proposal was defeated on the grounds that maternity leave in many countries is financed on a tripartite basis, through contributions from the employee as well as from the employer and the State. This decision is consistent with art. 10 of the ILO Maternity Protection Convention (Revised) (No. 103) and Recommendation (No. 95), 1952, ILO, CONVENTIONS AND RECOMMENDATIONS 1919-1966, at 835, 841 (1966), according to which such benefits may be provided on a tripartite basis. *See* Report of the Third Committee, *supra* note 23, at 15.

[110] Report of the Third Committee, *supra* note 23, at 15.

[111] *Id.*

[112] *Id.*

[113] *See,* e.g., Title 42 of the United States Code.

the principle that marriage must be based on the free consent of both spouses, as provided in paragraph 1, is followed without exception.

There is a noteworthy flaw which grows out of the Aid to Families with Dependent Children programs,[114] namely, the disqualification from benefits of family units where two actual or surrogate parents are present. If one parent (usually the man) is working over 100 hours per month, then the family unit is disqualified, even if the breadwinner is earning less than is required to support the family. If a mother with dependent children is receiving assistance, she may avoid marriage or avoid having a man in the house because, under the law, she then loses her welfare assistance. The so-called "man in the house" rule thus tends to disrupt the family unit or to discourage its full establishment, contrary to the intent of Article 10. On the other hand, it should be pointed out that the rule is being given less and less weight in practice and that the trend in the law is toward eliminating this anti-family factor. All current proposals for welfare reform would eliminate the rule.

### *Protection of Motherhood*

The U.S. welfare system protects mothers both before and after childbirth by providing both prenatal and postnatal care and by adjusting benefits because of the increased need during this period. Otherwise, even within the narrow definition of "mothers" applicable to Article 10, American mothers are disregarded. Working mothers, in particular, can suffer real hardship. Under state disability benefits programs, they can be denied disability benefits for their inability to work during the period immediately preceding and following childbirth. Indeed, there being no legal right even to unpaid maternity leave, much less to "paid leave or leave with adequate social security benefits" (as per paragraph 1), a woman who is unable to work because of pregnancy can be discharged for failure to report to work or denied reinstatement when she is ready to return to work. Of course, if the employer provides sick leave or sick leave pay for other disability causes, then a refusal to provide equivalent pregnancy leave benefits would probably constitute unlawful discrimination on the basis of sex. And it is true, too, that many collective agreements provide for pregnancy leaves. Nevertheless, except in a

[114] *See,* 42 U.S.C. §601 et seq. (1976).

few states,[115] the employer is not required to provide sick leave (paid or unpaid) due to pregnancy or any other reasons, and, as previously noted, about 85% of all employees in the United States are without the protection of collective agreements. On the other hand, amendments to Title VII of the Civil Rights Act of 1964 do prohibit discrimination on the basis of pregnancy, childbirth, or related medical conditions.[116]

### *Protection of Children*

Traditionally, in the United States there has been discrimination against illegitimate children in their rights to inherit, in their rights to social security benefits, and in other legal rights and status. This traditional pattern is in the process of being eliminated by statutory and other means as an unconstitutional denial of equal protection.[117] In addition, federal and state laws prohibit the employment of children, with the minimum age ranging from 14 to 18. Children under the age of 18 are barred from most employment in the absence of a permit limiting employment to times when school is not in session, and children under 18 are barred absolutely from certain kinds of work involving dangerous equipment or hazardous conditions. There does exist a variety of programs, as a result of the 1973 Comprehensive Employment and Training Act,[118] which try to cope with unemployment among minority youth.[119] Nonetheless, unemployment among black youths is more than double the rate of unemployment for white youths. Most child labor laws in the United States do not apply to farm labor, which results in a major gap in the protection of children and young persons from exploitation. Children and young persons from migrant labor families, often younger than ten years of age, are especially vulnerable to this omission.

### *Article 10 With or Without Qualification?*

No statement of understanding, declaration, or reservation would appear needed to safeguard United States interests. The gradualist

[115] E.g., California Civil Code §19991.6.
[116] *See* 42 U.S.C. §2000e(k) (Supp. II, 1978).
[117] *See,* e.g., 42 U.S.C. §426(h)(2) (1976).
[118] *See* 29 U.S.C. §801 et seq. (Supp. II, 1978); Mills v. Habluetzel, 456 U.S. 91 (1982); Levy v. Louisiana, 391 U.S. 68 (1968).
[119] For details, *see* COMM'M ON SECURITY AND COOPERATION IN EUROPE, *supra* note 101, at 113-117.

language of Article 2(1) affords adequate legal protection against deficiencies in United States law and practice.

## ARTICLE 11—RIGHT TO AN ADEQUATE STANDARD OF LIVING

*Clyde W. Summers, as revised by Joseph P. Grodin*

1. The States Parties to the present Covenant recognize the right of everyone to an adequate standard of living for himself and his family, including adequate food, clothing and housing, and to the continuous improvement of living conditions. The States Parties will take appropriate steps to ensure the realization of this right, recognizing to this effect the essential importance of international co-operation based on free consent.

2. The States Parties to the present Covenant, recognizing the fundamental right of everyone to be free from hunger, shall take, individually and through international co-operation, the measures, including specific programmes, which are needed:

(a) To improve methods of production, conservation and distribution of food by making full use of technical and scientific knowledge, by disseminating knowledge of the principles of nutrition and by developing or reforming agrarian systems in such a way as to achieve the most efficient development and utilization of natural resources;

(b) Taking into account the problems of both food-importing and food-exporting countries, to ensure an equitable distribution of world food supplies in relation to need.

Under Article 11, the States Parties "recognize" the right of "everyone" to an adequate standard of living for self and family (including adequate food, clothing, and housing), proclaimed earlier in Article 25 of the Universal Declaration as well as in the American Declaration,[120] the European Social Charter,[121] and the revised OAS Charter.[122] In so doing, they agree generally to "take appropriate steps to ensure the realization of this right" and, additionally, commit

[120] *Supra* note 15, arts. 11, 12, 14.
[121] *Supra* note 16, art. 4.
[122] *Supra* note 17, arts. 31, 43.

themselves specifically to certain implementing measures beyond those provided in Article 2 in respect of the "fundamental right of everyone to be free from hunger." All this is done within the gradualist norm of Article 2(1), including the subjective limitation of "available resources."

### *Analysis of Article 11*

The meaning of paragraph 1 is initially complicated by the fact that, under Article 7(a), the States Parties declare their support for remuneration for work commensurate with a "decent," as distinct from an "adequate," standard of living. One may wonder whether different meanings were meant to attach to the two adjectives used. This question was a matter of some debate among the Third Committee drafters, with proponents for the word "decent" contending that it connoted a higher standard of living than the word "adequate" which, it was argued, could be interpreted to mean only bare subsistence.[123] In the end the word "adequate" prevailed. It had been used already in Article 25 of the Universal Declaration of Human Rights and was adopted partly for this reason. It refers to the goal of a reasonably high level of economic existence, as determined by the availability of a State Party's resources and its ability to secure international assistance. The addition of the words "and to the continuous improvement of living conditions" may be understood both to reinforce this intention and to ensure recognition of the principle of continuous progress in this sphere,[124] consistent with the progressive aims of numerous ILO instruments affecting living conditions.[125]

Paragraph 2 may be interpreted to address freedom from malnutrition as well as freedom from starvation. Otherwise, the call in subparagraph (a) for increased understanding of "the principles of nutrition" would be meaningless. Also, while the States Parties commit themselves to "specific programmes" beyond those called for in Article 2, paragraph 2 must be read against the "available resources" and "progressive realization" language of Article 2(1) and the voluntary international cooperation language of paragraph 1. From this perspective, the understanding proposed by President Carter to

[123] Report of the Third Committee, *supra* note 23, at 18.
[124] *See U.N. Annotations, supra* note 1, at 110.
[125] *See,* e.g., the ILO conventions and recommendations cited *supra* notes 45 and 47.

the effect that Article 11 is not a legally binding obligation to provide foreign aid may be correct,[126] even though paragraph 2 does not refer specifically to foreign aid. Paragraph 2(a) obliges the States Parties only to use and disseminate pertinent food production knowledge, and paragraph 2(b) obliges them only to take the problems of food-importing and food-exporting countries into account when determining any level of aid.

### *Domestic Implications*

The right of "everyone" to an adequate standard of living is generally recognized in the United States, at least as an aspiration. The record of actual achievement is another matter. According to the federal government's own standards, for example, approximately 13% of the United States population lives below an adequate standard of living, reflecting "persistent poverty" even while income has risen for the upper 20% of the population.[127] Some would say that as much as 30% of the U.S. population does not enjoy an adequate standard of living and that it is therefore still true, as President Roosevelt decried about 45 years ago, that "[o]ne-third of the nation is ill-fed, ill-housed, and ill-clothed."[128] Much the same can be said about freedom from hunger. A notable segment of the United States population goes hungry each day, and an intolerable number of children suffer from malnutrition serious enough to cause permanent damage to mental and physical development.

Thus, it is at least arguable that the United States does not satisfy the objectives of Article 11 at the present time. Of course, when one considers the United States in light of standards used in other countries, particularly if those countries are outside Western Europe, few Americans could be said to have a standard of living below the level of adequacy. On the other hand, the standard to be achieved presumably is not that of the lowest common denominator. This observation would seem to be reinforced by the phrase "to the maximum of its available resources" in Article 2(1). The United

[126] *See* Message of the President, *supra* note 10, at ix.

[127] Rich, "Poverty Level Stabilizes at 31 Million," *Wash. Post,* 19 Oct. 1989, at A8, col. 1. In 1986, the poorest fifth of the U.S. population received only 4.6% of total income in the U.S., while the richest 20% received 43.7%. R. L. SIVARD, WORLD MILITARY AND SOCIAL EXPENDITURES 40 (12th ed. 1987).

[128] *Second Inaugural Address 1937,* in 4 THE PUBLIC PAPERS AND ADDRESSES OF FRANKLIN D. ROOSEVELT 4-5 (S. Roseman ed. 1938).

States, it is fair to conclude, does not meet the Article 11 test of adequacy.

Furthermore, the United States does not appear to be moving in any measurable way toward providing "everyone" with an adequate standard of living. It is true that certain programs, particularly in the areas of food assistance and medical aid, have made inroads on some of the harsher aspects of poverty; the median dollar income in the United States also has risen in recent years. But with the level of welfare benefits not keeping pace with the rate of inflation and with the level of real income actually declining in many areas, particularly in the South, the movement over the last decade has tended to be more retrogressive than progressive. In any event, the number of destitute people has not decreased, nor has the number of people at the level of bare subsistence.

On a more positive note, it is fair to say that the United States already complies fully with the limited terms of paragraph 2 of Article 11. Ever since 1954, with the enactment of the Agricultural Trade Development and Assistance Act[129] (better known as Public Law 480 or the Food for Peace Program), the United States has been actively involved in supporting programs designed to enhance worldwide food production and distribution. The minimal requirements of Article 11(2) would appear fully, even if not always wisely, met.[130]

The disparity between U.S. performance and the aspirations of the ESC Covenant is perhaps nowhere more apparent than with respect to Article 11. The plight of the homeless has become a national disgrace, and it appears that many national leaders see, at best, a minimal role for the government in securing the "right of everyone to an adequate standard of living." Even given the gradualist or progressive nature of the obligations imposed by the ESC Covenant, continuing U.S. rejection of the principles set forth in Article 11 would seem to require a more forthright statement upon ratification than the mere observation that the rights in the Covenant are to be implemented progressively. Alternatively, of course, the United States could renew its attempt to achieve the goal of an adequate standard of living for

[129] 7 U.S.C. §§1691, 1691a, 1701-36 (1976).

[130] For details, *see* R. BARD, FOOD AND INTERNATIONAL AGRICULTURAL TRADE (1972). *See also* Christensen, *The Right to Food: How to Guarantee,* 4 ALTERNATIVES—A JOURNAL OF WORLD POLICY 181 (1978); Walczak, *New Directions in United States Food Aid: Human Rights and Economic Development,* 8 DEN. J. INT'L. L & POL'Y 543 (1979).

everyone, in which case no reservation or other statement would be necessary.

## ARTICLE 12—RIGHT TO HEALTH

*Frank P. Grad, with the assistance of Ilise Levy Feitshans*

> 1. The States Parties to the present Covenant recognize the right of everyone to the enjoyment of the highest attainable standard of physical and mental health.
>
> 2. The steps to be taken by the States Parties to the present Covenant to achieve the full realization of this right shall include those necessary for:
>
> (a) The provision for the reduction of the stillbirth rate and of infant mortality and for the healthy development of the child;
>
> (b) The improvement of all aspects of environmental and industrial hygiene;
>
> (c) The prevention, treatment and control of epidemic, endemic, occupational and other diseases;
>
> (d) The creation of conditions which would assure to all medical service and medical attention in the event of sickness.

Under Article 12, the States Parties recognize the right to physical and mental health proclaimed earlier, though only indirectly, in Article 25 the Universal Declaration of Human Rights, the American Declaration of the Rights and Duties of Man,[131] and the European Social Charter.[132] Additionally, in paragraph 2, they commit themselves to a minimum of four "steps" to be taken to achieve the "full realization" of this right.

### *Analysis of Article 12*

Article 12 does not define "health." Paragraph 1 of the draft Covenant prepared under the auspices of the Commission on Human Rights, however, did define the term by applying the definition in the

[131] *Supra* note 15, art. 11.
[132] *Supra* note 16, arts. 1(11) and 2(11).

World Health Organization (WHO) Constitution: "a state of complete physical, mental and social well-being, and not merely the absence of disease or infirmity."[133] Like the ILO, in respect to Articles 6-11 of the ESC Covenant, WHO provided technical help in drafting Article 12. The Third Committee did not accept WHO's efforts to include a definition, arguing that such detail would be out of place in a legal text of this kind, that no other definitions were included in other articles of the Covenant, and that the proposed definition was incomplete.[134]

These arguments probably explain why the drafters did not define the qualifying phrase "highest attainable standard." Nevertheless, paragraph 2, adopted from a proposal submitted by the United States, details some of the "progressive" goals (as opposed to measures) which the drafters intended the States Parties to pursue in striving for "the highest attainable standard of physical and mental health."

### *Subparagraph (a)*

According to the preparatory record[135] and in keeping with WHO's definitions, the key term "infant mortality" is intended to refer to children who are born alive but who die within the first twelve months of birth.[136] Judging from WHO's first report to the U.N. Secretary-General pursuant to Article 18 of the Covenant, appropriate steps to curb infant mortality should include "particularly those promotive and preventive actions [which are] oriented towards the specific needs of mothers and children at various stages in the reproductive process and the growth and development of the child."[137] The report goes on to indicate that in 1979 the thirty-second World Health Assembly urged member States:

> 1. to promote specific Government regulations and laws to provide free health services at least during periods of high risk pregnancy, delivery, and

[133] Constitution of the World Health Organization, *reprinted in Basic Documents* (WHO, Geneva 1978).

[134] Report of the Third Committee, *supra* note 23, at 20.

[135] *Id.* at 20.

[136] 11 U.N. GAOR, C.3 (747th mtg.) 330, U.N. Doc. A/C.3/SR. 747 (1957). The Centers for Disease Control's recent study, entitled "National Infant Mortality Surveillance," reported that each year 40,000 infants in the U.S. die before their first birthday.

[137] First Report by the World Health Organization Concerning Rights Covered by Article 12 of the International Covenant on Economic, Social and Cultural Rights, U.N. Doc. E/1980/24, at 2 (1980) [hereinafter First WHO Report].

the first years of life when breast-feeding immunization and treatment of infectious and parasitic diseases are crucial for survival;

2. to promote the development of primary health care programmes with concrete plans for maternal and child health care as its essential component that includes care during pregnancy and childbirth, family planning, infant and child care with appropriate focus on improvement of nutrition, prevention of infections, promotion of physical and psychological development of the child, and education for family life;

3. to develop, as appropriate, health and related social services such as day-care services, school health services, and services for adolescents, and relevant social legislation in support of mothers and children.[138]

### *Subparagraph (b)*

The key words "environmental and industrial hygiene" are not clarified in the text or the preparatory record. Again, WHO's first report concerning Article 18 is helpful. The report refers, *inter alia,* to "[t]wo major thrusts [which] are identified in the organization's programme for the promotion of environmental health:

(1) provision of water supply and sanitation, with emphasis on rural and underserved populations, in accordance with the targets established for the International Drinking-Water Supply and Sanitation Decade (1980-1990); and

(2) assessment of adverse effects on human health of chemicals in the environment, and control of the pollution of air, water, food and land."[139]

Citing other resolutions of the 1979 World Health Assembly, the report expresses concern for "the uncontrolled introduction of some industrial and agricultural process(es) with physical, chemical, biological and psychosocial hazards,"[140] and notes that the Assembly further urged member States "to develop and strengthen occupational health institutions and to provide measures for preventing hazards in work places."[141]

[138] *Id.* at 3.
[139] *Id.* at 4.
[140] *Id.* at 5.
[141] *Id.*

### *Subparagraph (c)*

WHO's report also clarifies the concerns of this subparagraph: chronic diseases (cardiovascular diseases and cancer) in the developed world and communicable diseases (especially diarrheal diseases, sexually transmitted diseases, respiratory diseases, and malaria) in developing countries, with emphasis placed on biomedical research, improved nutrition, and immunization.[142] Despite the numerous ILO instruments on the subject, as well as a certain redundancy with Article 7(b), the preparatory work[143] shows that the drafters included "occupational diseases" to reaffirm the States' duties to protect workers.[144]

### *Subparagraph (d)*

The key word "conditions" is not defined in the preparatory record of Article 12, but it may be assumed that it does not require some form of "socialized" medicine to meet its standards. On the contrary, the drafters apparently contemplated diverse approaches to adequate medical care. As stated in the First WHO Report, the right to health is dependent upon "the development by each . . . State of a health system that is both accessible and acceptable to the total population, suited to its needs and to the socio-economic conditions of the country."[145] Judging from the same report, it is equally clear that the vagueness of subparagraph (d) was not intended to dilute a vigorous commitment to "primary" care (essential health care) in a given community or country. The fundamental components of primary care were outlined in detail in the Declaration of Alma Ata adopted by the International Conference on Primary Health Care in 1978.[146]

The provisions in the Alma Ata Declaration are an outgrowth of the Covenant. According to the Declaration and subsequent practice in the health professions, "primary health care" addresses the main health problems in the community providing preventive, promotive, curative and rehabilitative services, including prevention education to control health problems. Primary health care involves all sectors of

[142] *Id.* at 5-6.

[143] *See, e.g.*, Report of the Third Committee, *supra* note 23.

[144] First WHO Report, *supra* note 137, at 21.

[145] *Id.* at 7.

[146] World Health Organization, Primary Health Care: Report of the International Conference on Primary Health Care (1978).

national development, particularly agriculture, education, public works, and the further development of the health services infrastructure. These goals should be achieved through community organization, planning, and the work of community health care workers, especially in rural locations. Relying upon the Declaration, which calls on all governments to formulate national policies, strategies, and plans of action to launch and sustain primary health care as part of a comprehensive national health system, WHO's report urges governments "[t]o implement primary health care as an integral part of the national health system within overall socioeconomic development, and with the involvement of all sectors concerned."[147]

Finally, Article 12 contains no safeguards limiting the power of the State to impose medical treatment on the individual. The following amendment to Article 12 was defeated:

> Everyone is under a duty to care for his health and to undergo appropriate medical treatment. Nothing in this article may be interpreted as authorizing the compulsory imposition of particular medical treatment, except as provided by law for reasons of public health. The law may not go beyond the limits imposed by respect for the human person.[148]

The drafters chose not to include this or any equivalent provisions on the grounds, *inter alia,* that it could not deal adequately with the complex questions of consent to medical treatment or those cases where medical treatment should be given without patient consent, e.g., where the patient is unconscious. Most importantly, it was omitted because the problem is addressed by Articles 4 and 5 of this Covenant and by Article 7 of the CPR Covenant, which prohibits States from subjecting anyone "to medical or scientific experimentation" without that individual's free consent.

### *Domestic Implications*

"The right of everyone to the enjoyment of the highest attainable standard of physical and mental health" is a goal clearly shared by the United States. Though it is a goal that is hard to achieve, substantial progress has been made towards realization of basic health protection for all people in the United States. The nation's agenda for health protection has been disseminated in recent reports pertaining to

[147] First WHO Report at 7.
[148] *See* Report of the Third Committee, *supra* note 23, at 20.

"Health for All 2000," which map the control of fatal diseases, seek to increase life expectancy for older persons, and seek to achieve a significant reduction in infant mortality.[149]

The protection of health in the United States is largely a matter for state governments, working together with a wide variety of federal programs. The peculiar pattern of federal-state relations and the intricate interplay between federal and state law must therefore be taken into account when describing measures to protect public health in the United States. The protection of health is an important concern of government in the United States, as evidenced by huge and ever-growing appropriations for health programs.[150] Although the right to health is not guaranteed in the U.S. Constitution, legislation has created entitlements to health services.

In describing public health in the United States, the federal system of government must be considered. The federal government is a government of delegated powers, having received its powers from the original states. Hence, state governments, which came first in our system, have retained "police power" and the plenary power to provide for the "health, safety and welfare" of the people.[151] Under the Constitution, the federal government has no express delegated power to protect the public health, though it carries out vast programs for public health protection through the exercise of other delegated powers. Thus, it exercises many regulatory powers in the field of public health through its power to regulate interstate and foreign commerce.[152] In addition, the federal government exercises very broad

[149] *See* World Health Organization, *Global Strategy for Health for All by the Year 2000* (1981); Pan American Health Organization, *Plan of Action for the Implementation of Regional Strategies* (1982); Pan American Health Organization, *Health for all by the Year 2000/Strategies* (1980). Initiatives begun in 1978 at Alma-Ata reached a high point in the Americas in 1981 when PAHO approved the Plan of Action for implementing the regional strategies of health for all by the year 2000.

[150] *See* Institute of Medicine, *The Future of Public Health,* Appendix A at 165 (National Academy Press, Washington, DC, 1988).

[151] *See generally* F. GRAD, THE PUBLIC HEALTH LAW MANUAL (1990) [hereinafter PUBLIC HEALTH LAW MANUAL].

[152] *See* U.S. Const. Art. I, §8 cl.3. For discussion of the federal commerce power as a source of regulation of what passes in commerce and its health implications, *see* Cushman, *The National Policy Power Under the Commerce Clause of the Constitution,* 3 MINN. L. REV. 289, 381-412 (1919). For an early case, see Hopolite Egg Co. v. United States, 220 U.S. 45 (1911). Under the commerce power, the U.S. Government regulates the trade in, and the quality of, food, drugs and cosmetics [Federal Food, Drug and Cosmetic Act, 21 U.S.C. §§301-392. *See,* e.g., Note, *The Federal Food, Drug and Cosmetic Act,* 67 HARV. L. REV. 632 (1954); Mintena, *The Food and Drug Administration—A Protection of Public Health,* 10 FOOD DRUG COSM. L.J. 424 (1955)]; Wholesome Meat Act, 21 U.S.C. §601 et seq.; Wholesome Poultry Product Act, 21 U.S.C. §451 et seq.; Flammable Fabrics Act, 15 U.S.C. §1191 et seq.; 15 U.S.C. §1381 et seq. (automobiles with respect to safety features);

indirect regulatory activities through its delegated power to tax and spend for the general welfare. This "taxing and spending power" frequently is exercised through a variety of grant-in-aid programs, which provide federal funds for states and municipalities to establish certain public health programs.[153] An early grant-in-aid program, for instance, provided for the construction of hospitals if the states and municipalities provided in their state legislation for certain minimum standards for hospital facilities and personnel and if they undertook to provide a certain amount of free care. Grant-in-aid programs, in addition, may require the state or municipality to match part of the federal contribution.[154]

The grant-in-aid scheme, under the constitutional taxing and spending power, has allowed the federal government to originate many important public health programs. It also provides an opportunity for cooperative federal, state, and local involvement in public health programs, in the development of such programs, and in arranging for the delivery of services. Federal grant programs and federal programs relating to research and statistical information and program development also have counterparts on the state and local level where the delivery of services is likely to occur. If the state does not provide certain services, the service may be rendered with federal funding by private non-profit agencies or institutions.[155]

---

42 U.S.C. §7521 (with respect to emission of air pollutants); 42 U.S.C. §7547 (with respect to energy use and minimum mileage); and a variety of other goods in commerce. Under this power it also regulates air and water pollution; the disposition of solid wastes; noise resulting from interstate transportation and from particular manufactured products in interstate commerce; and occupational health and safety in places which manufacture, store, or deal in goods or merchandise in interstate commerce.

[153] For discussion of the grant-in-aid system *see, e.g.*, W. ANDERSON, INTERGOVERNMENTAL RELATIONS IN REVIEW 43-46, 61-64 (1960); W. ANDERSON, THE NATION AND THE STATES: RIVALS OR PARTNERS 175-190 (1955); COMMISSION ON INTERGOVERNMENTAL RELATIONS, A REPORT TO THE PRESIDENT FOR TRANSMITTAL TO CONGRESS 120 (Kestnbaum Rep. 1955); COMMISSION ON INTERGOVERNMENTAL RELATIONS, THE ADMINISTRATIVE AND FISCAL IMPACT OF GRANTS-IN-AID (1955); W. GRAVES, AMERICAN INTERGOVERNMENTAL RELATIONS 477-571, 932-68 (1964). Examples of federal grant-in-aid programs include programs for hospital construction [Hospital Survey and Construction Act (Hill-Burton Act), 42 U.S.C. §291 et seq.], programs for preventive disease care, programs for mental health services, 400 programs for the collection and study of public health statistics, as well as the vast system of "Medicaid," i.e., reimbursement of the cost of medical services for persons who are "medically indigent" and cannot pay for such services themselves.

[154] Hill-Burton Act, discussed in Public Health Law Manual, *supra* note 157, at 108-109.

[155] Federal grant programs often require that there be a single designated state agency to accept and supervise state-wide grant programs. For less than state-wide programs, the legislation may require management by a municipal or local government agency or by a private non-profit organization. For the variety of local and state patterns, *see* R. ROEMER, C. KRAMER, J. FRINK, PLANNING URBAN HEALTH SERVICES FROM JUNGLE TO SYSTEM (1975).

### *Provisions for the Reduction of the Stillbirth and Infant Mortality and for the Promotion of the Healthy Development of Children*

Stillbirth rates and infant mortality rates have long been used as major indicators of the effectiveness of efforts to promote public health. Collection of statistical data relating to stillbirths and infant mortality is required by state and federal law.[156] The greatly increased life expectancy of Americans is largely due to the reduction of stillbirths and infant mortality. On the other hand, regional and racial differences in the rate of stillbirths and infant mortality have long been a matter of concern, indicating that there are significant differences in the effectiveness of measures to promote public health among certain vulnerable populations.[157]

State or local laws or regulations address newborn and maternity services either separately or as part of the general regulation of hospitals. State laws often require or make provision for the following: (1) collection of vital statistics, including statistics on the rate of stillbirths or fetal deaths and on the occurrence of infant mortality; (2) collection of data on the occurrence of maternal deaths; (3) the reporting of communicable diseases, including early childhood disease; (4) immunizations for children; (5) the screening of persons, either during childhood or prior to marriage, for evidence of traits of congenital illness and genetic counselling for persons carrying such traits to advise them on the likelihood of the occurrence of genetic diseases in their offspring; (6) treatment of juvenile alcoholics and drug addicts; and (7) mental health services.

Health services for infants and children include provisions for prenatal services supported by grants from the federal government and

---

While administrative arrangements at the state and local level may at times be confusing, they are likely to be subject to general supervision by the federal grant-providing agency regardless of their location in the state or local governmental hierarchy.

[156] *See, e.g.*, National Center for Health Statistics, *Vital Statistics of the United States,* DHEW Pub., published annually; 42 U.S.C. §242k. For an account of the importance of accurate health statistics to the progress of public health, *see* Lawrence, *The Health Record of the American People,* in HEALTH IN AMERICA: 1776-1976, at 16-36 (K. Endicott ed. 1976, DHEW pub. No. (HRA) 76-616).

[157] Figures in the United States indicate significantly higher infant mortality rates among blacks than among whites, i.e., 18.2 black infant deaths per 1,000 live births versus 9.2 white infant deaths per 1,000 live births from 1984-1986. By region and by state the difference is even more dramatic. *See* U.S. Health and Human Services, *Health United States 1988* 55-59 (Mar. 1989). In addition, the incidence of low birthweight, defined as less than five pounds eight ounces, is on the rise, particularly among blacks, according to a study by the Centers for Disease Control. Such children are 90 to 100 times more likely to die in their first year than other infants. *Wall Street Journal,* 9 Mar. 1990, at B4.

preventive services to infants through well-baby clinics.[158] Yet, there are gaps in the provision of services, resulting in inadequate coverage in some parts of the nation. There is a structure that is designed to deal with these issues, but infant mortality and low birth-weight remain important problems in low-income areas and among underserved populations.[159]

Modern medicine has succeeded in controlling communicable disease and particularly in combatting infectious diseases in children. With most other communicable diseases controlled by immunization, there is now increasing concern over the rise in the number of pediatric cases of Acquired Immune Deficiency Syndrome (AIDS).[160]

The success in traditional areas of public health concern has caused the attention to shift towards genetic disorders. Encouraged by federal programs, most states have enacted legislation that provides for screening and genetic counselling when testing reveals the potential for genetic abnormalities in offspring. At the federal level, the Secretary of the Department of Health and Human Services (DHHS) is required to undertake surveillance and conduct epidemiological assessments of certain genetic diseases, and to consider the need for related programs. Additional funding has been obtained for experimental programs, such as gene therapies for persons with Huntington's and other genetic diseases. Federal programs dealing with genetic diseases and Sudden Infant Death Syndrome (SIDS) also provide funding for genetic testing, counselling programs and treatment of individuals who bear identifiable genetic traits. SIDS is also the subject of federal legislation that provides for an educational and statistical program and for assistance to state and local govern-

[158] *See* 42 U.S.C. §§701-716. Included in the grant authorization are services for reducing infant mortality and the promotion of maternal and child health; crippled children's services and services to children who are suffering from conditions that may lead to crippling; special project grants for maternity and infant care; children's dental health programs; and grants for research and training.

[159] The National Infant Mortality Surveillance study found that the most important predictor for infant survival is birth-weight and as noted previously in this paper infant mortality and low birth-weight are issues of great concern. *See* National Infant Mortality Surveillance, *supra* note 136.

[160] INSTITUTE OF MEDICINE, CONFRONTING AIDS 353 (1986). Acquired Immunodeficiency Syndrome (AIDS) is a severe manifestation of infection with human immunodeficiency virus. The Centers for Disease Control have established criteria to define cases of AIDS based on the presence of certain infections such as pneumonia and/or other conditions such as cancer. *Id.* at 7. Since pediatric AIDS was first recognized in 1980, a total of 348 cases in children under 13 years had been reported as of 8 Sept. 1986. *Id.* at 61. However, the Public Health Services' projection predicts the number of pediatric AIDS cases was more than 3,000 by 1991. *Id.* at 7.

ments for research into the identification of infants at risk of SIDS, and for the establishment of preventive programs.[161]

Federal legislation also provides grants for preventive health services, for example by providing technical assistance and funding to states that provide immunization services to protect children against communicable diseases.[162] Every state has enacted legislation relating to the control of communicable diseases.[163]

The important relationship among nutrition, health and growth is also a matter of substantial legislative concern in the United States. Nutritional programs created through federal legislation such as Aid to Families With Dependent Children,[164] Food Stamps,[165] and Women, Infants, and Children,[166] provide basic food and nutritional supplements to protect the health of children under age six and pregnant or nursing mothers. Additional programs provide grants for active service programs, including school breakfast and lunch programs,[167] as well as for research relating to children's nutrition.[168] There is continuing concern with childhood hunger and malnutrition in the United States, in spite of agricultural surpluses, though some progress has been made.[169] School health services, including examina-

[161] 42 U.S.C. §§300c-12.

[162] 42 U.S.C. §247b(j)(1)(A).

[163] The constitutionality of state and local laws authorizing compulsory immunization was upheld as early as 1905. Jacobson v. Massachusetts, 197 U.S. 11 (1905). Most states authorize compulsory examination for communicable disease and compulsory quarantine or exclusion from work or school when necessary to prevent the spread of communicable disease. The majority of states authorize immunization as a requirement of admission to school. For a summary of state laws and practices in the control of communicable disease, *see* PUBLIC HEALTH LAW MANUAL, *supra* note 151, at 67-83.

[164] 42 U.S.C. §602. *See also* Rowland, Lyons, and Edwards, *MEDICAID: Health Care for the Poor in the Reagan Era,* ANN. REV. PUBLIC HEALTH 427-450 (1988).

[165] Food Stamp Act of 1977, Pub. L. No. 98-36 (codified at 42 U.S.C. §610).

[166] 42 U.S.C. §1786. Special supplemental food program for pregnant, postpartum, and breastfeeding women, infants, and young children from families with inadequate income.

[167] 42 U.S.C. §1757 (school lunch program); 42 U.S.C. §1773 (school breakfast program). The programs are joint federal-state programs and the meals served use excess agricultural products. The federal government pays for the active cost of meals served to children from low income families and shares the cost of other meals with the states. Provision is made to assure that children eligible for the programs will not be identified or segregated in any way. 42 U.S.C. §1759a(f).

[168] 42 U.S.C. §§1771-1786. The Congressional finding relates good nutrition to the capacity of children to learn and to develop. The program has a research and training component, and provides also for special projects to encourage consumption of fluid milk. Another component provides a special supplementary food program for children one to five years of age, as well as for breastfeeding women. A National Advisory Council on Maternal, Infant and Fetal Nutrition is also established.

[169] The presence of malnutrition in the United States and its impact on child development were amply documented in the hearings held by the Senate Select Committee on Nutrition

tion and referral of children by their school physician or school nurse, are generally provided under state law. In many states, preventive dental health services may be provided through school programs,[170] community health centers, and fluoridation of the water supply to prevent dental caries.[171]

Mental health and prevention of mental illness among young persons is also a subject of special concern. While programs for research and development of treatment for mental illness are broadly provided for,[172] the needs of children and adolescents are specially mentioned in program legislation.[173] Problems of young persons which involve both mental and physical health include the use of tobacco and alcohol and chemical dependency on drugs. Federal programs concerning smoking and alcoholic beverage and drug use among children and adolescents support research to understand the biological and behavioral determinants of alcohol and drug abuse, with special emphasis on children age 12 and below. The federal government provides grants to states and local subdivisions for demonstration projects and school and community-based programs for the prevention of, treatment of, and rehabilitation after substance abuse.[174] Other federal grant programs address the increasingly serious problem of adolescent pregnancies and provide a variety of health services through private non-profit agencies.[175] These programs are highly cost-effective, because they save lives and reduce the expense of neo-natal intensive care unit stays for these high risk infants.

---

and Related Human Needs, and in the 1969 White House Conference on Food, Nutrition and Health which made many recommendations that are reflected in the Federal Foodstamps Program as well as in school breakfast and lunch programs.

[170] 42 U.S.C. §254c.

[171] For constitutionality of fluoridation programs, *see,* e.g., Schuringa v. City of Chicago, 30 Ill. 2d 504, 198 N.E.2d 326, *cert. denied,* 379 U.S. 964 (1965).

[172] *See* 42 U.S.C. §242a, authorizing training programs and research in mental health, and 42 U.S.C. §254c on Community Mental Health Centers.

[173] 42 U.S.C. §290cc-13. The teen suicide rate has generated concern in recent years, and the Director of the National Institute of Mental Health has been directed to develop and publish information on the causes and means of preventing suicide, with particular attention to individuals under 24 years old. 42 U.S.C. §290aa-3(f).

[174] 42 U.S.C. §300x et seq. *See also* HEW, ALCOHOL AND HEALTH NEW KNOWLEDGE (2nd Special Report to the U.S. Congress, June 1974).

[175] *See* U.S.C. §300z; 42 U.S.C. §300z-4.

## *The Improvement of all Aspects of Environmental Protection and Environmental Hygiene*

### Traditional Sanitary Controls

The vast field of environmental hygiene has many subdivisions in U.S. law and had historically been a matter for state and local regulation.[176] Established regulatory areas include: the hygiene of housing and related concerns for the disposal of ordinary domestic wastes and human wastes through appropriate waste disposal systems; sanitary controls for establishments where food is prepared or sold; the regulation of certain trades and occupations in which unhygienic conditions may increase human exposure to disease and where disease may be transmitted by close physical contact or by particular activities of the trade or occupation; and the regulation of nuisances or noisesome trades and occupations, which may involve stenches or malodorous emissions, provide breeding places and harbourages for rodent and insect pests, or offer a ready environment for the growth of pathogenic organisms. Although regulation in these areas is most frequently enforced by the city, county, town, or village government, it is increasingly required to comply with applicable state or federal standards.[177]

While much work needs to be done in the area of environmental hygiene, which by its "housekeeping" nature requires continuing enforcement efforts, it is fair to say that traditional local sanitary controls have been successful. The improved health of the population, particularly with respect to communicable diseases, is directly attributable to improved environmental and sanitary conditions which are the result partly of higher living standards and partly of improved sanitary controls.[178]

[176] *See,* e.g., Roemer, Frink, and Kramer, *Environmental Health Services—Multiplicity of Jurisdiction and Comprehensive Environmental Management,* in ORGANIZATIONAL ISSUES IN THE DELIVERY OF HEALTH SERVICES 181-270 (K. Zola and J. McKinlay eds. 1974).

[177] For comments on the complexity of local-state-federal interrelationships, including health regulations and sanitary controls, *see,* e.g., THE STATES AND THE URBAN CRISIS 22-24, 41-48, 140-151, A. Campbell ed. (1970); Grad, *The City is Here to Stay,* 1973 URB. L. ANN. 3, 6-8; M. GRODZINS, THE AMERICAN SYSTEM: A NEW VIEW OF GOVERNMENT IN THE UNITED STATES 60-88 (1966).

[178] For accounts of city conditions at the turn of the century, *see* J. FORD, SLUMS AND HOUSING (1936); R. LUBOVE, THE PROGRESSIVE AND THE SLUMS (1962); J. RIIS, HOW THE OTHER HALF LIVES (1890); L. VEILIER, HOUSING REFORM (1910).

All major urban areas have systems for the disposal of solid wastes, including industrial and household wastes,[179] and most urban areas have sewer systems to dispose of human wastes.[180] Many suburban areas and less highly populated areas or city areas with a relatively low population density rely on private sewage disposal systems such as septic tanks, which must meet local public health standards.[181] Thus, standards relating to disposal of human wastes and sanitary facilities generally are quite high. Reliance on water-flushed toilets and on sewer systems has shifted the focus from a localized problem of disposal to a more general one of water pollution of major rivers.

The emphasis on sound waste disposal has greatly reduced the incidence and prevalence of such diseases as typhoid, salmonellosis, or other enteric diseases. Other occupations, facilities, and conditions which may contribute to the dissemination of diseases have been placed under state and local licensure. For instance, barbershops and beauty parlors are required to obtain state or local licenses, and the conditions of licensure may induce physical examination of persons who are likely to come into contact with customers.[182] Facilities such as swimming pools or public baths are licensed by the state or the municipality, and the conditions of licensure include a requirement that facilities meet health standards with respect to recirculation of waters, sanitary disposal of wastes, and treatment of wastes or water supplies.[183]

Food establishments are commonly licensed, which usually requires not only that the facility be sanitary and in a condition which assures the safety of the patrons, but also that adequate sterilization equipment be available to clean tools and machinery. Common requirements include the physical examination of food handlers so that

[179] For a detailed account of the history and the traditional local role in solid waste collection and disposal and of the later impact of federal legislation on state involvement, see, F. GRAD, TREATISE ON ENVIRONMENTAL LAW §4.02[1], [2][a], [b] (1973, and supps.) *See also*, E.S. SAVAS, THE ORGANIZATION AND EFFICIENCY OF SOLID WASTE COLLECTION (1977).

[180] "In 1940, over 45 percent of all units were lacking some or all plumbing; by 1980, that percentage was below 5 percent." U.S. Council on Environmental Quality, *Environmental Quality—Fourteenth Annual Report* 56 (1983).

[181] *See*, e.g., New York City Health Code, art. 143. A common provision of law allows the use of private sewage disposal systems, such as septic tanks, only when there is no municipal sewer which can serve the home or other building.

[182] *See*, e.g., New York City Health Code, art. 163; N. Y. Gen. Bus. L. §403(3).

[183] E.g., New York City Health Code, art. 165.

persons who are involved in the preparation and serving of food will not spread disease.[184]

Finally, the field of housing demonstrates the profound influence of federal legislation on local and state initiatives to improve hygiene and environmental sanitation. Until the early 1960s, individual municipalities were free to decide whether to adopt housing codes to maintain minimally decent housing standards. Federal support for constructing and operating public waste treatment works[185] has had a direct impact on state and local law and on the increasing insistence on sewer disposal instead of private disposal. To address the decay of the nation's housing, particularly in large cities, the federal government has undertaken a program which provides funds for urban renewal and housing rehabilitation, conditioned on the municipalities' adoption of housing codes.[186] As a result, literally thousands of local jurisdictions adopted housing codes in order to become eligible for federal housing grants soon thereafter. Although the "workable program" requirement is no longer part of federal law, the reliance on municipal housing codes continues.

While substantial progress has been made in the hygiene of housing, this country still falls short of the aim of having a decent home for everyone.[187] On the other hand, acceptable housing standards in the United States are significantly more advanced than housing standards in many other parts of the world, and major efforts continue to be made at every level of government to improve the

[184] For discussion of licensure as a device of public health enforcement, *see* PUBLIC HEALTH LAW MANUAL, *supra* note 151, at 96-121. For related areas of licensure of health personnel, *see* U.S. Dept. of Health, Education, Welfare, State Licensing of Health Occupations (1968) and *id., Licensure and Related Health Personnel Credentialling* (1971).

[185] For discussion of this multi-billion dollar grant program, *see* GRAD, *supra* note 179, §3.03[3][b], which discusses 33 U.S.C. §1281 et seq.

[186] The condition for urban renewal funds was that the municipality have "a workable program for community improvement" including "a minimum standards housing code, related but not limited to health, sanitation and occupancy requirements, which is deemed adequate by the Secretary, and (B) the Secretary is satisfied that the locality is carrying out an effective program of enforcement to achieve compliance with such housing code." 42 U.S.C. §1451(c). The slum clearance and urban renewal title of the federal housing law was phased out in 1975, after Congress developed a new approach in the Housing and Community Development Act of 1974, Pub. L. No. 93-383, 88 Stat. 633 (1974), but the earlier law has had a lasting effect through the adoption of housing codes.

[187] National Commission on Urban Problems ("Douglas Commission"), *Building the American City* 1-30 (1969).

housing situation to provide for repair, rehabilitation, and urban renewal and by appropriate regulation to enforce housing standards.[188]

### Modern Pollution and Hazardous Waste Controls

The unprecedented growth of industry following World War II and developments in science and technology led to great social progress as well as to newer, more hazardous, and more plentiful pollutants. These environmental problems called for legislative responses which have developed into a significant system of environmental controls. Beginning in the late 1940s and early and mid-1950s, Congress enacted a succession of laws improving the regulation and management of pollutants. Although the patterns of regulatory control for air pollution, water pollution, control of solid wastes, radiation, and noise differ significantly, each level of government plays a part in the various regulatory schemes. Exercising its power to regulate interstate commerce, the federal government sets major environmental standards, while states and municipalities retain major enforcement and control jurisdiction.

The Clean Air Act regulates air pollution from both stationary and automotive sources.[189] The federal government sets national ambient air quality standards, i.e., the permissible concentration of pollutants which will be allowed in the environment in any part of the nation, and standards are then enforced by the states. To attain and maintain the ambient air quality standards, states must adopt "state implementation plans" subject to approval by the Administrator of the U.S. Environmental Protection Agency (EPA). State implementation plans establish the precise mode in which ambient air quality standards are to be attained and adopt emission limitations and enforcement machinery to meet the federal standards. If a state is unwilling or fails to do so, the federal government may adopt an implementation plan for a particular area and enforce the standards.

EPA directly enforces automotive standards by setting emissions limitations for each vehicle that is manufactured. An elaborate system requires automobiles and other automotive sources to meet certain certification standards before they may be sold. The regulation of

[188] *See*, e.g., Housing and Community Development Act of 1974. 79. 42 U.S.C. §7401 et seq.

[189] The Clean Air Act was first enacted in 1963 and has undergone a number of major amendments. For detailed analysis and comment on the provisions of the Act, *see* GRAD, *supra* note 179, §§2.03-2.05; W. RODGERS, HANDBOOK ON ENVIRONMENTAL LAW 208-353 (1977).

emissions controls relating to new vehicles is a matter of federal enforcement, but the control of vehicles on the road and the maintenance of their emission control apparatus then becomes a matter for state and local enforcement. In addition, the law also sets forth a system of permits and pre-construction review of sources of air pollution for areas where exceptionally good air quality must be maintained or in areas where air quality is poor and appropriate steps must be taken to improve the situation.

Emissions standards to protect human health are set for major new sources of air pollution as well as for sources of hazardous air pollution. There is clear evidence that not only the pulmonary system suffers from air pollution but that the intake of toxic substances and pollutants may give rise to other deteriorative diseases.

A different system applies to water pollution control.[190] The federal government, using its power to regulate interstate commerce, has imposed uniform effluent limits for different categories and classes of sources of water pollution. The scheme requires industry-wide uniformity of effluent limits for the country as a whole, regardless of the quality of the receiving waters. The legislation was intended to mandate "zero pollution" by the target date set in the law. Until the attainment of zero pollution, the law sets increasingly stringent regulations to attain fishable and swimmable water quality, i.e., water quality conducive to human health and the recreational uses of the waters of the nation.

Since the legislation emphasized protecting human health, the law provides for multi-billion dollar grants for the construction of public waste treatment works. It also provides for area-wide waste treatment management plans designed to integrate water pollution control with other planning efforts. The effluent standards promulgated under the law are enforced through an elaborate permit system, the National Pollution Discharge Elimination System (NPDES), whose purpose is to ascertain the nature of the pollutants that are being discharged and to limit the amount of pollution discharged, using detailed permit controls. Major industrial establishments must first secure a NPDES permit before they may discharge effluent into U.S. territorial waters.

[190] *See* Federal Water Pollution Control Act, 33 U.S.C. §1151 et seq. A number of earlier federal laws had dealt with aspects of water pollution, but the first Federal Water Pollution Control Act was passed in 1948. The present law is based on the Federal Water Pollution Control Act Amendments of 1972, as further amended by the Clean Water Act of 1977, Pub. L. No. 95-217, 91 Stat. 1567. For detailed analysis and comment on the provisions of the Act, *see* GRAD, *supra* note 179, §3.03; RODGERS, *supra* note 189, at 354-550.

The Federal Water Pollution Control Law also authorizes regulations to control hazardous pollutants and to control pollution from major new sources. There is also legislation to protect against ocean pollution, which prohibits in particular dumping of waste products near the continental shores.[191] Controls on the dumping of chemical wastes, radioactive wastes, or sludge from waste treatment works also emphasize protection of human health.

The Federal Safe Drinking Water Act seeks to protect the nation's supply of drinking water by preventing infusion of heavy metals, lead, dangerous chemicals, and other hazardous substances into the water supply.[192] Preservation of important aquifers and protection against adverse consequences of waste disposal by deep well injection which may have a long range effect on the safety of the water supply in major cities is also an area of special legislative concern.

Substantial federal controls also regulate solid waste disposal, particularly on land. With increasing concern for air pollution, the incineration of wastes has often proved to be impractical. The common alternative for solid waste disposal traditionally was the disposal of waste into open dumps, but with increasingly higher population concentration and more hazardous chemical and toxic wastes disposed of in such dumps, public dangers from open dumps increased. Sanitary land fills, in which layers of waste were alternated with layers of clean earth, also proved to be of limited usefulness when it came to hazardous wastes and wastes which were likely to leach into the water table and water supply. Moreover, it became apparent that many cities in the nation were rapidly running out of space for sanitary land fills. The entire management of solid wastes, which had earlier been a local responsibility, became a national problem when local land fill space ran out.

The problem was addressed in a succession of federal laws passed in the 1970s, such as the Federal Resource Conservation and Recovery Act (RCRA).[193] Many provisions in RCRA parallel the Clean Air Act in that major enforcement and management responsibility is carried

[191] Marine Protection, Research and Sanctuaries Act of 1972, Pub. L. No. 92-532, 86 Stat. 1051, as amended by Pub. L. No. 92-254, 88 Stat. 50 (1954), 33 U.S.C. §1401 et seq. For comment, *see* GRAD, *supra* note 179, §3.03[13][g].

[192] Pub. L. No. 93-523, 88 Stat. 1660 (1974), 42 U.S.C. §300f-300j-9. For comment, *see* GRAD, *supra* note 179, §3.03[13][h], §3.05[7].

[193] Pub. L. No. 94-579, 580, 90 Stat. 2795 (1976), 42 U.S.C. §6901 et seq.; in form, the 1976 Act is an amendment of a 1965 law. For detailed analysis and comment, see GRAD, *supra* note 179, §4.03[2]; RODGERS, *supra* note 189, at 619-696.

out through state implementation plans. As in the other laws, the federal government has assumed major standard-setting and supervisory authority as well as detailed regulatory authority over the management of hazardous wastes, which are controlled from their production until their final disposal through an elaborate system of permits and manifests. Aside from advancing the preservation of essential natural resources, federal solid waste legislation seeks to protect human health by preventing noxious, harmful, and hazardous substances from leaching into the water supply or otherwise infecting the environment and human beings who come in contact with it. Consistent with this policy, the Comprehensive Environmental Response, Compensation and Liability Act (CECLA), referred to as the "Superfund" law, initially provided $1.6 billion and ultimately $8.5 billion over five years for the clean-up of hazardous waste disposal sites and hazardous chemical spills.[194]

The history of nuclear power in the United States as a federal monopoly that began as a secret wartime technology explains the pre-emptive federal role in the field. The Nuclear Regulatory Commission has set increasingly more stringent standards relating to the so-called uranium cycle, i.e., the cycle from original mining of nuclear substances to their refinement and use in nuclear power plants and to their ultimate disposal as nuclear wastes. The effort has been to protect human health against untoward increases in background radiation and to protect workers in nuclear establishments against excessive exposure.[195] To protect people from the adverse affects of ionizing radiation, the federal government, through the Nuclear Regulatory Commission, has almost complete and pre-emptive authority.

There is increasing evidence that noise, too, is a significant health hazard rather than a mere annoyance. Noise adversely affects human hearing, the cardiovascular system, and the central nervous system. Although control of ambient noise in the environment is generally a matter for state and local governments, and regulations are enforced by the local police agencies as part of the general control of

[194] Comprehensive Environmental Responses, Compensation, and Liability Act of 1980, Pub. L. No. 96-510, 94 Stat. 2767 (1980), 42 U.S.C.A. §9611 et seq. (1986). *See* GRAD, *supra* note 179, §4A.02[f].

[195] Atomic Energy Act, 42 U.S.C. §2011 et seq. For discussion of the protection provisions of the Act and the limited state role in protecting against radiation hazards, *see* GRAD, *supra* note 179, §§6.02-6.03.

"nuisance,"[196] the federal government has enacted far-reaching legislation to regulate noise in interstate transportation, such as trains, planes, and buses.[197] It has also established noise emission regulations for machinery and products sold in interstate commerce which provide a recurring source of noise.

In summary, the federal government has created a vast and detailed scheme of regulatory controls for a wide range of environmental pollutants. This legislation is designed to improve human health by eliminating or reducing the environmental sources and origins of a variety of human ailments and diseases. While much remains to be done in the control of environmental pollution, very significant advances have been made. The air in our cities is cleaner and the waters of the United States are clearer and more wholesome than they were when the effort to control environmental pollution began.[198]

### The Improvement of Industrial Hygiene

The emphasis on improved industrial hygiene is consistent with Article 7(b) of the ESC Covenant, which calls for the assurance of safe and healthy working conditions. Health protection in the workplace is recognized as a matter of great significance, but it is also inextricably linked to the task of protecting the population generally.

Safe workplaces have been required under state laws for over a century. Early laws sought to reduce "visible" traumatic injuries from accidents and industrial catastrophes. Efforts in the later twentieth century have focussed on research and prevention of latent diseases, which result from the cumulative effects of years of exposure to carcinogens or toxic substances. Occupational disease is difficult to recognize and manage because it manifests itself many years after the initial exposure.[199] Recent studies have also examined the role of other

[196] For a discussion of nuisance, *see* PUBLIC HEALTH LAW MANUAL, *supra* note 151, at 163-167; for detailed analysis of state and local noise legislation, *see* GRAD, *supra* note 179, §5.03[e].

[197] Federal Noise Control Act of 1972, 42 U.S.C. §4901 et seq. For analysis and comment, *see* GRAD, *supra* note 179, §5.03[1][D].

[198] For a general appraisal of progress made, *see* U.S. Council on Environmental Quality—*Environmental Quality—Seventeenth Annual Report* (1987-88) which contains an overview of environmental regulatory efforts.

[199] Occupational diseases "cover all pathological conditions induced by prolonged work, e.g., by excessive exertion, or exposure to harmful factors inherent in materials, equipment or the working environment." ENCYCLOPEDIA OF OCCUPATIONAL SAFETY AND HEALTH 1488 (L. Parmeggianni ed. 1983). *Cf.* statutory presumption that radiation injuries, including cancer, are work-connected, New York Workmen's Compensation Law §3(2), 47; N.J. Stat. Ann. §4.15. *See also,* O'Toole, *Radiation, Causation, and Compensation,* 54 GA. L.J. 751, 775-776 (1966); Soble, *Proposals for the Administrative Compensation of Victims of Toxic Substance Pollution: A Model Act,* 14 HARV. J. LEGIS. 683 (1977).

occupational illnesses which cannot be traced to a particular exposure or specific traumatic event. Such illnesses include repetitive motion injuries, back injuries, harmful effects of video display terminal work, eye strain, and carpal tunnel syndrome.[200]

Early cases involved illnesses such as hearing loss and deafness resulting from extended exposure to excessive noise.[201] Later cases involved analysis of complex occupational diseases from exposure to silica dust, asbestos, coal dust, toxic chemicals, and ionizing radiation. Exposure to toxic substances or to radiation hazards are cumulative in their effects. Industrial workers are especially vulnerable because their workplace exposure is added to the general exposure which they share with the rest of the population. Reproductive hazards in the workplace from exposure to teratogens,[202] embryotoxins,[203] mutagens,[204] and lead has also been the subject of recent regulation[205] and litigation.[206] Concern about health care workers' exposure to AIDS patients and laboratory exposure to HIV infection[207] has brought

[200] The stress on occupational diseases is reflected in 29 U.S.C. §669, Research and Related Activities, which emphasizes exposure to substances and to toxic agents. *See also,* FE JOSEFINA F. DY, VISUAL DISPLAY UNITS: JOB CONTENT AND STRESS IN OFFICE WORK, 49-61 (International Labor Office, Geneva 1985); D.C. Commission for Women, *Video Display Terminal Ad-Hoc Committee Findings and Recommendations June, 1986* (1986).

[201] E.g., Slawinski v. F.J.H. Williams & Co., 273 A.D. 826, 76 N.Y.S.2d 888, *aff'd,* 298 N.Y. 546, 81 N.E. 2d 93 (1948) (an early workmen's compensation hearing loss case).

[202] Teratogens are substances or preparations having the effect of producing malformation in a fetus and is largely based on the experience of drug use or abuse by pregnant women and women in industry. Parmeggiani, *supra* note 199, at 585.

[203] Embryotoxins include various external, physical, chemical, and infectious factors that may perturb morphogenesis, arrest fetus development, or produce congenital malformations. *Id.* at 746.

[204] Mutagens are substances or agents that can induce biological activity and should be treated as dangerous. *Id.* at 585.

[205] Occupational Exposure to Lead, 55 Fed. Reg. 4998 (13 Feb. 1990) (codified at 29 C.F.R. Pt. 1910.1025).

[206] International Union UAW v. Johnson Controls, Inc., 886 F.2d 871 (7th Cir. 1989) reversed by the U.S. Supreme Court in March, 1992. In that case the Court found that exclusionary policies based on reproductive health hazards in the workplace constituted sex-based discrimination in violation of Title VII, 42 USC 2000-e, the Civil Rights Act of 1964. IUAW v. Johnson Controls, 111 S Ct 1196: — US —: 113 L Ed2d 158, (1991). *See also:* Wright v. Olin, 697 F2d 1172 (4th Cir 1982). But see OCAW v. American Cyanamid 741 F2d 444 (D.C. Cir 1984) as discussed in Feitshans, Ilise L., *The Law of Reproductive Health Protections in the Workplace After Johnson Controls* in HEALTH VALUES Vol 16, No. 1 January/February 1992 p. 29-38.

[207] Human immunodeficiency virus ("HIV"), the virus that causes AIDS and AIDS-related complex ("ARC"), is transmitted through sexual contact and exposure to infected blood or blood components. HIV has been isolated in blood, semen, vaginal secretions, saliva, tears, breast milk, and other body fluids and secretions. Increasingly, health care workers face the risk of exposure to patients with HIV. Studies undertaken in light of this rising risk have recommended certain precautions health care workers can take to prevent or decrease the risk of contracting the virus. Most of the recommendations involve increasing the awareness of

greater awareness of occupational transmission of hepatitis, rubella, and other infectious or communicable diseases.[208] These sources of occupational illness are the subject of federal regulations concerning bloodborne diseases.[209]

Earlier this century, most states had an industrial commissioner or department of industrial safety or other administrative agency within its department of labor. Each state promulgated its own separate industrial code to protect workers. In the last decade, the authority delegated to state agencies has markedly increased as states have attempted to fashion strong occupational safety and health programs.

In addition to hundreds of state and local ordinances governing sanitation, health inspections, building codes, and fire prevention, Congress, the states and municipalities have enacted worker and community "right-to-know" laws regarding the manufacture, use, and storage of toxic and hazardous substances in the workplace.[210] Parallel protections are provided in the federal government's Hazard Communication Standard,[211] which requires that workers be given protective equipment, access to Material Safety Data Sheets, instructions regarding the health hazards and safe use of toxic and hazardous substances, and periodic training.

The major federal law that requires employers to provide "safe and healthful" employment and places of employment is the Occupational Safety and Health Act (OSH Act) of 1970.[212] The emphasis of the law is two-fold: (1) enforcement via inspection and regulation through standard-setting by the Occupational Safety and Health Administration; and (2) research by the National Institute of Occupational Safety and Health (NIOSH). Under the OSH Act, the Occupational Safety and Health Review Commission (OSHRC) provides administrative

---

health care workers (beyond those that are in obvious contact with HIV-infected patients), proper sterilization and hygiene standards, and changes in disposal of needles and other instruments that pose the greatest risk of spreading the virus. *See* Centers for Disease Control, *Recommendations and Guidelines Concerning AIDS* (1987) [includes World Health Organization Guidelines, 1985].

[208] Vlahov, *Transmission of Human Immunodeficiency Virus Within the Health Care Setting*, in HEALTH PROBLEMS OF HEALTH CARE WORKERS 429 (*State of the Art Reviews*, Vol. 2, No. 3, E. Emmett ed. 1987).

[209] Occupational Exposure to Bloodborne Pathogens (Proposed Rule), 54 Fed. Reg. 23042 (30 May 1989).

[210] 29 C.F.R. §1910.1200 (1983). For discussion of OSHA's Hazard Communication Standard and Right-to-Know laws, *see* Feitshans, *Hazardous Substances in the Workplace: How Much Does the Employee Have the Right to Know?*, DETROIT COLL. L. REV. 697 (1985).

[211] 29 C.F.R. §1910.1900 (1984).

[212] 29 U.S.C. §651 et seq.; 29 U.S.C. §671 (NIOSH); 29 U.S.C. §661 (OSHRC).

review, and the courts provide judicial review, of their activities. The federal government funds state plans that adopt and implement OSH Act provisions and implement subsequent regulations. State plans must adopt federal standards and have their programs approved by the Secretary of Labor to obtain federal funding.

Although the OSH Act provides coverage for millions of workers in construction and general industry, its jurisdiction excludes significant portions of the working population, such as federal workers and state, county, and municipal employees, who may be covered by other legislation. By law, safety and health programs are required to be established for each federal agency. Other industrial hygiene standards were created under Parts 91 and 121 of the Federal Air Regulations of the Federal Aviation Administration, the Maritime Safety Amendments to the Longshoremen and Harbor Workers' Act,[213] the National Labor Relations Act,[214] the "Black Lung" acts,[215] the Mine Safety and Health Act,[216] the Atomic Energy Act,[217] the Federal Employees' Liability Act,[218] and statutes governing contracts with the federal government.

Agricultural workers also face the problem of protection against extended exposure to harmful pesticides, rodenticides, and herbicides. The Federal Insecticide, Fungicide and Rodenticide Act (FIFRA) seeks to protect the environment from harmful pesticide pollution and human beings against unintentional or excessive exposure.[219] The law regulates the application of pesticides, requires that people who apply hazardous pesticides be specially trained, and prohibits premature reentry in fields and areas that have been recently sprayed or otherwise treated with toxic substances.[220] Another major law governing industrial hygiene is the Toxic Substances Control Act of 1976 (TSCA), last amended in 1981.[221] TSCA regulates the use, manufac-

[213] 33 U.S.C. §901 et seq.
[214] 29 U.S.C. §151 et seq.
[215] 30 U.S.C. §901 et seq.
[216] 30 U.S.C. §801 et seq.
[217] 42 U.S.C. §2011 et seq.
[218] 45 U.S.C. §51 et seq.
[219] 7 U.S.C. §135 et seq., as last amended by the Federal Pesticide Act of 1978, Pub. L. No. 95-396, 92 Stat. 819. For analysis and comment, *see* GRAD, *supra* note 179, §8.03.

[220] EPA has the authority under the Act to promulgate rules governing farm worker exposure to pesticides. Organized Migrants in Community Action, Inc. v. Brennan, 520 F.2d 1161 (D.C. Cir. 1975).

[221] 15 U.S.C. §2601, Pub. L. No. 94-469, 90 Stat. 2003 (1976). While the TSCA calls for coordination with other agencies administering analogous legislation, it provides that action taken under TSCA shall not be considered an exercise of standard-setting authority under OSHA. 15 U.S.C. §2608(c).

ture, shipment, and disposal of toxic substances which have become an increasingly important part of our industrial life. TSCA protects the general public against unnecessary exposure and protects employees who work in plants that manufacture and use toxic substances.

In summary, there are many local, state and federal laws that protect occupational safety and health and assure adequate industrial hygiene in the United States. These laws are designed to improve the quality of life in the workplace and increase the life expectancy of all workers, consistent with the goals and requirements of the Covenant.

### *Prevention, Treatment and Control of Epidemic, Endemic, Occupational and Other Diseases*

The control of epidemic and endemic diseases requires activity on both the state and federal level. Federal laws govern the inspection and quarantine of persons and goods upon entry into the United States, to protect against the spread of pandemic disease. Many of these quarantine and inspection provisions are consistent with WHO requirements and are realized through cooperation with other nations. Within the United States, protection against potentially epidemic or endemic disease is a matter for substantial epidemiological controls which the federal government shares with the states. Known communicable diseases and the occurrence of specified "reportable" diseases (which may be of unknown etiology) are monitored by public health authorities under the laws and public health codes of the 50 states. To maintain this surveillance system, the federal government provides grants to the states for research and the collection of statistical data.[222] State statistical data are then forwarded to the federal government.

The Secretary of the Department of Health and Human Services, acting through the National Center for Health Services Research, the National Center for Health Statistics, and the National Center for Health Care Technology, conducts and supports research, demonstrations, evaluations, and statistical and epidemiological activities for the purpose of improving effectiveness, efficiency, and quality of health services in the United States.[223] The federal government also maintains the Centers for Disease Control (CDC), which maintain a

[222] *See* 42 U.S.C. §242k [National Center for Health Statistics].

[223] 42 U.S.C. §242b(a)(1) [general authority respecting research, evaluations, and demonstrations in health statistics, health services and health care technology-scope].

highly expert group of epidemiologists responsible for the identification and tracking of epidemics.[224] Their work has become well-known to the public since the discovery of HIV infection, but CDC has actively participated in the development of preventive measures and long-term longitudinal studies for decades. CDC produces a variety of health statistics that are published in the *Morbidity and Mortality Weekly Report* and also provides oversight and technical assistance to states after the outbreak of disease.

State prevention efforts are significant. The sanitary controls which are imposed at the state and local level, including the sanitary controls discussed above and state licensing activities of public health related professions and organizations, are directed primarily at disease prevention. Other state and local activities to prevent communicable disease involve vector control more directly, e.g., state and local programs to eradicate mosquitos that are potential vectors for plague, rickettsial pox, and a variety of other diseases. Another program for the prevention of communicable disease is the program carried out by the states, with federal funding, to control venereal disease.[225] A program of more limited nature is the federally-funded program to isolate, treat, and control Hansen's Disease (formerly known as "leprosy").[226]

Public health efforts in the last few decades have been concentrated on the prevention and treatment of chronic diseases.[227] The AIDS epidemic, however, has shifted both public awareness and health care resources back to infectious diseases which are associated with AIDS or "AIDS-related complex" (ARC) and communicable diseases that affect immunosuppressed persons.[228] In particular, efforts to provide health care services for persons with ARC requires the coordination of

[224] 42 U.S.C. §289(c). The CDC was established within the U.S. Public Health Service as an operating agency in 1973.

[225] 42 U.S.C. §247c.

[226] 42 U.S.C. §247e.

[227] *See* J. MAUSNER AND A. BAHN, EPIDEMIOLOGY: AN INTRODUCTORY TEXT 307 (1974). Chronic disease is defined as "all impairments or deviations from normal which have one or more of the following characteristics: are permanent; leave residual disability; are caused by non-reversible pathological alteration; require special training of the patient for rehabilitation; may be expected to require a long period of supervision, observation, or care." [citing National Commission on Chronic Illness Report, 1957].

[228] INSTITUTE OF MEDICINE, CONFRONTING AIDS 353 (1986). AIDS-related complex or ARC is a variety of chronic symptoms and physical findings in people who are infected with HIV which do not meet the Centers for Disease Control's definition of AIDS. Symptoms may include chronic swollen glands, fever, weight loss, chronic diarrhea, minor alterations of the immune system, and oral thrush.

governmental efforts by several agencies, because of the many types of pneumonia, opportunistic infections, and other illnesses that people who have ARC may suffer; even a relatively minor illness in other people may precipitate a major illness in people who have ARC.

The recent efforts to combat AIDS rely in large part upon existing federal laws that protect public health. In dealing with this new threat to the public health, federal, state, and local agencies have applied existing administrative and organizational systems and have used their accumulated experience in the attempt to manage the AIDS epidemic, although the dimension of the threat has stretched available resources.[229]

Since AIDS is largely a sexually transmissible disease or is transmitted via contaminated-needle use by intravenous drug users, the prevention of AIDS has relied heavily on public health education, particularly given the early absence of any medication to prevent either the spread or the ravages of the disease. While a cure for AIDS has proved elusive, efforts to postpone the impact of neurological damage and opportunistic infections have been partially successful, because of the development of AZT and other possible palliatives. The problem of preventing the spread of AIDS is aggravated by the large number of asymptomatic HIV positive persons, who, like other carriers, do not show the symptoms of AIDS or ARC, but who may spread the disease through sexual intercourse or needle sharing. The difficulty of control has been magnified because HIV positivity is not reportable in most states, and contact follow-up has not been generally authorized for fear of breaching confidentiality.[230]

Other diseases, which may be environmental, organic, or both in origin, have become the subject of special efforts of designated federal research institutes. The National Institutes of Health (NIH) are composed of many specialized institutes such as The National Heart, Lung and Blood Institute; The National Institute of Arthritis, Metabolism and Digestive Diseases; the National Eye Institute; the National Institute of General Medical Sciences Institute for Child Health and Human Development; the National Institute on Aging; and others. The work of these institutes influences most of the health research in the United States. For example, the National Cancer

[229] *See* Centers for Disease Control, Strategic Plan for Prevention of Human Immunodeficiency Virus (HIV) Infection 1990—and Beyond (1990).

[230] *See* Public Health Law Manual, *supra* note 151, at 78-82.

Institute directs a large research program and fosters cancer education and treatment activities. The research performed under the control and direction of the appropriate national institute is also reflected in further preventive efforts through other federal programs.

Similarly, the National Institutes for Mental Health (NIMH) work to prevent and treat mental illness. Federal law provides authority for clinical training, clinical traineeships, and grants to state and local agencies and private non-profit agencies for research into mental illness and for institutions which care for, treat, and rehabilitate people who suffer from mental illness.[231] Such research includes investigation into the effects of alcoholism, drug addiction, and other chemical dependencies.[232] Federal law also provides for the establishment of community mental health centers and authorizes grants for planning and operational assistance. Services include in-patient services, emergency services, out-patient services, and a broad range of diagnostic, treatment, and follow-up services for persons suffering from mental illnesses and disabilities due to alcoholism and chemical dependency.[233]

Viewed in the aggregate, NIH and NIMH research activities probably cover all of the human ailments. Although only a few people in clinical trials obtain treatment directly from NIH and NIMH programs, virtually no patient in the United States is untouched by their research. As a result, people in the United States benefit from one of the most advanced systems of health-related research in the world.

### *The Creation of Conditions Which Would Assure to All Medical Service and Medical Attention in the Event of Sickness*

The provision of medical services to all who need them may be divided into two parts. First, one must consider the availability of able and trained personnel, and, second, one must consider whether the potential patient has the access to these services. On the whole, the first condition is met in the United States. In contrast to other nations, there are only a few underserved areas in the nation where medical

[231] 42 U.S.C. §241a.
[232] 42 U.S.C. §242. *See* ALCOHOLISM AND CHEMICAL DEPENDENCY IN THE WORKPLACE (*State of the Art Reviews,* Vol. 4, No. 2, C. Wright ed. 1989).
[233] 42 U.S.C. §290cc-13.

care and health services cannot easily be obtained by those who can afford to pay for them. Even in inner-city slum areas, there may be more hospital beds, physicians specializing in non-primary care, and high-technology medical facilities than members of the local community can afford to use, although some sparsely-populated areas and poorer rural areas still face a dearth of primary case services.[234]

This maldistribution of resources led to the enactment of legislation authorizing DHHS to designate "health manpower shortage areas" and then to assign to them personnel of the National Health Service Corps.[235] Federal funds have been targeted to encourage physicians, nurses and other health professionals to serve in underserved areas.[236] The problem of underserved areas is being resolved to some extent by increasing urbanization, by improved means of transportation and communication, and by substantial planning efforts which have extended the network of available treatment resources.[237]

The availability of financial and other means to secure and pay for professional medical services is a distinct and problematic issue. There is no national health service in the United States, nor is there a national system of health insurance. There is no constitutional "right to treatment," but there are many government-sponsored and private systems that assure medical care to most, if not all, people in the United States. Efforts are being made to cover the people who need health care but cannot obtain access to health services because of their inability to pay or because they have not joined public or private medical programs.

Retired persons (usually past the age of sixty-five), blind persons, and certain categories of permanently disabled who qualify for Social Security, are covered by "Medicare" hospitalization insurance which provides in-hospital surgical benefits. By paying a minimal additional

[234] *See* Aday and Anderson, *The National Profile of Access to Medical Care: Where Do We Stand?*, 74 AM. J. PUBLIC HEALTH 1331 (1984). *See also* PRIMARY HEALTH CARE 2000, at 223-224 (J. Fry and J. C. Hasler eds. 1986).

[235] 42U.S.C. §254d-254g. A health manpower shortage area is defined to include a geographical area, a population group, or a public or private medical facility. Indicators of need include infant mortality, access to health services, health status, and the percentage of physicians serving the area who are foreign medical graduates.

[236] E.g., 42 U.S.C. §294h(c), which provides that a medical student or other health professional who has his or her education financed by a student loan may serve either in private practice or as a member of the National Health Service Corps and have up to $10,000 of the loan repayment forgiven for each 12-month period served.

[237] 42 U.S.C. §300k. *See also* 42 U.S.C. §300s-1a which provides for phasing out excess facilities in areas where they are no longer needed.

premium, they are also covered for most other ordinary medical costs, such as physicians' bills and office visits to a physician. Medicare is an entirely federal program, operated as a part of the Social Security System under Title XVIII of the Social Security Act.[238]

Another system of public payments for medical services is Medicaid, which is funded in part by the federal government and in part by the states under Title XIX of the Social Security Act. The federal government provides grants to the states to establish reimbursement programs for medical expenses of "medically indigent" persons—i.e., persons who are too poor to be able to meet their own medical expenses, though they may not be otherwise in need of public support or social welfare.[239] In addition, many states have supplemental welfare programs to provide health care and health services to vulnerable populations, such as poor families and near-poor single-parent households.

Approximately sixty percent of the working population in the United States has access to health care through employer-sponsored health benefits, as part of their employee fringe benefits.[240] Often these benefits are negotiated as part of a collective bargaining agreement between the employees' labor union and the employer, although there is a trend to sever hospital insurance from other health protection and to require employees to choose among different packages of health benefits programs. Some of these programs provide limited coverage and exclude many medical problems. Increasingly, they also require co-payment for many health services. Public and private insurance arrangements cover the largest part of the population—few Americans pay their own health costs directly. Many medical services are paid for by "third-party payers," including private insurers, such as Blue Cross/Blue Shield and Health Maintenance Organizations (HMOs) or through federally-funded programs. In spite of great progress, many reimbursement programs still exclude people who are uninsured or underinsured, a matter that is receiving continuing attention.

Many direct service systems are also available to people in the armed forces and their families, who receive medical care and hospital

[238] 42 U.S.C. §1395 et seq.

[239] 42 U.S.C. §1396 et seq.

[240] *See* Davis and Rowland, *Uninsured and Underserved: Inequities in Health Care in the U.S.*, 16 MILBANK MEMORIAL FUND QUARTERLY HEALTH AND SOCIETY (No. 2, 1983).

coverage in government facilities.[241] Veterans who suffer from service-connected ailments or disabilities, and veterans with non-service connected ailments who cannot afford to pay for care, are treated at veterans' hospitals and other facilities.[242]

On the state and local level, provision is made in most parts of the country for free services in state or municipal hospitals for indigent patients. Patients seeking such services must prove that they are indigent by meeting a "means test." With increasing reliance on Medicare, Medicaid, and private insurance reimbursement, the free service provided by public hospitals has waned. But poor and near-poor populations continue to depend on public hospitals and direct service programs that provide free services from private or voluntary hospitals. Such institutions are under an obligation to provide free care, but the quality of care and its availability has sometimes been controversial.

The present mechanisms for rendering and financing health services have led to significant differences in the quality of care. Persons with adequate means or insurance coverage are likely to get first-rate care in private or voluntary institutions. Persons with limited means or insurance coverage may have difficulty in obtaining care, even in emergencies. The quality of care may then depend on the institution to which they are referred or which will accept them. For these vulnerable populations, preventive care and early treatment is likely to be minimal. This gives rise to concern over a "two-track" system, where privately funded or well-insured patients obtain care but low-income patients have far less access to health care and health services. This approach is ultimately expensive, since public funds for underinsured and uninsured people are spent on acute care, which costs more money than prevention and early treatment.

### *Article 12 With or Without Qualifications?*

Although the United States has no constitutional requirement that health services be provided to all people who need them, and a national health service or national health insurance remains a matter

[241] 10 U.S.C. §§1074-1087. For history and contributions of military medicine, *see* Cowan and Burke, *The Evolution of Military Medicine,* in Endicott, *supra* note 156, at 37-50.

[242] 38 U.S.C. §601 et seq. For comments on the very substantial VA hospital system, *see* Chase, *Medical Care for America's Veterans,* in Endicott, *supra* note 156, at 51-65.

of political debate, both the legal framework and the availability of health services in general meet the requirements of Article 12.

There appears to be no need for a statement of understanding, declaration or reservation to account for the failure to establish a right of treatment for all. While unfavorable comparisons with other industrial States are possible, Article 2(1) affords adequate legal protection against potential allegations of non-compliance.

## ARTICLES 13 AND 14—RIGHT TO EDUCATION

*Mark G. Yudof*

Article 13

1. The States Parties to the present Covenant recognize the right of everyone to education. They agree that education shall be directed to the full development of the human personality and the sense of its dignity, and shall strengthen the respect for human rights and fundamental freedoms. They further agree that education shall enable all persons to participate effectively in a free society, promote understanding, tolerance and friendship among all nations and all racial, ethnic or religious groups, and further the activities of the United Nations for the maintenance of peace.

2. The States Parties to the present Covenant recognize that, with a view to achieving the full realization of this right:

(a) Primary education shall be compulsory and available free to all;

(b) Secondary education in its different forms, including technical and vocational secondary education, shall be made generally available and accessible to all by every appropriate means, and in particular by the progressive introduction of free education;

(c) Higher education shall be made equally accessible to all, on the basis of capacity, by every appropriate means, and in particular by the progressive introduction of free education;

(d) Fundamental education shall be encouraged or intensified as far as possible for those persons who have not received or completed the whole period of their primary education;

(e) The development of a system of schools at all levels shall be actively pursued, an adequate fellowship system shall be established, and the material conditions of teaching staff shall be continuously improved.

3. The States Parties to the present Covenant undertake to have respect for the liberty of parents and, when applicable, legal guardians, to choose for their children schools, other than those established by the public authorities, which conform to such minimum educational standards as may be laid down or approved by the State and to ensure the religious and moral education of their children in conformity with their own convictions.

4. No part of this article shall be construed so as to interfere with the liberty of individuals and bodies to establish and direct educational institutions, subject always to the observance of the principles set forth in paragraph 1 of this Article and to the requirement that the education given in such institutions shall conform to such minimum standards as may be laid down by the State.

Article 14

Each State Party to the present Covenant which, at the time of becoming a Party, has not been able to secure in its metropolitan territory or other territories under its jurisdiction compulsory primary education, free of charge, undertakes, within two years, to work out and adopt a detailed plan of action for the progressive implementation, within a reasonable number of years, to be fixed in the plan, of the principle of compulsory education free of charge for all.

Under Article 13, the States Parties "recognize" the right to education proclaimed earlier in Article 26 of the Universal Declaration as well as the American Declaration,[243] the European Social Charter,[244] and the revised OAS Charter.[245] Under Article 14, which appears to have little or no consequence for the United States domestically, States commit themselves to draw up plans of action for "the progressive implementation" of free and compulsory primary education.

### *Analysis of Articles 13 and 14*

The comparatively detailed character of these articles is due largely to the fact that UNESCO, with which the drafters consulted, favored detailed articles on the right to education.[246] It is to the work of

[243] *Supra* note 15, art. 12.
[244] *Supra* note 16, art. 10.
[245] *Supra* note 17, arts. 31(h), 45, and 46.
[246] *See U.N. Annotations, supra* note 1, at 112, para. 36.

UNESCO in the field of education, in fact, that one should look to fill gaps and clarify ambiguities.[247] UNESCO played the same role here that the ILO played with respect of Articles 6-11 and that the World Health Organization played with respect of Article 12.

Paragraph 1 of Article 13 sets out five educational objectives that were considered by the drafters to be the aims of education generally and which echo the spirit, even in part the letter, of Article 26 of the Universal Declaration. Even though such detail is not to be found elsewhere in the Covenant, it was believed necessary in light of the widely differing ends to which education can be put.[248] The Commission on Human Rights and Third Committee drafters, it seems, were adamant in their resolve to promote inexpensive, egalitarian, and comprehensive education for all, to the extent possible within the limits of available resources (per Article 2).

In a mandatory tone, but subject to the "progressive realization" qualification of Article 2(2), paragraph 2 of Article 13 sets out what the drafters believed to be the essential ingredients for the "full realization" of the aims of education: free compulsory education at the primary level; the "progressive introduction" of free, though not necessarily compulsory, education at the secondary and higher education levels; technical and vocational education, reflected in a 1975 UNESCO Recommendation stating that such education is or should be intended for the multiple purposes of "abolishing barriers between levels and areas of education, between education and employment, and between school and society";[249] "fundamental

[247] See, e.g., Convention Against Discrimination in Education, adopted 14 Dec. 1960, *entered into force* 22 May 1962, 429 U.N.T.S. 93; Recommendation Concerning Technical and Vocational Education, adopted 11 Dec. 1962, 12 UNESCO Gen. Conf. Rec., UNESCO Doc. 12C/Resolutions, at 129 (1963); Recommendation Concerning the Status of Teachers, *adopted* 5 Oct. 1966, by the UNESCO Special Intergovernmental Conference on the Status of Teachers, 14 UNESCO Gen. Conf. Rec., UNESCO Doc. 14C/Resolutions, at 29 (1967); Recommendation Concerning Education for International Understanding, Cooperation and Peace, and Education Relating to Human Rights and Fundamental Freedoms, *adopted* 19 Nov. 1974, 18 UNESCO Gen. Conf. Rec., UNESCO Doc. 18C/Resolutions, at 147 (1974); Revised Recommendation Concerning Technical and Vocational Education, *adopted* 19 Nov. 1974, 18 UNESCO Gen. Conf. Rec., UNESCO Doc. 18C/Resolutions, at 154 (1975); Recommendation on the Development of Adult Education, *adopted* 26 Nov. 1976 by the 19th General Conference of UNESCO, UNESCO Doc. 19C/Resolutions, Annex I, at 3 (1977).

[248] *See U.N. Annotations, supra* note 1, at 112-13, para. 37.

[249] Revised Recommendation Concerning Technical and Vocational Education, *supra* note 247. The Recommendation also makes explicit reference to equality of access to such education for men and women, to special forms of education for disadvantaged and handicapped persons, to participation by the representatives of different segments of society in policy formulation relative to such education, and to equal standards of quality in different educational streams to prevent discrimination between them.

education," by which is meant, according to UNESCO, complete programs of elementary instruction (not necessarily a part of formal educational programming) for illiterate children and adults, designed to help such people become fully participating and productive members of society; and finally, "a school system at all levels," "an adequate fellowship [i.e., scholarship] system," and the continuous improvement of "the material conditions of teaching staff," this last priority being the subject of fuller definition and discussion in a 1966 UNESCO Recommendation Concerning the Status of Teachers.[250]

In detailing these educational priorities the drafters took pains to affirm the "liberty" of parents and legal guardians to choose religious or secular non-State schools for their children, and, additionally, "to establish and direct [private] educational institutions" of their choice. Indeed, paragraphs 3 and 4 of Article 13 suggest, irrespective of the "progressive realization" terms of Article 2, an immediate undertaking on the part of the States Parties, consistent with Articles 18 and 19 of the CPR Covenant relative to freedom of thought, conscience, religion, opinion, and expression. It is important to note that, however, the drafters chose the word "liberty" rather than the word "right" in order to avoid any implication that the State might be obligated to provide material assistance for the education of children outside State schools.[251] Further, the State may prescribe and maintain "minimum educational standards." According to the preparatory history, this stress upon "minimal educational standards" was adopted partly to allay fears that the exercise of excessive individual liberty might result in teaching contrary to the objectives of paragraph 1 and partly to offset the undesirable possibility that "foreign bodies" might spread subversive propaganda under the guise of education.[252]

It also may be observed that Article 13, by referring to the right to education for "everyone" and "to all," implicitly endorses the concept of equality of educational opportunity. As such, of course, it is consistent with the non-discrimination language of Articles 2(2) and 3. Also, it is consistent with several UNESCO instruments which address the eradication of discrimination in education based on sex,

[250] *See supra* note 247.

[251] *See* Report of the Third Committee, 12 U.N. GAOR Annexes (Agenda Item 33) 1, at 4 (1957).

[252] *See id.*

race, or handicap.[253] Unclear, however, is whether Article 13 obligates the States Parties to provide education for linguistic minorities in their maternal or usual tongue. The preparatory history does not say. Yet, bearing in mind that Article 2(2) forbids discrimination on the basis of language and national origin, it is at least arguable that Article 13 does impose such a duty. On the other hand, guidance might be found in the decision of the European Court of Human Rights in the *Belgian Linguistic Cases*,[254] in which the Court construed Article 14 of the European Convention on Human Rights and Fundamental Freedoms[255] to mean that the obligation would arise only where *arbitrary* discrimination between linguistic groups could be established.

Finally, with regards to Article 14, it remains only to point out that the drafters, working in the climate of the 1960s "Development Decade," were keenly aware of the importance of free and compulsory primary education to economic development. Primary education, it was argued, "should not be made subject only to a general obligation to take steps to achieve progressive development."[256]

### *Domestic Implications*

Articles 13 and 14 are entirely consistent with the highest ideals of American education as frequently expressed in federal and state laws and constitutional provisions. If anything, these articles promise American children much of what already has been attained and much less than legislators and other education policymakers are striving for. While an entitlement to education is not embodied expressly or implied by the U. S. Constitution, a number of key clauses, in particular the Equal Protection and Due Process clauses, have been extended to protect particular education entitlements.[257] Equally or more importantly, every state has a state constitutional provision which, in varying language, contains an education guarantee through

[253] *See* Convention Against Discrimination in Education, *supra* note 247.

[254] *See* Case Relating to Certain Aspects of the Laws on the Use of Languages in Education in Belgium, Eur. Ct. Human Rts., Judgment of 23 July 1968, Ser. A No. 6, *reprinted in abridged form* in [1968] Y. B. EUR. CONV. ON HUMAN RIGHTS 832.

[255] Art. 14. of the European Convention provides: "The enjoyment of the rights and freedoms set forth in this Convention shall be secured without discrimination on any ground such as sex, race, colour, language, religion, political or other opinion, natural or social origin, association with a national minority, property, birth or other status."

[256] *U. N. Annotations, supra* note 1, at 114.

[257] *See generally* M. YUDOF, D. KIRP, T. VAN GEEL, B. LEVIN, EDUCATIONAL POLICY AND THE LAW chs. 3, 5-6 (3rd ed. 1992).

the secondary level;[258] these constitutional provisions are implemented, in turn, by state compulsory education statutes which generally require public school attendance for nearly all children, ages seven to sixteen.[259] Thus, virtually all American children have access to a public education through the secondary level, and national statistics show a high level of enrollment.[260] Compulsory attendance laws may be satisfied in approved private institutions[261] and, in many states, by home instruction,[262] but this is consistent with the constitutionally recognized right of parents to direct the education of their children,[263] and reflected, as observed above, in Article 13(3). Most states allow students to quit school upon completion of a particular grade or upon employment after a specified age, and there is grave concern about the drop-out rate, particularly among minority youngsters. But nearly all states make special efforts for "children at risk" and allow drop-outs to take adult education courses to qualify for high school equivalency diplomas.[264]

Some troublesome issues have surrounded certain traditional exemptions to compulsory attendance laws for children otherwise within the specified age bracket (e.g. children with mental, emotional, or physical disabilities; suspended or expelled students; incarcerated children; children excluded because of marriage or pregnancy).[265] For

[258] *See generally* T. VAN GEEL, THE COURTS AND AMERICAN EDUCATION LAW (1987). Responsibility for financing and operating public schools generally lies with the states, albeit the federal government provides some forms of categorical assistance and regulates some significant aspects of school operations. *See generally* B. LEVIN, THE COURTS AS EDUCATIONAL POLICYMAKERS AND THEIR IMPACT ON FEDERAL PROGRAMS 1 (1977); FEDERAL AID TO EDUCATION (J. Berke & M. Kirst eds. 1972).

[259] *See* VAN GEEL, *supra* note 258, at 18-21; NATIONAL INSTITUTE OF EDUCATION, STATE LEGAL STANDARDS FOR THE PROVISION OF PUBLIC EDUCATION (1978) [hereinafter cited as STATE LEGAL STANDARDS]. *See generally* M. Katz, A History of Compulsory Education Laws (1976); D. TYACK, T. JAMES & A. BENAVOT, LAW AND THE SHAPING OF PUBLIC EDUCATION, 1785-1954 (1987).

[260] Tyack, *Ways of Seeing: An Essay on the History of Compulsory Schooling,* 46 HARV. EDUC. REV. 355 (1976).

[261] *See* Lines, *Private Education Alternatives and State Regulation,* 12 J. LAW & EDUC. 189 (1983). *See generally* L. KOTIN & W. AIKMAN, LEGAL FOUNDATIONS OF COMPULSORY ATTENDANCE 93-110 (1980).

[262] *See,* e.g., Care and Protection of Charles, 399 Mass. 324, 504 N.E.2d 592 (1987); State v. Massa, 95 N.J. Super. 382, 231 A.2d 252 (1967). *See generally* Lines, *supra* note 261; Kahn, *Home Schooling,* THE ATLANTIC, 20 (April 1988).

[263] *See* Pierce v. Society of Sisters, 268 U.S. 510 (1925), a decision in which a state law allowing only public school attendance to satisfy compulsory education laws was found unconstitutional. *See also* Wisconsin v. Yoder, 406 U.S. 205 (1972).

[264] *See* STATE LEGAL STANDARDS, *supra* note 259, at 16, 25. In most states, a student may quit school between the ages of 14 to 16. *Id.* at 25.

[265] *See generally* VAN GEEL, *supra* note 258, at 117-120.

the most part, the problem has been resolved in the United States by statutes and court decisions declaring that these formerly exempted students have the right to receive an education at public expense.[266] For example, under the 1975 Education for All Handicapped Children Act,[267] students with certain physical and mental disabilities must be afforded an "appropriate education" by the states;[268] resident alien children also may not constitutionally be excluded from public schools.[269] Even the traditional power of public schools to suspend or expel miscreant students has been limited by due process protections.[270] Increasingly, the states themselves are circumscribing the power to suspend or expel, and often alternative instruction must be offered.

This does not mean that every child necessarily receives a public education, satisfactory to her and her parents. There has been grave difficulty in defining an adequate, minimum, or appropriate education for those who are in school.[271] In addition many children drop out of public schools under circumstances suggesting that school officials have not successfully attempted to meet their educational needs. But the overall thrust of American law is entirely consistent with the universal and compulsory education aims of Article 13.

The state-guaranteed entitlement to a *free* public education occasionally has raised legal problems. School districts are not permitted to charge tuition, but in some states a school district may impose a charge for non-resident students.[272] Another issue is whether fees for

[266] *See, e.g.*, Ordway v. Hargraves, 323 F.Supp. 1155 (D. Mass. 1971) (exclusion of pregnant, unmarried high school student unconstitutional); Bell v. Lone Oak Ind. School District, 507 S.W.2d 636 (Tex. Civ. App. 1979) (married students); Knight v. Board of Education, 48 F.R.D. 115 (E.D. N.Y. 1969) (nonattendance); Mills v. Board of Education, 348 F.Supp. 866 (D.D.C. 1972) (mentally retarded, emotionally disturbed, physically handicapped, hyperactive, etc.); Pennsylvania Ass'n for Retarded Children v. Pennsylvania, 343 F.Supp. 279 (E.D. Pa. 1972) (consent decree). *See generally* VAN GEEL, *supra* note 258, at 120-124; Haggerty & Sacks, *Education of the Handicapped,* 50 TEMPLE L.Q. 961 (1977); Comment, *Marriage, Pregnancy, and the Right to go to School,* 50 TEX. L. REV. 1196 (1972).

[267] 20 U.S.C. §1405-20 (1976). *See* Board of Education v. Rowley, 458 U.S. 176 (1982).

[268] Hosier v. Evans, 314 F.Supp. 316 (D. V.I. 1970).

[269] *See* Plyler v. Doe, 467 U.S. 202 (1982).

[270] *See* e.g., Goss v. Lopez, 419 U.S. 565 (1975); Banks v. Board of Public Instruction, 450 F.2d 1103 (5th Cir. 1971); Dixon v. Alabama State Bd. of Education, 294 F.2d 150 (1961). *See generally* Kirp, *Proceduralism and Bureaucracy: Due Process in the School Setting,* 28 STAN. L. REV. 841 (1976); Buss, *Procedural Due Process for School Discipline: Probing the Constitutional Outline,* 119 U. PA. L. REV. 545 (1971).

[271] *See* e.g., Board of Education v. Rowley, *supra* note 267.

[272] *See, e.g.*, Gray v. Board of Education, 389 P.2d 498 (Okla. 1964). *See generally,* VAN GEEL, *supra* note 258, at 124-125; E. G. GEE & D. SPERRY, EDUCATION LAW AND THE PUBLIC SCHOOLS; A COMPENDIUM T64-T65 (1978).

transportation, books, gym uniforms or extracurricular activities (e.g., band) are permissible under federal or state constitutions.[273] The trend is that charges related to the central educational mission of the school are unconstitutional under state education clauses, but incidental charges are allowed.[274]

Legal reform of education in the United States has tended to focus on non-discrimination and equal educational opportunity, and in this respect American education may have exceeded the minimum expectations articulated in Articles 13 and 14. To be sure, equal educational opportunity in the United States is highly dependent on the availability and distribution of public resources, family wealth, appropriate learning environments, non-discrimination against the poor and minorities, and effective teaching and educational strategies. Much remains to be done, as national reports have demonstrated.[275] But the initial steps have been taken, and in recent years the academic achievement of the bottom quartile of students has risen more rapidly than achievement in the top quartile.

The 1964 Civil Rights Act prohibits racial discrimination in public education,[276] and this statute has given great force to the effort to desegregate public education. Racial discrimination in admission to private schools has been declared to be unlawful,[277] and private schools engaging in discriminatory practices do not qualify for favorable tax treatment under federal income tax laws.[278] Discrimination against students with limited English-speaking ability has been outlawed by Congress,[279] and aid is provided by the federal govern-

[273] *See* Kadrmas v. Dickinson Public Schools, 108 S.Ct. 2481 (1988).

[274] *See* e.g., Board of Education v. Sinclair, 65 Wis.2d 179, 222 N.W.2d 143 (1974); Bond v. Public Schools of Ann Arbor School District, 338 Mich. 693, 178 N.W.2d 484 (1970); Paulson v. Minidoka Country Sch. Dist. No. 331, 93 Idaho 469, 463 P.2d 935 (1970). *But see* Hamer v. Board of Education, 47 Ill.2d 480, 265 N.E.2d 616 (1970). *See generally* VAN GEEL, *supra* note 258, at 124.

[275] *See,* e.g., National Commission on Excellence in Education, *A Nation at Risk* (1983).

[276] 42 U.S.C. §§2000a-h-6 (1976). *See generally* RADIN, IMPLEMENTATION, CHANGE, AND THE FEDERAL BUREAUCRACY; SCHOOL DESEGREGATION POLICY IN HEW 1964-1968 (1977); G. ORFIELD, THE RECONSTRUCTION OF SOUTHERN EDUCATION (1969).

[277] Runyon v. McCrary, 427 U.S. 160 (1976), *construing* 42 U.S.C. §1981 (1976) (originally section I of the 1866 Civil Rights Act). *See generally* Note, *Runyon v. McCrary and Private School Admission Policies,* 16 J. OF FAM. L. 77 (1977).

[278] Bob Jones University v. United States, 461 U.S. 574 (1983).

[279] Equal Educational Opportunities Act of 1974, §202, 20 U.S.C. §1701 (1976). *See also* Lau v. Nichols, 414 U.S. 563 (1974) (Title VI of Civil Rights Act of 1964); Castaneda v. Pickard, 648 F.2d 989 (5th Cir. 1981); Keyes v. School District No. 1, 521 F.2d 465, 482 (10th Cir. 1975).

ment (and by many state governments) for bilingual programs.[280] Title IX of the Education Amendments of 1972 prohibits many forms of sex discrimination, including the exclusion of females from particular courses or athletic activities.[281] Since 1965, the federal government has embarked on an ambitious program of providing compensatory education to educationally deprived youngsters, most notably those in areas with high concentrations of poor children.[282] Not all of these programs have been unmitigated successes, and there is still much to be learned about how to implement complex education reforms and how best to meet the needs of "at risk" children. Nonetheless, these regulatory and programmatic measures go well beyond the bare-bones guarantees of the Covenant.

The most intractable problem in public education in the United States is that of school segregation, which is scarcely mentioned in Articles 13 and 14. This should not be surprising, since the world community has in fact devoted little attention to the elaboration of the non-discrimination principle in the context of public schooling.[283] In *Brown v. Board of Education,*[284] the Fourteenth Amendment was construed as forbidding the deliberate separation of the races in public schools, but in subsequent cases the Supreme Court has had difficulty grappling with the question of what constitutes deliberate segregation.[285] In addition, the courts have been called upon to determine the appropriate remedy for past discrimination, and there has been much

[280] Bilingual Education Act, 20 U.S.C. §880b et seq. (1976). Bilingual education monies are available also under the Emergency School Aid Act for districts undergoing school desegregation. The magnitude of federal aid, however, is not great, and states and school districts still provide the bulk of the financial support for bilingual education. *See* LEVIN, *supra* note 257, at 40.

[281] 20 U.S.C. §§1681-86 (1976). *See also* Berkelman v. San Francisco Unified School District, 501 F.2d 1264 (9th Cir. 1974). Sex-based employment discrimination in public schools is covered by the Equal Pay Act (29 U.S.C. §206 (1970), as amended, 29 U.S.C. §206 (Supp. III, (1973)) and Title VII of the Civil Rights Act of 1964 (42 U.S.C. §2000e et seq. (1976)). *See also* Cleveland Board of Education v. LeFleur, 414 U.S. 632 (1974). The status of sex-separate high schools is less clear, although the Supreme Court upheld such separation without opinion. *See* Vorchheimer v. School District of Philadelphia, 532 F.2d 880 (3rd Cir.), *affirmed by an equally divided court,* 430 U.S. 703 (1977). With respect to public higher education, the Court has held that, at least in some circumstances, separate schools for women or men violate the constitutional guarantee of equal protection. *See* Mississippi University for Women v. Hogan, 458 U.S. 718 (1982).

[282] Title I of the Elementary and Secondary Education Act of 1965, 20 U.S.C. §241a-ff (1976), recodified in subchapter I, ch. 51 of the Elementary and Secondary Education Block Grant Act, 20 U.S.C. §3801 et seq. (1981).

[283] *See* Yudof, *International Human Rights and School Desegregation in the United States,* 15 TEX. INT. L.J. 101 (1979).

[284] 347 U.S. 483 (1954).

[285] *See,* e.g., Keyes v. School District No. 1, 413 U.S. 189 (1973).

dispute about whether the goal should be racially balanced public schools or color-blind neighborhood assignments.[286] The majority of students in most large, urban school districts are now minority, most frequently African Americans and Hispanics. Thus, the federal courts are confronted with a variety of complex and controversial issues that go beyond the simple moral imperative of *Brown*. Nonetheless, it is fair to say that American law and practice relative to racial desegregation in the education sector compares favorably with the racial non-discrimination principles that underpin Articles 13 and 14.

Finally, any comparison of Articles 13 and 14 and the existing legal rules in the United States would be incomplete without mention of *San Antonio Independent School District v. Rodriguez,* a 1973 Supreme Court decision in which the Court held that education is not a fundamental interest under the Equal Protection clause of the Constitution.[287] The impact of the *Rodriguez* decision was to uphold state school financing plans that result in unequal expenditures of dollars on the schooling of children living in different geographical areas, variations that are largely a function of disparate local property tax bases among school districts. Upon first reading, *Rodriguez* may appear inconsistent with the aims of Article 13, but this would be to attribute too much to the decision. First, as noted, state constitutions and federal statutes generally protect the education entitlements of school-age children. Second, many state legislatures have taken measures to redress inequities in school financing,[288] though few have completely addressed the problem. A number of state supreme courts also have undertaken school finance reform under applicable state constitutional provisions.[289] Third, the Court held only that differences in taxable property wealth in local school districts (resulting in different levels of educational expenditure for students living in those districts) were not unconstitutional. The majority opined that failure

[286] *See* Dayton Board of Education v. Brinkman, 443 U.S. 526 (1979) (Dayton II); Columbus Board of Education v. Penick, 443 U.S. 449 (1979) (Columbus II).

[287] 411 U.S. 1 (1973).

[288] *See generally* EDUCATION COMMISSION OF THE STATES, ANALYSIS AND COMPARISON OF FISCAL RESPONSES IN FOUR STATES (1979); S. CARROLL, THE SEARCH FOR EQUITY IN SCHOOL FINANCE; RESULTS FROM FIVE STATES (1979); J. CALLAHAN & W. WILKEN, SCHOOL FINANCE REFORM; A LEGISLATOR'S HANDBOOK (1976); N. GRUBB & S. MICHELSON, STATES AND SCHOOLS: THE POLITICAL ECONOMY OF SCHOOL FINANCE (1974).

[289] *See,* e.g., Edgewood Independent School District v. Kirby, 777 S.W.2d 391 (Tex. 1989); Rose v. The Council for Better Education, Inc., 790 S.W.2d 186 (Ky 1989); Robinson v. Cahill, 62 N.J. 473, 303 A.2d 273 (1973); Serrano v. Priest, 5 Cal.3d 584, 487 P.2d 1241, 96 Cal. Rptr. 601 (1971). *But see* Board of Education v. Nyquist, 57 N.Y.2d 27, 453 N.Y.S.2d 643 (1982).

to provide a minimum education might well be a constitutional violation, and the Court reached this result in a later case.[290] Finally, the Court left intact the decisional law forbidding invidious discrimination in education by race, gender and other arbitrary classifications.[291]

In summary, Articles 13 and 14 pose few or no significant problems of compliance for the United States. Universal, free and compulsory education is generally established by both law and practice. The parental right to guide the upbringing of children and to choose a private school has been constitutionally protected for more than sixty years. The aspirations of personal development, effective participation in a free society and equal educational opportunity, although by no means fully realized, remain central goals in education policy.

## ARTICLE 15—RIGHTS RELATING TO CULTURE AND SCIENCE

*Stephen P. Marks, with the assistance of Sofia Gruskin*

1. States Parties to the present Covenant recognize the right of everyone:

   (a) To take part in cultural life;

   (b) To enjoy the benefits of scientific progress and its applications;

   (c) To benefit from the protection of the moral and material interests resulting from any scientific, literary or artistic production of which he is the author.

2. The steps to be taken by the States Parties to the present Covenant to achieve the full realization of these rights shall include those necessary for the conservation, the development and the diffusion of science and culture.

3. The States Parties to the present Covenant undertake to respect the freedom indispensable for scientific research and creative activity.

[290] *See* Plyler v. Doe, *supra* note 269.
[291] *See generally* M. YUDOF et al., *supra* note 257, at chs. 5-7.

> 4. The States Parties to the present Covenant recognize the benefits to be derived from the encouragement and development of international contacts and cooperation in the scientific and cultural fields.

Under Article 15, the final substantive article in the ESC Covenant, the States Parties "recognize" the same three cultural and scientific rights proclaimed in Article 27 of the Universal Declaration of Human Rights and in Article 13 of the American Declaration on the Rights and Duties of Man. The Covenant adds indications regarding the steps States Parties are expected to take to achieve the rights, the freedoms considered "indispensable" in these fields, and the fact that international contacts and cooperation are deemed to be beneficial.

### *Analysis of Article 15*

UNESCO played an active role in drafting this article, as it did with respect to Articles 13 and 14.[292] Furthermore, UNESCO's standard-setting and program activities before and after the adoption of the Covenant have expanded and developed each of Article 15's provisions. The present analysis of the content of Article 15 will therefore draw on UNESCO definitions of culture and science and on the organization's normative activity with respect to each of the paragraphs of the article. While the United States is party to some but not all the UNESCO treaties and, at the time of writing, is no longer a member of UNESCO, it was an active participant in the drafting of virtually all UNESCO conventions and recommendations. Whatever the present U.S. attitude towards the organization, these instruments constitute a unique source of interpretation of the rights set forth in Article 15.

The broadest explanation of "culture" is to be found in the Recommendation on Participation by the People at Large in Cultural Life and Their Contribution to It (1976) [hereinafter "Recommendation on Participation in Cultural Life"].[293] While the Recommendation encountered opposition from some member States, including the United States,[294] the definition of culture on which it is based remains

[292] *See* Alston, *The United Nations Specialized Agencies and Implementation of the International Covenant on Economic, Social and Cultural Rights,* 18 COLUMBIA J. TRANSNAT'L L. 79, 84 (1979).

[293] Recommendation on Participation by the People at Large in Cultural Life and Their Contribution to It, *adopted* 26 Nov. 1976, *reprinted in UNESCO's Standard-Setting Instruments,* Sec. IV.B.7.

[294] The vote on the Recommendation at the 19th session of the General Conference was 63 in favor, 5 against, and 15 abstentions. *See* UNESCO, *Records of the General Conference, 19th session, proceedings,* vol. 2, part 2, Nairobi, 1976 19 C/Res. 131.5, p. 402 (1978). Before the vote, delegations from the United Kingdom, the Federal Republic of Germany, France, Belgium, Italy, Canada, the United States, Portugal, and Guatemala objected, variously, to references to "commercial mass culture," terminology, meanings, and philosophical style of the Recommenda-

valid. The text contains preambular paragraphs according to which "culture is, in its essence, a social phenomenon resulting from individuals joining and co-operating in creative activities." The text states further that culture "is at one and the same time the acquisition of knowledge, the demand for a way of life and the need to communicate."

The right to participate in cultural life, as stipulated in subparagraph 1(a) of the covenant, has been expanded by fifteen normative UNESCO instruments.[295] Of these, the Recommendation on Participation in Cultural Life, in spite of the above-noted criticisms by several States, provides the most comprehensive set of relevant principles (although they do not bind the United States).

The Recommendation specifies that "participation by the greatest possible number of people and associations in a wide variety of cultural activities of their own free choice is essential to the development of the basic human values and dignity of the individual" and that "access to culture and participation in cultural life are essential components of an overall social policy."[296] The Preamble stresses a non-elitist approach to cultural participation based on the idea:

---

tion, implied restrictions on freedom of expression and of individual creativity, and possible control of creative activity, by an oppressive bureaucracy. The Canadian and Japanese delegations urged postponement of the Recommendation. After the vote, the U.S. delegation disassociated itself from the Recommendation. *Id.,* paras. 96.1-134, pp. 393-402.

[295] Convention for the Protection of Cultural Property in the Event of Armed Conflict, with Regulations for the Execution of the Convention of 14 May 1954 (Hague Convention); Protocol for the Protection of Cultural Property in the Event of Armed Conflict, of 14 May 1954; Recommendation concerning the Most Effective Means of Rendering Museums Accessible to Everyone, of 14 Dec. 1960; Recommendation on the Means of Prohibiting and Preventing the Illicit Export, Import and Transfer of Ownership of Cultural Property, of 19 Nov. 1964; Declaration of the Principles of International Cultural Co-operation, of 4 Nov. 1966; Convention on the Means of Prohibiting and Preventing the Illicit Export, Import and Transfer of Ownership of Cultural Property, of 14 Nov. 1970; Declaration of Guiding Principles on the Use of Satellite Broadcasting for the Free Flow of Information, the Spread of Education and Greater Cultural Exchange, of 15 Nov. 1972; Recommendation concerning Protection, at the National Level, of the Cultural and Natural Heritage, of 16 Nov. 1972; Convention concerning the Protection of the World Cultural Heritage of 16 Nov. 1972; Recommendation concerning the Safeguarding and Contemporary Role of Historic Areas, of 26 Nov. 1976; Recommendation on Participation in Cultural Life, *supra* note 290; Declaration on Fundamental Principles concerning the Contribution of the Mass Media to Strengthening Peace and International Understanding, to the Promotion of Human Rights and to Countering Racism, *Apartheid* and Incitement to War, of 28 Nov. 1978; Recommendation on the Protection of Movable Cultural Property, of 28 Nov. 1978; Recommendation concerning the Status of the Artist, of 27 Oct. 1980; Recommendation for the Safeguarding and Preservation of Moving Images, of 27 Oct. 1980.

[296] *Supra* note 293, Preamble.

> that culture is not merely an accumulation of works and knowledge which an elite produces, collects and conserves in order to place it within reach of all; or that a people rich in its past and its heritage offers to others as a model which their own history has failed to provide for them; and that culture is not limited to access to works of art and the humanities.

While the definition of culture is (perhaps necessarily) vague, that of science is more detailed and precise. According to the Recommendation on the Status of Scientific Researchers (1974):

> The word "science" signifies the enterprise whereby mankind, acting individually or in small or large groups, makes an organized attempt, by means of the objective study of observed phenomena, to discover and master the chain of causalities; brings together in a coordinated form the resultant sub-systems of knowledge by means of systematic reflection and conceptualization, often largely expressed in the symbols of mathematics; and thereby furnishes itself with the opportunity of using, to its own advantage, understanding of the processes and phenomena occurring in nature and society.[297]

As few of the normative instruments adopted by the General Conferences of UNESCO deal with science and technology, they are not immediately relevant to the promotion of the right to enjoy the benefits of scientific progress and its applications as specified under subparagraph 1(b) of Article 15 of the ESC Covenant. This right, nevertheless, reflects a basic motivation of most of UNESCO's program activities in the area of science. The Recommendation on the Status of Scientific Researchers mentions the benefits for mankind, the preservation of peace, and the reduction of international tensions through scientific discoveries and related technological developments made possible by the optimum usage of science and scientific methods.[298] It also recalls the disparities between different countries regarding access to scientific and technological knowledge and urges governments to adopt approaches, policies, and programs to overcome these disparities, in particular by developing a cadre of talented and trained personnel; guaranteeing open communication of results, hypotheses, and opinions; and providing adequate support and essential equipment for research and experimental development.[299]

[297] Recommendation on the Status of Scientific Researchers, 18 C/Res. 40, *adopted* 20 Nov. 1974, *reprinted in UNESCO Standard-Setting Instruments,* Sect. II.B.1.

[298] *Id.,* Preamble.

[299] *Id.*

The right to benefit from protection of the moral and material interests resulting from any scientific, literary, or artistic production of which one is creator, as set out in Article 15(1)(c), is covered primarily by the Universal Copyright Convention of 1952, as revised in 1971,[300] as well as the Berne Convention for the Protection of Literary and Artistic Works of 1886, revised in 1908, 1928, 1948, 1967 and 1971.[301] According to the former, each contracting State must protect the rights of authors and other copyright holders and provide the same "adequate and effective" protection for authors of any contracting State publishing in its State as that provided for its own nationals publishing first in its own territory. The Berne Convention establishes the principle that aliens and residents enjoy the same protection for their works as nationals and sets some minimum standards of protection.

Besides the Universal Copyright Convention, five other normative instruments adopted by international conferences or the General Conference of UNESCO are relevant to the right to benefit from the protection of the moral and material interests in intellectual property.[302]

Paragraph 2 of Article 15 refers to conservation, development and diffusion of science and culture, and several UNESCO instruments develop the concepts and policies suggested therein. The Declaration of the Principles of International Cultural Cooperation[303] provides a

[300] *Adopted* 6 Sept. 1952, 6 U.S.T. 2731, T.I.A.S. No. 3324, *reprinted in UNESCO's Standard-Setting Instruments,* Sect. V.2A.1 (*entered into force* for U.S. 16 Sept. 1955), *revised* 24 July 1971, 25 U.S.T. 1341, T.I.A.S. No. 7868, *reprinted in UNESCO's Standard-Setting Instruments,* Sect. V.2.A.2.

[301] 331 U.N.T.S. 217. The Berne Convention Implementation Act, enabling the United States to adhere to the Convention, was signed by the President on 31 Oct. 1988, Pub. L. No. 100-568, 102 Stat. 2853 (1988) *codified at* 17 U.S.C.A. §§101, 104, 116, 116A, 205, 301, 401-8, 411, 501, 504, 801 (West Supp. 1989). The Convention entered into force for the U.S. on 1 Mar. 1989. *See* DuBoff, Winter, Flacks & Keplinger, *Out of UNESCO and into Berne: Has United States Participation in the Berne Convention for International Copyright Protection Become Essential?* 4 CARDOZO ARTS & ENT. L.J. 203 (1985); Damich, *State "Moral Rights" Statutes: An Analysis and Critique,* 13 COLUM. VLA. J. L. & ARTS 291-347; Ross, *The United States Joins the Berne Convention: New Obligations for Authors' Moral Rights?* 68 NORTH CAROLINA L. REV. 363 (1990).

[302] These are the International Convention for the Protection of Performers, Producers of Phonograms and Broadcasting Organizations, of 16 Oct. 1961, *reprinted in UNESCO's Standard-Setting Instruments,* Sect. V.2.A.3; Convention on the Means of Prohibiting and Preventing the Illicit Import, Export and Transfer of Ownership of Cultural Property, of 14 Nov. 1970, *id.,* Sect. IV.A.4; Convention for the Protection of Producers of Phonograms against Unauthorized Duplication of their Phonograms, of 29 Oct. 1971, *id.,* Sect. V.2.A.4; Multilateral Convention for the Avoidance of Double Taxation of Copyright Royalties, of 13 Dec. 1979, *id.,* Sect. V.2.A.6; and Recommendation on the Legal Protection of Translators and Translations and the Practical Means to Improve the Status of Translators, of 22 Nov. 1976, *id.,* Sect. V.2.B.1.

[303] *Adopted* 4 Nov. 1966, *reprinted in UNESCO's Standard-Setting Instruments,* Sect. IV.C.1.

normative framework for both "conservation" and "development." Article 1 of the Declaration reads as follows:

> 1. Each culture has a dignity and value which must be respected and preserved;
>
> 2. Every people has the right and the duty to develop its culture;
>
> 3. In their rich variety and diversity, and in the reciprocal influences they exert on one another, all cultures form part of the common heritage belonging to all mankind.

The term "diffusion," as it appears in Article 15(2), appears to apply to Article IV of the Declaration, which provides that the aims of international cultural cooperation in its various forms shall include the following:

> To spread knowledge, to stimulate talent and to enrich cultures;
>
> To develop peaceful relations and friendship among the peoples and bring about a better understanding of each other's way of life; . . .
>
> To enable everyone to have access to knowledge, to enjoy the arts and literature of all peoples, to share in advances made in science in all parts of the world and in the resulting benefits, and to contribute to the enrichment of cultural life. . . .

Other instruments of particular importance to "conservation" are the Recommendation (1964)[304] and Convention (1970)[305] on the Means of Prohibiting and Preventing the Illicit Export, Import and Transfer of Ownership of Cultural Property. While the Convention and Recommendation reflect a concern for *national* cultural heritage, "conservation" of culture may also be understood as a means of preserving an *international* heritage.[306] This latter approach is evident

[304] Recommendation on the Means of Prohibiting and Preventing the Illicit Export, Import and Transfer of Ownership of Cultural Property, *adopted* 19 Nov. 1964, *reprinted in UNESCO's Standard-Setting Instruments,* Sect. IV.B.4.

[305] Convention on the Means of Prohibiting and Preventing the Illicit Export, Import and Transfer of Ownership of Cultural Property, *adopted* 14 Nov. 1970, 823 U.N.T.S. 231, *reprinted in id.,* Sect. IV.A.4. In 1972, the U.S. Senate unanimously gave its advice and consent to ratification of the Convention, and in 1983 Congress adopted enabling legislation by means of the Cultural Property Act (Pub. L. 97-446).

[306] The distinction between "cultural internationalism" and "cultural nationalism" was the basis of a study of the protection of cultural property through the 1954 Hague Convention and the 1970 Convention. *See* Merryman, *Two Ways of Thinking About Cultural Property,* 80 AJIL 831 (1986).

in the 1954 Convention for the Protection of Cultural Property in the Event of Armed Conflict (the Hague Convention).[307]

The 1972 UNESCO Convention Concerning the Protection of the World Cultural and Natural Heritage[308] extends to the world's natural heritage a protection formerly reserved for cultural heritage. Pursuant to this convention, the Intergovernmental Committee for the Protection of the World Cultural and Natural Heritage ("World Heritage Committee") was established, which keeps a "World Heritage List" and a "List of World Heritage in Danger."[309]

Conservation, development and diffusion of culture through museums has been promoted through several other UNESCO instruments. For example, a Recommendation concerning the Most Effective Means of Rendering Museums Accessible to Everyone was adopted by the General Conference in 1960,[310] and a Recommendation concerning the Safeguarding of the Beauty and Character of Landscapes and Sites was adopted in 1986.[311] The Declaration of Guiding Principles on the Use of Satellite Broadcasting for the Free Flow of Information, the Spread of Education and Greater Cultural Exchange of 1972[312] provides additional guidelines on the diffusion of culture. Recognizing that satellite broadcasting "provides a new means of disseminating knowledge," this text seeks to balance the concern for transfer of technology to developing countries with freedom of expression. Other articles deal with the objectives of free flow of information, the spread of education, and the promotion of culture through satellite broadcasting.

Conservation of culture is the focus of yet another UNESCO instrument, the Recommendation concerning the Safeguarding and Contemporary Role of Historic Areas of 1976.[313] The Recommendation for the protection of Movable Cultural Property of 1978 is

[307] *Adopted* 14 May 1954, *entered into force* 7 Aug. 1956, 249 U.N.T.S. 356, *reprinted in UNESCO's Standard-Setting Instruments,* Sect. IV.A.3. On the implementation of this Convention, *see* Saba, *UNESCO and Human Rights,* in THE INTERNATIONAL DIMENSIONS OF HUMAN RIGHTS 401, 403-10 (K. Vasak & P. Alston eds. 1982); Marks, *UNESCO and Human Rights: Implementation of Rights Relating to Education, Science, Culture and Communication,* 13 TEXAS INT'L. L.J. 35, 59 (1977); Merryman, *supra* note 309, at 833-42.

[308] *Adopted* 18 Nov. 1972, 1037 U.N.T.S. 151, 27 U.S.T. 37; T.I.A.S. 8226; *reprinted in UNESCO's Standard-Setting Instruments,* Sect. IV.A.5 Convention, arts. 3, 5.

[309] *Id.,* arts. 8 and 11. *Also see* Recommendation on International Principles Applicable to Archaeological Excavations, *reprinted in UNESCO's Standard-Setting Instruments,* Sect. IV.B.1.

[310] *Adopted* 14 Dec. 1960, *reprinted in UNESCO's Standard-Setting Instruments,* Sect. IV.B.2.

[311] *Adopted* 11 Dec. 1986, *reprinted in UNESCO's Standard-Setting Instruments,* Sec. IV.B.3.

[312] *Adopted* 15 Nov. 1972, *reprinted in UNESCO's Standard-Setting Instruments,* Sect. IV.C.2.

[313] *Adopted* 26 Nov. 1976, *reprinted in UNESCO's Standard-Setting Instruments,* Sect. IV.B.9.

concerned with protecting property in museums and similar institutions, private collections, and in religious buildings and archaeological sites.[314]

As far back as 1948, the UNESCO General Conference adopted an Agreement for Facilitating the International Circulation of Visual and Auditory Materials of an Educational, Scientific and Cultural Character ("The Beirut Agreement").[315] This agreement applies to material whose primary purpose or effect is to instruct or inform or when the content is such as to maintain, increase or diffuse knowledge. Such material originating in a State Party is exempt from customs duties, quantitative restrictions, and the need for import licenses in any other State Party. The exemptions of the Beirut Agreement were considerably expanded in two subsequent treaties, the Florence Agreement of 1950 and its Protocol of 1976, both of which have been ratified by the United States.[316]

The Recommendation on the Status of Scientific Researchers[317] is relevant to the conservation, development, and diffusion of science insofar as it addresses the critical role scientific workers play in policy making, research, and the application of science and technology. In particular, the Recommendation encourages Member States to facilitate publication of the results obtained by scientific researchers, as well as their participation in international scientific meetings and foreign travel.

Respect for the freedom indispensable for scientific research and creative activity, as set out in paragraph 3 of Article 15, is covered primarily by the Recommendation on the Status of Scientific Researchers and the Recommendation concerning the Status of the Artist. The preamble to the former recognizes "that open communication of the results, hypotheses and opinions—as suggested by the phrase 'academic freedom'—lies at the very heart of the scientific process and provides the strongest guarantee of accuracy and objectivity of scientific results." With respect to publicly supported scientific

[314] *Adopted* 28 Nov. 1978, *reprinted in UNESCO's Standard-Setting Instruments,* Sect. IV.B.10.

[315] *Entered into force for U.S.* 12 Jan. 1967. 17 U.S.T. 1578, T.I.A.S. No. 6116, 197 U.N.T.S. 3, *reprinted in UNESCO's Standard-Setting Instruments,* Sect. IV.A.1

[316] Agreement on the Importation of Educational, Scientific and Cultural Materials (the "Florence Agreement"), *adopted* 17 June 1950, *entered into force for U.S.* 2 Nov. 1966. 17 U.S.T. 1835, T.I.A.S. No. 6129, 131 U.N.T.S. 25, *reprinted in UNESCO's Standard-Setting Instruments,* Sect. IV.A.2; Protocol to the Florence Agreement, *adopted* 26 Nov. 1976, *reprinted in id.,* Sect. IV.A.2.

[317] *Supra* note 297.

research, Member States are expected to allow researchers to enjoy "the degree of autonomy appropriate to their task and to the advancement of science and technology" and to take fully into account "that creative activities of scientific researchers should be promoted in the national science policy on the basis of utmost respect for the autonomy and freedom of research necessary to scientific progress."[318]

The Recommendation concerning the Status of the Artist recognizes "that the arts in their fullest and broadest definition are and should be an integral part of life and that it is necessary and appropriate for Governments to help create and sustain not only a climate encouraging freedom of artistic expression but also the material conditions facilitating the release of this creative talent."[319] The text is also based on the conviction:

> that action by the public authorities is becoming necessary and urgent in order to remedy the disquieting situation for artists in a large number of Member States, particularly with regard to human rights, economic and social circumstances and their conditions of employment, with a view to providing artists with the conditions necessary for the development and flowering of their talents and appropriate to the role that they are able to play in the planning and implementation of cultural policies and cultural development activities of communities and countries and in the improvement of the quality of life.[320]

Paragraph 4 of Article 15 of the ESC Covenant reiterates a basic objective of the United Nations and UNESCO that international contacts and cooperation in the scientific and cultural fields benefit international peace and the welfare of humanity. Particularly relevant in this regard is the Declaration of the Principles of International Cultural Co-operation[321] and a 1980 General Conference resolution entitled "International Cultural and Scientific Cooperation."[322] The resolution invites member States to take active measures towards broadening cultural and scientific cooperation, to eliminate impediments to the development of scientific and cultural exchanges, and to create a scientific environment for the full use of the potential of

[318] *Id.*, para. 8.

[319] Recommendation on the Status of the Artist, *adopted* 27 Oct. 1980, *reprinted in UNESCO's Standard-Setting Instruments,* Sect. IV.B., Preamble.

[320] *Id.*

[321] *Supra* note 303.

[322] 21 C/Res. 12.1, adopted 27 Oct. 1980.

scientists. The Director-General is called upon to continue "to make the general public...aware of the benefits of the further strengthening and development of cultural and scientific links among peoples."[323]

### *Domestic Implications*

The rights contained in Article 15 are all appropriately protected by U.S. law and policy. The compatibility of Article 15 with American domestic law can be attributed to the constitutional guarantees of speech and press embodied in the First Amendment, as well as to public policies favoring cultural and scientific development. Although the First Amendment is primarily related to Article 19 of the CPR Covenant, its scope also determines to a large extent the cultural and scientific freedoms to which Article 15 of the ESC Covenant refers. Under U.S. law, limitations on free expression apply to only a small range of activities deemed to fall outside the sweeping protection of the First Amendment. Obscenity,[324] speech seeking to incite or produce imminent lawless action and likely to bring it about,[325] and some forms of speech which conflict with legitimate regulations[326] are the only types of speech not constitutionally protected. However, broadly speaking, the First Amendment assures the freedom to engage in most every artistic, literary, cultural, or scientific activity.[327] Equally important, the U.S. Supreme Court's recognition of the public as the ultimate beneficiary of the First Amendment affirms the public's right to benefit from artistic, literary, and cultural activities, as

[323] *Id.*, operative para. 2.

[324] *See,* e.g., Miller v. California 413 U.S. 15 (1973); 18 U.S.C. §1464 (broadcasting obscene language).

[325] *See,* e.g., Brandenburg v. Ohio, 395 U.S. 444 (1969).

[326] *See,* e.g., regulations and ordinances concerning the use of streets or parks, or prescribing safety standards for buildings. Poulous v. New Hampshire, 345 U.S. 367 (1953); Cox v. Louisiana, 379 U.S. 536 (1965).

[327] Although the limits of artistic expression have not been tested in the courts, much concern has recently been expressed over the impact on artists of attempts to restrict these First Amendment freedoms. Jasper Johns, Robert Rauschenberg, Claes Oldenburg, and other artists expressed concern over the threat to artistic free speech in an amicus curiae brief submitted to the Supreme Court in Texas v. Johnson, 109 S. Ct. 2533 (1989), which overturned a Texas statute making it a crime to deface the American flag as a means of political expression. They stated, "The work of an artist is, obviously, meant to be seen. Artists do not usually communicate through words, but reach their audiences through the use of symbols and recognized images. Elimination of any particular 'tool of trade,' as does the Texas statute at issue, necessarily limits the visual vocabulary and stifles the creative process. Accordingly, the amicus curiae share an intense concern that a government not be permitted to bar or to impose criminal penalties for expression."

well as from scientific inquiry.[328] Whatever problems may arise in the complex area of First Amendment guarantees, the United States has a tradition of freedom of expression that goes well beyond the expectations of Article 15.[329]

However, Article 15 implies more than non-interference in the exercise of artistic or scientific creativity; it also implies positive duties. Unlike societies in which culture and science come within the full control of government, the U.S. government limits its role to supplementing, through government funding, private support for cultural and scientific discovery and dissemination. Funding for the National Endowment for the Arts, the National Gallery of Art, the Smithsonian Institution, and the National Academy of Sciences is just one example of the many ways in which the federal government ensures that artists and scientists continue to create, and the public continues to receive, the benefits of their expression.

Recent restrictions in federal funding may be viewed as a setback for artistic freedom domestically, but they do not jeopardize U.S. support for culture and science through "measures" envisaged by Article 15(2) of the ESC Covenant. In 1989, the House of Representatives reacted to the funding by the National Endowment in the Arts (NEA) of two controversial exhibits by withdrawing the costs of the exhibits from NEA's 1990 budget, and imposing limitations on the use of funds appropriated by the NEA and the National Endowment for the Humanities on grounds that have been sharply criticized.[330] Controversy of this type nevertheless occurs in a context of considerable artistic freedom, and occasional restrictive measures do not threaten "the freedom indispensable for...creative activity" which parties to the Covenant undertake to respect. The "chilling effect" funding restrictions might have on certain limited forms of artistic expression may be relevant to that obligation, but, seen in the context

[328] *See* Red Lion Broadcasting Co. v. FCC, 395 U.S. 367 (1969); Nat'l Broadcasting Co. v. U.S., 319 U.S. 190 (1943).

[329] *See,* e.g., L. TRIBE, AMERICAN CONSTITUTIONAL LAW, 785-1010 (2d ed. 1988) for an analysis of First Amendment protection and restrictions of speech.

[330] *See* Kramer, "Is Art Above the Law of Decency?" *N.Y. Times* (July 1, 1989); Regen, "Flinching and Fear, Is the Art World Doing Jesse Helms' Work for Him," *Village Voice* (October 17, 1989). The limitation relates to funds "used to promote, disseminate, or produce materials which in the judgment of the [NEA] or the [NEH] may be considered obscene...and which, when taken as a whole, do not have serious literary, artistic, political, or scientific value." Department of Interior on Related Agencies Appropriation Act of 1990, Pub. L. No. 101-121, §304, 103 Stat. 701, 741.

of overall U.S. support for science and the arts, it does not amount to non-compliance with the Covenant.

Electronic media play a major role in disseminating scientific knowledge and cultural expression, and U.S. law on broadcasting is therefore relevant to compliance with Article 15. Government regulation of broadcasting extends to programming.[331] In addition to regulation of radio and television stations, the pervasive influence of commercial advertising, even on public stations, clearly affects content. However, the system is designed to ensure, in accordance with the First Amendment, the effective functioning of the political process through dissemination of a plurality of ideas and information to American society. Regulations, the license renewal process, and commercial sponsorship, however much they affect the programming decisions of broadcasters, do not of themselves violate the letter or spirit of Article 15 of the ESC Covenant, but merely reflect one of the most complex dimensions of a democratic society in which scientific discovery and cultural creativity thrive.

The United States has a history of supporting free scientific inquiry. For example, the National Academy of Science was created in 1863 by a congressional charter signed by President Lincoln. Its aim is to further science and its use for the general welfare. Certain areas of scientific inquiry are regulated by federal law, such as weather modification, genetic engineering, and the development of new drugs in order to prevent harm to persons or the environment.

The most notable constraints on scientific research are not regulatory, but economic. Personnel and equipment are expensive, and the possibility of pursuing a certain line of scientific inquiry may depend entirely on the availability of funds, whether from private sources or from the federal government.[332] When scientific research results in a specific product or service, that product or service is usually subject to a private proprietary right, consistent with paragraph 1(c) of Article 15. While the public may benefit from that product or service, it can usually do so only at some financial cost, which may render the

[331] *See* T. Carter, M. Franklin & J. Wright, The First Amendment and the Fifth Estate: Regulation of Electronic Mass Media (1986), esp. chaps. VI and VII.

[332] The federal government sponsors several independent scientific agencies, e.g., the National Science Foundation, the National Aeronautics and Space Administration, and the National Institute of Health. Moreover, certain federal legislation, such as the Wilson Drug Act of 1982, indirectly benefits the public by providing incentives to pharmaceutical companies for the development of new drugs to treat rare diseases.

product or service inaccessible to the neediest segment of the population.

Financial limitations on access to cultural or scientific production result from the functioning of the free market. However, nothing in the ESC Covenant or in any other United Nations document on human rights or development renders a free market economy incompatible with respect for human rights. The fact that a particular economic system makes participation in or access to cultural and scientific production easier for some and virtually impossible for others is not in itself an obstacle to observance of Article 15, as long as the State Party seeks a balance between the benefits of paragraphs 1 and 2 and the freedom of paragraph 3. There can be no doubt that U.S. policy meets that basic standard, even if debate about to ways to improve performance in these fields continues.

Regarding paragraph 4 of Article 15, the United States clearly protects the material interests of creators of literary and artistic works, as well as scientists and engineers who develop new products. As part of that protection, the United States has long had a system of copyright and patent laws which shield most literary and musical works, as well as many products of scientific research, against infringement by outsiders.[333] However, Article 15 of the ESC Covenant recognizes the right of authors to benefit from the protection of "moral" as well as material interests resulting from scientific, literary, or artistic production. American copyright law is designed to protect financial interests in a work, whereas the concept of moral rights concerns the extension of the author's personality as embodied by the work, a concept which is reflected in Article 6*bis* of the Berne Convention for the Protection of Literary and Artistic Works,[334] but which is foreign to American law. However, when the United States ratified the Berne Convention, it did not modify U.S. copyright law to conform to Article 6*bis* of the Convention.[335] The two reasons cited by the Committee report for not modifying U.S. law in this respect are that other Berne members provide limited protection and that current federal and state law meets the require-

[333] *See,* e.g., Copyright Revision Act, 17 U.S.C. §§102, 103 (1988), and the basic patents legislation set forth in 35 U.S.C. §1 et seq.

[334] *Supra* note 301.

[335] *See* Damich, *supra* note 301, at 292; and Ross, *supra* note 301, at 364. The rights protected by art. 6*bis* are those of *attribution* of the work to the author and of *respect* of the integrity of the work, so as to prevent action prejudicial to the author's honor or reputation.

ments of Article 6*bis*.[336] The Committee found that federal law provides for certain protection relating to derivative works,[337] distortions of musical works,[338] termination of transfers and licenses,[339] and designation of origins and false descriptions.[340] Further, ten states have enacted statutes which, to varying degrees, protect and preserve certain moral rights of artists after the sale of their work.[341] Notwithstanding the view taken by Congress that current U.S. law meets the requirements of Article 6*bis,* doubts have been raised regarding the substantive protection of moral rights as measured by Article 6*bis* under both federal[342] and state[343] law. However, the problem with *how* moral rights are protected in the U.S. does not diminish U.S. recognition that everyone who produces a cultural or scientific work is entitled to the protection of his or her "moral interests" therein, which is the obligation of Article 15.

Finally, Article 15 requires States to recognize the benefits to be derived from international contacts and cooperation in the cultural and scientific fields. There are no legal restrictions in the United States on international contacts and cooperation in the scientific fields, except in cases concerning the transfer of technology with military application.[344]

In the cultural field, the principal issue regarding international contacts has been the denial of non-immigrant visas for ideological reasons. Cultural figures, including Gabriel Garciá Marquez, Dario Fo, Graham Greene, Carlos Fuentes, and Czeslaw Milosz have been denied non-immigrant visas to come to the United States pursuant to the McCarren-Walter Act of 1952.[345] Recent amendments to the

[336] *See* Damich, *supra* note 301, at 292.

[337] 17 U.S.C. §106.

[338] 17 U.S.C. §115(a)(2).

[339] 17 U.S.C. §203.

[340] Section 43(a) of the Lanham Act.

[341] California, Connecticut, Louisiana, Maine, Massachusetts, New Jersey, New Mexico, New York, Pennsylvania, and Rhode Island. *See* Damich, *supra* note 301.

[342] Damich, *Moral Rights in the United States and Article 6bis of the Berne Convention: A Comment on the Preliminary Report of the Ad Hoc Working Group on U.S. Adherence to the Berne Convention,* 10 COLUM. VLA J.L. & ARTS 143 (655) (1986).

[343] Damich, *supra* note 301.

[344] *See,* e.g., the Atomic Energy Act of 1954, 42 U.S.C. §§2011-2082, as amended by the Nuclear Nonproliferation Act of 1978, Pub. Law No. 95-242, 92 Stat. 120; International Security Assistance Act of 1976, 22 U.S.C. §2751 et seq.; and Export Administration Act of 1979, Pub. Law No. 97-145, 95 Stat. 1727, concerning restrictions on exports having both civilian and military applications.

[345] Pub. L. No. 82-414, §212(a), 66 Stat. 163, 182-87 (1952), *codified as amended* at 8 U.S.C. §1182(a) (1982). *See* Shapiro, *Ideological Exclusions: Closing the Border to Political Dissidents,* 100 HARV. L. REV. 931 (1987).

McCarren-Walter Act have eliminated the ideological grounds for visa denial of non-immigrant aliens,[346] although it continues to apply to immigrants. This remnant of the McCarthy era is, therefore, virtually abolished in law and practice.

In general, the United States is a leader in promoting international contacts in the scientific and cultural fields, and it certainly complies with the obligation of Article 15(4) to "recognize the benefits to be derived" from encouraging and developing such contacts.

#### *Article 15 With or Without Qualification?*

The United States is in full compliance with the provisions of Article 15, and no statement of understanding, declaration, or reservation is necessary to protect legitimate U.S. interests.

## 4.4 THE LIMITATION CLAUSES

*Oscar M. Garibaldi*

The scope of the rights set forth in the ESC Covenant is affected by certain limitation clauses, which closely parallel those of the CPR Covenant. The ESC Covenant also contains a minimum-standard clause, virtually identical with that of the CPR Covenant, restricting the grounds on which a State Party may limit the rights provided by its own domestic law. These clauses are discussed here only briefly, for their counterparts in the CPR Covenant are analyzed in detail in section 3.4.

It should be noted that the ESC Covenant does not authorize any derogation from the rights set forth in the treaty.

### 4.4.1 Limitations

The ESC Covenant contains two general limitation clauses (Article 4 and Article 5(1)), which apply generally to all the rights set forth in

[346] Foreign Relations Authorization Act, Pub. L. No. 100-204, §901, 101 Stat. 1331, 1399-1401 (1987) *as amended by* Pub. L. No. 101-246, §128, 104 Stat. 30 (1990).

the treaty, and several specific limitation clauses, which apply only to particular rights. Two of the specific limitation clauses (subparagraphs (a) and (c) of Article 8(1)) should be discussed together with the general limitation clauses, because they are patterned on Article 4 and the limitation clauses of the CPR Covenant. Of these four provisions (Articles 4 and 5(1), and subparagraphs (a) and (c) of Article 8(1)), only Article 5(1) directly restricts the scope of the defined rights, independently of governmental action. The remaining clauses provide for indirect limitations, i.e., they set forth the conditions under which a State Party is authorized to limit the rights in question.

Article 5(1), the counterpart of Article 5(1) of the CPR Covenant, provides that nothing in the ESC Covenant may be interpreted as implying for any group or person "any right to engage in any activity or to perform any act aimed at the destruction of any of the rights or freedoms" recognized in the ESC Covenant. This provision imposes a direct limitation on each of the rights defined in the treaty: acts that would otherwise fall within the exercise of a defined right are excluded from the scope of such right if they are also instances of the condemned acts or activities. As in the case of Article 5(1) of the CPR Covenant, such acts or activities are those that aim at or consist in the destruction of any of the rights set forth in the SEC Covenant.[347]

An indirect limitation is consistent with the ESC Covenant only if it satisfies four conditions: (i) it must have the form of (or be based on) domestic substantive law that complies with certain requirements of generality and certainty; (ii) it must bear a certain specified relation to one or more specified governmental interests; (iii) it must be consistent with the principles of a democratic society; and (iv) it must not consist in or aim at the destruction of the affected right.

These four conditions have already been analyzed in connection with the CPR Covenant.[348] Suffice it to add that the reference to a democratic society appears in all the clauses under consideration, and that the general welfare is the sole legitimate interest mentioned in Article 4. This article also requires that the limitation be "compatible with the nature" of the rights set forth in the Covenant. Although the matter is not entirely clear, this clause probably restates the principle

[347] *See* discussion *supra,* section 3.4.1(2)(iii).
[348] *See* discussion *supra,* section 3.4.1(2).

of non-destruction, i.e., the requirement that indirect limitations must not affect the centermost portion of the defined scope of each right.[349]

### 4.4.2 The Minimum-Standard Clause

Article 5(2) of the ESC Covenant provides as follows:

> No restriction upon or derogation from any of the fundamental human rights recognized or existing in any country in virtue of law, conventions, regulations or custom shall be admitted on the pretext that the present Covenant does not recognize such rights or that it recognizes them to a lesser extent.

This provision makes clear that the ESC Covenant was intended to lay down a minimum standard for economic, social and cultural rights, which would add to, and never detract from, the fundamental human rights (of any kind) recognized or existing in a State Party. Consequently, a State whose domestic law guarantees the right to own property, which is a fundamental civil and economic right, may not restrict or limit that right on the ground that it has been ignored by the ESC Covenant.[350]

## 4.5 COMPLIANCE MECHANISMS

*Hurst Hannum*

Like the CPR Covenant, the ESC Covenant creates a mandatory reporting procedure for States Parties, so that compliance with the Covenant will receive some degree of international review. However, there have been significant differences between the reporting procedures under the two Covenants, due to differences in the nature of the

[349] There is nothing in the label "economic, social and cultural" that would make the rights defined in the Covenant incompatible with certain limitations, nor is there any specific element in those definitions that would perform the same function. The "nature" of a right defined in the Covenant should be understood as a nucleus of meaning, i.e., the core of the extension (or denotation) of such right as defined in the treaty. This is probably the same nucleus of right which must in any case be preserved according to the principle of non-destruction.

[350] *See* discussion *supra,* section 3.4.3.

rights protected and the fact that no special oversight body was created by the ESC Covenant (unlike the Human Rights Committee established under the CPR Covenant). Instead, Articles 16-22 of the ESC Covenant simply entrust supervision of the Covenant to the U.N. Economic and Social Council (ECOSOC), a principal organ of the United Nations created under the Charter.

Reports on "the measures which they have adopted and the progress made in achieving the observance of the rights recognized" in the ESC Covenant are transmitted by the States Parties to ECOSOC via the U.N. Secretary-General. ECOSOC is given plenary authority under Article 17 of the Covenant to establish a program for State reports, and three different supervisory mechanisms have been adopted since the Covenant's entry into force in 1976.

The first procedure required States Parties to furnish reports to ECOSOC biennially on a six-year cycle: the initial report would address Articles 609 of the Covenant, and subsequent reports would address Articles 10-12 and 13-15, respectively.[351] The reports were considered by a sessional working group of ECOSOC, which first met in 1979. The working group adopted procedures roughly similar to those of the Human Rights Committee—inviting representatives of States whose reports were under consideration to be present when their reports were examined and discussing each report with the representative—but lack of time and expertise greatly hindered the effectiveness of the working group's review. In 1983, in an attempt to make the oversight process more effective, "governmental experts" replaced the regular representatives to ECOSOC who had participated in the working group.[352] Nevertheless, it was clear that the review process still left much to be desired.[353]

ECOSOC radically revised the oversight procedure in 1985 by creating a new body of experts, the Committee on Economic, Social and Cultural Rights (ESC Committee), which is generally comparable in composition and duties to the Human Rights Committee.[354] The eighteen ESC Committee members are elected for four-year terms by

[351] E.S.C. Res. 1988 (LX), 60 U.N. ESCOR, Supp. (No. 1) at 11, U.N. Doc. E/5850 (1976).

[352] E.S.C. Res. 1982/33, 1982 U.N. ESCOR, Supp. (No. 1) at 25, U.N. Doc. E/1982/82 (1982).

[353] *See generally* Alston, *Out of the Abyss: The Challenges Confronting the New U.N. Committee on Economic, Social and Cultural Rights,* 9 HUM. RTS. Q. 332, 340-42 (1987).

[354] *See* E.S.C. Res. 1985/17, 1985 U.N. ESCOR, Supp. (No. 1), at 15, U.N. Doc. E/1985/85 (1985).

the full Economic and Social Council, from among persons nominated by States Parties to the ESC Covenant. The Committee meets annually for three weeks; its first session was held in March 1987.[355]

Recognizing the burden placed on States Parties by the biennial reporting system devised in 1976, the ESC Committee decided at its second session to require an initial report within two years of the Covenant's entry into force for a State Party and subsequent reports every five years.[356] Each report would cover all of the rights in the ESC Covenant, although it is to be organized so as to deal separately with the three groups of rights contained in Articles 6-9, 10-12, and 13-15, respectively. A pre-sessional working group of five ESC Committee members identifies in advance questions which might be most usefully addressed to States whose reports are under consideration. The Committee has begun to adopt "general comments," similar to those prepared by the Human Rights Committee, on various rights set forth in the ESC Covenant.[357]

While the ESC Committee and its predecessor bodies had examined 191 initial or periodic State reports by the end of the 1990 session, a serious backlog of reports remains. The Committee requested a longer session or the scheduling of an additional session in order to deal with this backlog, but ECOSOC rejected this request in 1988.

Specialized agencies of the United Nations, such as the International Labour Organisation (ILO) and others, receive State reports pursuant to Article 16 of the Covenant. Article 18 permits the agencies to submit to ECOSOC their own reports on progress made by States in achieving observance of the Covenant falling within the scope of the agencies' activities, and representatives of the ILO and the U.N. Educational, Scientific and Cultural Organization (UNESCO) have regularly participated in the Committee's sessions.[358]

The ILO has been particularly active in contributing to the ESC Committee's work, and it has made available to the Committee reports and decisions by various ILO supervisory bodies regarding

[355] *See* Committee on Economic, Social and Cultural Rights, *Report on the First Session,* 1987 U.N. ESCOR, Supp. (No. 17), U.N. Doc. E/1987/28 (1987).

[356] *See* Committee on Economic, Social and Cultural Rights, *Report on the Second Session,* 1988 U.N. ESCOR, Supp. (No. 4) at 58-65, U.N. Doc. E/1988/14 (1988).

[357] A review of the Committee's methods of work may be found in its *Report on the Fourth Session,* 1990 U.N. ESCOR, Supp. (No. 3) at 6-11, U.N. Doc. E/1990/23 (1990).

[358] *Cf.* Alston, *supra* note 353, at 362-67.

respect for trade union and other rights which are guaranteed under Articles 6-10 of the Covenant. A recent report identified 103 ILO conventions which are relevant to the ESC Covenant, and, since 1979, the ILO has provided information to the Committee on over 50 countries.[359] The ILO reports include information on the status of ratifications of relevant ILO conventions and also refer to relevant comments of the various ILO supervisory bodies, such as the Committee of Experts on the Application of Conventions and Recommendations.

ECOSOC, the specialized agencies, and the Commission on Human Rights all have authority to make general recommendations on the basis of the State reports. States Parties and specialized agencies may comment to ECOSOC on any such recommendations. Although the drafting history indicates that the term "general recommendation" was chosen in order to exclude recommendations directed to a particular State, the reports of the ILO under Article 18, for example, do contain generally brief country-specific observations made in the context of the ILO's own supervisory procedures.

Any ECOSOC "recommendations of a general nature" are included in the report it transmits to the General Assembly, along with a summary of information from States Parties and the specialized agencies. Pursuant to Article 22, ECOSOC may draw the attention of other U.N. organs and agencies to "any matters arising out of the reports" it receives, in order to aid those agencies concerned with technical assistance in reaching decisions "on the advisability of international measures likely to contribute to the effective progressive implementation" of the Covenant.

Implementation and oversight of the ESC Covenant has clearly been inadequate thus far. Creation of the new ESC Committee in 1986 is a major advance, and there is every evidence that the Committee members are approaching their task with diligence and creativity. As has been the case with the Human Rights Committee, the contribution of individual members of the new Committee, in particular its Chairman and Rapporteur, has been of vital importance. An expanded role for non-governmental organizations also could

[359] *See* Note by the Secretary-General, *Implementation of the International Covenant on Economic, Social and Cultural Rights* [Eleventh report of the ILO under art. 18 of the ESC Covenant], U.N. Doc. E/1989/6 (1988) at 4-6, 19-21.

greatly assist the Committee in its work.[360] Nevertheless, the sheer volume of work and the broad scope of the substantive rights proclaimed in the Covenant will continue to pose problems for the effective international oversight of those rights.

[360] In 1988, ECOSOC invited NGOs in consultative status to submit to the Committee written statements "that might contribute to full and universal recognition and realization of the rights set forth in the Covenant." E.S.C. Res. 1988/4, 1988 U.N. ESCOR, Supp. (No. 1) at 8, U.N. Doc. 6/1988/88 (1988), para. 16.

# PART V
# ISSUES RAISED BY THE UNITED STATES RESERVATIONS, UNDERSTANDINGS, AND DECLARATIONS

# V
# ISSUES RAISED BY THE UNITED STATES RESERVATIONS, UNDERSTANDINGS, AND DECLARATIONS

*Dinah Shelton*

When the Carter administration transmitted the Covenants to the Senate in 1978, it proposed that ratification be accompanied by broad conditions. The conditions regarding the ESC Covenant await further Senate consideration of that agreement and include two reservations, one limiting United States obligations with regard to any subjects within state jurisdiction, the other declaring the Covenant non-self-executing. In addition, there are two statements: first, that the Covenant rights are to be achieved progressively and, that nothing in the Covenant affects free speech rights under the U.S. Constitution, laws, and practices. Finally, there is a declaration concerning international law responsibilities for expropriation.

The Carter proposals concerning the CPR Covenant were reformulated by the Bush administration and adopted by the Senate during the ratification process. The result is United States acceptance of the Covenant as modified or interpreted by five reservations, five understandings, and four declarations.[1] The existing reservations are narrower in scope than those first proposed and more limited than the understandings and declarations. However, there remain questions about the conformity of the "package" and some individual reservations to the object and purpose of the treaty, as well as about the legal effect of the understandings and declarations.

The reservations to the CPR Covenant limit or exclude the effect of Articles 20 (prohibitions on war propaganda and hate speech), 6 (limitations on application of the death penalty), 7 (definition of cruel, inhuman or degrading treatment or punishment), 15(1) (reduction of penalties for criminal offenses) and 10(2b) and (3) (segregation of adult and juvenile offenders). In addition, the understandings contain United States interpretive statements on the scope of state obligations of non-discrimination (Articles 2[1] and 26), compensation for wrongful arrest or detention (Articles 9[5] and 14[6]), segregation of accused and convicted persons (Article 10[2][a]), the purposes of incarceration (Article 10[3]), the due process rights to counsel and presentation of witnesses, and the prohibition of double jeopardy (Article 14[3][b], [d] and [e]); 14[7], and federal-state relations (Article 50).

The four declarations primarily concern the international obligations of states parties to the Covenant, including U.S. acceptance of the competence of the Human Rights Committee to receive interstate complaints. However, the first declaration states that the provisions of the Covenant are not self-executing and enforceable in United States courts. The same declaration is proposed for the ESC Covenant.

As a general policy toward the Covenants, President Carter unequivocally stated in his message to Congress, "Whenever a provision is in conflict with United States law, a reservation, understanding or declaration has been recommended." In addition to assuring that the Covenants did not modify United States law, the non-self-executing declaration aimed to preclude United States courts from giving effect to the rights they contain until and unless Congress

[1] The resolution of ratification also included a proviso, adopted as an amendment proposed by Senator Jesse Helms. However, the proviso is not included in the instrument of ratification and consequently does not modify or become part of the treaty. The proviso in essence restates Constitutional doctrine, stating that the Covenant will not be deemed to authorize un-Constitutional conduct by the United States. The text of the conditions may be found in Appendix 1.

implemented them by legislation. Moreover, the administration proposed to exclude subjects within the primary jurisdiction of states from the obligations undertaken by the United States.

The Bush administration and the Senate maintained the approach of attaching reservations where they found incompatibilities between United States law and the CPR Covenant. However, views about the degree and type of conflicts have undergone modification since 1978. In particular, the government has taken into consideration the practice of other states and the general comments of the Human Rights Committee, as well as changes in U.S. law. Thus, some of the adopted reservations are narrower in scope than those originally submitted, and the proposed federalism reservation has been reformulated as an understanding; in one case a new reservation was attached.

In addition to changing the language and scope of some of the Carter proposals, the Senate and administration expressed views of the Covenant that seem less hostile and more open to recognition of international concerns. The Senate report notes that:

> the overwhelming majority of the provisions in the Covenant are compatible with existing U.S. domestic law. In those few areas where the two diverge, the Administration has proposed a reservation or other form of condition to clarify the nature of the obligation being undertaken by the United States. This approach has caused concern among some private groups and individuals in the human rights field who argue that U.S. law should be brought into conformance with international human rights standards in those areas where international standards are superior.
>
> The Committee recognizes the importance of adhering to internationally recognized standards of human rights. Although the U.S. record of adherence has been good, there are some areas in which U.S. law differs from the international standard. For example, the Covenant prohibits the imposition of the death penalty for crimes committed by persons below the age of eighteen but U.S. law allows it for juveniles between the ages of 16 and 18. In areas such as these, it may be appropriate and necessary to question whether changes in U.S. law should be made to bring the United States into full compliance at the international level. However, the Committee anticipates that changes in U.S. law in these areas will occur through the normal legislative process.[2]

[2] United States: Senate Committee on Foreign Relations Report on the International Covenant on Civil and Political Rights, U.S. Senate Executive Report 102-23 (102nd Cong., 2d sess.), Jan. 30, 1992, p.4; *reprinted* in 31 I.L.M. 645 (1992).

This language is important in recognizing that there exist some broader human rights guarantees in the Covenants and that improvement in U.S. laws might be "appropriate and necessary."

As the Senate report notes, there has been considerable criticism of the United States approach, on grounds of both domestic domestic and international law and policy. In regard to the former, the scope of the conditions exceeds constitutional demands that treaties conform to the Constitution. There is no requirement that treaties yield to federal or state statutory or common law. Under well-established U.S. jurisprudence, treaties and federal statutes possess equal stature; when they conflict, which is to be avoided by interpretation where possible, the latter in time prevails.[3] As for state law, the Constitution subordinates it to all federal law, including treaties. Thus, the actual and proposed reservations conforming the Covenants to state and federal law are not constitutionally required, although they may have been important in securing Senate approval.

In international law, any reservation (including an understanding or declaration that excludes or modifies the legal effect of any provision of the CPR Covenant) could be judged invalid if other states or the Human Rights Committee view it as incompatible with the object and purpose of the treaty. More generally, other parties may object to the U.S. limiting the effect of the Covenants in all cases of incompatibility with domestic law. Treaty ratification normally implies a purpose of conforming domestic law to international obligations, not the reverse. Particularly because the Covenants are deemed to constitute the minimum standard of state conduct towards individuals and groups, there may be objections to the number and scope of U.S. conditions taken together.

Individually, of the five reservations attached by the Senate to the CPR Covenant, the two most problematic are those concerning Articles 6 and 7. Article 6 protects the right to life and Article 7 guarantees freedom from torture or cruel, inhuman or degrading treatment or punishment. Both are non-derogable rights and no other state has maintained any reservation to them.[4] The U.S. reservation to Article 6:

[3] *See supra* chapt. II, sec. 2.2; AMERICAN LAW INSTITUTE, 1 RESTATEMENT (THIRD) OF THE FOREIGN RELATIONS LAW OF THE UNITED STATES §111 (2 vols. 1987).

[4] Upon ratification in 1972, Norway reserved to Article 6, para. 4 on the right to seek commutation or pardon in case of a death penalty. This reservation was withdrawn in 1979.

> reserves the right, subject to its Constitutional restraints, to impose capital punishment on any person (other than a pregnant woman) duly convicted under existing or future laws permitting the imposition of capital punishment, including such punishment for crimes committed by persons below 18 years of age.

This reservation is significantly narrower than the proposed Carter reservation, which reserved the possibility of executing pregnant women as well.[5] However, it clearly foresees the possibility of expanding application of the death penalty and thus raises questions of compatibility not only with the letter of para. 5 (prohibiting the execution of those under the age of 18), but also para. 2 (permitting imposition only for "serious crimes") and the spirit of para. 6. The latter provides that nothing in the Article "shall be invoked to delay or to prevent the abolition of capital punishment." The adoption of a protocol to the Covenant abolishing the death penalty for those states that ratify it reinforces the general abolitionist approach of Article 6. In light of this, the reservation that permits future U.S. expansion in application of the death penalty is likely to be questioned.[6]

The reservation to Article 7 limits application of the prohibition against cruel, inhuman or degrading treatment or punishment to that prohibited by the Fifth, Eighth and/or Fourteenth Amendments to the Constitution. It considerably narrows the protections of the Covenant, particularly insofar as treatment is concerned. The same reservation was proposed to the United Nations Convention against Torture and Other Cruel, Inhuman or Degrading Treatment or Punishment and the same objection may be raised there. It appears that the reservation, which was not proposed by the Carter administration, is a direct result of the *Soering Case*[7] before the European Court of Human Rights. The Senate Report notes that the Court, and the Human Rights Committee, have concluded that prolonged judicial proceedings in cases involving capital punishment may, under certain circumstances, violate this provision or similar ones in other

[5] This reservation was dropped "since neither the Federal nor the state governments in fact carry out executions until after the birth of the condemned woman's child." Senate Report, p. 12.

[6] For an analysis of the legality of reservations to provisions concerning the death penalty in regard to another human rights treaty, *see* Inter-American Court of Human Rights, "Restrictions to the Death Penalty", Articles 4(2) and 4(4), American Convention on Human Rights, Advisory Opinion OC-3/83 of September 8, 1983.

[7] Eur. Ct. Hum. Rts., Soering Case, *Judgment* of July 7, 1989, Ser. A. No. 161, *reprinted in* 28 I.L.M. 1063 (1989).

instruments. However, the reservation also excludes corporal punishment, solitary confinement, and similar practices, from the scope of Article 7 protections.

The remaining reservations are similar to those filed by other states parties to the Convention. Germany, Italy and Trinidad and Tobago have each filed similar reservations to Article 15(1) (guaranteeing post-offense reduction in penalties) similar to the United States condition. Although the limited number of reservations indicates widespread acceptance in principle of the rights contained in Article 15(1), no objections have been raised by states parties to the three reservations already on file.

The provisions of Article 10(b)(2) and (3) concerning the treatment of juvenile offenders have not been universally accepted and the proposed reservation of the United States finds parallel in reservations submitted by Australia, Austria, Barbados, Belgium, Denmark, Finland, Iceland, Luxembourg (a declaration), the Netherlands, New Zealand, Norway, Sweden, Trinidad and Tobago, and the United Kingdom. The Netherlands objected to the scope of the Australian reservations, while the others passed without comment.

The remaining United States reservation, concerning the limitations on free speech contained in Article 20, is similar to those filed by most European states as well as Australia and New Zealand. In these countries, strong legal protections for free speech limit state actions to prohibit hate speech and war propaganda. No objections have been raised to the reservations, although members of the Human Rights Committee have questioned states about the subject during presentations of their state reports.

Turning to the United States understandings, the first issue is whether the Committee may interpret them as reservations, to the extent that the legal interpretations they provide conflict with those adopted by the Committee. The Senate states that its advice and consent to ratification is "subject to" them and that they "shall apply to the obligations of the United States" under the Covenant". If the understandings modify the legal impact of the Covenant, then they would be tested like reservations for compatibility with the object and purpose of the treaty.

Most of the understandings, even if they are interpreted as reservations, conform to state practice. Articles 9, 10, and 14 have been the objects of the most numerous reservations; generally, the scope of provisions on non-discrimination is unique and narrows the scope of the Covenant in some respects, although it appears to largely adopt the definition of discrimination established by the Human Rights Committee in its case law and general comments.

The last of the understandings concerns federalism and Article 50 of the Covenant. Originally proposed in broader terms as a reservation by the Carter administration, the understanding now seems to accept the general obligation of federal states to ensure compliance with the Covenants at all levels of government. The change seems in part to reflect the experience of Australia, which had a broad federalism reservation similar to that proposed by the Carter administration. After widespread criticism by states parties and the Human Rights Committee, Australia withdrew the reservation.[8]

Only one of the declarations, adopted for the CPR Covenant and proposed for the ESC Covenant, raises substantial legal issues. The Senate states in regard to the CPR Covenant that "the provisions of Articles 1 through 27 of the Covenant are not self-executing."[9] According to the Senate, "the intent is to clarify that the Covenant will not create a private cause of action in U.S. courts."[10] Moreover, it is explicitly stated that implementing legislation is not contemplated to execute the Covenant because U.S. law generally complies with the Covenant.

Internationally, there is no general rule of law that treaties must be incorporated into the national legal systems of States Parties, but the Covenant clearly requires execution through domestic legal measures. This requirement derives from the general commitment of each State Party to the Covenant "to respect and ensure to all individuals within its territory and subject to its jurisdiction the rights recognized in the present Covenant" (Article 2(1)). The means of compliance are left to the laws of each State Party. However, legislative or other measures must be adopted if necessary to give effect to the rights recognized (Article 2(2)), and States Parties are required to ensure an effective remedy to any persons whose rights are violated (Article 2(3)). Specifically, States are obliged to "develop the possibilities of a judicial remedy."

Article 2(2) requires legislation be enacted only "where not already provided for by existing legislative or other measures." Thus, if the

[8] *See* U.N. Doc. CCPR/SR.402 (1982) and U.N. Doc CCPR/C/142/Add.2 (1987) at 13.
[9] Senate Report, *supra* note 2, p. 19.
[10] *Id.*

Senate is correct and all rights guaranteed by the Covenant are fully extant and enforceable in U.S. law, then no substantive guarantees need be added. If the Senate is mistaken, then implementation either through legislation or judicial enforcement is required. In any case, the right to an effective remedy in case of violation must be present and probably requires legislative expansion of access to administrative or judicial tribunals, because of current limitations on private rights of action and liability in the civil rights area.

The impact of the non-self-executing declaration on domestic law is uncertain. The Supremacy Clause makes valid treaties "the Law of the Land" and envisages automatic incorporation of international treaty law into municipal law. Whether treaties are directly enforceable (self-executing) or not is ultimately a question for the courts. The declaration attempts to foreclose judicial consideration of the matter by asserting that the Covenants are entirely non-self-executing. Interpretation of treaties, including the self-executing issue, is a judicial function. Under the rationale used by the court in the Power Authority case, a declaration of this kind could be seen as merely hortatory.[11] It is not binding on the courts because the restrictive language is not an integral part of the treaty, operates purely domestically, and does not involve international obligations within the exclusive competence of the legislative and executive branches.

If given effect, the non-self-executing declaration will limit enforcement of the Covenants. Potential victims are those most likely to be vigilant in protesting lack of compliance with the rights guaranteed. U.S. courts have previously recognized executive limitations in monitoring government infringement of individual rights and implied a private right of action to enforce civil rights legislation, e.g., Title IX of the 1964 Civil Rights Act[12] and the 1965 Voting Rights Act.[13] The policies that led the court to imply a right of individual enforcement of these laws apply equally to international human rights protections. Furthermore, the rights in the Covenant are as detailed

[11] Power Authority of New York v. Federal Power Commission, 247 F.2d 538, 540 (App. D.C. 1957) (vacated on remand). But *cf.* United States v. Stuart, 109 S. Ct. 1183 (1989), where the majority of the Court looked beyond the clear language of a treaty to the legislative history of Senate ratification. Three of the justices concurred in the judgment but rejected relying upon Senate debates or documents not in the form of a formal reservation.

[12] 20 U.S.C. 1681-1683 (1976); *see* Cannon v. University of Chicago, 441 U.S. 677 (1979).

[13] 42 U.S.C. 1973 et seq. (Supp. I, 1964); *see* Allen v. Board of Education, 393 U.S. 544 (1968).

and specific as most U.S. legislation and certainly more so than most Constitutional guarantees.

Finally, the declarations do not serve the apparent purpose of prohibiting judicial application of the Covenants, but instead creates confusion and possible conflict between the Senate and the courts. As a principle of interpretation, domestic law is construed as fully as possible in conformity with the international law. Thus, courts may make use of the standards of the Covenants, as interpreted by their respective Committees, in interpreting domestic rights, even if the treaties are declared non-self-executing. Provisions of the CPR Covenant, as well as decisions of the Human Rights Committee, can be used by State and federal courts to interpret or clarify constitutional or legislative standards.[14]

In conclusion, it should be noted that only Australia filed as many conditions as the United States to its acceptance of the CPR Covenant. All but three Australian reservations were subsequently withdrawn. Finland, France, the Netherlands, Norway and Korea also have withdrawn reservations as their legislation has come into compliance with Covenant standards, or in response to criticism that their reservations were illegal.[15] These precedents are well worth keeping in mind as the United States begins participating in the Covenant system.

[14] *See,* e.g., Thompson v. Oklahoma, 108 S.Ct. 2687 (1988); Sterling v. Cupp, 290 Or. 611, 625 P.2d 123 (1981); Boehm v. Superior Court, 178 Cal. App. 3d 494, 223 Ca. Rptr. 716 (1986); Pauley v. Kelly, 255 S.E. 2d 859 (W. Va. Sup. Ct. 1979).

[15] Human Rights Committee, Reservations, Declarations, Notifications and Objections relating to the International Covenant on Civil and Political Rights and the Optional Protocols Thereto, CCPR/C/2/Rev.3, May 12, 1992.

# PART VI
# CONCLUSION

# VI
# CONCLUSION

*Hurst Hannum and Dana D. Fischer*

The Covenants represent an international consensus forged over three decades of negotiations, in which the United States played an active and positive role. Over 100 countries of all political persuasions have formally accepted the minimum standards the Covenants establish respecting the conduct of governments toward their own citizens. For the United States, ratification of the CPR Covenant acknowledges, at long last, that national interest in the treatment of individuals in other countries and its effect on international peace and security can be served effectively by participating in at least one of these treaty regimes. Although they recognize certain weaknesses in both treaties, the editors of this volume agree that "the United States can adhere to these treaties without cost to our domestic legal order and with genuine, if modest, benefit" to that order, in addition to substantial benefits to the United States in its international relations.[1]

The Covenant on Civil and Political Rights embodies rights already found in the U.S. Constitution and which have been enhanced and strengthened over the life of the country by the Supreme Court and Congress. The philosophy which underlies the rights set forth in the

[1] Prepared statement of John Lawrence Hargrove, International Human Rights Treaties, Hearings before the Committee on Foreign Relations, United States Senate, 96th Cong., 1st Sess. on Ex. C, D, E, and F, 95-2; Four Treaties Relating to Human Rights, November 14, 15, 16 and 19, 1979 (hereafter Senate Hearings) at 336.

CPR Covenant is, broadly speaking, that of America's political and constitutional forefathers. These rights are inalienable and "derive from the inherent dignity of the human person."[2] They are neither granted by the State nor are they the result of one's own actions.[3]

Values recognized as rights in the United States have traditionally concerned "rights deriving from, and vindicating, individual freedom and autonomy, but not claims upon society to do for the individual what he cannot do for himself. It tells government only what not to do, not what to do."[4] The fact that economic and social rights in the United States are not always Constitutional rights has fostered a number of misunderstandings about the compatibility of the Covenant on Economic, Social and Cultural Rights with American traditions. The ESC Covenant affirms a collection of rights and public policy goals which have been considered part and parcel of American aspirations since the 1930s and which echo Franklin Roosevelt's Four Freedoms message to Congress in 1944. Declaring the right to be free from want, he said: "We have come to a clear realization of the fact that true individual freedom cannot exist without economic security and independence....People who are hungry and out of a job are the stuff of which dictatorships are made."[5]

Although there may be no constitutional right in the United States to be free from want, subsequent practice and legislation have created a network of federal and state laws which reflect, in large part, the goals of the ESC Covenant. The United States does and will continue to recognize a commitment by the government to the individual to provide a minimum level of individual welfare. These expectations are deeply embedded in national life and increasingly expressed in the language of social obligations and individual rights.[6]

One cannot deny that the Reagan and Bush years led to a lower commitment by the federal government to social and economic programs, although that commitment has often been concommitantly increased at the state and local level. While cultural rights have generally remained secure, larger segments of American society now

[2] CPR Covenant, Preamble.

[3] *See* Donnelly, *Human Rights and Human Dignity: An Analytic Critique of Non-Western Conceptions of Human Rights,* 76 AM. POL. SCI. REV. 303 (1982).

[4] Henkin, *Economic-Social Rights as "Rights": A United States Perspective,* 2 HUM. RTS. Q. 223, 228 (1981).

[5] 90-I Cong. Rec. 55 (1944).

[6] *See* Henkin, *supra* note 4, at 229.

live in poverty and hopelessness than was the case a decade ago, despite overall economic growth. At the same time, however, the rhetoric of politicians from both major parties continues to espouse the goals of economic and social advancement for all Americans—albeit with varying degrees of direct governmental assistance. Indeed, tax breaks and other government support for business are most often justified on the grounds that they will benefit society as a whole and not just its privileged elite.

Thus, although a particular administration may deny the status of "rights" to economic and social demands, such a temporary reversal of governmental priorities cannot alter the fundamental expectations of American citizens, i.e., that their government will continue to intervene actively in the fields of education, health care, housing, social security, support for children, and other areas, in order to promote economic progress and ensure that all Americans do have an equal opportunity to share in the American dream.

## 6.1 DOMESTIC OBSTACLES TO RATIFICATION

There are no overriding legal obstacles to United States ratification of either Covenant, with such reservations as may be constitutionally required.

The arguments that the United States may not ratify the Covenants because they interfere with federal/state relations or because they are not matters of international concern are but two sides of the same coin. The Constitution grants broad treaty-making powers to the federal government while imposing few limitations on these powers.[7] What is within that power is not reserved to the states, and treaties are not limited by any implicit constraints in the Tenth Amendment.[8] Although the United States can conclude a treaty even on matters on which Congress has no power to legislate, there are few, if any, matters covered by the Covenants that are subject exclusively to state jurisdiction. Under the Fourteenth Amendment and other Constitu-

[7] *See generally supra* chap. II, sec. 2.2.

[8] *But see* De Geofroy v. Riggs, 133 U.S. 258, 267 (1890): "It would not be contended that [the treaty power] extends so far as to authorize what the Constitution forbids, or a change in the character of the government or in that of one of the states, or a cession of any portion of the territory of the latter without its consent." The treaty power also is subject to the constitutional prohibitions of the first eight amendments, safeguarding individual rights. *See* Reid v. Covert, 354 U.S. 1 (1957).

tional provisions, these matters have been extensively treated in federal legislation and are within the jurisdiction of the federal courts.

While it has been suggested that treaties entered into by the United States must deal with matters which are "of international concern," there is no agreement either on how this term is to be defined or, indeed, on whether any such limitation exists. "There is no principle either in international law or in United States constitutional law that some subjects are intrinsically 'domestic' and hence impermissible subjects for an international agreement."[9] Indeed, what is of international concern to the United States—what is considered relevant to its foreign policy and therefore an appropriate subject for negotiation and treaty making—varies with the ever-changing character of its relations with other States. In any event, human rights have been treated by the United States as proper subjects for treaties since the seventeenth century, and thus can be considered as matters of international concern.[10] Certainly the ratification in recent years of treaties concerned with genocide, torture, and civil rights has laid such arguments definitively to rest.

While the arguments which would preclude United States ratification on constitutional grounds are unpersuasive, there remains the question of what kinds of conditions the United States would be obliged to attach to its adherence to the Covenants. In many cases, the contributors to the present book have criticized the reservations, understandings, and declarations proposed by the Executive Branch and ultimately accepted by the Senate as either unnecessary or inappropriate. The avowed intent of the Carter and Bush Administrations to prevent any conflict with existing municipal law goes well beyond constitutional requirements. Indeed, where local or state laws or practices fall below the minimum standards established in the Covenants, consideration should be given to changing such practices so that U.S. citizens can enjoy the rights accepted by the rest of the world community and unnecessary reservations can be withdrawn.

Of course, no international agreement can detract from the individual constitutional rights set forth in the Bill of Rights,[11] and it is appropriate for the United States to submit a reservation in such

[9] American Law Institute, 1 Restatement (Third) of the Foreign Relations Law of the United States §302 Reporters Note 2 at 156 (2 vols. 1987).

[10] *See* Henkin, *The Constitution, Treaties, and International Human Rights*, 1216 U. Pa. L. Rev. 1012 (1968).

[11] *See* Reid v. Covert, *supra* note 8.

cases. In addition, there may be appropriately narrow reservations, declarations, or understandings which could be submitted either to preserve long-standing U.S. practice or to reflect a carefully considered unwillingness or clear inability to implement certain Covenant provisions fully. However, the broad formulations adopted—which essentially declare that U.S. law and practice is perfect and the United States will accept no international norm as an appropriate goal—do little credit either to the U.S. concept of rights or to the international community.

## 6.2 THE NATIONAL INTEREST IN RATIFICATION

The Covenants serve a foreign relations purpose for the United States, which is to help influence the behavior of other countries in ways which the United States deems desirable. American concern over the treatment of individuals and minorities in other countries is immediate and compelling. Where there are widespread domestic conditions of misery and tyranny, the risk of international conflict increases. Those conditions tend to encourage external intervention and often cause leaders to begin disruptive foreign adventures in order to divert attention from internal misery or disorder. America cannot isolate itself from the effects of gross violations of human rights abroad, human rights:

> breed refugees, exiles and dissidents who come knocking at our doors. We must choose between bolting the doors, thus increasing misery and violence outside, and opening them, at some cost to our own well-being. Or else these violations will breed revolt against them, and our own enterprises, or our security interests, will be affected, if the country in turmoil is one with close links to our own.[12]

But, it is argued, the United States has been championing the observance of human rights by foreign governments since 1776; why do we need the Covenants to continue such advocacy? The issue is the relative efficacy of an *ad hoc* policy of human rights advocacy on the basis of unilateral standards which lack a commonly accepted definition, versus an approach which utilizes *international* legal standards accepted by the entire world community as well as by the United States.

[12] S. Hoffman, Duties Beyond Borders 111 (1981).

Since the 1970s, human rights has become an integral part of U.S. foreign policy. Legislation and administrative measures have been adopted to punish human rights violators by terminating economic assistance, withholding diplomatic support, opposing multilateral loans, and refraining from licensing crime control equipment or supplying military assistance and training.[13] This legislation refers to "internationally recognized human rights," and the United States should not refuse to participate in the process with which such rights are defined. Each year, the Department of State is mandated to report on the human rights practices of all U.N. member states, whether or not they receive U.S. assistance.[14] The United States also plays an active role in deliberations of the U.N. Commission on Human Rights, the review process of the Conference on Security and Cooperation in Europe, and other international bodies concerned with the political aspects of human rights.

Allegations and denials of human rights violations have become politicized in the international arena, and the Reagan Administration (and others) complained of a "double standard" at the United Nations with respect to human rights matters. Apart from accusations that the United States is guilty of its own double standard when it comes to criticizing the human rights performance of its allies, the United States obviously is open to unanswerable charges of hypocrisy if it accuses others of violating standards it refuses itself to accept.

Ratification of the CPR Covenant goes half-way to meeting these charges, even with the reservations and other qualifications which the United States has attached to it. But the United States remains vulnerable to accusations that is insufficiently concerned with the economic and social rights that are of at least of immediate importance to most people in the world. In the post-cold war era, the refusal of the United States to submit its concept of "happiness" to the scrutiny of the international community is difficult to understand, particularly

[13] *See, e.g.*, INTERNATIONAL HUMAN RIGHTS LAW GROUP, U.S. LEGISLATION RELATING HUMAN RIGHTS TO U.S. FOREIGN POLICY (4th ed. 1991) for a compilation of such statutes. *Also see, e.g.*, D. KOMMERS AND G. LOESCHER, HUMAN RIGHTS AND AMERICAN FOREIGN POLICY (1979); Cohen, *Conditioning U.S. Security Assistance on Human Rights Practices*, 75 AJIL 246 (1982); Forsythe, *Congress and Human Rights in U.S. Foreign Policy: The Fate of General Legislation*, 9 HUMAN RTS. Q. 382 (1987); Weissbrodt, *Human Rights Legislation and U.S. Foreign Policy*, 7 GA. J. INT'L & COMP. L. 231 (1977).

[14] *See* §§116(d)(1), 502B(b) of the Foreign Assistance Act of 1961, *as amended*, 22 U.S.C. §§2151n(a), 2304. *Cf.* de Neufville, *Human Rights Reporting as Policy Tool: An Examination of the State Department Country Reports*, 8 HUMAN RTS. Q. 681 (1986).

as U.S. foreign policy seeks to convert the world to the U.S. form of capitalism as well as democracy.

The implementation procedures by which the Covenants are interpreted and applied, along with their *ad hoc* invocation in unilateral statements of governments or bilateral exchanges, offer an opportunity to increase the sophistication of U.S. attempts to promote human rights and begin to search for points of agreement. Within the Human Rights Committee, there is an opportunity to clarify the philosophical underpinnings of human rights as well as the precise nature of States Parties' obligations under the CPR Covenant.

The language of human rights can best be defended within the institutions established by the Covenants. The activities of these institutions can either weaken or strengthen international standards, depending on the vigor and clarity of the arguments put forward and—to a considerable extent—the relative political power of the contenders. The same processes that hold out promise of a gradual strengthening of human rights standards also offer opponents of human rights an opportunity to try to narrow, dilute, and otherwise undermine their effective development.

The language of both treaties is broad, although concepts such as "general welfare," "public interest," and "*ordre public*" are no more vague than nineteenth-century definitions of "due process" or "equal protection." The object of U.S. policy should be to prevent the trivialization of the Covenants and to exert every effort to preserve and protect human rights concepts which reflect American values. This is the primary reason why the United States must be in a position to influence the bodies in which the treaties are being interpreted. Although the Human Rights Committee established by the CPR Covenant is composed of independent experts, in the long run its future depends on "the sound commitment of sympathetically disposed governments to the integrity of the treaty regime."[15] One noted English human rights lawyer has noted with regret "the continued isolation of American constitutional law from international human rights law" and suggested that "it is...a misfortune for the United States itself, not only in diminishing American influence overseas, but also in separating American constitutional law from the

[15] Hargrove, *supra* note 1, at 337.

ideas and values of other advanced democratic nations and their courts."[16]

The ESC Covenant raises special problems in this regard, as compliance with this Covenant is by its nature more difficult to judge. The standards of the ESC Covenant must be implemented by programs and policies constrained by national resources and political will, and the disappointing history of the bodies created to oversee the ESC Covenant compound the difficulties. However, there is reason to be more optimistic about the future of the new Committee on Economic, Social and Cultural Rights, which met for the first time in 1987, and U.S. participation in its definitional and interpretative debates would do much to promote U.S. values. Indeed, the United States *does* have a commitment to "the pursuit of happiness," and U.S. economic achievements have created the possibility of fulfilling many of the ESC Covenant's goals. Why should the United States "be prepared to abandon the interpretation and administration of the broad principles of economic, social and cultural life to our antagonists any more than the basic principles of civil liberty?"[17]

As the product of three decades of negotiations, the Covenants reflect a consensus forged among States with diverse political and economic systems. Although they do not perfectly mirror the values of Western liberal democracy, they do embody more of our values than the United States could ever expect to renegotiate.

Ratification of the Covenants presents an opportunity for the United States to decrease the isolationism from multilateral institutions which has occurred in the past decade, to reaffirm its somewhat bruised image as a country dedicated to the rule of law, and to admit that U.S. society may have something to learn from others. Although the human rights situation in the United States is not perfect, we should have little to fear from international scrutiny—and if fear is what motivates the opponents of ratification, then they are selling the United States short. Where U.S. policies are out of step with the rest of the world—and we may well lag behind other Western democracies in the economic and social spheres—international dialogue should result in more rights for Americans, not fewer.

Ultimately, U.S. participation in the Covenants and other international human rights treaties is not a legal but a political issue. The

[16] Lester, *The Overseas Trade in the American Bill of Rights,* 88 COL. L. REV. 537, 560, 561 (1988).

[17] *Id.* at 338.

United States can stand by, aloof and proud, or it can exercise the leadership role its 200-year history of democracy justifies, by accepting that human rights norms are truly universal and worthy of support.

# ANNEXES

# ANNEXES

## INTERNATIONAL COVENANT ON CIVIL AND POLITICAL RIGHTS

### Preamble

*The States Parties to the present Covenant,*

*Considering* that, in accordance with the principles proclaimed in the Charter of the United Nations, recognition of the inherent dignity and of the equal and inalienable rights of all members of the human family is the foundation of freedom, justice and peace in the world,

*Recognizing* that these rights derive from the inherent dignity of the human person,

*Recognizing* that, in accordance with the Universal Declaration of Human Rights, the ideal of free human beings enjoying civil and political freedom and freedom from fear and want can only be achieved if conditions are created whereby everyone may enjoy his civil and political rights, as well as his economic, social and cultural rights,

*Considering* the obligation of States under the Charter of the United Nations to promote universal respect for, and observance of, human rights and freedoms,

*Realizing* that the individual, having duties to other individuals and to the community to which he belongs, is under a responsibility to strive for the promotion and observance of the rights recognized in the present Covenant,

*Agree* upon the following articles:

## PART I

### *Article 1*

1. All peoples have the right of self-determination. By virtue of the right they freely determine their political status and freely pursue their economic, social and cultural development.

2. All peoples may, for their own ends, freely dispose of their natural wealth and resources without prejudice to any obligations arising out of international economic co-operation, based upon the principle of mutual benefit, and international law. In no case may a people be deprived of its own means of subsistence.

3. The States Parties to the present Covenant, including those having responsibility for the administration of Non-Self-Governing and Trust Territories, shall promote the realization of the right of self-determination, and shall respect that right, in conformity with the provisions of the Charter of the United Nations.

### *Article 2*

1. Each State Party to the present Covenant undertakes to respect and to ensure to all individuals within its territory and subject to its jurisdiction the rights recognized in the present Covenant, without distinction of any kind, such as race, colour, sex, language, religion, political or other opinion, national or social origin, property, birth or other status.

2. Where not already provided for by existing legislative or other measures, each State Party to the present Covenant undertakes to take the necessary steps, in accordance with its constitutional processes and with the provisions of the present Covenant, to adopt such legislative or other measures as may be necessary to give effect to the rights recognized in the present Covenant.

3. Each State Party to the present Covenant undertakes:

(a) To ensure that any person whose rights or freedoms as herein recognized are violated shall have an effective remedy, notwithstanding that the violation has been committed by persons acting in an official capacity;

(b) To ensure that any person claiming such a remedy shall have his right thereto determined by competent judicial, administrative or legislative authorities, or by any other competent authority provided for by the legal system of the State, and to develop the possibilities of judicial remedy;

(c) To ensure that the competent authorities shall enforce such remedies when granted.

### *Article 3*

The States Parties to the present Covenant undertake to ensure the equal right of men and women to the enjoyment of all civil and political rights set forth in the present Covenant.

### *Article 4*

1. In time of public emergency which threatens the life of the nation and the existence of which is officially proclaimed, the States Parties to the present Covenant may take measures derogating from their obligations under the present Covenant to the extent strictly required by the exigencies of the situation, provided that such measures are not inconsistent with their other obligations under international law and do not involve discrimination solely on the ground of race, colour, sex, language, religion or social origin.
2. No derogation from articles 6, 7, 8 (paragraphs 1 and 2), 11, 15, 16 and 18 may be made under this provision.
3. Any State Party to the present Covenant availing itself of the right of derogation shall immediately inform the other States Parties to the present Covenant, through the intermediary of the Secretary-General of the United Nations of the provisions from which it has derogated and of the reasons by which it was actuated. A further communication shall be made, through the same intermediary, on the date on which it terminates such derogation.

### *Article 5*

1. Nothing in the present Covenant may be interpreted as implying for any State, group or person any right to engage in any activity or perform any act aimed at the destruction of any of the rights and freedoms recognized herein or at their limitation to a greater extent than is provided for in the present Covenant.
2. There shall be no restriction upon or derogation from any of the fundamental human rights recognized or existing in any State Party to the present Covenant pursuant to law, conventions, regulations or custom on the pretext that the present Covenant does not recognize such rights or that it recognizes them to a lesser extent.

## PART III

### *Article 6*

1. Every human being has the inherent right to life. This right shall be protected by law. No one shall be arbitrarily deprived of his life.

2. In countries which have not abolished the death penalty, sentence of death may be imposed only for the most serious crimes in accordance with law in force at the time of the commission of the crime and not contrary to the provisions of the present Covenant and to the Convention on the Prevention and Punishment of the Crime of Genocide. This penalty can only be carried out pursuant to a final judgement rendered by a competent court.

3. When deprivation of life constitutes the crime of genocide, it is understood that nothing in this article shall authorize any State Party to the present Covenant to derogate in any way from any obligation assumed under the provisions of the Convention on the Prevention and Punishment of the Crime of Genocide.

4. Anyone sentenced to death shall have the right to seek pardon or commutation of the sentence. Amnesty, pardon or commutation of the sentence of death may be granted in all cases.

5. Sentence of death shall not be imposed for crimes committed by persons below eighteen years of age and shall not be carried out on pregnant women.

6. Nothing in this article shall be invoked to delay or to prevent the abolition of capital punishment by any State Party to the present Covenant.

### *Article 7*

No one shall be subjected to torture or to cruel, inhuman or degrading treatment or punishment. In particular, no one shall be subjected without his free consent to medical or scientific experimentation.

### *Article 8*

1. No one shall be held in slavery; slavery and the slave-trade in all their forms shall be prohibited.

2. No one shall be held in servitude.

3.(a) No one shall be required to perform forced or compulsory labour;

(b) Paragraph 3(a) shall not be held to preclude in countries where imprisonment with hard labour may be imposed as a punishment for a crime, the performance of hard labour in pursuance of a sentence to such punishment by a competent court;

(c) For the purpose of this paragraph the term "forced or compulsory labour" shall not include:

(i) Any work or service, not referred to in sub-paragraph (b), normally required of a person who is under detention in consequence of a lawful order of a court, or of a person during conditional release from such detention;

(ii) Any service of a military character and, in countries where conscientious objection is recognized, any national service required by law of conscientious objectors;

(iii) Any service exacted in cases of emergency or calamity threatening the life or well-being of the community;

(iv) Any work or service which forms part of normal civil obligations.

### *Article 9*

1. Everyone has the right to liberty and security of person. No one shall be subjected to arbitrary arrest or detention. No one shall be deprived of his liberty except on such grounds and in accordance with such procedures as are established by law.

2. Anyone who is arrested shall be informed, at the time of arrest, of the reasons for his arrest and shall be promptly informed of any charges against him.

3. Anyone arrested or detained on a criminal charge shall be brought promptly before a judge or other officer authorized by law to exercise judicial power and shall be entitled to trial within a reasonable time or to release. It shall not be the general rule that persons awaiting trial shall be detained in custody, but release may be subject to guarantees to appear for trial, at any other stage of the judicial proceedings, and, should occasion arise, for execution of the judgement.

4. Anyone who is deprived of his liberty by arrest or detention shall be entitled to take proceedings before a court, in order that that court may decide without delay on the lawfulness of his detention and order his release if the detention is not lawful.

5. Anyone who has been the victim of unlawful arrest or detention shall have an enforceable right to compensation.

### *Article 10*

1. All persons deprived of their liberty shall be treated with humanity and with respect for the inherent dignity of the human person.

2. (a) Accused persons shall, save in exceptional circumstances, be segregated from convicted persons, and shall be subject to separate treatment appropriate to their status as unconvicted persons;

(b) Accused juvenile persons shall be separated from adults and brought as speedily as possible for adjudication.

3. The penitentiary system shall comprise treatment of prisoners the essential aim of which shall be their reformation and social rehabilitation. Juvenile offenders shall be segregated from adults and be accorded treatment appropriate to their age and legal status.

### *Article 11*

No one shall be imprisoned merely on the ground of inability to fulfil a contractual obligation.

### *Article 12*

1. Everyone lawfully within the territory of a State shall, within that territory, have the right to liberty of movement and freedom to choose his residence.

2. Everyone shall be free to leave any country, including his own.

3. The above-mentioned rights shall not be subject to any restrictions except those which are provided by law, are necessary to protect national security, public order (*ordre public*), public health or morals or the rights and freedoms of others, and are consistent with the other rights recognized in the present Covenant.

4. No one shall be arbitrarily deprived of the right to enter his own country.

### *Article 13*

An alien lawfully in the territory of a State Party to the present Covenant may be expelled therefrom only in pursuance of a decision reached in accordance with law and shall, except where compelling reasons of national security otherwise require, be allowed to submit the reasons against his expulsion and to have his case reviewed by, and be represented for the purpose before, the competent authority or a person or persons especially designated by the competent authority.

### *Article 14*

1. All persons shall be equal before the courts and tribunals. In the determination of any criminal charge against him, or of his rights and obligations in a suit at law, everyone shall be entitled to a fair and public hearing by a competent, independent and impartial tribunal established by law. The press and the public may be excluded from all or part of a trial for reasons of morals, public order ("*ordre public*") or national security in a democratic society, or when the interest of the private lives of the Parties so requires, or to the extent strictly necessary in the opinion of the court in special circumstances where publicity would prejudice the interests of justice; but any judgement rendered in a criminal case or in a suit at law shall be made public except where the interest of juveniles otherwise requires or the proceedings concern matrimonial disputes or the guardianship of children.

2. Everyone charged with a criminal offence shall have the right to be presumed innocent until proved guilty according to law.

3. In the determination of any criminal charge against him, everyone shall be entitled to the following minimum guarantees, in full equality:

(a) To be informed promptly and in detail in a language which he understands of the nature and cause of the charge against him;

(b) To have adequate time and facilities for the preparation of his defence and to communicate with counsel of his own choosing;

(c) To be tried without undue delay;

(d) To be tried in his presence, and to defend himself in person or through legal assistance of his own choosing; to be informed, if he does not have legal assistance, of this right; and to have legal assistance assigned to him, in any case where the interests of justice so require, and without payment by him in any such case if he does not have sufficient means to pay for it;

(e) To examine, or have examined, the witnesses against him and to obtain the attendance and examination of witnesses on his behalf under the same conditions as witnesses against him;

(f) To have the free assistance of an interpreter if he cannot understand or speak the language used in court;

(g) Not to be compelled to testify against himself or to confess guilt.

4. In the case of juvenile persons, the procedure shall be such as will take account of their age and the desirability of promoting their rehabilitation.

5. Everyone convicted of a crime shall have the right to his conviction and sentence being reviewed by a higher tribunal according to law.

6. When a person has by a final decision been convicted of a criminal offence and when subsequently his conviction has been reversed or he has been pardoned on the ground that a new or newly discovered fact shows conclusively that there has been a miscarriage of justice, the person who has suffered punishment as a result of such conviction shall be compensated according to law, unless it is proved that the non-disclosure of the unknown fact in time is wholly or partly attributable to him.

7. No one shall be liable to be tried or punished again for an offence for which he has already been finally convicted or acquitted in accordance with the law and penal procedure of each country.

### *Article 15*

1. No one shall be held guilty of any criminal offence on account of any act or omission which did not constitute a criminal offence, under national or international law, at the time when it was committed. Nor shall a heavier penalty be imposed than the one that was applicable at the time when the criminal offence was committed. If, subsequently to the commission of the offence, provision is made by law for the imposition of the lighter penalty, the offender shall benefit thereby.

2. Nothing in this article shall prejudice the trial and punishment of any person for any act or omission which, at the time when it was committed, was criminal according to the general principles of law recognized by the community of nations.

### *Article 16*

Everyone shall have the right to recognition everywhere as a person before the law.

### *Article 17*

1. No one shall be subjected to arbitrary or unlawful interference with his privacy, family, home or correspondence, nor to unlawful attacks on his honour and reputation.

2. Everyone has the right to the protection of the law against such interference or attacks.

### *Article 18*

1. Everyone shall have the right to freedom of thought, conscience and religion. This right shall include freedom to have or to adopt a religion or belief of his choice, and freedom either individually or in community with others and in public or private, to manifest his religion or belief in worship, observance, practice and teaching.

2. No one shall be subject to coercion which would impair his freedom to have or to adopt a religion or belief of his choice.

3. Freedom to manifest one's religion or beliefs may be subject only to such limitations as are prescribed by law and are necessary to protect public safety, order, health, or morals or the fundamental rights and freedoms of others.

4. The States Parties to the present Covenant undertake to have respect for the liberty of parents and, when applicable, legal guardians, to ensure the religious and moral education of their children in conformity with their own convictions.

### *Article 19*

1. Everyone shall have the right to hold opinions without interference.

2. Everyone shall have the right to freedom of expression; this right shall include freedom to seek, receive and impart information and ideas of all kinds, regardless of frontiers, either orally, in writing or in print, in the form of art, or through any other media of his choice.

3. The exercise of the rights provided for in paragraph 2 of this article carries with it special duties and responsibilities. It may therefore be subject to certain restrictions, but these shall only be such as are provided by law and are necessary: (a) for respect of the rights or reputations of others; (b) for the protection of national security or of public order ("*ordre public*"), or of public health or morals.

### *Article 20*

1. Any propaganda for war shall be prohibited by law.

2. Any advocacy of national, racial, or religious hatred that constitutes incitement to discrimination, hostility or violence shall be prohibited by law.

### *Article 21*

The right of peaceful assembly shall be recognized. No restrictions may be placed on the exercise of this right other than those imposed in conformity with the law and which are necessary in a democratic society in the interests of national security or public safety, public order ("*ordre public*"), the protection of public health or morals or the protection of the rights and freedoms of others.

### *Article 22*

1. Everyone shall have the right to freedom of association with others, including the right to form and join trade unions for the protection of his interests.

2. No restrictions may be placed on the exercise of this right other than those prescribed by law and which are necessary in a democratic society in the interests of national security or public safety, public order ("*ordre public*"), the protection of public health or morals or the protection of the rights and freedoms of others. This article shall not prevent the imposition of lawful restrictions on members of the armed forces and of the police in their exercise of this right.

3. Nothing in this article shall authorize States Parties to the International Labour Organisation Convention of 1948 concerning Freedom of Association and Protection of the Right to Organize to take legislative measures which would prejudice, or to apply the law in such a manner as to prejudice the guarantees provided for in that Convention.

### *Article 23*

1. The family is the natural and fundamental group unit of society and is entitled to protection by society and the State.

2. The right of men and women of marriageable age to marry and to found a family shall be recognized.

3. No marriage shall be entered into without the free and full consent of the intending spouses.

4. States Parties to the present Covenant shall take appropriate steps to ensure equality of rights and responsibilities of spouses as to marriage, during marriage and at its dissolution. In the case of dissolution, provision shall be made for the necessary protection of any children.

### *Article 24*

1. Every child shall have, without any discrimination as to race, colour, sex, language, religion, national or social origin, property or birth, the right to such measures of protection as required by his status as a minor, on the part of his family, society and the State.
2. Every child shall be registered immediately after birth and shall have a name.
3. Every child has the right to acquire a nationality.

### *Article 25*

Every citizen shall have the right and the opportunity, without any of the distinctions mentioned in article 2 and without unreasonable restrictions:

(a) To take part in the conduct of public affairs, directly or through freely chosen representatives;

(b) To vote and to be elected at genuine periodic elections which shall be by universal and equal suffrage and shall be held by secret ballot, guaranteeing the free expression of the will of the electors;

(c) To have access, on general terms of equality, to public service in his country.

### *Article 26*

All persons are equal before the law and are entitled without any discrimination to equal protection of the law. In this respect the law shall prohibit any discrimination and guarantee to all persons equal and effective protection against discrimination on any ground such as race, colour, sex, language, religion, political or other opinion, national or social origin, property, birth or other status.

### *Article 27*

In those States in which ethnic, religious or linguistic minorities exist, persons belonging to such minorities shall not be denied the right, in community with the other members of their group, to enjoy their own culture, to profess and practise their own religion, or to use their own language.

## PART IV

### *Article 28*

1. There shall be established a Human Rights Committee (hereafter referred to in the present Covenant as "the Committee"). It shall consist of eighteen members and shall carry out the functions hereinafter provided.

2. The Committee shall be composed of nationals of the States Parties to the present Covenant who shall be persons of high moral character and recognized competence in the field of human rights, consideration being given to the usefulness of the participation of some persons having legal experience.

3. The members of the Committee shall be elected and shall serve in their personal capacity.

### *Article 29*

1. The members of the Committee shall be elected by secret ballot from a list of persons possessing the qualifications prescribed in article 28 and nominated for the purpose by the States Parties to the present Covenant.

2. Each State Party to the present Covenant may nominate not more than two persons. These persons shall be nationals of the nominating State.

3. A person shall be eligible for renomination.

### *Article 30*

1. The initial election shall be held no later than six months after the date of the entry into force of the present Covenant.

2. At least four months before the date of each election to the Committee, other than an election to fill a vacancy declared in accordance with article 34, the Secretary-General of the United Nations shall address a written invitation to the States Parties to the present Covenant to submit their nominations for membership of the Committee within three months.

3. The Secretary-General of the United Nations shall prepare a list in alphabetical order of all the persons thus nominated, with an indication of the States Parties which have nominated them, and shall

submit it to the States Parties to the present Covenant no later than one month before the date of each election.

4. Elections of the members of the Committee shall be held at a meeting of the States Parties to the present Covenant convened by the Secretary-General of the United Nations at the Headquarters of the United Nations. At that meeting, for which two thirds of the States Parties to the present Covenant shall constitute a quorum, the persons elected to the Committee shall be those nominees who obtain the largest number of votes and an absolute majority of the votes of the representatives of States Parties present and voting.

### *Article 31*

1. The Committee may not include more than one national of the same State.

2. In the election of the Committee, consideration shall be given to equitable geographical distribution of membership and to the representation of the different forms of civilization and of the principal legal systems.

### *Article 32*

1. The members of the Committee shall be elected for a term of four years. They shall be eligible for re-election if renominated. However, the terms of nine of the members elected at the first election shall expire at the end of two years; immediately after the first election the names of these nine members shall be chosen by lot by the Chairman of the meeting referred to in article 30, paragraph 4.

2. Elections at the expiry of office shall be held in accordance with the preceding articles of this part of the present Covenant.

### *Article 33*

1. If, in the unanimous opinion of the other members, a member of the Committee has ceased to carry out his functions for any cause other than absence of a temporary character, the Chairman of the Committee shall notify the Secretary-General of the United Nations who shall then declare the seat of that member to be vacant.

2. In the event of the death or the resignation of a member of the Committee, the Chairman shall immediately notify the Secretary-General of the United Nations, who shall declare the seat vacant from the date of death or the date on which the resignation takes effect.

### *Article 34*

1. When a vacancy is declared in accordance with article 33 and if the term of office of the member to be replaced does not expire within six months of the declaration of the vacancy, the Secretary-General of the United Nations shall notify each of the States Parties to the present Covenant which may within two months submit nominations in accordance with article 29 for the purpose of filling the vacancy.

2. The Secretary-General of the United Nations shall prepare a list in alphabetical order of the persons thus nominated and shall submit it to the States Parties to the present Covenant. The election to fill the vacancy shall then take place in accordance with the relevant provisions of this part of the present Covenant.

3. A member of the Committee elected to fill a vacancy declared in accordance with article 33 shall hold office for the remainder of the term of the member who vacated the seat on the Committee under the provisions of that article.

### *Article 35*

The members of the Committee shall, with the approval of the General Assembly of the United Nations, receive emoluments from United Nations resources on such terms and conditions as the General Assembly may decide, having regard to the importance of the Committee's responsibilities.

### *Article 36*

The Secretary-General of the United Nations shall provide the necessary staff and facilities for the effective performance of the functions of the Committee under the present Covenant.

### *Article 37*

1. The Secretary-General of the United Nations shall convene the initial meeting of the Committee at the Headquarters of the United Nations.

2. After its initial meeting, the Committee shall meet at such times as shall be provided in its rules of procedure.

3. The Committee shall normally meet at the Headquarters of the United Nations or at the United Nations Office at Geneva.

### *Article 38*

Every member of the Committee shall, before taking up his duties, make a solemn declaration in open committee that he will perform his functions impartially and conscientiously.

### *Article 39*

1. The Committee shall elect its officers for a term of two years. They may be re-elected.

2. The Committee shall establish its own rules of procedure, but these rules shall provide, *inter alia*, that:

(a) Twelve members shall constitute a quorum;

(b) Decisions of the Committee shall be made by a majority vote of the members present.

### *Article 40*

1. The States Parties to the present Covenant undertake to submit reports on the measures they have adopted which give effect to the rights recognized herein and on the progress made in the enjoyment of those rights: (a) Within one year of the entry into force of the present Covenant for the States Parties concerned; (b) Thereafter whenever the Committee so requests.

2. All reports shall be submitted to the Secretary-General of the United Nations who shall transmit them to the Committee for consideration. Reports shall indicate the factors and difficulties, if any, affecting the implementation of the present Covenant.

3. The Secretary-General of the United Nations may, after consultation with the Committee, transmit to the specialized agencies concerned copies of such parts of the reports as may fall within their field of competence.

4. The Committee shall study the reports submitted by the States Parties to the present Covenant. It shall transmit its reports, and such general comments as it may consider appropriate, to the States Parties. The Committee may also transmit to the Economic and Social Council these comments along with the copies of the reports it has received from States Parties to the present Covenant.

5. The States Parties to the present Covenant may submit to the Committee observations on any comments that may be made in accordance with paragraph 4 of this article.

### *Article 41*

1. A State Party to the present Covenant may at any time declare under this article that it recognizes the competence of the Committee to receive and consider communications to the effect that a State Party claims that another State Party is not fulfilling its obligations under the present Covenant. Communications under this article may be received and considered only if submitted by a State Party which has made a declaration recognizing in regard to itself the competence of the Committee. No communication shall be received by the Committee if it concerns a State Party which has not made such a declaration. Communications received under this article shall be dealt with in accordance with the following procedure:

(a) If a State Party to the present Covenant considers that another State Party is not giving effect to the provisions of the present Covenant, it may, by written communication, bring the matter to the attention of that State Party. Within three months after the receipt of the communication the receiving State shall afford the State which sent the communication an explanation, or any other statement in writing clarifying the matter which should include, to the extent possible and pertinent, reference to domestic procedures and remedies taken, pending, or available in the matter;

(b) If the matter is not adjusted to the satisfaction of both States Parties concerned within six months after the receipt by the receiving State of the initial communication, either State shall have the right to refer the matter to the Committee, by notice given to the Committee and to the other State;

(c) The Committee shall deal with a matter referred to it only after it has ascertained that all available domestic remedies have been invoked and exhausted in the matter, in conformity with the generally recognized principles of international law. This shall not be the rule where the application of the remedies is unreasonably prolonged;

(d) The Committee shall hold closed meetings when examining communications under this article;

(e) Subject to the provisions of sub-paragraph (c), the Committee shall make available its good offices to the States Parties concerned with a view to a friendly solution of the matter on the basis of respect for human rights and fundamental freedoms as recognized in the present Covenant;

(f) In any matter referred to it, the Committee may call upon the States Parties concerned, referred to in subparagraph (b), to supply any relevant information;

(g) The States Parties concerned, referred to in subparagraph (b), shall have the right to be represented when the matter is being considered in the Committee and to make submissions orally and/or in writing;

(h) The Committee shall, within twelve months after the date of receipt of notice under subparagraph (b), submit a report:

(i) If a solution within the terms of sub-paragraph (e) is reached, the Committee shall confine its report to a brief statement of the facts and of the solution reached;

(ii) If a solution within the terms of subparagraph (e) is not reached, the Committee shall confine its report to a brief statement of the facts; the written submissions and record of the oral submissions made by the States Parties concerned shall be attached to the report.

In every matter the report shall be communicated to the States Parties concerned.

2. The provisions of this article shall come into force when ten States Parties to the present Covenant have made declarations under paragraph 1 of this article. Such declarations shall be deposited by the States Parties with the Secretary-General of the United Nations who shall transmit copies thereof to the other States Parties. A declaration may be withdrawn at any time by notification to the Secretary-General. Such a withdrawal shall not prejudice the consideration of any matter which is the subject of a communication already transmitted under this article; no further communication by any State Party shall be received after the notification of withdrawal of the declaration has been received by the Secretary-General, unless the State Party concerned has made a new declaration.

### *Article 42*

1. (a) If a matter referred to the Committee in accordance with article 41 is not resolved to the satisfaction of the States Parties concerned, the Committee may, with the prior consent of the States Parties concerned, appoint an *ad hoc* Conciliation Commission (hereinafter referred to as "the Commission"). The good offices of the Commission shall be made available to the States Parties concerned with a view to an amicable solution of the matter on the basis of respect for the present Covenant;

(b) The Commission shall consist of five persons acceptable to the States Parties concerned. If the States Parties concerned fail to reach agreement within three months on all or part of the composition of the Commission, the members of the Commission concerning whom no agreement has been reached shall be elected by secret ballot by a two-thirds majority vote of the Committee from among its members.

2. The members of the Commission shall serve in their personal capacity. They shall not be nationals of the States Parties concerned, or of a State not Party to the present Covenant, or of a State Party which has not made a declaration under article 41.

3. The Commission shall elect its own Chairman and adopt its own rules of procedure.

4. The meetings of the Commission shall normally be held at the Headquarters of the United Nations or at the United Nations Office at Geneva. However, they may be held at such other convenient places as the Commission may determine in consultation with the Secretary-General of the United Nations and the States Parties concerned.

5. The secretariat provided in accordance with article 36 shall also service the Commissions appointed under this article.

6. The information received and collated by the Committee shall be made available to the Commission and the Commission may call upon the States Parties concerned to supply any other relevant information.

7. When the Commission has fully considered the matter, but in any event not later than twelve months after having been seized of the matter, it shall submit to the Chairman of the Committee a report for communication to the States Parties concerned:

(a) If the Commission is unable to complete its consideration of the matter within twelve months, it shall confine its report to a brief statement of the status of its consideration of the matter;

(b) If an amicable solution to the matter on the basis of respect for human rights as recognized in the present Covenant is reached, the Commission shall confine its report to a brief statement of the facts and of the solution reached;

(c) If a solution within the terms of subparagraph (b) is not reached, the Commission's report shall embody its findings on all questions of fact relevant to the issues between the States Parties concerned, and its views on the possibilities of an amicable solution of the matter. This report shall also contain the written submissions and a record of the oral submissions made by the States Parties concerned;

(d) If the Commission's report is submitted under subparagraph (c), the States Parties concerned shall, within three months of the receipt of the report, notify the Chairman of the Committee whether or not they accept the contents of the report of the Commission.

8. The provisions of this article are without prejudice to the responsibilities of the Committee under article 41.

9. The States Parties concerned shall share equally all the expenses of the members of the Commission in accordance with estimates to be provided by the Secretary-General of the United Nations.

10. The Secretary-General of the United Nations shall be empowered to pay the expenses of the members of the Commission, if necessary, before reimbursement by the States Parties concerned in accordance with paragraph 9 of this article.

### *Article 43*

The members of the Committee and of the *ad hoc* conciliation commissions which may be appointed under article 42, shall be entitled to the facilities, privileges and immunities of experts on mission for the United Nations as laid down in the relevant sections of the Convention on the Privileges and Immunities of the United Nations.

### *Article 44*

The provisions for the implementation of the present Covenant shall apply without prejudice to the procedures prescribed in the field of human rights by or under the constituent instruments and the conventions of the United Nations and of the specialized agencies and shall not prevent the States Parties to the present Covenant from having recourse to other procedures for settling a dispute in accordance with general or special international agreements in force between them.

### *Article 45*

The Committee shall submit to the General Assembly, through the Economic and Social Counsel, an annual report on its activities.

## PART V

### *Article 46*

Nothing in the present Covenant shall be interpreted as impairing the provisions of the Charter of the United Nations and of the constitutions of the specialized agencies which define the respective responsibilities of the various organs of the United Nations and of the specialized agencies in regard to the matters dealt with in the present Covenant.

### *Article 47*

Nothing in the present Covenant shall be interpreted as impairing the inherent right of all peoples to enjoy and utilize fully and freely their natural wealth and resources.

## PART VI

### *Article 48*

2. The present Covenant is open for signature by any State Member of the United Nations or member of any of its specialized agencies, by any State Party to the Statute of the International Court of Justice, and by any other State which has been invited by the General Assembly of the United Nations to become a party to the present Covenant.

3. The present Covenant is subject to ratification. Instruments of ratification shall be deposited with the Secretary-General of the United Nations.

4. The present Covenant shall be open to accession by any State referred to in paragraph 1 of this article.

5. Accession shall be effected by the deposit of an instrument of accession with the Secretary-General of the United Nations.

6. The Secretary-General of the United Nations shall inform all States which have signed this Covenant or acceded to it of the deposit of each instrument of ratification or accession.

### *Article 49*

1. The present Covenant shall enter into force three months after the date of the deposit with the Secretary-General of the United Nations of the thirty-fifth instrument of ratification or instrument of accession.

2. For each State ratifying the present Covenant or acceding to it after the deposit of the thirty-fifth instrument of ratification or instrument of accession, the present Covenant shall enter into force three months after the date of the deposit of its own instrument of ratification or instrument of accession.

### *Article 50*

The provisions of the present Covenant shall extend to all parts of federal States without any limitations or exceptions.

### *Article 51*

1. Any State Party to the present Covenant may propose an amendment and file it with the Secretary-General of the United Nations. The Secretary-General of the United Nations shall thereupon communicate any proposed amendments to the States Parties to the present Covenant with a request that they notify him whether they favour a conference of States Parties for the purpose of considering and voting upon the proposals. In the event that at least one third of the States Parties favours such conference, the Secretary-General of the United Nations shall convene the conference under the auspices of the United Nations. Any amendment adopted by a majority of the States Parties present and voting at the conference shall be submitted to the General Assembly of the United Nations for approval.

2. Amendments shall come into force when they have been approved by the General Assembly and accepted by a two-thirds majority of the States Parties to the present Covenant in accordance with their respective constitutional processes.

3. When amendments come into force, they shall be binding on those States Parties which have accepted them, other States Parties still being bound by the provisions on the present Covenant and any earlier amendment which they have accepted.

### *Article 52*

Irrespective of the notifications made under article 48, paragraph 5, the Secretary-General of the United Nations shall inform all States referred to in paragraph 1 of the same article of the following particulars:

(a) Signatures, ratifications and accessions under article 48;

(b) The date of the entry into force of the present Covenant under article 49 and the date of the entry into force of any amendments under article 51.

### *Article 53*

1. The present Covenant, of which the Chinese, English, French, Russian and Spanish texts are equally authentic, shall be deposited in the archives of the United Nations.

2. The Secretary-General of the United Nations shall transmit certified copies of the present Covenant to all States referred to in article 48.

# INTERNATIONAL COVENANT ON ECONOMIC, SOCIAL AND CULTURAL RIGHTS

*Preamble*

*Considering* that, in accordance with the principles proclaimed in the Charter of the United Nations, recognition of the inherent dignity and of the equal and inalienable rights of all members of the human family is the foundation of freedom, justice and peace in the world,

*Recognizing* that these rights derive from the inherent dignity of the human person,

*Recognizing* that, in accordance with the Universal Declaration of Human Rights, the ideal of free human beings enjoying freedom from fear and want can only be achieved if conditions are created whereby everyone may enjoy his economic, social and cultural rights, as well as his civil and political rights,

*Considering* the obligation of States under the Charter of the United Nations to promote universal respect for, and observance of, human rights and freedoms,

*Realizing* that the individual, having duties to other individuals and to the community to which he belongs, is under a responsibility to strive for the promotion and observance of the rights recognized in the present Covenant,

*Agree* upon the following articles:

## PART I

### *Article 1*

1. All peoples have the right of self-determination. By virtue of the right they freely determine their political status and freely pursue their economic, social and cultural development.

2. All peoples may, for their own ends, freely dispose of their natural wealth and resources without prejudice to any obligations arising out of international economic co-operation, based upon the principle of mutual benefit, and international law. In no case may a people be deprived of its own means of subsistence.

3. The States Parties to the present Covenant, including those having responsibility for the administration of Non-Self-Governing and Trust Territories, shall promote the realization of the right of self-determination, and shall respect that right, in conformity with the provisions of the United Nations Charter.

## PART II

### *Article 2*

1. Each State Party to the present Covenant undertakes to take steps, individually and through international assistance and co-operation, especially economic and technical, to the maximum of its available resources, with a view to achieving progressively the full realization of the rights recognized in the present Covenant by all appropriate means, including particularly the adoption of legislative measures.

2. The States Parties to the present Covenant undertake to guarantee that the rights enunciated in the present Covenant will be exercised without discrimination of any kind as to race, colour, sex, language, religion, political or other opinion, national or social origin, property, birth or other status.

3. Developing countries, with due regard to human rights and their national economy, may determine to what extent they would guarantee the economic rights recognized in the present Covenant to non-nationals.

### *Article 3*

The States Parties to the present Covenant undertake to ensure the equal right of men and women to the enjoyment of all economic, social and cultural rights set forth in the present Covenant.

### *Article 4*

The States Parties to the present Covenant recognize that, in the enjoyment of those rights provided by the State in conformity with the present Covenant, the State may subject such rights only to such limitations as are determined by law only in so far as this may be compatible with the nature of these rights and solely for the purpose of promoting the general welfare in a democratic society.

### *Article 5*

1. Nothing in the present Covenant may be interpreted as implying for any State, group or person, any right to engage in any activity or to perform any act aimed at the destruction of any of the rights or freedoms recognized herein, or at their limitation to a greater extent than is provided for in the present Covenant.

2. No restriction upon or derogation from any of the fundamental human rights recognized or existing in any country in virtue of law, conventions, regulations or custom shall be admitted on the pretext that the present Covenant does not recognize such rights or that it recognizes them to a lesser extent.

## PART III

### *Article 6*

1. The States Parties to the present Covenant recognize the right to work, which includes the right of everyone to the opportunity to gain his living by work which he freely chooses or accepts, and will take appropriate steps to safeguard this right.

2. The steps to be taken by a State Party to the present Covenant to achieve the full realization of this right shall include technical and vocational guidance and training programmes, policies and techniques to achieve steady economic, social and cultural development and full and productive employment under conditions safeguarding fundamental political and economic freedoms to the individual.

### *Article 7*

The States Parties to the present Covenant recognize the right of everyone to the enjoyment of just and favourable conditions of work which ensure, in particular:

(a) Remuneration which provides all workers, as a minimum, with:

(i) Fair wages and equal remuneration for work of equal value without distinction of any kind, in particular women being guaranteed conditions of work not inferior to those enjoyed by men, with equal pay for equal work;

(ii) A decent living for themselves and their families in accordance with the provisions of the present Covenant;

(b) Safe and healthy working conditions;

(c) Equal opportunity for everyone to be promoted in his employment to an appropriate higher level, subject to no considerations other than those of seniority and competence;

(d) Rest, leisure and reasonable limitation of working hours and periodic holidays with pay, as well as remuneration for public holidays.

*Article 8*

1. The States Parties to the present Covenant undertake to ensure:

(a) The right of everyone to form trade unions and join the trade union of his choice, subject only to the rules of the organization concerned, for the promotion and protection of his economic and social interests. No restrictions may be placed on the exercise of this right other than those prescribed by law and which are necessary in a democratic society in the interests of national security or public order or for the protection of the rights and freedom of others;

(b) The right of trade unions to establish national federations or confederations and the right of the latter to form or join international trade-union organizations;

(c) The right of trade unions to function freely subject to no limitations other than those prescribed by law and which are necessary in a democratic society in the interests of national security or public order or for the protection of the rights and freedoms of others;

(d) The right to strike, provided that it is exercised in conformity with the laws of the particular country.

2. This article shall not prevent the imposition of lawful restrictions on the exercise of these rights by members of the armed forces, or of the police or of the administration of the State.

3. Nothing in this article shall authorize States Parties to the International Labour Convention of 1948 concerning Freedom of Association and Protection of the Rights to Organize to take legislative measures which would prejudice, or apply the law in such a manner as would prejudice, the guarantees provided for in that Convention.

*Article 9*

The States Parties to the present Covenant recognize the right of everyone to social security, including social insurance.

*Article 10*

The States Parties to the present Covenant recognize that:

1. The widest possible protection and assistance should be accorded to the family, which is the natural and fundamental group unit of society, particularly for its establishment and while it is responsible for the care and education of dependent children. Marriage must be entered into with the free consent of the intending spouses,

2. Special protection should be accorded to mothers during a reasonable period before and after childbirth. During such period working mothers should be accorded paid leave or leave with adequate social security benefits,

3. Special measures of protection and assistance should be taken on behalf of all children and young persons without any discrimination for reasons of parentage or other conditions. Children and young persons should be protected from economic and social exploitation. Their employment in work harmful to their morals or health or dangerous to life or likely to hamper their normal development should be punishable by law. States should also set age limits below which the paid employment of child labour should be prohibited and punishable by law.

### *Article 11*

1. The States Parties to the present Covenant recognize the right of everyone to an adequate standard of living for himself and his family, including adequate food, clothing and housing, and to the continuous improvement of living conditions. The States Parties will take appropriate steps to ensure the realization of this right, recognizing to this effect the essential importance of international co-operation based on free consent.

2. The States Parties to the present Covenant, recognizing the fundamental right of everyone to be free from hunger, shall take, individually and through international co-operation, the measures, including specific programmes, which are needed:

(a) To improve methods of production, conservation and distribution of food by making full use of technical and scientific knowledge, by disseminating knowledge of the principles of nutrition and by developing or reforming agrarian systems in such a way as to achieve the most efficient development and utilization of natural resources;

(b) Taking into account the problems of both food-importing and food-exporting countries, to ensure an equitable distribution of world food supplies in relation to need.

### *Article 12*

1. The States Parties to the present Covenant recognize the right of everyone to the enjoyment of the highest attainable standard of physical and mental health.

2. The steps to be taken by the States Parties to the present Covenant to achieve the full realization of this right shall include those necessary for:

(a) The provision for the reduction of the stillbirth-rate and of infant mortality and for the healthy development of the child;

(b) The improvement of all aspects of environmental and industrial hygiene;

(c) The prevention, treatment and control of epidemic, endemic, occupational and other diseases;

(d) The creation of conditions which would assure to all medical service and medical attention in the event of sickness.

### *Article 13*

1. The States Parties to the present Covenant recognize the right of everyone to education. They agree that education shall be directed to the full development of the human personality and the sense of its dignity, and shall strengthen the respect for human rights and fundamental freedoms. They further agree that education shall enable all persons to participate effectively in a free society, promote understanding, tolerance and friendship among all nations and all racial, ethnic or religious groups, and further the activities of the United Nations for the maintenance of peace.

2. The States Parties to the present Covenant recognize that, with a view to achieving the full realization of this right:

(a) Primary education shall be compulsory and available free to all;

(b) Secondary education in its different forms, including technical and vocational secondary education, shall be made generally available and accessible to all by every appropriate means, and in particular by the progressive introduction of free education;

(c) Higher education shall be made equally accessible to all, on the basis of capacity, by every appropriate means, and in particular by the progressive introduction of free education;

(d) Fundamental education shall be encouraged or intensified as far as possible for those persons who have not received or completed the whole period of their primary education;

(e) The development of a system of schools at all levels shall be actively pursued, an adequate fellowship system shall be established, and the material conditions of teaching staff shall be continuously improved.

3. The States Parties to the present Covenant undertake to have respect for the liberty of parents and, when applicable, legal guardians, to choose for their children schools, other than those established by the public authorities, which conform to such minimum educational standards as may be laid down or approved by the State and to ensure the religious and moral education of their children in conformity with their own convictions.

4. No part of this article shall be construed so as to interfere with the liberty of individuals and bodies to establish and direct educational institutions, subject always to the observance of the principles set forth in paragraph 1 of this article and to the requirement that the education given in such institutions shall conform to such minimum standards as may be laid down by the State.

### *Article 14*

Each State Party to the present Covenant which, at the time of becoming a Party, has not been able to secure in its metropolitan territory or other territories under its jurisdiction compulsory primary education, free of charge, undertakes, within two years, to work out and adopt a detailed plan of action for the progressive implementation, within a reasonable number of years, to be fixed in the plan, of the principle of compulsory education free of charge for all.

### *Article 15*

1. The States Parties to the present Covenant recognize the right of everyone:

(a) To take part in cultural life;

(b) To enjoy the benefits of scientific progress and its applications;

(c) To benefit from the protection of the moral and material interests resulting from any scientific, literary or artistic production of which he is the author.

2. The steps to be taken by the States Parties to the present Covenant to achieve the full realization of this right shall include those necessary for the conservation, the development and the diffusion of science and culture.

3. The States Parties to the present Covenant undertake to respect the freedom indispensable for scientific research and creative activity.

4. The States Parties to the present Covenant recognize the benefits to be derived from the encouragement and development of international contacts and co-operation in the scientific and cultural fields.

## PART IV

### *Article 16*

1. The States Parties to the present Covenant undertake to submit in conformity with this part of the Covenant reports on the measures which they have adopted and the progress made in achieving the observance of the rights recognized herein.

2. (a) All reports shall be submitted to the Secretary-General of the United Nations, who shall transmit copies to the Economic and Social Council for consideration in accordance with the provisions of the present Covenant;

(b) The Secretary-General of the United Nations shall also transmit to the specialized agencies copies of the reports, or any relevant parts therefrom, from States Parties to the present Covenant which are also members of these specialized agencies in so far as these reports, or parts therefrom, relate to any matters which fall within the responsibilities of the said agencies in accordance with their constitutional instruments.

### *Article 17*

1. The States Parties to the present Covenant shall furnish their reports in stages, in accordance with a programme to be established by the Economic and Social Council within one year of the entry into force of the present Covenant after consultation with the States Parties and the specialized agencies concerned.

2. Reports may indicate factors and difficulties affecting the degree of fulfilment of obligations under the present Covenant.

3. Where relevant information has previously been furnished to the United Nations or to any specialized agency by any State Party to the present Covenant it will not be necessary to reproduce that information but a precise reference to the information so furnished will suffice.

### *Article 18*

Pursuant to its responsibilities under the Charter of the United Nations in the field of human rights and fundamental freedoms, the Economic and Social Council may make arrangements with the specialized agencies in respect of their reporting to it on the progress made in achieving the observance of the provisions of the present Covenant falling within the scope of their activities. These reports may include particulars of decisions and recommendations on such implementation adopted by their competent organs.

### *Article 19*

The Economic and Social Council may transmit to the Commission on Human Rights for study and general recommendation or, as appropriate, for information the reports concerning human rights submitted by States in accordance with articles 16 and 17, and those concerning human rights submitted by the specialized agencies in accordance with article 18.

### *Article 20*

The States Parties to the present Covenant and the specialized agencies concerned may submit comments to the Economic and Social Council on any general recommendation under article 19 or reference to such general recommendation in any report of the Commission on Human Rights or any documentation referred to therein.

### *Article 21*

The Economic and Social Council may submit from time to time to the General Assembly reports with recommendations of a general nature and a summary of the information received from the States Parties to the present Covenant and the specialized agencies on the measures taken and the progress made in achieving general observance of the rights recognized in the present Covenant.

### *Article 22*

The Economic and Social Council may bring to the attention of other organs of the United Nations, their subsidiary organs and specialized agencies concerned with furnishing technical assistance any matters arising out of the reports referred to in this part of the present Covenant which may assist such bodies in deciding, each within its field of competence, on the advisability of international measures likely to contribute to the effective progressive implementation of the present Covenant.

### *Article 23*

The States Parties to the present Covenant agree that international action for the achievement of the rights recognized in the present

Covenant includes such methods as the conclusion of conventions, the adoption of recommendations, the furnishing of technical assistance and the holding of regional meetings and technical meetings for the purpose of consultation and study organized in conjunction with the Governments concerned.

*Article 24*

Nothing in the present Covenant shall be interpreted as impairing the provisions of the Charter of the United Nations and of the constitutions of the specialized agencies which define the respective responsibilities of the various organs of the United Nations and of the specialized agencies in regard to the matters dealt with in the present Covenant.

*Article 25*

Nothing in the present Covenant shall be interpreted as impairing the inherent right of all peoples to enjoy and utilize fully and freely their natural wealth and resources.

## PART V

*Article 26*

1. The present Covenant is open for signature by any State Member of the United Nations or member of any of its specialized agencies, by any State Party to the Statute of the International Court of Justice, and by any other State which has been invited by the General Assembly of the United Nations to become a party to the present Covenant.
2. The present Covenant is subject to ratification. Instruments of ratification shall be deposited with the Secretary-General of the United Nations.
3. The present Covenant shall be open to accession by any State referred to in paragraph 1 of this article.
4. Accession shall be effected by the deposit of an instrument of accession with the Secretary-General of the United Nations.
5. The Secretary-General of the United Nations shall inform all States which have signed the present Covenant or acceded to it of the deposit of each instrument of ratification or accession.

### *Article 27*

1. The present Covenant shall enter into force three months after the date of the deposit with the Secretary-General of the United Nations of the thirty-fifth instrument of ratification or instrument of accession.

2. For each State ratifying the present Covenant or acceding to it after the deposit of the thirty-fifth instrument of ratification or instrument of accession, the present Covenant shall enter into force three months after the date of the deposit of its own instrument of ratification or instrument of accession.

### *Article 28*

The provisions of the present Covenant shall extend to all parts of federal States without any limitations or exceptions.

### *Article 29*

1. Any State Party to the present Covenant may propose an amendment and file it with the Secretary-General of the United Nations. The Secretary-General shall thereupon communicate any proposed amendments to the States Parties to the present Covenant with a request that they notify him whether they favour a conference of States Parties for the purpose of considering and voting upon the proposals. In the event that at least one third of the States Parties favours such a conference, the Secretary-General shall convene the conference under the auspices of the United Nations. Any amendment adopted by a majority of the States Parties present and voting at the conference shall be submitted to the General Assembly of the United Nations for approval.

2. Amendments shall come into force when they have been approved by the General Assembly and accepted by a two-thirds majority of the States Parties to the present Covenant in accordance with their respective constitutional processes.

3. When amendments come into force they shall be binding on those States Parties which have accepted them, other States Parties still being bound by the provisions of the present Covenant and any earlier amendment which they have accepted.

### *Article 30*

Irrespective of the notifications made under article 26, paragraph 5, the Secretary-General of the United Nations shall inform all States referred to in paragraph 1 of the same article of the following particulars:

(a) Signatures, ratifications and accessions under article 26;

(b) The date of the entry into force of the present Covenant under article 27 and the date of the entry into force of any amendments under article 29.

### *Article 31*

1. The present Covenant, of which the Chinese, English, French, Russian and Spanish texts are equally authentic, shall be deposited in the archives of the United Nations.

2. The Secretary-General of the United Nations shall transmit certified copies of the present Covenant to all States referred to in article 26.

# U.S. RESERVATIONS, DECLARATIONS AND UNDERSTANDINGS*

## A. Reservations

### *1. Free Speech*

Article 20 does not authorize or require legislation or other action by the United States that would restrict the right of free speech and association protected by the Constitution and laws of the United States.

### *2. Capital Punishment*

The United States reserves the right, subject to its Constitutional constraints, to impose capital punishment on any person (other than a pregnant woman) duly convicted under existing or future laws permitting the imposition of capital punishment, including such punishment for crimes committed by persons below eighteen years of age.

### *3. Cruel, Inhuman or Degrading Treatment or Punishment*

The United States considers itself bound by Article 7 to the extent that "cruel, inhuman or degrading treatment or punishment" means the cruel and unusual treatment or punishment prohibited by the Fifth, Eighth and/or Fourteenth Amendments to the Constitution of the United States.

### *4. Criminal Penalties*

Because the U.S. law generally applies to an offender the penalty in force at the time the offense was committed, the United States does not adhere to the third clause of paragraph 1 of Article 15.

### *5. Juveniles*

The policy and practice of the United States are generally in compliance with and supportive of the Covenant's provisions regarding treatment of juveniles in the criminal justice system. Nevertheless, the United States reserves the right, in exceptional circumstances, to

*The administration's explanation of the reservations, declarations, and understandings may be found in the Senate Foreign Relations Committee's Report, International Covenant on Civil and Political Rights, S. EXEC. DOC. No. 102-23, d Cong. 2d Sess. 6-21 (1992), *reprinted in* 31 I.L.M. 645 (1992).

treat juveniles as adults, notwithstanding paragraphs 2(b) and 3 of Article 10 and paragraph 4 of Article 14. The United States further reserves to these provisions with respect to individuals who volunteer for military service prior to age 18.

## B. Understandings

### *1. Non-Discrimination and Equal Protection*

The Constitution and laws of the United States guarantee all persons equal protection of the law and provide extensive protections against discrimination. The United States understands distinctions based upon race, colour, sex, language, religion, political or other opinion, national or social origin, property, birth or any other status — as those terms are used in Article 2, paragraph 1 and Article 26 — to be permitted when such distinctions are, at minimum, rationally related to a legitimate governmental objective. The United States further understands the prohibition in paragraph 1 of Article 4 upon discrimination, in time of public emergency, based "solely" on the status of race, colour, sex, language, religion or social origin not to bar distinctions that may have a disproportionate effect upon persons of particular status.

### *2. Right to Compensation for Illegal Arrest and Miscarriage of Justice*

The United States understands the right to compensation referred to in Articles 9(5) and 14(6) to require the provision of effective and enforceable mechanisms by which a victim of an unlawful arrest or detention or a miscarriage of justice may seek and, where justified, obtain compensation from either the responsible individual or the appropriate governmental entity. Entitlement to compensation may be subject to the reasonable requirements of domestic law.

### *3. Separate Treatment of the Accused and Juveniles*

The United States understands the reference to "exceptional circumstances" in paragraph 2(a) of Article 10 to permit the imprisonment of an accused person with convicted persons where appropriate in light of an individual's overall dangerousness, and to permit accused persons to waive their right to segregation from convicted persons. The United States further understands that paragraph 3 of Article 10 does not diminish the goals of punishment, deterrence, and incapacitation as additional legitimate purposes for a penitentiary system.

*4. Right to Counsel, Compelled Witnesses, Double Jeapordy*

The United States understands that subparagraphs 3(b) and (d) of Article 14 do not require the provision of a criminal defendant's counsel of choice when the defendant is provided with court-appointed counsel on grounds of indigence, when the defendant is financially able to retain alternative counsel, or when imprisonment is not imposed. The United States further understands that paragraph 3(e) does not prohibit a requirement that the defendant make a showing that any witness whose attendance he seeks to compel is necessary for his defense. The United States understands the prohibition upon double jeapordy in paragraph 7 to apply only when the judgment of acquittal has been rendered by a court of the same governmental unit, whether the Federal Government or a constituent unit, as is seeking a new trial for the same cause.

*5. Federalism*

The United States understands that this Convention shall be implemented by the Federal Government to the extent that it exercises legislative and judicial jurisdiction over the matters covered therein, and otherwise by the state and local governments: to the extent that state and local governments exercise jurisdiction over such matters, the Federal Government shall take measures appropriate to the Federal system to the end that the competent authorities of the state or local governments may take appropriate measures for the fulfillment of the Convention.

## C. Declarations

*1. Non-Self-Executing*

The United States declares that the provisions of Articles 1 through 27 of the covenant are not self-executing.

*2. Limitations on Rights*

It is the view of the United States that States Party to the Covenant should wherever possible refrain from imposing any restrictions or limitations on the exercise of the rights recognized and protected by the Covenant, even when such restrictions and limitations are permissible under the terms of the Covenant. For the United States, Article 5, paragraph 2, which provides that fundamental human rights existing in any State Party may not be diminished on the pretext that the Covenant recognizes them to a lesser extent, has particular relevance to Article 19, paragraph 3, which would permit certain restrictions on the freedom of expression. The United States declares that it will continue to adhere to the requirements and constraints of its Constitution in respect of all such restrictions and limitations.

### *3. Competence of the Human Rights Committee*

The United States declares that it accepts the competence of the Human Rights Committee to receive and consider communications under Article 41 in which a State Party claims that another State Party is not fulfilling its obligations under the Covenant.

### *4. Natural Wealth and Resources*

The United States declares that the right referred to in Article 47 may be exercised only in accordance with international law.

# CONTRIBUTORS

*David B. Filvaroff* is the Dean and Professor of Law at the State University of New York at Buffalo Law School, where he teaches courses on civil rights, constitutional law and human rights. A former Fellow at the Institute of Politics, John F. Kennedy School of Government, Harvard University, Professor Filvaroff has published numerous articles in the area of civil rights.

*Dana D. Fischer* is a Foreign Service Officer with the Agency for International Development. She is currently Officer-in-Charge of Regional Programs in the Office of Sahel and West African Affairs. Prior to joining the Foreign Service, she was Assistant Professor of Political Science and International Affairs at George Washington University.

*Oscar M. Garibaldi* is a member of the District of Columbia Bar and a partner in the law firm of Covington & Burling in Washington, D.C. He is the recipient of the first Romulo Gallegos Fellowship, instituted by the Inter-American Commission of Human Rights, in support of advanced studies on international human rights law.

*Frank P. Grad* is Chamberlain Professor of Legislation and Director of the Legislative Drafting Research Fund at Columbia Law School. He is the author of a five-volume *Treatise on Environmental Law*, which he updates semi-annually, as well as the *Public Health Law Manual* and other works on public health law, housing law, legislation and state and local government law.

*Joseph R. Grodin* is Professor of Law at the University of California, Hastings College of Law, where he teaches classes and seminars in labor law, employment discrimination, alternative dispute resolution, and other subjects. A former Associate Justice of the California Court of Appeals, he was appointed to the California Supreme Court in 1982.

*Hurst Hannum* is Associate Professor of International Law at The Fletcher School of Law and Diplomacy of Tufts University. He has been a visiting or adjunct professor at Harvard Law School and the American University School of Law. He is author or editor of *Guide to International Human Rights Practice, Basic Documents on Autonomy and Minority Rights* and *The Right to Leave and Return in International Law and Practice.*

*Virginia A. Leary* has been Professor of International Law at the State University of New York at Buffalo since 1976. She has been an active member of the American Society of International Law, serving as Vice-President from 1990-1992. She is the author of two books and a number of monographs, book chapters, and articles on international law and human rights.

*Stephen P. Marks* was recently Professor of Law and Director of the Program in International Law and Human Rights at Cardozo School of Law, as well as University Fellow at the New School for Social Research. He is currently working with United Nations Transitional Authority in Cambodia (UNTAC). His writings relate to various aspects of human rights, peace and international organizations.

*Dinah Shelton* is professor of international law and human rights at Santa Clara University School of Law. She is co-author of the prize-winning book *Protecting Human Rights in the Americas* and *International Environmental Law*, as well as the author of numerous articles on international law and human rights.

*Clyde W. Summers* is the Fordham Professor of Law at the University of Pennsylvania. Professor Summers has been awarded Honorary Doctor of Law degrees from the University of Leuven, Belgium, and from the University of Stockholm, Sweden. He has been a consultant to the Department of Labor and Department of Housing and Urban Development and is the author of several books on labor law.

*Burns H. Weston* is the Bessie Dutton Murray Distinguished Professor of Law, Associate Dean for International and Comparative Legal Studies, and Chair of the Graduate Program of International and Comparative Law at the University of Iowa. His most recent books include *Human Rights in the World Community: Issues and Action* and *Alternative Security: Living Without Nuclear Deterrence.*

*Anne M. Williams* is currently the A.I.D. Representative to Chad. She has worked for the US Agency for International Development since 1979. Having lived and worked in Africa from 1962 to 1970 and 1979 to 1980, she has followed carefully the recent movement towards democracy in Africa and its effect on the human rights situation there.

*Mark G. Yudof* is Dean of the University of Texas School of Law in Austin and holds the John Jeffers Research Chair in Law. Recipient of the Scribes Most Meritorious Book Award for *When Government Speaks*, he is the co-author of *Educational Policy and the Law* and articles on law, property taxation and other subjects.

# INDEX